Introduction to 3D Game Programming with DirectX® 9.0

Frank D. Luna
Technical review by Rod Lopez

Wordware Publishing, Inc.

Library of Congress Cataloging-in-Publication Data

Luna, Frank D.
  Introduction to 3D game programming with DirectX 9.0 / by Frank D. Luna.
    p. cm.
  ISBN-10: 1-55622-913-5 (pbk.)
  1. Computer games--Programming.   2. DirectX. I. Title.
  QA76.76.C672L83 2003
  794.8'15268--dc21   2003005834
                                                       CIP

ISBN-13: 978-1-55622-913-8
ISBN-10: 1-55622-913-5

10 9 8 7 6 5
0305

All inquiries for volume purchases of this book should be addressed to Wordware
Publishing, Inc., at the above address. Telephone inquiries may be made by calling:

(972) 423-0090

To my parents, Frank and Kathryn

Contents

Acknowledgments

I would like to thank my technical editor Rod Lopez for putting in the time to review this book for both accuracy and improvements. I would also like to thank Jim Leiterman (author of *Vector Game Math Processors* from Wordware Publishing) and Hanley Leung (programmer for Kush Games), who both reviewed portions of this book. Next, I want to thank Adam Hault and Gary Simmons, who both teach the BSP/PVS course at www.gameinstitute.com, for their assistance. In addition, I want to thank William Chin who helped me out many years ago. Lastly, I want to thank the staff at Wordware Publishing, in particular, Jim Hill, Wes Beckwith, Beth Kohler, Heather Hill, Denise McEvoy, and Alan McCuller.

Introduction

This book is an introduction to programming interactive 3D computer graphics using DirectX 9.0, with an emphasis on game development. It teaches you the fundamentals of Direct3D, after which you will be able to go on to learn and apply more advanced techniques. Assumingly, since you have this book in your hands, you have a rough idea of what DirectX is about. From a developer's perspective, DirectX is a set of APIs (application programming interfaces) for developing multimedia applications on the Windows platform. In this book we are concerned with a particular DirectX subset, namely Direct3D. As the name implies, Direct3D is the API used for developing 3D applications.

This book is divided into four main parts. Part I explains the mathematical tools that will be used throughout this book. Part II covers elementary 3D techniques, such as lighting, texturing, alpha blending, and stenciling. Part III is largely about using Direct3D to implement a variety of interesting techniques and applications, such as picking, terrain rendering, particle systems, a flexible virtual camera, and loading and rendering 3D models (XFiles). The theme of Part IV is vertex and pixel shaders, including the effects framework and the new (to DirectX 9.0) High-Level Shading Language. The present and future of 3D game programming is the use of shaders, and by dedicating an entire part of the book to shaders, we have an up-to-date and relevant book on modern graphics programming.

For the beginner, this book is best read front to back. The chapters have been organized so that the difficulty increases progressively with each chapter. In this way, there are no sudden jumps in complexity, leaving the reader lost. In general, for a particular chapter we will use the techniques and concepts previously developed. Therefore, it is important that you have mastered the material of a chapter before continuing. Experienced readers can pick the chapters of interest.

Finally, you may wonder what kinds of games you can develop after reading this book. The answer to that question is best obtained by skimming through this book and seeing the types of applications that are developed. From that you should be able to visualize the types of games that can be developed based on the techniques taught in this book and some of your own ingenuity.

Prerequisites

This book is designed to be an introductory level textbook. However, that does not imply that it is easy for people with no programming experience. Readers are expected to be comfortable with algebra, trigonometry, their development environment (e.g., Visual Studio), C++, and fundamental data structures such as arrays and lists. Being familiar with Windows programming is also helpful but not imperative; refer to the appendix for an introduction to Windows programming.

Required Development Tools

This book uses C++ as its programming language for the sample programs. To quote the DirectX documentation, "DirectX 9.0 supports only Microsoft Visual C++ 6.0 and later." Therefore, as of publication, in order to write C++ applications using DirectX 9.0, you need either Visual C++ (VC++) 6.0 or VC++ 7.0 (.NET).

Note: The sample code for this book was compiled and built using VC++ 7.0. For the most part, it should compile and build on VC++ 6.0 also, but be aware of the following difference. In VC++ 7.0 the following will compile and is legal because the variable cnt is considered to be local to the for loop.

```
int main()
{
    for(int cnt = 0; cnt < 10; cnt++)
    {
        std::cout << "hello" << std::endl;
    }

    for(int cnt = 0; cnt < 10; cnt++)
    {
        std::cout << "hello" << std::endl;
    }
    return 0;
}
```

However, in VC++ 6.0 this will not compile. It gives the error message *error C2374: 'cnt' : redefinition; multiple initialization* because in VC++ 6.0 the variable cnt is not treated as being local to the for loop. Therefore, when porting to VC++ 6.0, you may need to make some minor changes to get it to compile due to this difference.

Recommended Hardware

The following hardware recommendations are if you wish to be able to run the sample programs at an acceptable frame rate; all the samples can be run using the REF device, which emulates Direct3D functionality in software. Because things are being emulated in software, they run very slow. We discuss the REF more in Chapter 1.

The sample programs in Part II of this book are fairly basic and should run on low-end cards, such as the Riva TNT or an equivalent graphics card. The sample programs in Part III push more geometry and use some newer features, such as point sprites. For these samples we recommend a graphics card at the level of a GeForce2. The sample programs in Part IV use vertex and pixel shaders; therefore, to run these programs in real time, you will need a graphics card that supports shaders such as the GeForce3.

Intended Audience

This book was designed with the following three audiences in mind:

- Intermediate level C++ programmers who would like an introduction to 3D programming using the latest iteration of Direct3D— Direct3D 9.0
- 3D programmers experienced with an API other than DirectX (e.g., OpenGL) who would like an introduction to Direct3D 9.0
- Experienced Direct3D programmers who would like an up-to-date book covering the latest version of Direct3D, including vertex and pixel shaders, the High-Level Shading Language, and the effects framework

Installing DirectX 9.0

To write and execute DirectX 9.0 programs, you need both the DirectX 9.0 runtime and the DirectX 9.0 SDK (Software Development Kit) installed on your computer. Note that the runtime will be installed when you install the SDK. The DirectX SDK can be obtained at http://msdn.microsoft.com/library/default.asp?url=/downloads/list/ directx.asp. The installation is straightforward; however, there is one important point. When you get to the dialog box shown in Figure I.1, make sure that you select the Debug option.

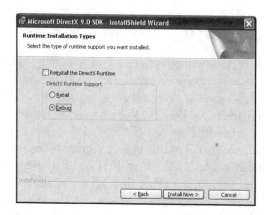

Figure I.1: For developing DirectX applications, it is best to select the Debug option so that you can debug your DirectX applications easier.

The Debug option installs both the debug and retail builds of the DirectX DLLs onto your computer, whereas the Retail option installs just the retail DLLs. For development, you want the debug DLLs, since these DLLs will output Direct3D-related debug information into the Visual Studio output window when the program is run in debug mode, which is obviously very useful when debugging DirectX applications. Figure I.2 shows the debug spew when a Direct3D object hasn't been properly released.

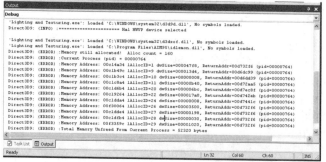

Figure I.2: The debug spew resulting from not releasing a Direct3D resource

Note: Be aware that the debug DLLs are slower than the retail DLLs, so for shipping applications, use the retail version.

Setting Up the Development Environment

The types of projects that you will want to create for writing DirectX applications are *Win32 Application* projects. In VC++ 6.0 and 7.0 you will also want to specify the directory paths at which the DirectX header files and library files are located, so VC++ can find these files. The DirectX header files and library files are located at the paths D:\DXSDK\Include and D:\DXSDK\Lib, respectively.

> **Note:** The location of the DirectX directory DXSDK on your computer may differ; it depends on the location that you specified during installation.

Typically, the DirectX SDK installation will add these paths to VC++ for you. However, in case it doesn't, you can do it manually as follows:

In VC++ 6.0 go to the menu and select **Tools > Options > Directories** and enter the DirectX header file and library paths, as Figure I.3 shows.

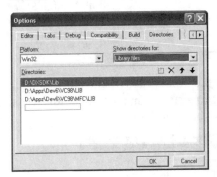

Figure I.3: Adding the DirectX include and library paths to VC++ 6.0

In VC++ 7.0 go to the menu and select **Tools > Options > Projects Folder > VC++ Directories** and enter the DirectX header and library paths, as Figure I.4 shows.

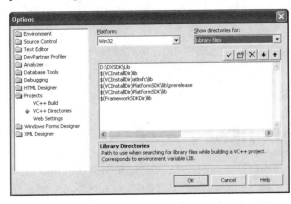

Figure I.4: Adding the DirectX include and library paths to VC++ 7.0

Then, in order to build the sample programs, you will need to link the library files d3d9.lib, d3dx9.lib, and winmm.lib into your project. Note that winmm.lib isn't a DirectX library file; it is the Windows multimedia library file, and we use it for its timer functions.

In VC++ 6.0 you can specify the library files to link in by going to the menu and selecting Project > Settings > Link tab and then entering the library names, as shown in Figure I.5.

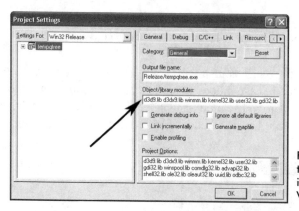

Figure I.5: Specifying the library files to link into the project in VC++ 6.0

In VC++ 7.0 you can specify the library files to link in by going to the menu and selecting Project>Properties>Linker>Input folder and then entering the library names, as shown in Figure I.6.

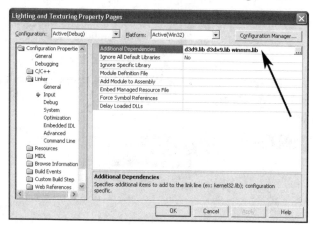

Figure I.6: Specifying the library files to link into the project in VC++ 7.0

Use of the D3DX Library

Since version 7.0, DirectX has shipped with the D3DX (Direct3D Extension) library. This library provides a set of functions, classes, and interfaces that simplify common 3D graphics-related operations, such as math operations, texture and image operations, mesh operations, and shader operations (e.g., compiling and assembling). That is to say, D3DX contains many features that would be a chore to implement on your own.

We use the D3DX library throughout this book because it allows us to focus on more interesting material. For instance, we'd rather not spend pages explaining how to load various image formats (e.g., .bmp, .jpeg) into a Direct3D texture interface when we can do it in a single call to the D3DX function `D3DXCreateTextureFromFile`. In other words, D3DX makes us more productive and lets us focus more on actual content rather than spending time reinventing the wheel.

Other reasons to use D3DX:

■ D3DX is general and can be used with a wide range of different types of 3D applications.

■ D3DX is fast (at least as fast as general functionality can be).

■ Other developers use D3DX. Therefore, you will most likely encounter code that uses D3DX. Consequently, whether you choose to use D3DX or not, you should become familiar with it so that you can read code that uses it.

■ D3DX already exists and has been thoroughly tested. Furthermore, it becomes more improved and feature rich with each iteration of DirectX.

Using the DirectX SDK Documentation and SDK Samples

Direct3D is a huge API, and we cannot hope to cover all of its details in this one book. Therefore, to obtain extended information, it is imperative that you learn how to use the DirectX SDK documentation. You can launch the C++ DirectX online documentation by executing the DirectX9_c file in the \DXSDK\Doc\DirectX9 directory, where DXSDK is the directory to which you installed DirectX.

The DirectX documentation covers just about every part of the DirectX API; therefore, it is very useful as a reference, but because the documentation doesn't go into much depth, it isn't the best learning tool. However, it does get better and better with every new DirectX version released.

As said, the documentation is primarily useful as a reference. Suppose you come across a DirectX-related type or function (say the function `D3DXMatrixInverse`) that you would like more information on. You simply do a search in the documentation index and get a description of the object type, or in this case function, as shown in Figure I.7.

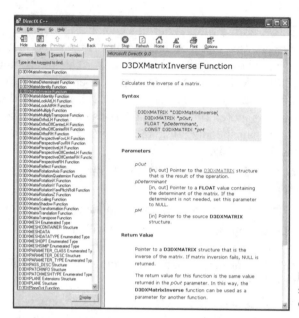

Figure I.7: A screen shot of the C++ SDK documentation viewer

Note: In this book we may direct you to the documentation for further details from time to time.

The SDK documentation also contains some introductory tutorials at the URL /DirectX9_c.chm::/directx/graphics/programmingguide/tutorialsandsamplesandtoolsandtips/tutorials/tutorials.htm. These tutorials correspond to some of the topics in Part II of this book. Therefore, we recommend that you study these tutorials at the same time you read through that part of the book so that you can get alternative explanations and examples.

We would also like to point out the available Direct3D sample programs that ship with DirectX SDK. The C++ Direct3D samples are located in the \DXSDK\Samples\C++\Direct3D directory. Each sample illustrates how to implement a particular effect in Direct3D. These samples are fairly advanced for a beginning graphics programmer, but by the end of this book you should be ready to study them. Examination of the samples is a good "next step" after finishing this book.

Code Conventions

The coding conventions for the sample code are fairly clear-cut. The only two things worth mentioning are that we prefix member variables with an underscore. For example:

```
class C
{
public:
    // ...define public interface
private:
    float _x; // prefix member variables with an underscore.
    float _y;
    float _z;
};
```

And global variable and function names begin with a capital letter, whereas local variable and method names begin with a lowercase letter. We find this useful for determining variable/function scope.

Error Handling

In general, we don't do any error handling in the sample programs because we don't want to take your attention away from the more important code that is demonstrating a particular concept or technique. In other words, we feel the sample code illustrates a concept more clearly without error-handling code. Keep this in mind if you are using any of the sample code in your own projects, as you will probably want to rework it to include error handling.

Clarity

We want to emphasize that the program samples for this book were written with clarity in mind and not performance. Thus, many of the samples may be implemented inefficiently. Keep this in mind if you are using any of the sample code in your own projects, as you may wish to rework it for better efficiency.

Sample Programs and Additional Online Supplements

The web site for this book (www.moon-labs.com) plays an integral part in getting the most out of this book. On the web site you will find the complete source code for every one of the samples in this book. We advise readers to study the corresponding sample(s) for each chapter, either as they read through the chapter or after they have read the chapter. As a general rule, the reader should be able to implement a chapter's sample(s) on his or her own after reading the chapter and spending some time studying the sample's source code. In fact, a good exercise is trying to implement the samples on your own using the book and sample code as a reference.

In addition to sample programs, the web site also contains a message board and chat program. We urge readers to communicate with each other and post questions on topics they do not understand or need clarification on. In many cases, getting alternative perspectives and explanations of a concept speeds up the time it takes to comprehend it.

Lastly, we plan to add additional program samples and tutorials to the web site on topics that we could not fit into this book for one reason or another. Also, if reader feedback indicates readers are struggling with a particular concept, additional examples and explanations may be uploaded to the web site as well.

The companion files can also be downloaded from www.wordware.com/files/dx9.

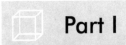 **Part I**

Mathematical Prerequisites

In this prerequisite part we introduce the mathematical tools that are used throughout this book. The major theme is the discussion on vectors, matrices, and transformations, which are used in just about every sample program of this book. Planes and rays are covered as well because some applications in this book make reference to them; these sections are considered optional on a first reading.

This discussion is kept light and informal so that the material is accessible to readers with various math backgrounds. For readers desiring a more thorough and complete understanding of the topics covered here, a linear algebra course in a classroom is the best place to learn these topics thoroughly. Readers who have already studied linear algebra will find Part I a light read and can use it as a refresher if necessary.

In addition to the math explanations, we show the D3DX math-related classes used to model these mathematical objects and the functions used to execute a particular operation.

Objectives

- To learn the geometry and algebra of vectors and their applications to 3D computer graphics
- To learn about matrices, their algebra, and how we use them to transform 3D geometry
- To learn how to model planes and rays algebraically and their applications to 3D graphics
- To become familiar with a subset of the classes and functions provided by the D3DX library that are used for 3D math operations

1

Vectors in 3-Space

Geometrically, we represent a vector as a directed line segment, as shown in Figure 1. The two properties of vectors are their length (also known as the magnitude and the norm) and the direction in which they point. Thus, vectors are useful for modeling physical quantities that possess both a magnitude and direction. For example, in Chapter 14 we implement a particle system. We use vectors to model the velocity and acceleration of our particles. Other times in 3D computer graphics we use vectors to model directions only. For instance, we often want to know the direction in which a ray of light is traveling, the direction a polygon is facing, or the direction the camera is looking in the 3D world. Vectors provide a convenient mechanism for describing such directions in 3-space.

Since location is not a property of vectors, two vectors that have the same length and point in the same direction are considered equal, even if they are in different locations. Observe that two such vectors are parallel to each other. For example, in Figure 1, the vectors **u** and **v** are equal.

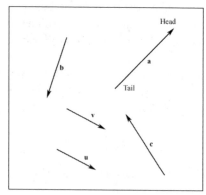

Figure 1: Free vectors defined independently of a particular coordinate system

Figure 1 shows that vectors can be discussed independently of a particular coordinate system because the vector itself (directed line segment) contains the meaningful information—the direction and magnitude. Introducing a coordinate system does not give the vector meaning; rather the vector, which inherently contains its meaning, is simply described relative to that particular system. And as we change coordinate systems we are just describing the *same* vector relative to different systems.

That said, we move on to learning how we describe vectors relative to the left-handed rectangular coordinate system. Figure 2 shows a left-handed system as well as a right-handed system. The difference between the two is the directions in which the positive z-axis runs. In the left-handed system, the positive z-axis goes into the page. In the right-handed system, the positive z-axis comes out of the page.

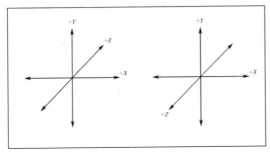

Figure 2: On the left we have a left-handed coordinate system. Observe that the positive z-axis goes into the page. On the right we have a right-handed coordinate system. Observe that the positive z-axis comes out of the page.

Because the location of a vector doesn't change its properties, we can translate all the vectors parallel to themselves so that their tail coincides with the origin of the coordinate system. When a vector's tail coincides with the origin it is in *standard position*. Thus, when a vector is in standard position we can describe the vector by specifying the coordinates of its head point. We call these coordinates the *components* of a vector. Figure 3 shows the vectors from Figure 1 described in standard position.

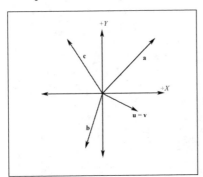

Figure 3: Fixed vectors in standard position defined relative to a particular coordinate system. Observe that **u** and **v** now coincide with each other exactly because they are equal.

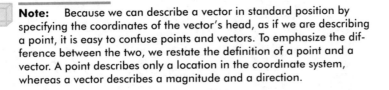

Note: Because we can describe a vector in standard position by specifying the coordinates of the vector's head, as if we are describing a point, it is easy to confuse points and vectors. To emphasize the difference between the two, we restate the definition of a point and a vector. A point describes only a location in the coordinate system, whereas a vector describes a magnitude and a direction.

We usually denote a vector in lowercase bold but sometimes in upper-case bold as well. Examples of two-, three-, and four-dimensional vectors, respectively: $\mathbf{u} = (u_x, u_y)$, $\mathbf{N} = (N_x, N_y, N_z)$, $\mathbf{c} = (c_x, c_y, c_z, c_w)$.

We now introduce four special 3D vectors, which are illustrated in Figure 4. The first is called the *zero vector* and has zeros for all of its components; it is denoted by a bold zero: $\mathbf{0} = (0, 0, 0)$. The next three special vectors are referred to as the standard basis vectors for $\mathfrak{R}^3$. These vectors, called the $\mathbf{i}, \mathbf{j}$, and $\mathbf{k}$ vectors, run along the x-, y-, and z-axes of our coordinate system, respectively, and have a magnitude of one: $\mathbf{i} = (1, 0, 0)$, $\mathbf{j} = (0, 1, 0)$, and $\mathbf{k} = (0, 0, 1)$.

Note: A vector with a magnitude of one is called a *unit vector*.

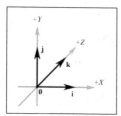

Figure 4: The zero vector and the standard basis vectors for $\mathfrak{R}^3$

In the D3DX library, we can use the `D3DXVECTOR3` class to represent a vector in 3-space. Its class definition is:

```
typedef struct D3DXVECTOR3 : public D3DVECTOR {
public:
    D3DXVECTOR3 () {};
    D3DXVECTOR3 ( CONST FLOAT * );
    D3DXVECTOR3 ( CONST D3DVECTOR& );
    D3DXVECTOR3 ( FLOAT x, FLOAT y, FLOAT z );

    // casting
    operator FLOAT* ();
    operator CONST FLOAT* () const;

    // assignment operators
    D3DXVECTOR3& operator += ( CONST D3DXVECTOR3& );
    D3DXVECTOR3& operator -= ( CONST D3DXVECTOR3& );
    D3DXVECTOR3& operator *= ( FLOAT );
    D3DXVECTOR3& operator /= ( FLOAT );

    // unary operators
    D3DXVECTOR3 operator + () const;
    D3DXVECTOR3 operator - () const;

    // binary operators
    D3DXVECTOR3 operator + ( CONST D3DXVECTOR3& ) const;
    D3DXVECTOR3 operator - ( CONST D3DXVECTOR3& ) const;
    D3DXVECTOR3 operator * ( FLOAT ) const;
    D3DXVECTOR3 operator / ( FLOAT ) const;
```

```
    friend D3DXVECTOR3 operator * ( FLOAT,
                                     CONST struct D3DXVECTOR3& );

    BOOL operator == ( CONST D3DXVECTOR3& ) const;
    BOOL operator != ( CONST D3DXVECTOR3& ) const;

} D3DXVECTOR3, *LPD3DXVECTOR3;
```

Note that `D3DXVECTOR3` inherits its component data from
`D3DVECTOR`, which is defined as:

```
typedef struct _D3DVECTOR {
    float x;
    float y;
    float z;
} D3DVECTOR;
```

Like scalar quantities, vectors have their own arithmetic, as you can
see from the mathematical operations that the `D3DXVECTOR3` class
defines. You are not expected to know what these methods do at this
time. The following subsections introduce these vector operations as
well as some other D3DX vector utility functions and other important
details about vectors.

Note: Although we are primarily concerned with 3D vectors, we
sometimes work with 2D and 4D vectors in 3D graphics programming.
The D3DX library provides a `D3DXVECTOR2` and `D3DXVECTOR4` class for
representing 2D and 4D vectors, respectively. Vectors of different
dimensions have the same properties as 3D vectors, namely they
describe magnitudes and directions, only in different dimensions. In
addition, the mathematical operations of vectors can be generalized to
any dimensional vector with the exception of the vector cross product
(see the section titled "Cross Products"), which is only defined in $\Re^3$.
Thus, with the exception of the cross product, the operations we discuss for 3D vectors carry over to 2D, 4D, and even n-dimensional
vectors.

Vector Equality

Geometrically, two vectors are equal if they point in the same direction
and have the same length. Algebraically, we say they are equal if they
are of the same dimension and their corresponding components are
equal. For example, $(u_x, u_y, u_z) = (v_x, v_y, v_z)$ if $u_x = v_x$, $u_y = v_y$, and $u_z = v_z$.

In code we can test if two vectors are equal using the overloaded
equals operator:

```
D3DXVECTOR u(1.0f, 0.0f, 1.0f);
D3DXVECTOR v(0.0f, 1.0f, 0.0f);

if( u == v ) return true;
```

Similarly, we can test if two vectors are not equal using the overloaded not equals operator:

```
if( u != v ) return true;
```

Note: When comparing floating-point numbers, care must be taken because, due to floating-point imprecision, two floating-point numbers that we expect to be equal may differ slightly; therefore, we test if they are approximately equal. We do this by defining an EPSILON constant, which is a very small value that we use as a "buffer." We say two values are approximately equal if their distance is less than EPSILON. In other words, EPSILON gives us some tolerance for floating-point imprecision. The following function illustrates how EPSILON can be used to test if two floating-point values are equal:

```
const float EPSILON = 0.001f;
bool Equals(float lhs, float rhs)
{
    // if lhs == rhs their difference should be zero
    return fabs(lhs - rhs) < EPSILON ? true : false;
}
```

We do not have to worry about doing this when using the D3DXVEC-TOR3 class, as its overloaded comparison operations will do this for us, but comparing floating-point numbers properly is important to know in general.

Computing the Magnitude of a Vector

Geometrically, the magnitude of a vector is the length of the directed line segment. Given the components of a vector, we can algebraically compute its magnitude with the following formula:

$$(1) \quad \|\mathbf{u}\| = \sqrt{u_x^2 + u_y^2 + u_z^2}$$

The double vertical bars in $\|\mathbf{u}\|$ denotes the magnitude of $\mathbf{u}$.

Example: Find the magnitude of the vectors $\mathbf{u} = (1, 2, 3)$ and $\mathbf{v} = (1, 1)$.

Solution: For $\mathbf{u}$ we have:

$$(2) \quad \|\mathbf{u}\| = \sqrt{1^2 + 2^2 + 3^2} = \sqrt{1 + 4 + 9} = \sqrt{14}$$

Generalizing formula (1) to two dimensions, for $\mathbf{v}$ we have:

$$(3) \quad \|\mathbf{v}\| = \sqrt{1^2 + 1^2} = \sqrt{2}$$

Using the D3DX library, we can compute the magnitude of a vector using the following function:

```
FLOAT D3DXVec3Length(      // Returns the magnitude.
    CONST D3DXVECTOR3* pV // The vector to compute the length of.
);


D3DXVECTOR3 v(1.0f, 2.0f, 3.0f);
float magnitude = D3DXVec3Length( &v ); // = sqrt(14)
```

Normalizing a Vector

Normalizing a vector makes a vector's magnitude equal to one, which is called a unit vector. We can normalize a vector by dividing each component by the vector's magnitude, as shown here:

$$\hat{u} = \frac{u}{\|u\|} = \left(\frac{u_x}{\|u\|}, \quad \frac{u_y}{\|u\|}, \quad \frac{u_z}{\|u\|} \right)$$

We denote a unit vector by putting a hat over it: û.

<u>Example</u>: Normalize the vectors **u** = (1, 2, 3) and **v** = (1, 1).

<u>Solution</u>: From equations (2) and (3) we have $\|u\| = \sqrt{14}$ and $\|v\| = \sqrt{2}$, so:

$$\hat{u} = \frac{u}{\sqrt{14}} = \left(\frac{1}{\sqrt{14}}, \quad \frac{2}{\sqrt{14}}, \quad \frac{3}{\sqrt{14}} \right)$$

$$\hat{v} = \frac{v}{\sqrt{2}} = \left(\frac{1}{\sqrt{2}}, \quad \frac{1}{\sqrt{2}} \right)$$

Using the D3DX library, we can normalize a vector using the following function:

```
D3DXVECTOR3 *D3DXVec3Normalize(
    D3DXVECTOR3* pOut,      // Result.
    CONST D3DXVECTOR3* pV // The vector to normalize.
);
```

Note: This function returns a pointer to the result so that it can be passed as a parameter to another function. For the most part, unless otherwise stated, a D3DX math function returns a pointer to the result. We will not explicitly say this for every function.

Vector Addition

We can add two vectors by adding their corresponding components together; note that the vectors being added must be of the same dimension:

$$u + v = \left(u_x + v_x, \quad u_y + v_y, \quad u_z + v_z \right)$$

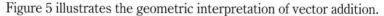

Figure 5 illustrates the geometric interpretation of vector addition.

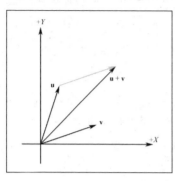

Figure 5: Vector addition. Notice how we translate **v** parallel to itself so that its tail coincides with the head of **u**; then the sum is the vector originating at the tail of **u** and ending at the head of the translated **v**.

To add two vectors in code, we use the overloaded addition operator:

```
D3DXVECTOR3 u(2.0f,  0.0f, 1.0f);
D3DXVECTOR3 v(0.0f, -1.0f, 5.0f);

// (2.0 + 0.0, 0.0 + (-1.0), 1.0 + 5.0)
D3DXVECTOR3 sum = u + v; // = (2.0f, -1.0f, 6.0f)
```

Vector Subtraction

Similar to addition, two vectors are subtracted by subtracting their corresponding components. Again, the vectors must be of the same dimension.

$$\mathbf{u}-\mathbf{v}=\mathbf{u}+\left(-\mathbf{v}\right)=\left(u_x-v_x, \; u_y-v_y, \; u_z-v_z\right)$$

Figure 6 illustrates the geometric interpretation of vector subtraction.

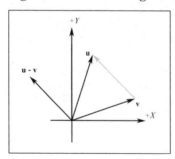

Figure 6: Vector subtraction

To subtract two vectors in code, we use the overloaded subtraction operator:

```
D3DXVECTOR3 u(2.0f,  0.0f, 1.0f);
D3DXVECTOR3 v(0.0f, -1.0f, 5.0f);

D3DXVECTOR3 difference = u - v; // = (2.0f, 1.0f, -4.0f)
```

As Figure 6 shows, vector subtraction returns a vector from the head of **v** to the head of **u**. If we interpret the components of **u** and **v** as the coordinates of points, we can use vector subtraction to find the vector from one point to another. This is a very convenient operation because we will often want to find the vector describing the direction from one point to another.

Scalar Multiplication

We can multiply a vector by a scalar, as the name suggests, and this scales the vector. This operation leaves the direction of the vector unchanged, unless we scale by a negative number, in which case the direction is flipped (inverted).

$$k\mathbf{u} = \left(ku_x, \quad ku_y, \quad ku_z \right)$$

The D3DXVECTOR3 class provides a scalar multiplication operator:

```
D3DXVECTOR3 u(1.0f, 1.0f, -1.0f);
D3DXVECTOR3 scaledVec = u * 10.0f; // = (10.0f, 10.0f, -10.0f)
```

Dot Products

The dot product is one of two products that vector algebra defines. It is computed as follows:

$$\mathbf{u} \cdot \mathbf{v} = u_x v_x + u_y v_y + u_z v_z = s$$

The above formula does not present an obvious geometric meaning. Using the law of cosines, we can find the relationship $\mathbf{u} \cdot \mathbf{v} = \|\mathbf{u}\|\|\mathbf{v}\| \cos \vartheta$, which says that the dot product between two vectors is the cosine of the angle between them scaled by the vectors' magnitudes. Thus, if both **u** and **v** are unit vectors, then **u** · **v** is the cosine of the angle between them.

Some useful properties of the dot product:

■ If $\mathbf{u} \cdot \mathbf{v} = 0$, then $\mathbf{u} \perp \mathbf{v}$.

■ If $\mathbf{u} \cdot \mathbf{v} > 0$, then the angle, ϑ, between the two vectors is less than 90 degrees.

■ If $\mathbf{u} \cdot \mathbf{v} < 0$, then the angle, ϑ, between the two vectors is greater than 90 degrees.

Note: The $\perp$ symbol means "orthogonal," which is synonymous with the term "perpendicular."

We use the following D3DX function to compute the dot product between two vectors:

```
FLOAT D3DXVec3Dot (          // Returns the result.
    CONST D3DXVECTOR3* pV1, // Left sided operand.
    CONST D3DXVECTOR3* pV2  // Right sided operand.
);


D3DXVECTOR3 u(1.0f, -1.0f, 0.0f);
D3DXVECTOR3 v(3.0f,  2.0f, 1.0f);

//    1.0*3.0 + -1.0*2.0 + 0.0*1.0
// = 3.0 + -2.0
float dot = D3DXVec3Dot( &u, &v ); // = 1.0
```

Cross Products

The second form of multiplication that vector math defines is the cross product. Unlike the dot product, which evaluates to a scalar, the cross product evaluates to another vector. Taking the cross product of two vectors, **u** and **v**, yields another vector, **p**, that is mutually orthogonal to **u** and **v**. By that we mean **p** is orthogonal to **u**, and **p** is orthogonal to **v**. The cross product is computed like so:

$$\mathbf{p} = \mathbf{u} \times \mathbf{v} = [(u_y v_z - u_z v_y),\ \ (u_z v_x - u_x v_z),\ \ (u_x v_y - u_y v_x)]$$

In component form:

$$p_x = (u_y v_z - u_z v_y)$$

$$p_y = (u_z v_x - u_x v_z)$$

$$p_z = (u_x v_y - u_y v_x)$$

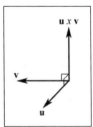

Figure 7: Cross product. The vector $\mathbf{u} \times \mathbf{v} = \mathbf{p}$ is orthogonal to both **u** and **v**.

Example: Find $\mathbf{j} = \mathbf{k} \times \mathbf{i} = (0, 0, 1) \times (1, 0, 0)$ and verify that **j** is orthogonal to both **k** and **i**.

Solution:

$$j_x = (0(0) - 1(0)) = 0$$

$$j_y = (1(1) - 0(0)) = 1$$

$$j_z = (0(0) - 0(1)) = 0$$

So, $\mathbf{j} = (0, 1, 0)$. Recall from the section titled "Dot Products" that if $\mathbf{u} \cdot \mathbf{v} = 0$, then $\mathbf{u} \perp \mathbf{v}$. Since $\mathbf{j} \cdot \mathbf{k} = 0$ and $\mathbf{j} \cdot \mathbf{i} = 0$, we know $\mathbf{j}$ is orthogonal to both $\mathbf{k}$ and $\mathbf{i}$.

We use the following D3DX function to compute the cross product between two vectors:

```
D3DXVECTOR3 *D3DXVec3Cross(
    D3DXVECTOR3* pOut,        // Result.
    CONST D3DXVECTOR3* pV1,   // Left sided operand.
    CONST D3DXVECTOR3* pV2    // Right sided operand.
);
```

It is obvious from Figure 7 that the vector $-\mathbf{p}$ is also mutually orthogonal to both $\mathbf{u}$ and $\mathbf{v}$. The order in which we perform the cross product determines whether we get $\mathbf{p}$ or $-\mathbf{p}$ as a result. In other words, $\mathbf{u} \times \mathbf{v} = -(\mathbf{v} \times \mathbf{u})$. This shows that the cross product is not commutative. You can determine the vector returned by the cross product by the *left-hand thumb rule*. (We use a left-hand rule because we are using a left-handed coordinate system. We would switch to the right-hand rule if we were using a right-handed coordinate system.) If you curve the fingers of your left hand in the direction of the first vector toward the second vector, your thumb points in the direction of the returned vector.

Matrices

In this section we concentrate on the mathematics of matrices. Their applications to 3D graphics are explained in the next section.

An $m \times n$ *matrix* is a rectangular array of numbers with m rows and n columns. The number of rows and columns give the dimension of the matrix. We identify a matrix entry by specifying the row and column that it is in using a double subscript, where the first subscript identifies the row and the second subscript identifies the column. Examples of a 3 $\times$ 3 matrix $\mathbf{M}$, a 2×4 matrix $\mathbf{B}$, and a 3×2 matrix $\mathbf{C}$ follow:

$$\mathbf{M} = \begin{bmatrix} m_{11} & m_{12} & m_{13} \\ m_{21} & m_{22} & m_{23} \\ m_{31} & m_{32} & m_{33} \end{bmatrix} \quad \mathbf{B} = \begin{bmatrix} b_{11} & b_{12} & b_{13} & b_{14} \\ b_{21} & b_{22} & b_{23} & b_{24} \end{bmatrix} \quad \mathbf{C} = \begin{bmatrix} c_{11} & c_{12} \\ c_{21} & c_{22} \\ c_{31} & c_{32} \end{bmatrix}$$

We generally use uppercase bold letters to denote matrices.

Sometimes a matrix will contain a single row or column. We give the special names *row vector* and *column vector* to describe such matrices. Examples of a row and column vector follow:

$$\mathbf{v} = \begin{bmatrix} v_1, & v_2, & v_3, & v_4 \end{bmatrix} \qquad \mathbf{u} = \begin{bmatrix} u_x \\ u_y \\ u_z \end{bmatrix}$$

When using row or column vectors, we only need a single subscript, and sometimes we use letters as the subscripts used to identify an entry in the row or column.

Equality, Scalar Multiplication, and Addition

Refer to the following four matrices throughout this subsection:

$$\mathbf{A} = \begin{bmatrix} 1 & 5 \\ -2 & 3 \end{bmatrix} \quad \mathbf{B} = \begin{bmatrix} 6 & 2 \\ 5 & -8 \end{bmatrix} \quad \mathbf{C} = \begin{bmatrix} 1 & 5 \\ -2 & 3 \end{bmatrix} \quad \mathbf{D} = \begin{bmatrix} 1 & 2 & -1 & 3 \\ -6 & 3 & 0 & 0 \end{bmatrix}$$

- Two matrices are equal if they are of the same dimension and their corresponding entries are equal. For example, $\mathbf{A} = \mathbf{C}$ because $\mathbf{A}$ and $\mathbf{C}$ have the same dimension and their corresponding entries are equal. We note that $\mathbf{A} \neq \mathbf{B}$ and $\mathbf{A} \neq \mathbf{D}$ because either the corresponding entries are not equal or the matrices are of different dimensions.

- We can multiply a matrix by a scalar by multiplying each entry of the matrix by the scalar. For example, multiplying $\mathbf{D}$ by the scalar k gives:

$$k\mathbf{D} = \begin{bmatrix} k(1) & k(2) & k(-1) & k(3) \\ k(-6) & k(3) & k(0) & k(0) \end{bmatrix}$$

If $k = 2$, we have:

$$k\mathbf{D} = 2\mathbf{D} = \begin{bmatrix} 2(1) & 2(2) & 2(-1) & 2(3) \\ 2(-6) & 2(3) & 2(0) & 2(0) \end{bmatrix} = \begin{bmatrix} 2 & 4 & -2 & 6 \\ -12 & 6 & 0 & 0 \end{bmatrix}$$

- Two matrices can be added only if they are of the same dimension. The sum is found by adding the corresponding entries of the two matrices together. For example:

$$\mathbf{A} + \mathbf{B} = \begin{bmatrix} 1 & 5 \\ -2 & 3 \end{bmatrix} + \begin{bmatrix} 6 & 2 \\ 5 & -8 \end{bmatrix} = \begin{bmatrix} 1+6 & 5+2 \\ -2+5 & 3+(-8) \end{bmatrix} = \begin{bmatrix} 7 & 7 \\ 3 & -5 \end{bmatrix}$$

- As with addition, in order to be able to subtract two matrices, they must have the same dimensions. Matrix subtraction is illustrated by the following example:

$$\mathbf{A} - \mathbf{B} = \mathbf{A} + (-\mathbf{B}) = \begin{bmatrix} 1 & 5 \\ -2 & 3 \end{bmatrix} - \begin{bmatrix} 6 & 2 \\ 5 & -8 \end{bmatrix} = \begin{bmatrix} 1 & 5 \\ -2 & 3 \end{bmatrix} + \begin{bmatrix} -6 & -2 \\ -5 & 8 \end{bmatrix} = \begin{bmatrix} 1-6 & 5-2 \\ -2-5 & 3+8 \end{bmatrix} = \begin{bmatrix} -5 & 3 \\ -7 & 11 \end{bmatrix}$$

Multiplication

Matrix multiplication is the most important operation that we use with matrices in 3D computer graphics. Through matrix multiplication we can transform vectors and combine several transformations together. Transformations are covered in the next section.

In order to take the matrix product $\mathbf{AB}$, the number of columns of $\mathbf{A}$ must equal the number of rows of $\mathbf{B}$. If that condition is satisfied, the product is defined. Consider the following two matrices, $\mathbf{A}$ and $\mathbf{B}$, of dimensions 2×3 and 3×3, respectively:

$$\mathbf{A} = \begin{bmatrix} a_{11} & a_{12} & a_{13} \\ a_{21} & a_{22} & a_{23} \end{bmatrix} \qquad \mathbf{B} = \begin{bmatrix} b_{11} & b_{12} & b_{13} \\ b_{21} & b_{22} & b_{23} \\ b_{31} & b_{32} & b_{33} \end{bmatrix}$$

We see that the product $\mathbf{AB}$ is defined because the number of columns of $\mathbf{A}$ equals the number of rows of $\mathbf{B}$. Note that the product $\mathbf{BA}$, found by switching the order of multiplication, is not defined because the number of columns of $\mathbf{B}$ does *not* equal the number of rows of $\mathbf{A}$. This suggests that matrix multiplication is generally not commutative (that is, $\mathbf{AB} \neq \mathbf{BA}$). We say "generally not commutative" because there are some instances where matrix multiplication does work out to be commutative.

Now that we know when matrix multiplication is defined, we can give its definition as follows: If $\mathbf{A}$ is an $m \times n$ matrix and $\mathbf{B}$ is an $n \times p$ matrix, the product $\mathbf{AB}$ is defined and is an $m \times p$ matrix $\mathbf{C}$, where the ij^{th} entry of the product $\mathbf{C}$ is found by taking the dot product of the ith row vector in $\mathbf{A}$ with the jth column vector in $\mathbf{B}$:

(4) $\quad c_{ij} = \mathbf{a}_i \cdot \mathbf{b}_j$

where $\mathbf{a}_i$ denotes the ith row vector in $\mathbf{A}$, and $\mathbf{b}_j$ denotes the jth column vector in $\mathbf{B}$.

As an example, find the product:

$$\mathbf{AB} = \begin{bmatrix} 4 & 1 \\ -2 & 1 \end{bmatrix} \begin{bmatrix} 1 & 3 \\ 2 & 1 \end{bmatrix}$$

We verify the product is defined because the number of columns of **A** equals the number of rows of **B**. Also note that the resulting matrix is a 2×2 matrix. Using formula (4), we have:

$$\mathbf{AB} = \begin{bmatrix} 4 & 1 \\ -2 & 1 \end{bmatrix} \begin{bmatrix} 1 & 3 \\ 2 & 1 \end{bmatrix} = \begin{bmatrix} \mathbf{a_1 \cdot b_1} & \mathbf{a_1 \cdot b_2} \\ \mathbf{a_2 \cdot b_1} & \mathbf{a_2 \cdot b_2} \end{bmatrix} = \begin{bmatrix} (4 \ 1)\cdot(1 \ 2) & (4 \ 1)\cdot(3 \ 1) \\ (-2 \ 1)\cdot(1 \ 2) & (-2 \ 1)\cdot(3 \ 1) \end{bmatrix} = \begin{bmatrix} 6 & 13 \\ 0 & -5 \end{bmatrix}$$

As an exercise, verify for this particular example that $\mathbf{AB} \neq \mathbf{BA}$.

A more general example:

$$\mathbf{AB} = \begin{bmatrix} a_{11} & a_{12} & a_{13} \\ a_{21} & a_{22} & a_{23} \end{bmatrix} \begin{bmatrix} b_{11} & b_{12} \\ b_{21} & b_{22} \\ b_{31} & b_{32} \end{bmatrix} = \begin{bmatrix} a_{11}b_{11} + a_{12}b_{21} + a_{13}b_{31} & a_{11}b_{12} + a_{12}b_{22} + a_{13}b_{32} \\ a_{21}b_{11} + a_{22}b_{21} + a_{23}b_{31} & a_{21}b_{12} + a_{22}b_{22} + a_{23}b_{32} \end{bmatrix} = \mathbf{C}$$

The Identity Matrix

There is a special matrix called the *identity matrix*. The identity matrix is a square matrix that has zeros for all elements except along the main diagonal, and the elements along the main diagonal are all ones. For example, below are 2×2, 3×3, and 4×4 identity matrices:

$$\begin{bmatrix} 1 & 0 \\ 0 & 1 \end{bmatrix} \quad \begin{bmatrix} 1 & 0 & 0 \\ 0 & 1 & 0 \\ 0 & 0 & 1 \end{bmatrix} \quad \begin{bmatrix} 1 & 0 & 0 & 0 \\ 0 & 1 & 0 & 0 \\ 0 & 0 & 1 & 0 \\ 0 & 0 & 0 & 1 \end{bmatrix}$$

The identity matrix acts as a multiplicative identity:

MI = IM = M

That is, multiplying a matrix by the identity does not change the matrix. Further, multiplying with the identity matrix is a particular case when matrix multiplication is commutative. The identity matrix can be thought of as the number "1" for matrices.

Example: Verify that multiplying the matrix $\mathbf{M} = \begin{bmatrix} 1 & 2 \\ 0 & 4 \end{bmatrix}$ by the 2×2 identity matrix results in **M**.

$$\begin{bmatrix} 1 & 2 \\ 0 & 4 \end{bmatrix}\begin{bmatrix} 1 & 0 \\ 0 & 1 \end{bmatrix} = \begin{bmatrix} (1 \ \ 2)\cdot(1 \ \ 0) & (1 \ \ 2)\cdot(0 \ \ 1) \\ (0 \ \ 4)\cdot(1 \ \ 0) & (0 \ \ 4)\cdot(0 \ \ 1) \end{bmatrix} = \begin{bmatrix} 1 & 2 \\ 0 & 4 \end{bmatrix}$$

Inverses

In matrix math there is not an analog to division but there is a multiplicative inverse operation. The following list summarizes the important information about inverses:

- Only square matrices have inverses; therefore when we speak of matrix inverses, we assume we are dealing with a square matrix.
- The inverse of an $n \times n$ matrix $\mathbf{M}$ is an $n \times n$ matrix denoted as $\mathbf{M}^{-1}$.
- Not every square matrix has an inverse.
- Multiplying a matrix with its inverse results in the identity matrix: $\mathbf{MM}^{-1} = \mathbf{M}^{-1}\mathbf{M} = \mathbf{I}$. Note that matrix multiplication is commutative when multiplying a matrix with its inverse.

Matrix inverses are useful for solving for other matrices in a matrix equation. For example, consider the equation $\mathbf{p}' = \mathbf{pR}$ and suppose that we know $\mathbf{p}'$ and $\mathbf{R}$ and wish to solve for $\mathbf{p}$. The first task is to find $\mathbf{R}^{-1}$ (assuming it exists). Once $\mathbf{R}^{-1}$ is known, we can solve for $\mathbf{p}$, like so:

$$\mathbf{p}'\mathbf{R}^{-1} = \mathbf{p}(\mathbf{R}\mathbf{R}^{-1})$$
$$\mathbf{p}'\mathbf{R}^{-1} = \mathbf{pI}$$
$$\mathbf{p}'\mathbf{R}^{-1} = \mathbf{p}$$

Techniques for finding inverses are beyond the scope of this book, but they are described in any linear algebra textbook. In the section titled "Basic Transformations" we give the inverses for the particular matrices that we work with. In the section titled "D3DX Matrices" we learn about a D3DX function that finds the inverse of a matrix for us.

To conclude this section on inverses we present the following useful property for the inverse of a product: $(\mathbf{AB})^{-1} = \mathbf{B}^{-1}\mathbf{A}^{-1}$. This property assumes both $\mathbf{A}$ and $\mathbf{B}$ are invertible and that they are both square matrices of the same dimension.

The Transpose of a Matrix

The *transpose* of a matrix is found by interchanging the rows and columns of the matrix. Thus, the transpose of an $m \times n$ matrix is an $n \times m$ matrix. We denote the transpose of a matrix $\mathbf{M}$ as $\mathbf{M}^T$.

Example: Find the transpose for the following two matrices:

$$\mathbf{A} = \begin{bmatrix} 2 & -1 & 8 \\ 3 & 6 & -4 \end{bmatrix} \quad \mathbf{B} = \begin{bmatrix} a & b & c \\ d & e & f \\ g & h & i \end{bmatrix}$$

To reiterate, the transposes are found by interchanging the rows and columns. Thus:

$$\mathbf{A}^T = \begin{bmatrix} 2 & 3 \\ -1 & 6 \\ 8 & -4 \end{bmatrix} \quad \mathbf{B}^T = \begin{bmatrix} a & d & g \\ b & e & h \\ c & f & i \end{bmatrix}$$

D3DX Matrices

When programming Direct3D applications, we typically use 4×4 matrices and 1×4 row vectors exclusively. Note that using these two sizes of matrices implies the following matrix multiplications are defined:

- **Vector-matrix multiplication.** That is, if **v** is a 1×4 row vector and **T** is a 4×4 matrix, the product **vT** is defined and the result is a 1×4 row vector.

- **Matrix-matrix multiplication.** That is, if **T** is a 4×4 matrix and **R** is a 4×4 matrix, the products **TR** and **RT** are defined and both result in a 4×4 matrix. Note that the product **TR** does not necessarily equal the product **RT** because matrix multiplication is not commutative.

To represent 1×4 row vectors in D3DX, we typically use the D3DXVECTOR3 and D3DXVECTOR4 vector classes. Of course, D3DXVECTOR3 only has three components, not four. However, the fourth component is typically an understood one or zero (more on this in the next section).

To represent 4×4 matrices in D3DX, we use the D3DXMATRIX class, defined as follows:

```
typedef struct D3DXMATRIX : public D3DMATRIX
{
public:
    D3DXMATRIX() {};
    D3DXMATRIX(CONST FLOAT*);
    D3DXMATRIX(CONST D3DMATRIX&);
    D3DXMATRIX(FLOAT _11, FLOAT _12, FLOAT _13, FLOAT _14,
              FLOAT _21, FLOAT _22, FLOAT _23, FLOAT _24,
              FLOAT _31, FLOAT _32, FLOAT _33, FLOAT _34,
              FLOAT _41, FLOAT _42, FLOAT _43, FLOAT _44);
```

```
// access grants
FLOAT& operator () (UINT Row, UINT Col);
FLOAT  operator () (UINT Row, UINT Col) const;

// casting operators
operator FLOAT* ();
operator CONST FLOAT* () const;

// assignment operators
D3DXMATRIX& operator *= (CONST D3DXMATRIX&);
D3DXMATRIX& operator += (CONST D3DXMATRIX&);
D3DXMATRIX& operator -= (CONST D3DXMATRIX&);
D3DXMATRIX& operator *= (FLOAT);
D3DXMATRIX& operator /= (FLOAT);

// unary operators
D3DXMATRIX operator + () const;
D3DXMATRIX operator - () const;

// binary operators
D3DXMATRIX operator * (CONST D3DXMATRIX&) const;
D3DXMATRIX operator + (CONST D3DXMATRIX&) const;
D3DXMATRIX operator - (CONST D3DXMATRIX&) const;
D3DXMATRIX operator * (FLOAT) const;
D3DXMATRIX operator / (FLOAT) const;

friend D3DXMATRIX operator * (FLOAT, CONST D3DXMATRIX&);

BOOL operator == (CONST D3DXMATRIX&) const;
BOOL operator != (CONST D3DXMATRIX&) const;
} D3DXMATRIX, *LPD3DXMATRIX;
```

The D3DXMATRIX class inherits its data entries from the simpler D3DMATRIX structure, which is defined as:

```
typedef struct _D3DMATRIX {
    union {
        struct {
            float _11, _12, _13, _14;
            float _21, _22, _23, _24;
            float _31, _32, _33, _34;
            float _41, _42, _43, _44;
        };
        float m[4][4];
    };
} D3DMATRIX;
```

Observe that the D3DXMATRIX class has a myriad of useful operators, such as testing for equality, adding and subtracting matrices, multiplying a matrix by a scalar, casting, and—most importantly—multiplying two D3DXMATRIXs together. Because matrix multiplication is so important, we give a code example of using this operator:

```
D3DXMATRIX A(…); // initialize A
D3DXMATRIX B(…); // initialize B
```

```
D3DXMATRIX C = A * B; // C = AB
```

Another important operator of the `D3DXMATRIX` class is the parenthesis operator, which allows us to conveniently access entries in the matrix. Note that when using the parenthesis operator, we index starting into the matrix starting at zero like a C array. For example, to access entry $ij = 11$ of a matrix, we would write:

```
D3DXMATRIX M;
M(0, 0) = 5.0f; // Set entry ij = 11 to 5.0f.
```

The D3DX library also provides the following useful functions that set a `D3DXMATRIX` to the identity matrix, take the transpose of a `D3DXMATRIX`, and find the inverse of a `D3DXMATRIX`:

```
D3DXMATRIX *D3DXMatrixIdentity(
    D3DXMATRIX *pout        // The matrix to be set to the identity.
);

D3DXMATRIX M;
D3DXMatrixIdentity( &M );   // M = identity matrix


D3DXMATRIX *D3DXMatrixTranspose(
    D3DXMATRIX *pOut,       // The resulting transposed matrix.
    CONST D3DXMATRIX *pM    // The matrix to take the transpose of.
);

D3DXMATRIX A(...);          // initialize A
D3DXMATRIX B;
D3DXMatrixTranspose( &B, &A ); // B = transpose(A)


D3DXMATRIX *D3DXMatrixInverse(
    D3DXMATRIX *pOut,       // returns inverse of pM
    FLOAT *pDeterminant,    // determinant, if required, else pass 0
    CONST D3DXMATRIX *pM    // matrix to invert
);
```

The inverse function returns null if the matrix that we are trying to invert does not have an inverse. Also, for this book we can ignore the second parameter and set it to 0 every time.

```
D3DXMATRIX A(...);              // initialize A
D3DXMATRIX B;
D3DXMatrixInverse( &B, 0, &A ); // B = inverse(A)
```

Basic Transformations

When programming using Direct3D, we use 4×4 matrices to represent transformations. The idea is this: We set the entries of a 4×4 matrix **X** to describe a specific transformation. Then we place the coordinates of a point or the components of a vector into the columns of a 1×4 row vector **v**. The product **vX** results in a new transformed vector **v**′. For example, if **X** represented a 10-unit translation on the x-axis and **v** = [2, 6, –3, 1], the product **vX** = **v**′ = [12, 6, –3, 1].

A few things need to be clarified. We use 4×4 matrices because that particular size can represent all the transformations that we need. A 3×3 may at first seem more suitable to 3D. However, there are many types of transformations that we would like to use that we cannot describe with a 3×3 matrix, such as translations, perspective projections, and reflections. Remember that we are working with a vector-matrix product, and so we are limited to the rules of matrix multiplication to perform transformations. Augmenting to a 4×4 matrix allows us to describe more transformations with a matrix and the defined vector-matrix multiplication.

We said that we place the coordinates of a point or the components of a vector into the columns of a 1×4 row vector. But our points and vectors are 3D! Why are we using 1×4 row vectors? We must augment our 3D points/vectors to 4D row vectors in order to make the vector-matrix product defined—the product of a 1×3 row vector and a 4×4 matrix is *not* defined.

So then, what do we use for the fourth component, which, by the way, we denote as w? When placing *points* in a 1×4 row vector, we set the w component to 1. This allows translations of points to work correctly. Because vectors have no location, the translation of vectors is not defined, and attempting to translate a vector results in a meaningless vector. In order to prevent translation on vectors, we set the w component to 0 when placing *vectors* into a 1×4 row vector. For example, the point **p** = (p_1, p_2, p_3) would be placed in a row vector as $[p_1, p_2, p_3, 1]$, and the vector **v** = (v_1, v_2, v_3) would be placed in a row vector as $[v_1, v_2, v_3, 0]$.

Note: We set $w = 1$ to allow points to be translated correctly, and we set $w = 0$ to prevent translations on vectors. This is made clear when we examine the actual translation matrix.

Note: The augmented 4D vector is called a *homogenous* vector and because homogeneous vectors can describe points and vectors, we use the term "vector," knowing that we may be referring to either points or vectors.

Sometimes a matrix transformation we define changes the w component of a vector so that $w \neq 0$ and $w \neq 1$. Consider the following:

$$\mathbf{p}=\begin{bmatrix} p_1, & p_2, & p_3, & 1 \end{bmatrix}\begin{bmatrix} 1 & 0 & 0 & 0 \\ 0 & 1 & 0 & 0 \\ 0 & 0 & 1 & 1 \\ 0 & 0 & 0 & 0 \end{bmatrix}=\begin{bmatrix} p_1, & p_2, & p_3, & p_3 \end{bmatrix}=\mathbf{p'}, \text{ for } p_3 \neq 0$$

and $p_3 \neq 1$.

We note that $w = p_3$. When $w \neq 0$ and $w \neq 1$, we say that we have a vector in *homogeneous space*, as opposed to a vector in 3-space. We can map a vector in homogeneous space back to three dimensions by dividing each component of the vector by the w component. For example, to map the vector $(x,\ y,\ z,\ w)$ in homogeneous space to the 3D vector $\mathbf{x}$ we would write:

$$\left(\frac{x}{w},\ \frac{y}{w},\ \frac{z}{w},\ \frac{w}{w}\right)=\left(\frac{x}{w},\ \frac{y}{w},\ \frac{z}{w},\ 1\right)=\left(\frac{x}{w},\ \frac{y}{w},\ \frac{z}{w}\right)=\mathbf{x}$$

Going to homogeneous space and then mapping back to 3D space is used to do perspective projections in 3D graphics programming.

Note: When we write a point $(x,\ y,\ z)$ as $(x,\ y,\ z,\ 1)$ we are technically describing our 3D space on a 4D plane in 4-space, namely the 4D plane $w = 1$. (Note that a plane in 4D is a 3D space, just like a plane in 3D is a 2D space.) Thus, when we set w to something else, we move off the $w = 1$ plane. In order to get back onto that plane, which corresponds with our 3D space, we project back onto it by dividing each component by w.

The Translation Matrix

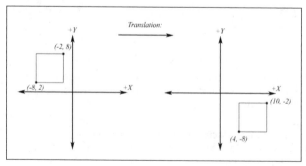

Figure 8: Translating 12 units on the x-axis and −10 units on the y-axis

We can translate the vector $(x,\ y,\ z,\ 1)$ p_x units on the x-axis, p_y units on the y-axis, and p_z units on the z-axis by multiplying it with the following matrix:

$$\mathbf{T(p)}=\begin{bmatrix} 1 & 0 & 0 & 0 \\ 0 & 1 & 0 & 0 \\ 0 & 0 & 1 & 0 \\ p_x & p_y & p_z & 1 \end{bmatrix}$$

The D3DX function to build a translation matrix is:

```
D3DXMATRIX *D3DXMatrixTranslation(
    D3DXMATRIX* pOut,      // Result.
    FLOAT x,               // Number of units to translate on x-axis.
    FLOAT y,               // Number of units to translate on y-axis.
    FLOAT z                // Number of units to translate on z-axis.
);
```

Exercise: Let $\mathbf{T(p)}$ be a matrix representing a translation transformation, and let $\mathbf{v} = [v_1, v_2, v_3, 0]$ be any vector. Verify $\mathbf{vT(p)} = \mathbf{v}$ (that is, verify the vector is not affected by translations if $w = 0$).

The inverse of the translation matrix is found by simply negating the translating vector $\mathbf{p}$.

$$\mathbf{T}^{-1} = \mathbf{T(-p)} = \begin{bmatrix} 1 & 0 & 0 & 0 \\ 0 & 1 & 0 & 0 \\ 0 & 0 & 1 & 0 \\ -p_x & -p_y & -p_z & 1 \end{bmatrix}$$

The Rotation Matrices

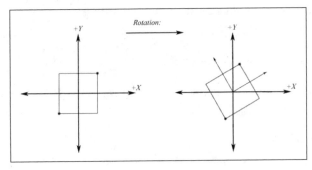

Figure 9: Rotating 30 degrees counterclockwise around the z-axis from our perspective

We can rotate a vector ϑ radians around the x-, y-, and z-axes using the following matrices. Note that angles are measured clockwise when looking down the axis of rotation toward the origin.

$$\mathbf{X}(\vartheta) = \begin{bmatrix} 1 & 0 & 0 & 0 \\ 0 & \cos\theta & \sin\theta & 0 \\ 0 & -\sin\theta & \cos\theta & 0 \\ 0 & 0 & 0 & 1 \end{bmatrix}$$

The D3DX function to build an x-axis rotation matrix is:

```
D3DXMATRIX *D3DXMatrixRotationX(
    D3DXMATRIX* pOut,      // Result.
```

```
        FLOAT Angle                // Angle of rotation measured in radians.
);
```

$$\mathbf{Y}(\vartheta)=\begin{bmatrix} \cos\theta & 0 & -\sin\theta & 0 \\ 0 & 1 & 0 & 0 \\ \sin\theta & 0 & \cos\theta & 0 \\ 0 & 0 & 0 & 1 \end{bmatrix}$$

The D3DX function to build a y-axis rotation matrix is:

```
D3DXMATRIX *D3DXMatrixRotationY(
    D3DXMATRIX* pOut,      // Result.
    FLOAT Angle            // Angle of rotation measured in radians.
);
```

$$\mathbf{Z}(\vartheta)=\begin{bmatrix} \cos\theta & \sin\theta & 0 & 0 \\ -\sin\theta & \cos\theta & 0 & 0 \\ 0 & 0 & 1 & 0 \\ 0 & 0 & 0 & 1 \end{bmatrix}$$

The D3DX function to build a z-axis rotation matrix is:

```
D3DXMATRIX *D3DXMatrixRotationZ(
    D3DXMATRIX* pOut,      // Result.
    FLOAT Angle            // Angle of rotation measured in radians.
);
```

The inverse of a rotation matrix $\mathbf{R}$ is its transpose, $\mathbf{R}^T = \mathbf{R}^{-1}$. Such a matrix is said to be orthogonal.

The Scaling Matrix

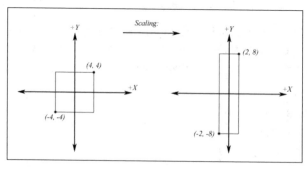

Figure 10: Scaling by one-half units on the x-axis and two units on the y-axis

We can scale a vector q_x units on the x-axis, q_y units on the y-axis, and q_z units on the z-axis by multiplying a vector with the following matrix:

$$S(q) = \begin{bmatrix} q_x & 0 & 0 & 0 \\ 0 & q_y & 0 & 0 \\ 0 & 0 & q_z & 0 \\ 0 & 0 & 0 & 1 \end{bmatrix}$$

The D3DX function to build a scaling matrix is:

```
D3DXMATRIX *D3DXMatrixScaling(
    D3DXMATRIX* pOut,    // Result.
    FLOAT sx,            // Number of units to scale on the x-axis.
    FLOAT sy,            // Number of units to scale on the y-axis.
    FLOAT sz             // Number of units to scale on the z-axis.
);
```

The inverse of a scaling matrix is found by taking the reciprocal of each scaling factor:

$$S^{-1} = S\left(\frac{1}{q_x}, \frac{1}{q_y}, \frac{1}{q_z}\right) = \begin{bmatrix} \dfrac{1}{q_x} & 0 & 0 & 0 \\ 0 & \dfrac{1}{q_y} & 0 & 0 \\ 0 & 0 & \dfrac{1}{q_z} & 0 \\ 0 & 0 & 0 & 1 \end{bmatrix}$$

Combining Transformations

Often we apply a sequence of transformations to a vector. For instance, we may scale a vector, then rotate it, and finally translate it into its desired position.

Example: Scale the vector $\mathbf{p} = [5, 0, 0, 1]$ by one-fifth on all axes, then rotate it $\pi/4$ radians on the y-axis, and finally translate it 1 unit on the x-axis, 2 units on the y-axis, and –3 units on the z-axis.

Solution: Note that we must perform a scaling, a y-axis rotation, and a translation. We set up our transformation matrices $\mathbf{S}$, $\mathbf{R}_y$, $\mathbf{T}$ for scaling, rotating, and translating, respectively, as follows:

$$S\left(\frac{1}{5}, \frac{1}{5}, \frac{1}{5}\right) = \begin{bmatrix} \dfrac{1}{5} & 0 & 0 & 0 \\ 0 & \dfrac{1}{5} & 0 & 0 \\ 0 & 0 & \dfrac{1}{5} & 0 \\ 0 & 0 & 0 & 1 \end{bmatrix} \qquad R_y\left(\frac{\pi}{4}\right) = \begin{bmatrix} .707 & 0 & -.707 & 0 \\ 0 & 1 & 0 & 0 \\ .707 & 0 & .707 & 0 \\ 0 & 0 & 0 & 1 \end{bmatrix}$$

$$T(1, 2, -3) = \begin{bmatrix} 1 & 0 & 0 & 0 \\ 0 & 1 & 0 & 0 \\ 0 & 0 & 1 & 0 \\ 1 & 2 & -3 & 1 \end{bmatrix}$$

Applying the sequence of transformations in the order scaling, rotating, and translating, we obtain:

$$pS = \begin{bmatrix} 1, & 0, & 0, & 1 \end{bmatrix} = p'$$

$$(5) \quad p'R_y = \begin{bmatrix} .707, & 0, & -.707, & 1 \end{bmatrix} = p''$$

$$p''T = \begin{bmatrix} 1.707, & 2, & -3.707, & 1 \end{bmatrix}$$

One of the key benefits of matrices is that we can use matrix multiplication to combine several transformations into one matrix. For example, let's reconsider the example at the beginning of this section. Let's combine the three transformation matrices into one matrix representing all three through matrix multiplication. Note that the order in which we multiply the transformations is the order that they are applied.

$$(6) \quad SR_y T = \begin{bmatrix} \frac{1}{5} & 0 & 0 & 0 \\ 0 & \frac{1}{5} & 0 & 0 \\ 0 & 0 & \frac{1}{5} & 0 \\ 0 & 0 & 0 & 1 \end{bmatrix} \begin{bmatrix} .707 & 0 & -.707 & 0 \\ 0 & 1 & 0 & 0 \\ .707 & 0 & .707 & 0 \\ 0 & 0 & 0 & 1 \end{bmatrix} \begin{bmatrix} 1 & 0 & 0 & 0 \\ 0 & 1 & 0 & 0 \\ 0 & 0 & 1 & 0 \\ 1 & 2 & -3 & 1 \end{bmatrix}$$

$$= \begin{bmatrix} .1414 & 0 & -.1414 & 0 \\ 0 & 1 & 0 & 0 \\ .1414 & 0 & .1414 & 0 \\ 1 & 2 & -3 & 1 \end{bmatrix} = Q$$

Then $pQ = [1.707, 2, -3.707, 1]$.

The ability to combine transformations has performance implications. Suppose that we need to apply the same scaling, rotation, and translation transformations to a large set of vectors (a common task in 3D graphics). Instead of applying a sequence of transformations, as we did in equation (5), per vector, we can combine all three transformations into one matrix, as we did in equation (6). Then we only have to multiply each vector by one matrix that contains all three transformations combined. This saves a significant amount of vector-matrix multiplication operations.

Some Functions to Transform Vectors

The D3DX library provides the following two functions for transforming points and vectors, respectively. The `D3DXVec3TransformCoord` function transforms points and assumes the fourth component of the vector is an understood 1. The `D3DXVec3TransformNormal` function transforms vectors and assumes the fourth component of the vector is an understood 0.

```
D3DXVECTOR3 *D3DXVec3TransformCoord(
        D3DXVECTOR3* pOut,          // Result.
        CONST D3DXVECTOR3* pV,      // The point to transform.
        CONST D3DXMATRIX* pM        // The transformation matrix.
    );

D3DXMATRIX T(...);     // initialize a transformation matrix
D3DXVECTOR3 p(...);    // initialize a point
D3DXVec3TransformCoord( &p, &p, &T );  // transform the point


D3DXVECTOR3 *WINAPI D3DXVec3TransformNormal(
        D3DXVECTOR3 *pOut,          // Result.
        CONST D3DXVECTOR3 *pV,      // The vector to transform.
        CONST D3DXMATRIX *pM        // The transformation matrix.
    );

D3DXMATRIX T(...);     // initialize a transformation matrix
D3DXVECTOR3 v(...);    // initialize a vector
D3DXVec3TransformNormal( &v, &v, &T);  // transform the vector
```

Note: The D3DX library also provides `D3DXVec3Transform-CoordArray` and `D3DXVec3TransformNormalArray` for transforming an array of points and an array of vectors, respectively.

Planes (Optional)

A plane can be described with a vector **n** and a point on the plane **p**$_0$. The vector **n** is called the plane's *normal vector* and is perpendicular to the plane (see Figure 11).

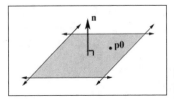

Figure 11: A plane defined by a normal vector **n** and a point on the plane **p**$_0$

In Figure 12 we see that the graph of a plane is all the points **p** that satisfy the equation.

(7) $\mathbf{n} \cdot (\mathbf{p} - \mathbf{p}_0) = 0$

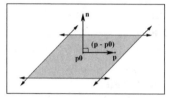

Figure 12: If $\mathbf{p}_0$ is a point on the plane, then the point **p** is also on the plane if the vector formed from $(\mathbf{p} - \mathbf{p}_0)$ is orthogonal to the plane's normal vector.

When describing a particular plane, the normal **n** and a known point on the plane $\mathbf{p}_0$ are fixed, so it is typical to write equation (7) as:

(8) $\mathbf{n} \cdot \mathbf{p} + d = 0$

where $d = -\mathbf{n} \cdot \mathbf{p}_0$.

Note: If the plane's normal vector **n** is of unit length, $d = -\mathbf{n} \cdot \mathbf{p}_0$ gives the shortest signed distance from the origin to the plane.

D3DXPLANE

When representing a plane in code, it suffices to store only the normal vector **n** and the constant d. It is useful to think of this as a 4D vector, which we denote as $(\mathbf{n}, d)$. The D3DX library uses the following structure for a plane:

```
typedef struct D3DXPLANE
{
#ifdef __cplusplus
public:
    D3DXPLANE() {}
    D3DXPLANE( CONST FLOAT* );
    D3DXPLANE( CONST D3DXFLOAT16* );
    D3DXPLANE( FLOAT a, FLOAT b, FLOAT c, FLOAT d );

    // casting
    operator FLOAT* ();
    operator CONST FLOAT* () const;

    // unary operators
    D3DXPLANE operator + () const;
    D3DXPLANE operator - () const;

    // binary operators
    BOOL operator == ( CONST D3DXPLANE& ) const;
    BOOL operator != ( CONST D3DXPLANE& ) const;
```

Part I

```
#endif //__cplusplus
    FLOAT a, b, c, d;
} D3DXPLANE, *LPD3DXPLANE;
```

where a, b, and c form the components of the plane's normal vector **n** and d is the constant d, from equation (8).

Point and Plane Spatial Relation

Equation (8) is primarily useful for testing the location of points relative to the plane. For example, given the plane $(\mathbf{n}, d)$, we can test how a particular point **p** is in relation with the plane:

If $\mathbf{n} \cdot \mathbf{p} + d = 0$, then **p** is coplanar with the plane.

If $\mathbf{n} \cdot \mathbf{p} + d > 0$, then **p** is in front of the plane and in the plane's positive half-space.

If $\mathbf{n} \cdot \mathbf{p} + d < 0$, then **p** is in back of the plane and in the plane's negative half-space.

Note: If the plane's normal vector **n** is of unit length, then $\mathbf{n} \cdot \mathbf{p} + d$ gives the shortest signed distance from the plane to the point **p**.

This next D3DX function evaluates $\mathbf{n} \cdot \mathbf{p} + d$ for a particular plane and point:

```
FLOAT D3DXPlaneDotCoord(
    CONST D3DXPLANE *pP,              // plane.
    CONST D3DXVECTOR3 *pV             // point.
);

// Test the locality of a point relative to a plane.
D3DXPLANE p(0.0f, 1.0f, 0.0f, 0.0f);

D3DXVECTOR3 v(3.0f, 5.0f, 2.0f);

float x = D3DXPlaneDotCoord( &p, &v );

if( x approximately equals 0.0f )     // v is coplanar to the plane.
if( x > 0 )                           // v is in positive half-space.
if( x < 0 )                           // v is in negative half-space.
```

Note: We say "approximately equals" due to floating-point imprecision. See the note in the section titled "Vector Equality."

Note: Methods similar to D3DXPlaneDotCoord are D3DXPlaneDot and D3DXPlaneDotNormal. See the DirectX documentation for details.

Construction

Besides directly specifying the normal and signed distance of a plane, we can calculate these two components in two ways. Given the normal **n** and a known point on the plane $\mathbf{p}_0$, we can solve for the d component:

$$\mathbf{n} \cdot \mathbf{p}_0 + d = 0$$
$$\mathbf{n} \cdot \mathbf{p}_0 = -d$$
$$-\mathbf{n} \cdot \mathbf{p}_0 = d$$

The D3DX library provides the following function to perform this calculation:

```
D3DXPLANE *D3DXPlaneFromPointNormal(
    D3DXPLANE* pOut,              // Result.
    CONST D3DXVECTOR3* pPoint,    // Point on the plane.
    CONST D3DXVECTOR3* pNormal    // The normal of the plane.
);
```

The second way that we can construct a plane is by specifying three points on the plane.

Given the points $\mathbf{p}_0$, $\mathbf{p}_1$, $\mathbf{p}_2$, we can form two vectors on the plane:

$$\mathbf{u} = \mathbf{p}_1 - \mathbf{p}_0$$
$$\mathbf{v} = \mathbf{p}_2 - \mathbf{p}_0$$

From that we can compute the normal of the plane by taking the cross product of the two vectors on the plane. Remember the left-hand thumb rule.

$$\mathbf{n} = \mathbf{u} \times \mathbf{v}$$

Then, $-(\mathbf{n} \cdot \mathbf{p}_0) = d$.

The D3DX library provides the following function to compute a plane, given three points on the plane:

```
D3DXPLANE *D3DXPlaneFromPoints(
    D3DXPLANE* pOut,           // Result.
    CONST D3DXVECTOR3* pV1,    // Point 1 on the plane.
    CONST D3DXVECTOR3* pV2,    // Point 2 on the plane.
    CONST D3DXVECTOR3* pV3     // Point 3 on the plane.
);
```

Normalizing a Plane

Sometimes we might have a plane and would like to normalize the normal vector. At first thought, it would seem that we could just normalize the normal vector as we would any other vector. But recall that $d = -\mathbf{n} \cdot \mathbf{p}_0$ in $\mathbf{n} \cdot \mathbf{p} + d = 0$. We see that the length of the normal vector influences the constant d. Therefore, if we normalize the normal vector, we must also recalculate d. Note that $\dfrac{d}{\|\mathbf{n}\|} = -\dfrac{\mathbf{n}}{\|\mathbf{n}\|} \cdot \mathbf{p}_0$.

Thus, we have the following formula to normalize the normal vector of the plane $(\mathbf{n}, d)$:

$$\frac{1}{\|\mathbf{n}\|}(\mathbf{n} \quad d) = \left(\frac{\mathbf{n}}{\|\mathbf{n}\|} \quad \frac{d}{\|\mathbf{n}\|}\right)$$

We can use the following D3DX function to normalize a plane's normal vector:

```
D3DXPLANE *D3DXPlaneNormalize(
    D3DXPLANE *pOut,            // Resulting normalized plane.
    CONST D3DXPLANE *pP         // Input plane.
);
```

Transforming a Plane

Lengyel shows in *Mathematics for 3D Game Programming & Computer Graphics* that we can transform a plane $(\hat{\mathbf{n}}, d)$ by treating it as a 4D vector and multiplying it by the inverse-transpose of the desired transformation matrix. Note that the plane's normal vector must be normalized first.

We use the following D3DX function to do this:

```
D3DXPLANE *D3DXPlaneTransform(
    D3DXPLANE *pOut,            // Result
    CONST D3DXPLANE *pP,        // Input plane.
    CONST D3DXMATRIX *pM        // Transformation matrix.
);
```

Sample code:

```
D3DXMATRIX T(...);              // Init. T to a desired transformation.
D3DXMATRIX inverseOfT;
D3DXMATRIX inverseTransposeOfT;

D3DXMatrixInverse( &inverseOfT, 0, &T );
D3DXMatrixTranspose( &inverseTransposeOfT, &inverseOfT );

D3DXPLANE p(...);              // Init. Plane.
D3DXPlaneNormalize( &p, &p ); // make sure normal is normalized.

D3DXPlaneTransform( &p, &p, &inverseTransposeOfT );
```

Nearest Point on a Plane to a Particular Point

Suppose that we have a point $\mathbf{p}$ in space and would like to find the point $\mathbf{q}$ on the plane $(\hat{\mathbf{n}}, d)$ that is closest to $\mathbf{p}$. Note that the plane's normal vector is assumed to be of unit length—this simplifies the problem a bit.

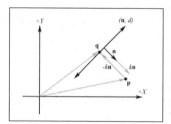

Figure 13: The point **q** on the plane $(\hat{n}, d)$ nearest to **p**. Observe that the shortest signed distance k from **p** to the plane is positive, since **p** is in the positive half-space of $(\hat{n} \; d)$. If **p** were behind the plane, then $k < 0$.

From Figure 13 we can see that $\mathbf{q} = \mathbf{p} + (-k\hat{n})$, where k is the shortest signed distance from **p** to the plane, which is also the shortest signed distance between the points **p** and **q**. Recall that if the plane's normal vector **n** is of unit length, then $\mathbf{n} \cdot \mathbf{p} + d$ gives the shortest signed distance from the plane to the point **p**.

Rays (Optional)

Suppose a player in a game that we are working on fires his gun at an enemy. How would we determine whether the bullet starting from a particular position and aimed in a direction hit the target? One approach would be to model the bullet with a ray and model the enemy with a bounding sphere. (A bounding sphere is simply a sphere that tightly surrounds an object, thus roughly approximating its volume. Bounding spheres are explained in Chapter 11.) Then mathematically we can determine whether the ray hit the sphere and where. In this section we learn how to model rays mathematically.

Rays

A ray can be described with an origin and a direction. The parametric equation of a ray is:

(9) $\quad \mathbf{p}(t) = \mathbf{p}_0 + t\mathbf{u}$

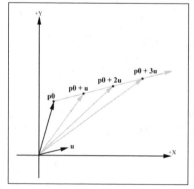

Figure 14: A ray described by an origin **p0** and direction **u**. We can generate points on the ray by plugging in scalars for t that are greater than or equal to zero.

$\mathbf{p}_0$ is the origin of the ray, $\mathbf{u}$ is the direction of the ray, and t is the parameter. By plugging in different values for t, we compute different points on the ray. The parameter t must be in the interval $[0, \infty)$ to describe a ray. Values less than zero will generate points behind the ray (that is, on the line that the ray is on). In fact, if we let $t \in (-\infty, \infty)$, then we have a line in 3-space.

Ray/Plane Intersection

Given a ray $\mathbf{p}(t) = \mathbf{p}_0 + t\mathbf{u}$ and a plane $\mathbf{n} \cdot \mathbf{p} + d = 0$, we would like to know if the ray intersects the plane and the point of intersection. To do this, we plug the ray into the plane equation and solve for the parameter t that satisfies the plane equation, giving us the parameter that yields the intersection point.

Plugging equation (9) into the plane equation:

$\mathbf{n} \cdot \mathbf{p}(t) + d = 0$ Plug ray into plane equation

$\mathbf{n} \cdot (\mathbf{p}_0 + t\mathbf{u}) + d = 0$

$\mathbf{n} \cdot \mathbf{p}_0 + \mathbf{n} \cdot t\mathbf{u} + d = 0$ Distributive property

$\mathbf{n} \cdot t\mathbf{u} = -d - (\mathbf{n} \cdot \mathbf{p}_0)$

$t(\mathbf{n} \cdot \mathbf{u}) = -d - (\mathbf{n} \cdot \mathbf{p}_0)$ Associative property

$t = \dfrac{-d - (\mathbf{n} \cdot \mathbf{p}_0)}{(\mathbf{n} \cdot \mathbf{u})}$ Solve for t.

If t is not in the interval $[0, \infty)$, the ray does not intersect the plane.

If t is in the interval $[0, \infty)$, the intersection point is found by plugging the parameter that satisfies the plane equation into the ray equation:

$$\mathbf{p}\left(\frac{-d - (\mathbf{n} \cdot \mathbf{p}_0)}{(\mathbf{n} \cdot \mathbf{u})}\right) = \mathbf{p}_0 + \frac{-d - (\mathbf{n} \cdot \mathbf{p}_0)}{(\mathbf{n} \cdot \mathbf{u})}\mathbf{u}$$

Summary

- Vectors are used to model physical quantities that possess a magnitude and direction mathematically. Geometrically, we represent a vector with a directed line segment. A vector is in standard position when it is translated parallel to itself so that its tail coincides with the origin of the coordinate system. A vector in standard position can be described algebraically by specifying the coordinates of its head.

- We can use 4×4 matrices to represent transformations and 1×4 homogeneous vectors to describe points and vectors. The vector-matrix product of a 1×4 row vector and a 4×4 transformation matrix results in a new transformed 1×4 row vector. Several transformation matrices can be combined into one transformation matrix through matrix-matrix multiplication.

- We use 4D homogeneous vectors to represent both vectors and points. We specify 0 for the w component to denote a vector and 1 for the w component to denote a point. If $w \neq 0$ and $w \neq 1$, then we have a vector (x, y, z, w) in homogeneous space that can be mapped back to 3-space by dividing each component by w:

$$\left(\frac{x}{w} \quad \frac{y}{w} \quad \frac{z}{w} \quad \frac{w}{w} \right) = \left(\frac{x}{w} \quad \frac{y}{w} \quad \frac{z}{w} \quad 1 \right) = \left(\frac{x}{w} \quad \frac{y}{w} \quad \frac{z}{w} \right)$$

- Planes divide 3D space into two parts: a positive half-space, which is the space in front of the plane, and a negative half-space, which is the space behind the plane. Planes are useful for testing the locality of points relative to them (in other words, what half-space a point exists in relative to a particular plane).

- Rays are described parametrically with an origin and direction vector. Rays are useful for modeling various physical quantities, such as light rays and projectiles that approximately follow a linear path such as bullets and rockets.

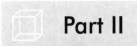

Part II

Direct3D Fundamentals

In this part, we study fundamental Direct3D concepts and techniques that are used throughout the rest of this book. With these fundamentals mastered, we can move on to writing more interesting applications. A brief description of the chapters in this part follows.

Chapter 1, "Direct3D Initialization"—In this chapter, we learn what Direct3D is about and how to initialize it in preparation for 3D drawing.

Chapter 2, "The Rendering Pipeline"—The first theme of this chapter is to learn, mathematically, how to describe a 3D world and represent a virtual camera that describes the perspective from which the world is viewed. The second theme is to learn the steps necessary to take a 2D "picture" of the 3D world based on what the camera "sees"; these steps as a whole are referred to as the *rendering pipeline*.

Chapter 3, "Drawing in Direct3D"—This chapter shows how to draw 3D geometry in Direct3D. We learn how to store geometric data in a form that is usable by Direct3D, and we learn the Direct3D drawing commands. In addition, we learn how to configure the way that Direct3D draws geometry using render states.

Chapter 4, "Color"—In this chapter, we learn how color is represented in Direct3D and how to apply color to solid 3D geometric primitives. Finally, we describe two ways that colors specified per vertex can be shaded across a primitive.

Chapter 5, "Lighting"—In this chapter, we learn how to create light sources and define the interaction between light and surfaces. Lighting adds to the scene's realism and helps depict the solid form and volume of objects.

Chapter 6, "Texturing"—This chapter describes texture mapping. *Texture mapping* is a technique used to increase the realism of the scene by mapping 2D image data onto a 3D primitive. For example, using texture mapping, we can model a brick wall by applying a 2D brick wall image onto a 3D rectangle.

Chapter 7, "Blending"—In this chapter, we look at a technique called *blending*. This technique allows us to implement a number of special effects—in particular, glass-like transparency.

Chapter 8, "Stenciling"—This chapter describes the stencil buffer, which, like a stencil, allows us to block pixels from being drawn. To illustrate the ideas of this chapter, we include thorough discussions on implementing reflections and planar shadows using the stencil buffer.

Chapter 1

Direct3D Initialization

Initialization of Direct3D has historically been a tedious chore. Fortunately, version 8.0 adopted a simplified initialization model, and Direct3D 9.0 follows that same model. However, the initialization process still assumes that the programmer is familiar with basic graphics concepts and some fundamental Direct3D types. The first few sections of this chapter address these requirements. With these prerequisites met, the remainder of the chapter explains the initialization process.

Objectives

- To learn how Direct3D interacts with graphics hardware
- To understand the role that COM plays with Direct3D
- To learn fundamental graphics concepts, such as how 2D images are stored, page flipping, and depth buffering
- To learn how to initialize Direct3D
- To become familiar with the general structure that the sample applications of this book employ

1.1 Direct3D Overview

Direct3D is a low-level graphics API (application programming interface) that enables us to render 3D worlds using 3D hardware acceleration. Direct3D can be thought of as a mediator between the application and the graphics device (3D hardware). For example, to instruct the graphics device to clear the screen, the application would call the Direct3D method `IDirect3DDevice9::Clear`. Figure 1.1 shows the relationship between the application, Direct3D, and the hardware.

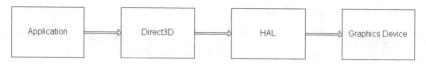

Figure 1.1: The relationship between the application, Direct3D, and the hardware

The Direct3D part of Figure 1.1 is the defined set of interfaces and functions Direct3D exposes to the application/programmer. These interfaces and functions represent the entire features set that the current version of Direct3D supports. Note that just because Direct3D exposes a feature, it doesn't imply that available graphics hardware supports it.

As Figure 1.1 shows, there is an intermediate step between Direct3D and the graphics device—the HAL (Hardware Abstraction Layer). Direct3D cannot interact directly with graphics devices because there are a variety of different cards on the market, and each card has different capabilities and ways of implementing things. For instance, two different graphics cards may implement the clear screen operation differently. Therefore, Direct3D requires device manufacturers to implement a HAL. The HAL is the set of device-specific code that instructs the device to perform an operation. In this way Direct3D avoids having to know the specific details of a device, and its specification can be made independent of hardware devices.

Device manufacturers implement all the features that their device supports into the HAL. Features exposed by Direct3D but not supported by the device are not implemented into the HAL. Calling a Direct3D function that is not implemented by the HAL results in failure, unless it's a vertex processing operation, in which case the desired functionality can be emulated in software by the Direct3D runtime (provided software vertex processing was specified). Therefore, when using esoteric features that are only supported by a minority of devices on the market, be sure to verify that the device supports the feature (device capabilities are explained in section 1.3.8).

1.1.1 The REF Device

You may wish to write programs that use functionality that Direct3D exposes but is not implemented on your device. For this purpose, Direct3D provides a reference rasterizer (known as a REF device), which emulates the entire Direct3D API in software. This allows you to write and test code that uses Direct3D features that are not available on your device. For example, in Part IV of this book we use vertex and pixel shaders, which many cards do not support. If your graphics card does not support shaders, you can still test the sample code with the REF device. It is important to understand that the REF device is for development only. It ships only with the DirectX SDK and cannot be distributed to end users. In addition, the REF is slow enough that it's not practical to use for anything but testing.

1.1.2 **D3DDEVTYPE**

In code, a HAL device is specified by D3DDEVTYPE_HAL, which is a member of the D3DDEVTYPE enumerated type. Similarly, a REF device is specified by D3DDEVTYPE_REF, which is also a member of the D3DDEVTYPE enumerated type. These types are important to remember because we will be asked to specify which type to use when creating our device.

1.2 **COM**

Component Object Model (COM) is the technology that allows DirectX to be language independent and have backward compatibility. We usually refer to a COM object as an interface, which for our purposes can be thought of and used as a C++ class. Most of the details of COM are transparent to us when programming DirectX with C++. The only thing that we must know is that we obtain pointers to COM interfaces through special functions or the methods of another COM interface; we do not create a COM interface with the C++ new keyword. In addition, when we are done with an interface, we call its Release method (all COM interfaces inherit functionality from the IUnknown COM interface, which provides the Release method) rather than delete it. COM objects perform their own memory management.

There is, of course, much more to COM, but more detail is not necessary for using DirectX effectively.

 Note: COM interfaces are prefixed with a capital I. For example, the COM interface that represents a surface is called IDirect3DSurface9.

1.3 **Some Preliminaries**

The initialization process of Direct3D requires us to be familiar with some basic graphics concepts and Direct3D types. We introduce these ideas and types in this section, making the next section that discusses Direct3D initialization more focused.

Part II

1.3.1 **Surfaces**

A *surface* is a matrix of pixels that Direct3D uses primarily to store 2D image data. Figure 1.2 identifies some components of a surface. Note that while we visualize the surface data as a matrix, the pixel data is actually stored in a linear array.

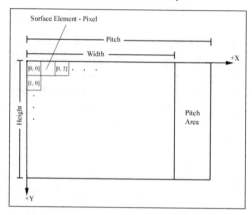

Figure 1.2: A surface

The width and height of a surface are measured in pixels. The pitch is measured in bytes. Furthermore, the pitch may be wider than the width, depending on the underlying hardware implementation, so you *cannot* assume that *pitch = width · sizeof(pixelFormat)*.

In code, we describe surfaces with the IDirect3DSurface9 interface. This interface provides several methods for reading and writing data directly to a surface as well as a method to retrieve information about the surface. The most important methods of IDirect3DSurface9 are:

■ LockRect—This method allows us to obtain a pointer to the surface memory. Then, with some pointer arithmetic, we can read and write to each pixel in the surface.

■ UnlockRect—After you have called LockRect and are done accessing the surface's memory, you must unlock the surface by calling this method.

■ GetDesc—This method retrieves a description of the surface by filling out a D3DSURFACE_DESC structure.

Locking a surface and writing to each pixel can be somewhat confusing at first, considering the surface pitch, so we have provided the following code block that locks a surface and colors each pixel red:

```
// Assume _surface is a pointer to an IDirect3DSurface9 interface.
// Assumes a 32-bit pixel format for each pixel.

// Get the surface description.
D3DSURFACE_DESC surfaceDesc;
_surface->GetDesc(&surfaceDesc);

// Get a pointer to the surface pixel data.
D3DLOCKED_RECT lockedRect;
_surface->LockRect(
    &lockedRect,// pointer to receive locked data
    0,          // lock entire surface
    0);         // no lock flags specified

// Iterate through each pixel in the surface and set it to red.
DWORD* imageData = (DWORD*)lockedRect.pBits;
for(int i = 0; i < surfaceDesc.Height; i++)
{
    for(int j = 0; j < surfaceDesc.Width; j++)
    {
        // index into texture, note we use the pitch and divide by
        // four since the pitch is given in bytes and there are
        // 4 bytes per DWORD.
        int index = i * lockedRect.Pitch / 4 + j;

        imageData[index] = 0xffff0000; // red
    }
}

_surface->UnlockRect();
```

The D3DLOCKED_RECT structure is defined as:

```
typedef struct _D3DLOCKED_RECT {
    INT Pitch;   // the surface pitch
    void *pBits; // pointer to the start of the surface memory
} D3DLOCKED_RECT;
```

Here are a few comments about the surface lock code. The 32-bit pixel format assumption is important since we cast the bits to DWORDs, which are 32 bits. This lets us treat every DWORD as representing a pixel. Also, do not worry about understanding how 0xffff0000 represents red, as colors are covered in Chapter 4.

1.3.2 Multisampling

Multisampling is a technique used to smooth out blocky-looking images that can result when representing images as a matrix of pixels. One of the common uses of multisampling a surface is for full-screen antialiasing (see Figure 1.3).

Figure 1.3: On the left we have a jagged line. On the right we have a sampled antialiased line, which is smoother.

The D3DMULTISAMPLE_TYPE enumerated type consists of values that allow us to specify the level of multisampling of a surface. They are:

■ D3DMULTISAMPLE_NONE—Specifies no multisampling

■ D3DMULTISAMPLE_1_SAMPLE... D3DMULTISAMPLE_16_ SAMPLE—Specifies multisampling levels from 1 to 16

There is also a quality level associated with the multisampling type. This is described as a DWORD.

In this book's sample programs we do not use multisampling because it slows down the application too much. If you wish to include it, remember to use the IDirect3D9::CheckDeviceMultiSampleType method to verify that your graphics device supports the multisampling type that you wish to use and check for valid quality levels.

1.3.3 Pixel Formats

We often need to specify the pixel format of Direct3D resources when we create a surface or texture. The format of a pixel is defined by specifying a member of the D3DFORMAT enumerated type. Some formats are:

■ D3DFMT_R8G8B8—Specifies a 24-bit pixel format where, starting from the leftmost bit, 8 bits are allocated for red, 8 bits are allocated for green, and 8 bits are allocated for blue

■ D3DFMT_X8R8G8B8—Specifies a 32-bit pixel format where, starting from the leftmost bit, 8 bits are not used, 8 bits are allocated for red, 8 bits are allocated for green, and 8 bits are allocated for blue

■ D3DFMT_A8R8G8B8—Specifies a 32-bit pixel format where, starting from the leftmost bit, 8 bits are allocated for alpha, 8 bits are allocated for red, 8 bits are allocated for green, and 8 bits are allocated for blue

■ D3DFMT_A16B16G16R16F—Specifies a 64-bit, floating-point pixel format. Starting from the leftmost bit, 16 bits are allocated for alpha, 16 bits are allocated for blue, 16 bits are allocated for green, and 16 bits are allocated for red.

■ `D3DFMT_A32B32G32R32F`—Specifies a 128-bit, floating-point pixel format. Starting from the leftmost bit, 32 bits are allocated for alpha, 32 bits are allocated for blue, 32 bits are allocated for green, and 32 bits are allocated for red.

For a complete list of supported pixel formats, look up `D3DFORMAT` in the SDK documentation.

> **Note:** The first three formats (`D3DFMT_R8G8B8`, `D3DFMT_X8R8G8B8`, and `D3DFMT_A8R8G8B8`) are common and supported on most hardware. The floating-point pixel format and some of the other formats available (see the SDK docs) are not as widely supported. When using these not-so-widely supported formats, be sure to verify that your card supports a particular format before using it.

1.3.4 Memory Pools

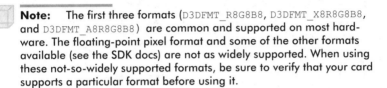

Surfaces and other Direct3D resources can be placed in a variety of memory pools. The memory pool is specified by one of the members of the `D3DPOOL` enumerated type. The memory pools available are:

■ `D3DPOOL_DEFAULT`—The default memory pool instructs Direct3D to place the resource in the memory that is best suited for the resource type and its usage. This may be video memory, AGP memory, or system memory. Note that resources in the default pool must be destroyed (released) prior to an `IDirect-3DDevice9::Reset` call, and must be reinitialized after the reset call.

■ `D3DPOOL_MANAGED`—Resources placed in the manage pool are managed by Direct3D (that is, they are moved to video or AGP memory as needed by the device automatically). In addition, a backup copy of the resource is maintained in system memory. When resources are accessed and changed by the application, they work with the system copy. Then, Direct3D automatically updates them to video memory as needed.

■ `D3DPOOL_SYSTEMMEM`—Specifies that the resource be placed in system memory

■ `D3DPOOL_SCRATCH`—Specifies that the resource be placed in system memory. The difference between this pool and `D3DPOOL_SYSTEMMEM` is that these resources must not follow the graphics device's restrictions. Consequently, the device cannot access resources in this pool, but the resources can be copied to and from each other.

1.3.5 **The Swap Chain and Page Flipping**

Direct3D maintains a collection of surfaces—usually two or three—called a swap chain that is represented by the `IDirect3DSwap-Chain9` interface. We do not go into the specifics of this interface since Direct3D manages it and we rarely need to manipulate it. Instead we will simply outline the purpose of it.

Swap chains and, more specifically, the technique of page flipping are used to provide smooth animation between frames. Figure 1.4 shows a swap chain with two surfaces.

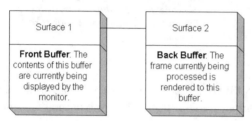

Figure 1.4: A swap chain with two surfaces: a front buffer and a back buffer

In Figure 1.4, the surface in the *front buffer* slot is the surface that corresponds to the image presently being displayed on the monitor. The monitor does not display the image represented by the front buffer instantaneously; it takes one-sixtieth of a second on a monitor with a refresh rate of 60 hertz, for instance. The application's frame rate is often out of sync with the monitor's refresh rate (for example, the application may be able to render frames faster than the monitor can display them). However, we do not want to update the contents of the front buffer with the next frame of animation until the monitor has finished drawing the current frame, but we do not want to halt our rendering while waiting for the monitor to finish displaying the contents of the front buffer either. Therefore, we render to an off-screen surface (*back buffer*); then when the monitor is done displaying the surface in the front buffer, we move it to the end of the swap chain and the next back buffer in the swap chain is promoted to be the front buffer. This process is called *presenting*. Figure 1.5 shows the swap chain before and after a presentation.

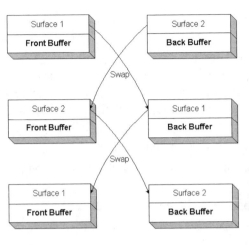

Figure 1.5: Presenting two times. When using a swap chain that contains two surfaces, we see that presenting basically amounts to swapping the surfaces.

Thus, the structure of our rendering code is:

1. Render to back buffer.
2. Present the back buffer.
3. Go to (1).

1.3.6 Depth Buffers

The *depth buffer* is a surface that does not contain image data but rather depth information about a particular pixel. There is an entry in the depth buffer that corresponds to each pixel in the final rendered image. So if the rendered image had a resolution of 640x480, there would be 640x480 depth entries.

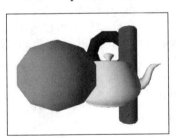

Figure 1.6: A group of objects that partially obscure each other because one is in front of another

Figure 1.6 shows a simple scene where some objects partially obscure the objects behind them. In order for Direct3D to determine which pixels of an object are in front of another, it uses a technique called *depth buffering* or *z-buffering*.

Depth buffering works by computing a depth value for each pixel and performing a depth test. The depth test basically compares the depths of pixels competing to be written to a particular pixel location.

The pixel with the depth value closest to the camera wins, and that pixel gets written. This makes sense because the pixel closest to the camera obscures the pixels behind it.

The format of the depth buffer determines the accuracy of the depth test. That is, a 24-bit depth buffer is more accurate than a 16-bit depth buffer. In general, most applications work fine with a 24-bit depth buffer, although Direct3D also exposes a 32-bit depth buffer.

- D3DFMT_D32—Specifies a 32-bit depth buffer

- D3DFMT_D24S8—Specifies a 24-bit depth buffer with 8 bits reserved as the stencil buffer

- D3DFMT_D24X8—Specifies a 24-bit depth buffer only

- D3DFMT_D24X4S4—Specifies a 24-bit buffer with 4 bits reserved for the stencil buffer

- D3DFMT_D16—Specifies a 16-bit depth buffer only

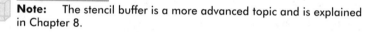

Note: The stencil buffer is a more advanced topic and is explained in Chapter 8.

1.3.7 Vertex Processing

Vertices are the building blocks for 3D geometry, and they can be processed in two different ways, either in software (*software vertex processing*) or in hardware (*hardware vertex processing*). Software vertex processing is always supported and can always be used. On the other hand, hardware vertex processing can only be used if the graphics card supports vertex processing in hardware.

Hardware vertex processing is always preferred since dedicated hardware is faster than software. Furthermore, performing vertex processing in hardware unloads calculations from the CPU, which implies that the CPU is free to perform other calculations.

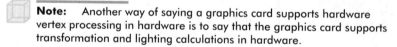

Note: Another way of saying a graphics card supports hardware vertex processing in hardware is to say that the graphics card supports transformation and lighting calculations in hardware.

1.3.8 Device Capabilities

Every feature that Direct3D exposes has a corresponding data member or bit in the D3DCAPS9 structure. The idea is to initialize the members of a D3DCAPS9 instance based on the capabilities of a particular hardware device. Then, in our application, we can check if a device supports a feature by checking the corresponding data member or bit in the D3DCAPS9 instance.

The following example illustrates this. Suppose we wish to check if a hardware device is capable of doing vertex processing in hardware (or in other words, whether the device supports transformation and lighting calculations in hardware). By looking up the `D3DCAPS9` structure in the SDK documentation, we find that the bit `D3DDEVCAPS_HWTRANS-FORMANDLIGHT` in the data member `D3DCAPS9::DevCaps` indicates whether the device supports transformation and lighting calculations in hardware. Our test then, assuming `caps` is a `D3DCAPS9` instance and has already been initialized, is:

```
bool supportsHardwareVertexProcessing;

// If the bit is "on" then that implies the hardware device
// supports it.
if( caps.DevCaps & D3DDEVCAPS_HWTRANSFORMANDLIGHT )
{
    // Yes, the bit is on, so it is supported.
    supportsHardwareVertexProcessing = true;
}
else
{
    // No, the bit is off, so it is not supported.
    hardwareSupportsVertexProcessing = false;
}
```

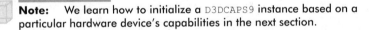

Part II

Note: `DevCaps` stands for "device capabilities."

Note: We learn how to initialize a `D3DCAPS9` instance based on a particular hardware device's capabilities in the next section.

Note: We recommend that you look up the `D3DCAPS9` structure in the SDK documentation and examine the complete list of capabilities that Direct3D exposes.

1.4 Initializing Direct3D

The following subsections show how to initialize Direct3D. The process of initializing Direct3D can be broken down into the following steps:

1. Acquire a pointer to an `IDirect3D9` interface. This interface is used for finding out information about the physical hardware devices on a system and creating the `IDirect3DDevice9` interface, which is our C++ object that represents the physical hardware device we use for displaying 3D graphics.

2. Check the device capabilities (`D3DCAPS9`) to see if the primary display adapter (primary graphics card) supports hardware vertex

processing or not. We need to know if it can in order to create the `IDirect3DDevice9` interface.

3. Initialize an instance of the `D3DPRESENT_PARAMETERS` structure. This structure consists of a number of data members that allow us to specify the characteristics of the `IDirect3DDevice9` interface that we are going to create.

4. Create the `IDirect3DDevice9` object based on an initialized `D3DPRESENT_PARAMETERS` structure. As said, the `IDirect3D-Device9` object is our C++ object that represents the physical hardware device that we use for displaying 3D graphics.

Keep in mind that in this book we use the primary display adapter for drawing 3D graphics. If your system only has one graphics card, that is the primary display adapter. If you have more than one graphics card, then the card you are presently using is the primary display adapter (e.g., the one displaying the Windows desktop, etc.).

1.4.1 Acquiring an IDirect3D9 Interface

Initialization of Direct3D begins by acquiring a pointer to an `IDirect3D9` interface. This is easily done using a special Direct3D function, as the following lines of code show:

```
IDirect3D9* _d3d9;
_d3d9 = Direct3DCreate9(D3D_SDK_VERSION);
```

The single parameter to `Direct3DCreate9` should always be `D3D_SDK_VERSION`, which guarantees that the application is built against the correct header files. If this function fails, it returns a null pointer.

The `IDirect3D9` object is used for two things: device enumeration and creating the `IDirect3DDevice9` object. Device enumeration refers to finding out the capabilities, display modes, formats, and other information about each graphics device available on the system. For instance, to create the `IDirect3DDevice9` object that represents a physical device, we need to create it using a configuration of display modes and formats that the physical device supports. To find such a working configuration, we must use the `IDirect3D9` enumeration methods.

However, because device enumeration can be quite an involved task and we want to get up and running as quickly as possible with Direct3D, we have elected *not* to perform any enumeration, except for one check as shown in the next section. In order to safely skip enumeration, we have chosen a "safe" configuration that almost all hardware devices will support.

1.4.2 Checking for Hardware Vertex Processing

When we create an `IDirect3DDevice9` object to represent the primary display adapter, we must specify the type of vertex processing to use with it. We want to use hardware vertex processing if we can, but because not all cards support hardware vertex processing, we must check if the card supports it first.

To do this, we must first initialize a `D3DCAPS9` instance based on the capabilities of the primary display adapter. We use the following method:

```
HRESULT IDirect3D9::GetDeviceCaps(
    UINT Adapter,
    D3DDEVTYPE DeviceType,
    D3DCAPS9 *pCaps
);
```

■ `Adapter`—Specifies the physical display adapter that we are going to get the capabilities of

■ `DeviceType`—Specifies the device type to use (e.g., hardware device (`D3DDEVTYPE_HAL`) or software device (`D3DDEVTYPE_REF`))

■ `pCaps`—Returns the initialized capabilities structure

Then we can check the capabilities, as we did in section 1.3.8. The following code snippet illustrates this:

```
// Fill D3DCAPS9 structure with the capabilities of the
// primary display adapter.

D3DCAPS9 caps;
d3d9->GetDeviceCaps(
    D3DADAPTER_DEFAULT, // Denotes primary display adapter.
    deviceType, // Specifies the device type, usually D3DDEVTYPE_HAL.
    &caps);     // Return filled D3DCAPS9 structure that contains
                // the capabilities of the primary display adapter.

// Can we use hardware vertex processing?
int vp = 0;
if( caps.DevCaps & D3DDEVCAPS_HWTRANSFORMANDLIGHT )
{
    // yes, save in 'vp' the fact that hardware vertex
    // processing is supported.
    vp = D3DCREATE_HARDWARE_VERTEXPROCESSING;
}
else
{
    // no, save in 'vp' the fact that we must use software
    // vertex processing.
```

Part II

```
        vp = D3DCREATE_SOFTWARE_VERTEXPROCESSING;
}
```

Observe that we save the type of vertex processing that we are going to use in the variable `vp`. This is because we are going to need to specify the vertex processing type that we are going to use later on when we create the `IDirect3DDevice9` object.

Note: The identifiers `D3DCREATE_HARDWARE_VERTEXPROCESSING` and `D3DCREATE_SOFTWARE_VERTEXPROCESSING` are just predefined values that denote hardware vertex processing and software vertex processing, respectively.

Tip: When developing applications and using new, special, or advanced features (in other words, features that are not widely supported), it is recommended that you always check the device capabilities (`D3DCAPS9`) to see if the device supports the particular feature before using it. Never assume that a feature is available. Also, be aware that the sample applications in this book generally do not follow this advice — we generally do not check device capabilities.

Note: If a particular sample application isn't working, it is most likely because your hardware doesn't support the feature that the sample is using; try switching to the REF device.

1.4.3 Filling Out the **D3DPRESENT_PARAMETERS** Structure

The next step in the initialization process is to fill out an instance of the `D3DPRESENT_PARAMETERS` structure. This structure is used to specify some of the characteristics of the `IDirect3DDevice9` object that we are going to create, and is defined as:

```
typedef struct _D3DPRESENT_PARAMETERS_ {
    UINT       BackBufferWidth;
    UINT       BackBufferHeight;
    D3DFORMAT BackBufferFormat;
    UINT       BackBufferCount;
    D3DMULTISAMPLE_TYPE MultiSampleType;
    DWORD      MultiSampleQuality;
    D3DSWAPEFFECT SwapEffect;
    HWND       hDeviceWindow;
    BOOL       Windowed;
    BOOL       EnableAutoDepthStencil;
    D3DFORMAT AutoDepthStencilFormat;
    DWORD      Flags;
    UINT       FullScreen_RefreshRateInHz;
    UINT       PresentationInterval;
} D3DPRESENT_PARAMETERS;
```

Note: In the following data member descriptions for the `D3DPRESENT_PARAMETERS` structure, we only cover the flags and options that we feel are the most important to a beginner at this point.

For a description of further flags, options, and configurations, we refer you to the SDK documentation.

- `BackBufferWidth`—Width of the back buffer surface in pixels

- `BackBufferHeight`—Height of the back buffer surface in pixels

- `BackBufferFormat`—Pixel format of the back buffer (e.g., 32-bit pixel format: `D3DFMT_A8R8G8B8`)

- `BackBufferCount`—The number of back buffers to use. Usually we specify "1" to indicate that we want only one back buffer.

- `MultiSampleType`—The type of multisampling to use with the back buffer. See the SDK documentation for details.

- `MultiSampleQuality`—The quality level of multisampling. See the SDK documentation for details.

- `SwapEffect`—A member of the `D3DSWAPEFFECT` enumerated type that specifies how the buffers in the flipping chain will be swapped. Specifying `D3DSWAPEFFECT_DISCARD` is the most efficient.

- `hDeviceWindow`—The window handle associated with the device. Specify the application window onto which you want to draw.

- `Windowed`—Specify `true` to run in windowed mode or `false` for full-screen mode.

- `EnableAutoDepthStencil`—Set to `true` to have Direct3D create and maintain the depth/stencil buffer automatically.

- `AutoDepthStencilFormat`—The format of the depth/stencil buffer (e.g., 24-bit depth with 8 bits reserved for the stencil buffer: `D3DFMT_D24S8`).

- `Flags`—Some additional characteristics. Specify zero (no flags) or a member of the `D3DPRESENTFLAG` set. See the documentation for a complete list of valid flags. Two common ones are:

  - `D3DPRESENTFLAG_LOCKABLE_BACKBUFFER`—Specifies that the back buffer can be locked. Note that using a lockable back buffer can degrade performance.

  - `D3DPRESENTFLAG_DISCARD_DEPTHSTENCIL`—Specifies that the depth/stencil buffer will be discarded after the next back buffer is presented. By "discard" we mean just that—the depth/stencil buffer memory will be discarded or invalid. This can improve performance.

- `FullScreen_RefreshRateInHz`—Refresh rate; use the default refresh rate by specifying `D3DPRESENT_RATE_DEFAULT`.

- `PresentationInterval`—A member of the `D3DPRESENT` set. See the documentation for a complete list of valid intervals. Two common ones are:

  □ `D3DPRESENT_INTERVAL_IMMEDIATE`—Presents immediately

  □ `D3DPRESENT_INTERVAL_DEFAULT`—Direct3D will choose the present rate. Usually this is equal to the refresh rate.

An example of filling this structure out is:

```
D3DPRESENT_PARAMETERS d3dpp;
d3dpp.BackBufferWidth          = 800;
d3dpp.BackBufferHeight         = 600;
d3dpp.BackBufferFormat         = D3DFMT_A8R8G8B8; //pixel format
d3dpp.BackBufferCount          = 1;
d3dpp.MultiSampleType          = D3DMULTISAMPLE_NONE;
d3dpp.MultiSampleQuality       = 0;
d3dpp.SwapEffect               = D3DSWAPEFFECT_DISCARD;
d3dpp.hDeviceWindow            = hwnd;
d3dpp.Windowed                 = false; // fullscreen
d3dpp.EnableAutoDepthStencil   = true;
d3dpp.AutoDepthStencilFormat   = D3DFMT_D24S8; // depth format
d3dpp.Flags                    = 0;
d3dpp.FullScreen_RefreshRateInHz = D3DPRESENT_RATE_DEFAULT;
d3dpp.PresentationInterval     = D3DPRESENT_INTERVAL_IMMEDIATE;
```

1.4.4 Creating the IDirect3DDevice9 Interface

With the `D3DPRESENT_PARAMETERS` filled out, we can create the `IDirect3DDevice9` object with the following method:

```
HRESULT IDirect3D9::CreateDevice(
    UINT Adapter,
    D3DDEVTYPE DeviceType,
    HWND hFocusWindow,
    DWORD BehaviorFlags,
    D3DPRESENT_PARAMETERS *pPresentationParameters,
    IDirect3DDevice9** ppReturnedDeviceInterface
);
```

- `Adapter`—Specifies the physical display adapter that we want the created `IDirect3DDevice9` object to represent

- `DeviceType`—Specifies the device type to use (e.g., hardware device (`D3DDEVTYPE_HAL`) or software device (`D3DDEVTYPE_REF`))

- `hFocusWindow`—Handle to the window that the device will be associated with. This is typically the window that the device will draw onto, and for our purposes it is the same handle that we specify for the data member `d3dpp.hDeviceWindow` of the `D3DPRESENT_PARAMETERS` structure.

- `BehaviorFlags`—Specify either `D3DCREATE_HARDWARE_VERTEXPROCESSING` or `D3DCREATE_SOFTWARE_VERTEX-PROCESSING` for this parameter
- `pPresentationParameters`—Specifies an initialized `D3DPRESENT_PARAMETERS` instance that defines some of the characteristics of the device
- `ppReturnedDeviceInterface`—Returns the created device

Example call:

```
IDirect3DDevice9* device = 0;
hr = d3d9->CreateDevice(
    D3DADAPTER_DEFAULT,     // primary adapter
    D3DDEVTYPE_HAL,         // device type
    hwnd,                   // window associated with device
    D3DCREATE_HARDWARE_VERTEXPROCESSING, // vertex processing type
    &d3dpp,                 // present parameters
    &device);               // returned created device

if( FAILED(hr) )
{
    ::MessageBox(0, "CreateDevice() - FAILED", 0, 0);
    return 0;
}
```

1.5 Sample Application: Initializing Direct3D

For this chapter's sample, we initialize a Direct3D application and clear the screen to black (see Figure 1.7).

Figure 1.7:
Screen shot of the sample for this chapter

This sample and all the samples in this book use code from the
d3dUtility.h and d3dUtility.cpp files, which can be found on this chapter's web page on the book's web site. These files contain functions
that implement common tasks that every Direct3D application will
need to do, such as creating a window, initializing Direct3D, and entering the application message loop. By wrapping up these common tasks
in functions, the samples are more focused on the particular chapter's
topic. In addition, we add useful utility code to these files as we prog-
ress through the book.

1.5.1 d3dUtility.h/cpp

Before we get started on this chapter's sample, let's spend some time
getting familiar with the functions provided by d3dUtility.h/cpp. The
d3dUtility.h file looks like this:

```cpp
// Include the main Direct3DX header file. This will include the
// other Direct3D header files we need.
#include <d3dx9.h>

namespace d3d
{
    bool InitD3D(
        HINSTANCE hInstance,         // [in] Application instance.
        int width, int height,       // [in] Back buffer dimensions.
        bool windowed,               // [in] Windowed (true) or
                                     //      full screen (false).
        D3DDEVTYPE deviceType,       // [in] HAL or REF
        IDirect3DDevice9** device);  // [out] The created device.

    int EnterMsgLoop(
        bool (*ptr_display)(float timeDelta));

    LRESULT CALLBACK WndProc(
        HWND hwnd,
        UINT msg,
        WPARAM wParam,
        LPARAM lParam);

    template<class T> void Release(T t)
    {
        if( t )
        {
            t->Release();
            t = 0;
        }
    }

    template<class T> void Delete(T t)
    {
        if( t )
        {
            delete t;
```

```
            t = 0;
     }
  }
}
```

- ◼ `InitD3D`—This function initializes a main application window and implements the Direct3D initialization code discussed in section 1.4. It outputs a pointer to a created `IDirect3DDevice9` interface if the function returns successfully. Observe that the parameters allow us to specify the window's dimensions and whether it should run in windowed mode or full-screen mode. See the sample code for further details on its implementation.

- ◼ `EnterMsgLoop`—This function wraps the application message loop. It takes a pointer to a function that is to be the *display function*. The display function is the function that implements the sample's drawing code. The message loop function needs to know the display function so that it can call it and display the scene during idle processing:

```
int d3d::EnterMsgLoop( bool (*ptr display)(float timeDelta) )
{
    MSG msg;
    ::ZeroMemory(&msg, sizeof(MSG));

    static float lastTime = (float)timeGetTime();

    while(msg.message != WM QUIT)
    {
        if(::PeekMessage(&msg, 0, 0, 0, PM REMOVE))
        {
            ::TranslateMessage(&msg);
            ::DispatchMessage(&msg);
        }
        else
        {
            float currTime  = (float)timeGetTime();
            float timeDelta = (currTime -
               lastTime)*0.001f;

            ptr_display(timeDelta); // call display function

            lastTime = currTime;
        }
    }
    return msg.wParam;
}
```

The "time" code is used to calculate the time elapsed between calls to `ptr_display`, that is, the time between frames.

- ◼ `Release`—This template function is designed as a convenience function to release COM interfaces and set them to null.

Part II

- `Delete`—This template function is designed as a convenience function to delete an object on the free store and set the pointer to null.

- `WndProc`—The window procedure declaration for the main application window

1.5.2 Sample Framework

By *sample framework* we are referring to the general way that we structure the sample applications of this book. For each sample we consistently implement three functions, not counting the message procedure and `WinMain`. These three functions are used to implement the code specific to the particular sample. They are:

- `bool Setup()`—This function is where we set up anything that needs to be set up for this sample, such as allocating resources, checking device capabilities, and setting application states.

- `void Cleanup()`—This function is where we free anything that we allocated in the Setup function, such as deallocating memory.

- `bool Display(float timeDelta)`—This function is where we implement all of our drawing code and code that occurs on a frame-by-frame basis, such as updating object positions. The parameter `timeDelta` is the time elapsed between each frame and is used to sync animations with the frames per second.

1.5.3 Sample: D3D Init

As stated, the sample application creates and initializes a Direct3D application, and then clears the screen to black. Note that we make use of our utility functions to simplify initialization. The complete project can be found on this chapter's page on the book's web site.

Note: This sample closely follows the ideas discussed in Tutorial 1 in the DirectX SDK documentation. You may wish to read Tutorial 1 after this chapter to gain a different perspective.

We start out by including d3dUtility.h and instantiating a global variable for the device:

```
#include "d3dUtility.h"


IDirect3DDevice9* Device = 0;
```

Next we implement our framework functions:

```
bool Setup()
{
```

```
      return true;
}

void Cleanup()
{

}
```

We don't have any resources or things to set up in this sample, so the
`Setup` and `Cleanup` methods are empty.

```
bool Display(float timeDelta)
{
    if( Device )
    {
        Device->Clear(0, 0, D3DCLEAR_TARGET | D3DCLEAR_ZBUFFER,
                   0x00000000, 1.0f, 0);

        Device->Present(0, 0, 0, 0);// present backbuffer
    }
    return true;
}
```

The `Display` method calls the `IDirect3DDevice9::Clear`
method, which clears the back buffer and depth/stencil buffer to the
color black and 1.0, respectively. Notice that we only perform the drawing code if the application is not paused. The declaration of
`IDirect3DDevice9::Clear` is:

```
HRESULT IDirect3DDevice9::Clear(
    DWORD Count,
    const D3DRECT* pRects,
    DWORD Flags,
    D3DCOLOR Color,
    float Z,
    DWORD Stencil
);
```

- `Count`—Number of rectangles in the `pRects` array
- `pRects`—An array of screen rectangles to clear. This allows us to
  only clear parts of a surface.
- `Flags`—Specifies which surfaces to clear. We can clear one or
  more of the following surfaces:
  - ☐ `D3DCLEAR_TARGET`—The render target surface, usually the
    back buffer
  - ☐ `D3DCLEAR_ZBUFFER`—The depth buffer
  - ☐ `D3DCLEAR_STENCIL`—The stencil buffer
- `Color`—The color we wish to clear the render target to
- `Z`—The value we wish to set the depth buffer (z-buffer) to
- `Stencil`—The value we wish to set the stencil buffer to

After the surfaces have been cleared, we present the back buffer by calling the `IDirect3DDevice9::Present` method.

The window procedure method handles a couple of events; namely it allows us to exit the application by pressing the Escape key.

```
LRESULT CALLBACK d3d::WndProc(HWND hwnd, UINT msg, WPARAM wParam,
    LPARAM lParam)
{
    switch( msg )
    {
    case WM_DESTROY:
        ::PostQuitMessage(0);
        break;

    case WM_KEYDOWN:
        if( wParam == VK_ESCAPE )
            ::DestroyWindow(hwnd);
        break;
    }
    return ::DefWindowProc(hwnd, msg, wParam, lParam);
}
```

Finally, `WinMain` performs the following steps:

1. Initializes the main display window and Direct3D
2. Calls the `Setup` routine to set up the application
3. Enters the message loop using `Display` as the display function
4. Cleans up the application and finally releases the `IDirect3D-Device9` object

```
int WINAPI WinMain(HINSTANCE hinstance,
                   HINSTANCE prevInstance,
                   PSTR cmdLine,
                   int showCmd)
{
    if(!d3d::InitD3D(hinstance,
        800, 600, true, D3DDEVTYPE_HAL, &Device))
    {
        ::MessageBox(0, "InitD3D() - FAILED", 0, 0);
        return 0;
    }

    if(!Setup())
    {
        ::MessageBox(0, "Setup() - FAILED", 0, 0);
        return 0;
    }

    d3d::EnterMsgLoop( Display );

    Cleanup();

    Device->Release();
```

```
    return 0;
}
```

As you can see, our sample template structure is quite clean with our utility function handling the window and Direct3D initialization processes. For almost every sample program in this book, our task is to fill out the implementations for the `Setup`, `Cleanup`, and `Display` functions.

 Note: Remember to link in d3d9.lib, d3dx9.lib, and winmm.lib if you are building these samples on your own.

1.6 Summary

- Direct3D can be thought of as a mediator between the programmer and the graphics hardware. The programmer calls a Direct3D function, which in turn, indirectly, has the physical hardware perform the operation by interfacing with the device's HAL (Hardware Abstraction Layer).

- The REF device allows developers to test features that Direct3D exposes but are not implemented by available hardware.

- Component Object Model (COM) is the technology that allows DirectX to be language independent and have backward compatibility. Direct3D programmers don't need to know the details of COM and how it works; they only need to know how to acquire COM interfaces and release them.

- Surfaces are special Direct3D interfaces used to store 2D images. A member of the `D3DFORMAT` enumerated type specifies the pixel format of a surface. Surfaces and other Direct3D resources can be stored in several different memory pools as is specified by a member of the `D3DPOOL` enumerated type. In addition, surfaces can be multisampled, which creates a smoother image.

- The `IDirect3D9` interface is used to find out information about the system's graphics devices. For example, through this interface we can obtain the capabilities of a device. It is also used to create the `IDirect3DDevice9` interface.

- The `IDirect3DDevice9` interface can be thought of as our software interface for controlling the graphics device. For instance, calling the `IDirect3DDevice9::Clear` method will indirectly have the graphics device clear the specified surfaces.

Part II

■ The sample framework is used to provide a consistent interface that all sample applications in this book follow. The utility code provided in the d3dUtility.h/cpp files wraps initialization code that every application must implement. By wrapping this code up, we hide it, which allows the samples to be more focused on demonstrating the current topic.

Chapter 2

The Rendering Pipeline

The primary theme of this chapter is the rendering pipeline. The rendering pipeline is responsible for creating a 2D image given a geometric description of the 3D world and a virtual camera that specifies the perspective from which the world is being viewed.

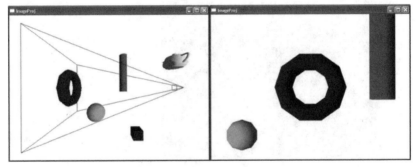

Figure 2.1: The left image shows some objects set up in the 3D world with a camera positioned and aimed. The image on the right shows the 2D image created based on what the camera "sees."

Objectives

- To find out how we represent 3D objects in Direct3D
- To learn how we model the virtual camera
- To understand the rendering pipeline—the process of taking a geometric description of a 3D scene and generating a 2D image from it

2.1 Model Representation

A *scene* is a collection of objects or models. An object is represented as a *triangle mesh* approximation, as Figure 2.2 illustrates. The triangles of the mesh are the building blocks of the object that we are modeling. We use the following terms all interchangeably to refer to the triangles of a mesh: polygons, primitives and mesh geometry. (Although triangles are primitives, Direct3D also supports line and point primitives. However, since lines and points aren't useful for modeling 3D solid objects, we omit a discussion of these primitive types. We do discuss some applications of points in Chapter 14.)

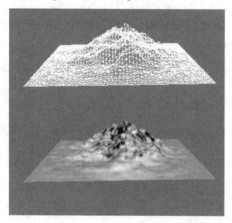

Figure 2.2: A terrain approximated by triangles

The point where two edges on a polygon meet is a *vertex*. To describe a triangle we specify the three point locations that correspond to the three vertices of the triangle (see Figure 2.3). Then to describe an object, we specify the triangles that make it up.

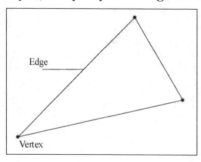

Edge

Vertex

Figure 2.3: A triangle defined by its three vertices

2.1.1 Vertex Formats

The previous definition of a vertex is correct mathematically, but it is an incomplete definition when used in the context of Direct3D. This is because a vertex in Direct3D can consist of additional properties besides a spatial location. For instance, a vertex can have a color property as well as a normal property (colors and normals are discussed in Chapters 4 and 5, respectively). Direct3D gives us the flexibility to construct our own vertex formats; in other words it allows us to define the components of a vertex.

To create a custom vertex format, we first create a structure that holds the vertex data that we choose. For instance, below we illustrate two different kinds of vertex formats; one consists of position and color, and the second consists of position, normal, and texture coordinates (see Chapter 6, "Texturing").

Part II

```
struct ColorVertex
{
    float _x, _y, _z;    // position
    DWORD _color;
};

struct NormalTexVertex
{
    float _x, _y, _z;    // position
    float _nx, _ny, _nz; // normal vector
    float _u, _v;        // texture coordinates
};
```

Once we have the vertex structure completed, we need to describe the way that the vertices are formatted by using a combination of flexible vertex format (FVF) flags. Using the previous two vertex structures, we have the following *vertex formats*:

```
#define FVF_COLOR (D3DFVF_XYZ | D3DFVF_DIFFUSE)
```

Put into words, the above says that the vertex structure that corresponds to this vertex format contains a position property and a diffuse color property.

```
#define FVF_NORMAL_TEX (D3DFVF_XYZ | D3DFVF_NORMAL | D3DFVF_TEX1)
```

The above says that the vertex structure that corresponds to this vertex format contains position, normal, and texture coordinate properties.

One restriction that must be taken into consideration is that the order in which you specify the flexible vertex flags must be the same order in which you specify the data in the vertex structure.

Look up `D3DFVF` in the documentation for a complete list of the available vertex format flags.

2.1.2 Triangles

Triangles are the basic building blocks of 3D objects. To construct an object, we create a triangle list that describes the shape and contours of the object. A triangle list contains the data for each individual triangle that we wish to draw. For example, to construct a rectangle, we break it into two triangles, as seen in Figure 2.4, and specify the vertices of each triangle.

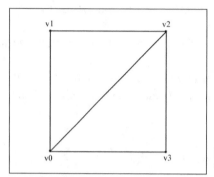

Figure 2.4: A rectangle built from two triangles

```
Vertex rect[6] = {v0, v1, v2,  // triangle0
                  v0, v2, v3}; // triangle1
```

Note: The order in which you specify the vertices of a triangle is important and called the winding order. See section 2.3.4 for information.

2.1.3 Indices

Often the triangles that form a 3D object share many of the same vertices, as the rectangle in Figure 2.4 illustrates. Although only two vertices are duplicated in the rectangle example, the number of duplicate vertices can increase as the detail and complexity of the model increases. For instance, the cube in Figure 2.5 has eight unique vertices, but many of them would be duplicated to form the triangle list for the cube.

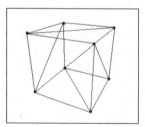

Figure 2.5: A cube defined by triangles

To solve this problem we introduce the concept of indices. It works like this: We create a vertex list and an index list. The vertex list consists of all the unique vertices, and the index list contains values that index into the vertex list to define how they are to be put together to form triangles. Returning to the rectangle example, the vertex list would be constructed as follows:

```
Vertex vertexList[4] = {v0, v1, v2, v3};
```

Then the index list needs to define how the vertices in the vertex list are to be put together to form the two triangles.

```
WORD indexList[6] = {0, 1, 2,  // triangle0
                     0, 2, 3}; // triangle1
```

Put into words, the `indexList` definition says to build triangle0 from elements zero (`vertexList[0]`), one (`vertexList[1]`), and two (`vertexList[2]`) of the vertex list and build triangle1 from elements zero (`vertexList[0]`), two (`vertexList[2]`), and three (`vertexList[3]`) of the vertex list.

2.2 The Virtual Camera

The camera specifies what part of the world the viewer can see and thus what part of the world for which we need to generate a 2D image. The camera is positioned and oriented in the world and defines the volume of space that is visible. Figure 2.6 shows a diagram of our camera model.

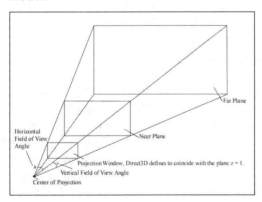

Figure 2.6: A frustum that defines the volume of space that the camera "sees"

The volume of space is a *frustum* and defined by the field of view angles and the near and far planes. The reasons for using a frustum should be made clear when you consider that your monitor screen is rectangular. Objects that are not inside this volume cannot be seen and should be discarded from further processing. The process of discarding such data is called *clipping*.

The *projection window* is the 2D area that the 3D geometry inside the frustum gets projected onto to create the 2D image representation of the 3D scene. It is important to know that we define the projection window with the dimensions min = (–1, –1) and max = (1, 1).

To simplify some of the drawings that are to follow in this book, we make the near plane and *projection plane* (plane the projection window lies on) coincide. Also, note that Direct3D defines the projection plane to be the plane $z = 1$.

2.3 The Rendering Pipeline

Once we have described our 3D scene geometrically and set up a virtual camera, we have the task of producing a 2D representation of that scene on the monitor. The series of operations that must be performed to achieve this is called the rendering pipeline. Figure 2.7 provides a simplified overview of the pipeline, and the following subsections explain each stage.

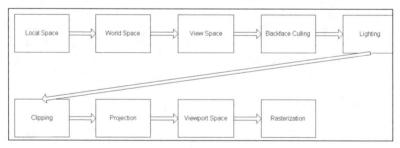

Figure 2.7: An abridged rendering pipeline

Several of the stages in the pipeline transform geometry from one coordinate system to another. The transformations are done using matrices. Direct3D is set up to do the transformation calculations for us. This is advantageous because the transformations may be done on the graphics hardware, if the hardware is capable of doing hardware transformations. To use Direct3D for the transformations, all we must do is supply the desired transformation matrix that describes the transformation needed to go from one system to the next. We supply a matrix using the `IDirect3DDevice->SetTransform` method. This method takes a parameter describing the transformation type and a matrix that represents the transformation. For example, from Figure

2.7, to set the transformation needed to go from local space to world space, we would write:

```
Device->SetTransform(D3DTS_WORLD, &worldMatrix);
```

You see more of this method in the subsequent sections, where we examine each stage.

2.3.1 Local Space

Local space, or modeling space, is the coordinate system in which we define an object's triangle list. Local space is useful because it simplifies the modeling process. Building a model around its own local coordinate system is easier than building a model directly into the world. For instance, local space allows us to construct a model without regard to its position, size, or orientation in relation to other objects in the world.

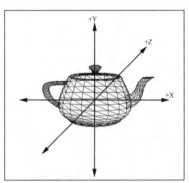

Figure 2.8: A teapot defined around its own local coordinate system

2.3.2 World Space

Once we have constructed various models, each residing in their own local coordinate system, we need to bring them together to form the scene in one global (world) coordinate system. Objects in local space are transformed to world space through a process called the *world transform*, which usually consists of translations, rotations, and scaling operations that set the position, orientation, and size of the model in the world. The world transformation sets up all the objects in the world in relationship to each other in position, size, and orientation.

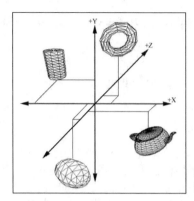

Figure 2.9: Several 3D objects described relative to one world coordinate system

The world transformation is represented with a matrix and set with Direct3D using the `IDirect3DDevice9::SetTransform` method with `D3DTS_WORLD` as the transform type. For example, suppose we want to position a cube at the point (–3, 2, 6) in the world and a sphere at the point (5, 0, –2). We would write:

```
// Build the cube world matrix that only consists of a translation.
D3DXMATRIX cubeWorldMatrix;
D3DXMatrixTranslation(&cubeWorldMatrix, -3.0f, 2.0f, 6.0f);
// Build the sphere world matrix that only consists of a translation.
D3DXMATRIX sphereWorldMatrix;
D3DXMatrixTranslation(&sphereWorldMatrix, 5.0f, 0.0f, -2.0f);

// Set the cube's transformation
Device->SetTransform(D3DTS_WORLD, &cubeWorldMatrix);
drawCube(); // draw the cube

// Now since the sphere uses a different world transformation, we
// must change the world transformation to the sphere's. If we
// don't change this, the sphere would be drawn using the previously
// set world matrix - the cube's.
Device->SetTransform(D3DTS_WORLD, &sphereWorldMatrix);
drawSphere(); // draw the sphere
```

This is a simplistic example, as the objects would most likely need to be oriented and scaled as well, but it shows how the world transformation works.

2.3.3 View Space

In world space the world geometry and the camera are defined relative to the world coordinate system, as Figure 2.10 shows. However, projection and other operations are difficult or less efficient when the camera is at an arbitrary position and orientation in the world. To make things easier, we transform the camera to the origin of the world system and rotate it so that the camera is looking down the positive z-axis. All geometry in the world is transformed along with the camera so that the view of the world remains the same. This transformation is called the *view space transformation*, and the geometry is said to reside in view space after this transformation.

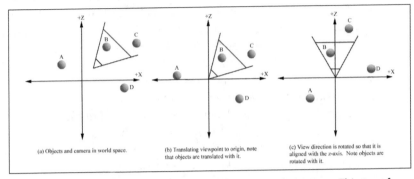

(a) Objects and camera in world space.

(b) Translating viewpoint to origin, note that objects are translated with it.

(c) View direction is rotated so that it is aligned with the z-axis. Note objects are rotated with it.

Figure 2.10: The transformation from world space to view space. This transformation transforms the camera to the origin of the system looking down the positive z-axis. Notice that the objects in space are transformed along with the camera so that the camera's view of the world remains the same.

The view space transformation matrix can be computed using the following D3DX function:

```
D3DXMATRIX *D3DXMatrixLookAtLH(
    D3DXMATRIX* pOut, // pointer to receive resulting view matrix
    CONST D3DXVECTOR3* pEye, // position of camera in world
    CONST D3DXVECTOR3* pAt,  // point camera is looking at in world
    CONST D3DXVECTOR3* pUp   // the world's up vector - (0, 1, 0)
);
```

The `pEye` parameter specifies the position where you want the camera to be in the world. The `pAt` parameter specifies the point in the world where you want to aim the camera. The `pUp` parameter is the vector that indicates which direction is "up" in the 3D world; this is usually always the vector coincident with the y-axis—(0, 1, 0).

Example: Suppose we want to position the camera at the point (5, 3, −10) and have the camera look at the center of the world (0, 0, 0). We can then build the view transformation matrix by writing:

```
D3DXVECTOR3 position(5.0f, 3.0f, -10.0f);
D3DXVECTOR3 targetPoint(0.0f, 0.0f, 0.0f);
D3DXVECTOR3 worldUp(0.0f, 1.0f, 0.0f);

D3DXMATRIX V;
D3DXMatrixLookAtLH(&V, &position, &targetPoint, &worldUp);
```

The view space transformation is set with the `IDirect3DDevice9::SetTransform` method with `D3DTS_VIEW` as the transform type:

```
Device->SetTransform(D3DTS_VIEW, &V);
```

Part II

2.3.4 Backface Culling

A polygon has two sides, and we label one side as the front side and the other as the back side. In general, the back sides of polygons are never seen. This is because the majority of objects in a scene are enclosed volumes, such as boxes, cylinders, tanks, characters, etc., and the camera should never be allowed to enter the solid volume of space inside the object. Thus, the camera will never see the back sides of the polygons. This is important to know because if we were ever allowed to see the back side of a polygon, backface culling wouldn't work.

Figure 2.11 shows an object in view space where the front sides have an arrow sticking out. A polygon whose front side *faces* the camera is called a *front-facing* polygon, and a polygon whose front side *faces away* from the camera is called a *back-facing* polygon.

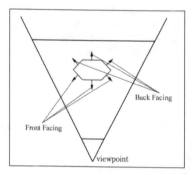

Figure 2.11: An object with front-facing and back-facing polygons

Upon examination of Figure 2.11, we can see that the front-facing polygons obscure the back-facing polygons that are behind them. Direct3D takes advantage of this by culling (discarding from further processing) the back-facing polygons; this is called *backface culling*. Figure 2.12 shows the same object after the back faces have been culled. From the camera's viewpoint, the same scene will be drawn because the back faces were obscured anyway and would never have been seen.

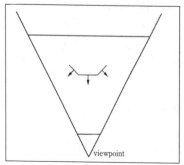

Figure 2.12: The scene after back-facing polygons have been culled

Of course, in order for this to work, Direct3D needs to know which polygons are front facing and which are back facing. By default, Direct3D treats triangles with vertices specified in a clockwise winding order (in view space) as front facing. Triangles with vertices specified in counterclockwise winding orders (in view space) are considered back facing.

> **Note:** Notice that we said "in view space." This is because when a triangle is rotated 180 degrees, its winding order is flipped. Thus, a triangle that had a clockwise winding order when it was defined in its local space might not have a clockwise winding order when it's transformed to view space due to possible rotations.

If for some reason we are not happy with the default culling behavior, we can change it by changing the D3DRS_CULLMODE render state.

```
Device->SetRenderState(D3DRS_CULLMODE, Value);
```

where Value can be one of the following:

- D3DCULL_NONE—Disables back-face culling entirely
- D3DCULL_CW—Triangles with a clockwise wind are culled.
- D3DCULL_CCW—Triangles with a counterclockwise wind are culled. This is the default state.

2.3.5 Lighting

Light sources are defined in world space but transformed into view space by the view space transformation. In view space these light sources are applied to light the objects in the scene to give a more realistic appearance. Lighting in the fixed function pipeline is covered in detail in Chapter 5. Later, in Part IV of this book, we implement our own lighting scheme using the programmable pipeline.

2.3.6 Clipping

At this point we need to cull the geometry that is outside the viewing volume; this process is called *clipping*. There are three locations where a triangle can be with regards to the frustum.

- Completely inside—If the triangle is completely inside the frustum, it is kept and will move onto the next stage.
- Completely outside—If the triangle is completely outside the frustum, it is culled.
- Partially inside (partially outside)—If the triangle is partially inside and partially outside the frustum, the triangle is split into two

parts. The part inside the frustum is kept, while the part outside is culled.

Figure 2.13 shows the three possible scenarios.

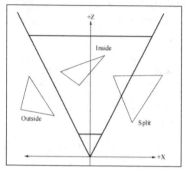

Figure 2.13: Clipping geometry outside the viewing volume

2.3.7 Projection

In view space we have the task of obtaining a 2D representation of the 3D scene. The process of going from an n dimension to an $n - 1$ dimension is called *projection*. There are many ways of performing a projection, but we are interested in a particular way called *perspective projection*. A perspective projection projects geometry in such a way that foreshortening occurs. That is, objects farther away from the camera appear smaller than those near the camera. This type of projection allows us to represent a 3D scene on a 2D image. Figure 2.14 shows a 3D point being projected onto the projection window with a perspective projection.

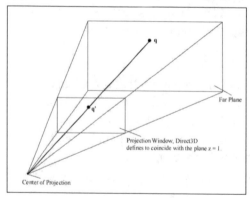

Figure 2.14: Projection of a 3D point onto the projection window

The projection transformation defines our viewing volume (frustum) and is responsible for projecting the geometry in the frustum onto the projection window. The projection matrix is complex and we omit a derivation of it. Instead we use the following D3DX function, which creates a projection matrix based on a frustum description.

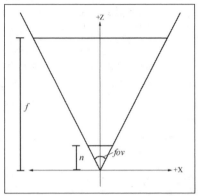

Figure 2.15: The components of a frustum

Part II

```
D3DXMATRIX *D3DXMatrixPerspectiveFovLH(
    D3DXMATRIX* pOut,    // returns projection matrix
    FLOAT fovY,          // vertical field of view angle in radians
    FLOAT Aspect,        // aspect ratio = width / height
    FLOAT zn,            // distance to near plane
    FLOAT zf             // distance to far plane
);
```

The aspect ratio parameter deserves some elaboration. The geometry on the projection window is eventually transformed to screen space (see section 2.3.8). The transformation from a square (projection window) to the screen, which is a rectangle, causes a stretching distortion. The aspect ratio is simply the ratio between the screen's two dimensions and is used to correct the distortion caused when mapping from a square to a rectangle.

$$aspectRatio = screenWidth/screenHeight$$

The projection matrix is set with the `IDirect3DDevice9::Set-Transform` method, passing `D3DTS_PROJECTION` as the transform type. The following example creates a projection matrix based on a frustum with a 90-degree field of view, a near plane with a distance of 1, and a far plane with a distance of 1000.

```
D3DXMATRIX proj;
D3DXMatrixPerspectiveFovLH(
    &proj, PI * 0.5f, (float)width / (float)height, 1.0, 1000.0f);
Device->SetTransform(D3DTS_PROJECTION, &proj);
```

Note: The interested reader can read about projection in depth in *3D Computer Graphics*, third edition, by Alan Watt.

2.3.8 **Viewport Transform**

The viewport transform is responsible for transforming coordinates on the projection window to a rectangle on the screen, which we call the *viewport*. For games, the viewport is usually the entire screen rectangle. However, it can be a subset of the screen or client area if we are running in windowed mode. The viewport rectangle is described relative to the window it resides in and is specified in window coordinates. Figure 2.16 shows a viewport.

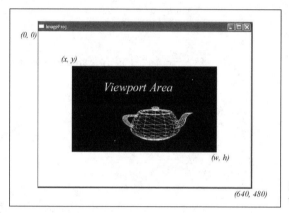

Figure 2.16: The viewport rectangle

In Direct3D a viewport is represented by the D3DVIEWPORT9 structure. It is defined as:

```
typedef struct _D3DVIEWPORT9 {
    DWORD   X;
    DWORD   Y;
    DWORD   Width;
    DWORD   Height;
    DWORD   MinZ;
    DWORD   MaxZ;
} D3DVIEWPORT9;
```

The first four data members define the viewport rectangle relative to the window in which it resides. The MinZ member specifies the minimum depth buffer value, and MaxZ specifies the maximum depth buffer value. Direct3D uses a depth buffer range of zero to one, so MinZ and MaxZ should be set to those values respectively unless a special effect is desired.

Once we have filled out the D3DVIEWPORT9 structure, we set the viewport with Direct3D like so:

```
D3DVIEWPORT9 vp = { 0, 0, 640, 480, 0, 1 };
Device->SetViewport(&vp);
```

Direct3D handles the viewport transformation for us automatically, but for reference the viewport transformation is described with the following matrix. The variables are the same as for the `D3DVIEWPORT9` structure.

$$\begin{bmatrix} \dfrac{Width}{2} & 0 & 0 & 0 \\ 0 & -\dfrac{Height}{2} & 0 & 0 \\ 0 & 0 & MaxZ - MinZ & 0 \\ X + \dfrac{Width}{2} & Y + \dfrac{Height}{2} & MinZ & 1 \end{bmatrix}$$

2.3.9 Rasterization

After the vertices are transformed to screen coordinates, we have a list of 2D triangles. The rasterization stage is responsible for computing the individual pixel color values needed to draw each triangle (see Figure 2.17).

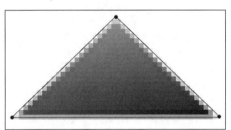

Figure 2.17: A screen triangle being rasterized

The rasterization process is very intensive computationally and should always be done by dedicated graphics hardware. The end result of the rasterization stage is the 2D image that is displayed by the monitor.

2.4 Summary

- 3D objects are represented as triangle meshes—a list of triangles that approximates the shape and contours of the object.
- The virtual camera is modeled as a frustum. The volume of space inside the frustum is what the camera "sees."
- 3D objects are defined in local space and are then all brought into one world space system. To facilitate projection, culling, and other operations, the objects are then transformed to view space, where the camera is positioned at the origin and looking down the positive

Part II

z-axis. Once in view space, the objects are projected to the projection window. The viewport transformation transforms the geometry on the projection window to the viewport. Finally, the rasterization stage computes the individual pixel colors of the final 2D image.

Chapter 3

Drawing in Direct3D

In the last chapter we learned the concepts of creating and rendering a scene. In this chapter we put that into practice and learn how to draw some geometric objects in Direct3D. The Direct3D interfaces and methods covered in this chapter are of some importance, for they are used throughout the rest of this book.

Objectives

- To find out how vertex and index data is stored in Direct3D
- To discover how to change the way geometry is rendered using render states
- To learn how to render a scene
- To learn how to create more complex 3D shapes using the `D3DXCreate*` functions

3.1 Vertex/Index Buffers

Vertex and index buffers are similar interfaces and share similar methods; therefore we cover them together. A vertex buffer is simply a chunk of contiguous memory that contains vertex data. Similarly, an index buffer is a chunk of contiguous memory that contains index data. We use vertex and index buffers to hold our data rather than arrays because vertex and index buffers can be placed in video memory. Rendering data from video memory is done much faster than rendering data in system memory.

In code, a vertex buffer is represented by the `IDirect3DVertexBuffer9` interface and an index buffer is represented by the `IDirect3DIndexBuffer9` interface.

3.1.1 **Creating Vertex and Index Buffers**

We can create a vertex and index buffer with the following two methods:

```
HRESULT IDirect3DDevice9::CreateVertexBuffer(
    UINT Length,
    DWORD Usage,
    DWORD FVF,
    D3DPOOL Pool
    IDirect3DVertexBuffer9** ppVertexBuffer,
    HANDLE* pSharedHandle
);

HRESULT IDirect3DDevice9::CreateIndexBuffer(
    UINT Length,
    DWORD Usage,
    D3DFORMAT Format,
    D3DPOOL Pool,
    IDirect3DIndexBuffer9** ppIndexBuffer,
    HANDLE* pSharedHandle
);
```

The majority of the parameters are identical for both methods, so let's cover the parameters of both methods together.

- `Length`—The number of bytes to allocate for the buffer. If we wanted a vertex buffer to have enough memory to store eight vertices, we would set this parameter to `8 * sizeof(Vertex)`, where `Vertex` is our vertex structure.

- `Usage`—Specifies some additional properties about how the buffer is used. This value can be zero, indicating no additional properties, or a combination of one or more of the following flags:

  - `D3DUSAGE_DYNAMIC`—Setting this flag makes the buffer dynamic. See the notes on static and dynamic buffers on the following page.

  - `D3DUSAGE_POINTS`—This flag specifies that the buffer will hold point primitives. Point primitives are covered in the section called "Particle Systems" in Chapter 14. This flag is used only for vertex buffers.

  - `D3DUSAGE_SOFTWAREPROCESSING`—Vertex processing is done in software.

  - `D3DUSAGE_WRITEONLY`—Specifies that the application will only write to the buffer. This allows the driver to place the buffer in the best memory location for write operations. Note that reading from a buffer created with this flag will result in an error.

- `FVF`—The flexible vertex format of the vertices that is stored in the vertex buffer
- `Pool`—The memory pool in which the buffer is placed
- `ppVertexBuffer`—Pointer to receive the created vertex buffer
- `pSharedHandle`—Not used; set to zero
- `Format`—Specifies the size of the indices; use `D3DFMT_INDEX16` for 16-bit indices or `D3DFMT_INDEX32` for 32-bit indices. Note that not all devices support 32-bit indices; check the device capabilities.
- `ppIndexBuffer`—Pointer to receive the created index buffer

> **Note:** A buffer created *without* the `D3DUSAGE_DYNAMIC` flag is called a *static buffer*. A static buffer is generally placed in video memory where its contents can be processed most efficiently. However, the trade-off of making a buffer static is that writing to and reading from the memory of a static buffer is inherently slow because accessing video memory is slow. For this reason we use static buffers to hold static data (data that will not need to be changed (accessed) very frequently). Terrains and city buildings are examples of good candidates for static buffers because the terrain and building geometry will usually not change during the course of the application. Static buffers should be filled with geometry at application initialization time and never at run time.

> **Note:** A buffer created *with* the `D3DUSAGE_DYNAMIC` flag is called a *dynamic buffer*. A dynamic buffer is generally placed in AGP memory where its memory can be updated quickly. Dynamic buffers are not processed as quickly as static buffers because the data must be transferred to video memory before rendering, but the benefit of dynamic buffers is that they can be updated reasonably fast (fast CPU writes). Therefore, if you need to update the contents of a buffer frequently, it should be made dynamic. Particle systems are good candidates for dynamic buffers because they are animated, and thus their geometry is usually updated every frame.

> **Note:** Reading video memory and AGP memory from your application is very slow. Therefore, if you need to read your geometry at run time, it is best to keep a local system memory copy and then read from that.

The following example creates a static vertex buffer that has enough memory to hold eight vertices of type `Vertex`.

```
IDirect3DVertexBuffer9* vb;
_device->CreateVertexBuffer(
    8 * sizeof( Vertex ),
    0,
    D3DFVF_XYZ,
    D3DPOOL_MANAGED,
```

```
    &vb,
    0);
```

This next code example shows how to create a dynamic index buffer that has enough memory to hold 36 16-bit indices.

```
IDirect3DIndexBuffer9* ib;
_device->CreateIndexBuffer(
    36 * sizeof( WORD ),
    D3DUSAGE_DYNAMIC | D3DUSAGE_WRITEONLY,
    D3DFMT_INDEX16,
    D3DPOOL_MANAGED,
    &ib,
    0);
```

3.1.2 Accessing a Buffer's Memory

To access the memory of a vertex/index buffer, we need to get a pointer to its internal memory contents. We obtain a pointer to its contents by using the `Lock` method. It is important to unlock the buffer when we are done accessing it. Once we have a pointer to the memory, we can read and write information to it.

Note: If the vertex/index buffer was created with the usage flag `D3DUSAGE_WRITEONLY`, you must not read from the buffer. Doing so will result in a failed read.

```
HRESULT IDirect3DVertexBuffer9::Lock(
    UINT OffsetToLock,
    UINT SizeToLock,
    BYTE** ppbData,
    DWORD Flags
);
HRESULT IDirect3DIndexBuffer9::Lock(
    UINT OffsetToLock,
    UINT SizeToLock,
    BYTE** ppbData,
    DWORD Flags
);
```

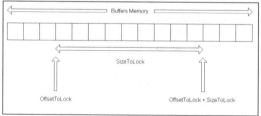

Figure 3.1: The `Offset ToLock` and `SizeToLock` parameters specify the block of memory to lock. Specifying zero for both of these parameters is a shortcut to lock the entire buffer.

The parameters for both methods are exactly the same.

- `OffsetToLock`—Offset, in bytes, from the start of the buffer to the location to begin the lock. See Figure 3.1.

- `SizeToLock`—Number of bytes to lock
- `ppbData`—A pointer to the start of the locked memory
- `Flags`—Flags describing how the lock is done. This can be zero or a combination of one or more of the following flags:
  - `D3DLOCK_DISCARD`—This flag is used only for dynamic buffers. It instructs the hardware to discard the buffer and return a pointer to a newly allocated buffer. This is useful because it allows the hardware to continue rendering from the discarded buffer while we access the newly allocated buffer. This prevents the hardware from stalling.
  - `D3DLOCK_NOOVERWRITE`—This flag is used only for dynamic buffers. It states that you are only going to append data to a buffer. That is, you will not overwrite any memory that is currently being rendered. This is beneficial because it allows the hardware to continue rendering at the same time you add new data to the buffer.
  - `D3DLOCK_READONLY`—This flag states that you are locking the buffer only to read data and that you won't be writing to it. This allows for some internal optimizations.

The flags `D3DLOCK_DISCARD` and `D3DLOCK_NOOVERWRITE` address the fact that a portion of the buffer's memory could be in use (being rendered) at the time of a lock call. If circumstances allow these flags to be used, they prevent a rendering stall when locking, which otherwise would occur.

The following example shows how the `Lock` method is commonly used. Note how we call the `Unlock` method when we are done.

```
Vertex* vertices;
vb->Lock(0, 0, (void**)&vertices, 0);   // lock the entire buffer

vertices[0] = Vertex(-1.0f, 0.0f, 2.0f); // write vertices to
vertices[1] = Vertex( 0.0f, 1.0f, 2.0f); // the buffer
vertices[2] = Vertex( 1.0f, 0.0f, 2.0f);

vb->Unlock(); // unlock when you're done accessing the buffer
```

3.1.3 Retrieving Information about Vertex and Index Buffers

Sometimes we need to get information about the vertex/index buffer. The following example demonstrates the methods used to obtain such information:

```
D3DVERTEXBUFFER_DESC vbDescription;
_vertexBuffer->GetDesc(&vbDescription); // get vb info

D3DINDEXBUFFER_DESC ibDescription;
_indexBuffer->GetDesc(&ibDescription);  // get ib info
```

The `D3DVERTEXBUFFER_DESC` and `D3DINDEXBUFFER_DESC` structures are defined as follows:

```
typedef struct _D3DVERTEXBUFFER_DESC {
    D3DFORMAT Format;
    D3DRESOURCETYPE Type;
    DWORD Usage;
    D3DPOOL Pool;
    UINT Size;
    DWORD FVF;
} D3DVERTEXBUFFER_DESC;

typedef struct _D3DINDEXBUFFER_DESC {
    D3DFORMAT Format;
    D3DRESOURCETYPE Type;
    DWORD Usage;
    D3DPOOL Pool;
    UINT Size;
} D3DINDEXBUFFER_DESC;
```

3.2 Render States

Direct3D encapsulates a variety of rendering states that affect how geometry is rendered. Render states have default values, so you only need to change them if your application requires something other than the default. A render state stays in effect until you change the particular state again. To set a render state, we use the following method:

```
HRESULT IDirect3DDevice9::SetRenderState(
    D3DRENDERSTATETYPE State, // the state to change
    DWORD Value               // value of the new state
);
```

For example, in this chapter's samples we are going to render our objects in wireframe mode. Therefore, we set the following render state:

```
_device->SetRenderState(D3DRS_FILLMODE, D3DFILL_WIREFRAME);
```

Note: Look up `D3DRENDERSTATETYPE` in the DirectX SDK to see all the possible render states.

3.3 **Drawing Preparations**

Once we have created a vertex buffer and, optionally, an index buffer, we are almost ready to render its contents, but there are three steps that must be taken first.

1. Set the stream source. Setting the stream source hooks up a vertex buffer to a stream that essentially feeds geometry into the rendering pipeline.

    The following method is used to set a stream source:

    ```
    HRESULT IDirect3DDevice9::SetStreamSource(
        UINT StreamNumber,
        IDirect3DVertexBuffer9* pStreamData,
        UINT OffsetInBytes,
        UINT Stride
    );
    ```

    - `StreamNumber`—Identifies the stream source to which we are hooking the vertex buffer. In this book we do not use multiple streams; thus we always use stream zero.

    - `pStreamData`—A pointer to the vertex buffer that we want to hook up to the stream

    - `OffsetInBytes`—An offset from the start of the stream, measured in bytes, that specifies the start of the vertex data to be fed into the rendering pipeline. To set this parameter to something besides zero, check if your device supports it by checking the `D3DDEVCAPS2_STREAMOFFSET` flag in the `D3DCAPS9` structure.

    - `Stride`—Size in bytes of each element in the vertex buffer that we are attaching to the stream

    For example, suppose `vb` is a vertex buffer that has been filled with vertices of type `Vertex`:

    ```
    _device->SetStreamSource( 0, vb, 0, sizeof( Vertex ) );
    ```

2. Set the vertex format. This is where we specify the vertex format of the vertices that we use in subsequent drawing calls.

    ```
    _device->SetFVF( D3DFVF_XYZ | D3DFVF_DIFFUSE | D3DFVF_TEX1 );
    ```

3. Set the index buffer. If we are using an index buffer, we must set the index buffer that is used in subsequent drawing operations. Only one index buffer can be used at a time; therefore if you need to draw an object with a different index buffer, you must switch to the other. The following code sets an index buffer:

    ```
    _device->SetIndices( _ib ); // pass copy of index buffer pointer
    ```

Part II

3.4 Drawing with Vertex/Index Buffers

After we have created our vertex/index buffers and done our preparation work, we can draw our geometry, which sends the geometry through the rendering pipeline using either `DrawPrimitive` or `DrawIndexedPrimitive`. These methods obtain the vertex info from the vertex streams and the index info from the currently set index buffer.

3.4.1 IDirect3DDevice9::DrawPrimitive

This method is used to draw primitives that do not use index info.

```
HRESULT IDirect3DDevice9::DrawPrimitive(
    D3DPRIMITIVETYPE PrimitiveType,
    UINT StartVertex,
    UINT PrimitiveCount
);
```

- `PrimitiveType`—The type of primitive that we are drawing. For instance, we can draw points and lines in addition to triangles. Since we are using a triangle, use `D3DPT_TRIANGLELIST` for this parameter.

- `StartVertex`—Index to an element in the vertex streams that marks the starting point from which to begin reading vertices. This parameter gives us the flexibility to only draw certain portions of a vertex buffer.

- `PrimitiveCount`—The number of primitives to draw

Example:

```
// draw four triangles.
_device->DrawPrimitive( D3DPT_TRIANGLELIST, 0, 4 );
```

3.4.2 IDirect3DDevice9::DrawIndexedPrimitive

This method is used to draw primitives using index info.

```
HRESULT IDirect3DDevice9::DrawIndexedPrimitive(
    D3DPRIMITIVETYPE Type,
    INT BaseVertexIndex,
    UINT MinIndex,
    UINT NumVertices,
    UINT StartIndex,
    UINT PrimitiveCount
);
```

- `Type`—The type of primitive that we are drawing. For instance, we can draw points and lines in addition to triangles. Since we are using a triangle, use `D3DPT_TRIANGLELIST` for this parameter.

- `BaseVertexIndex`—A base number to be added to the indices used in this call. See the following note.
- `MinIndex`—The minimum index value that will be referenced
- `NumVertices`—The number of vertices that will be referenced in this call
- `StartIndex`—Index to an element in the index buffer that marks the starting point from which to begin reading indices
- `PrimitiveCount`—The number of primitives to draw

Example:

```
_device->DrawIndexedPrimitive(D3DPT_TRIANGLELIST, 0, 0, 8, 0, 12);
```

Note: The `BaseVertexIndex` parameter deserves some explanation. Refer to Figure 3.2 during this explanation.

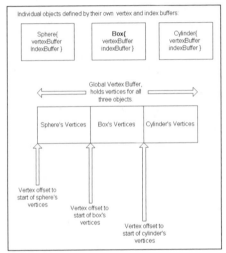

Figure 3.2: Separately defined vertex buffers merged into one global vertex buffer

The local index buffers reference vertices in the corresponding local vertex buffer. However, suppose that we want to combine the vertices of the sphere, box, and cylinder into one global vertex buffer. For each object we would have to recompute the indices to index correctly into the global vertex buffer. The new indices are computed by adding an offset value that specifies the start of the object's vertices in the global vertex buffer to each index. Note that the offset is measured in vertices, not bytes.

Rather than having to compute the indices relative to where the object is in the global vertex buffer ourselves, Direct3D allows us to pass in a vertex-offset value through the `BaseVertexIndex` parameter. Direct3D will then recompute the indices internally.

Part II

3.4.3 Begin/End Scene

The last bit of information to mention is that all drawing methods must be called inside an `IDirect3DDevice9::BeginScene` and `IDirect3DDevice9::EndScene` pair. For example, we would write:

```
_device->BeginScene();
    _device->DrawPrimitive(...);
_device->EndScene();
```

3.5 D3DX Geometric Objects

Building 3D objects by constructing each triangle in code is tedious. Fortunately, the D3DX library provides some methods to generate the mesh data of simple 3D objects for us.

The D3DX library provides the following six mesh creation functions:

- ▆ `D3DXCreateBox`
- ▆ `D3DXCreateSphere`
- ▆ `D3DXCreateCylinder`
- ▆ `D3DXCreateTeapot`
- ▆ `D3DXCreatePolygon`
- ▆ `D3DXCreateTorus`

Figure 3.3: Objects created and rendered using the `D3DXCreate*` functions

All six are used similarly and use the D3DX mesh data structure `ID3DXMesh` as well as the `ID3DXBuffer` interface. These interfaces are covered in Chapters 10 and 11. For now, we ignore their details and concentrate on using them in the simplest way.

```
HRESULT D3DXCreateTeapot(
    LPDIRECT3DDEVICE9 pDevice,  // device associated with the mesh
    LPD3DXMESH* ppMesh,         // pointer to receive mesh
    LPD3DXBUFFER* ppAdjacency   // set to zero for now
);
```

An example of using the `D3DXCreateTeapot` function:

```
ID3DXMesh* mesh = 0;
D3DXCreateTeapot(_device, &mesh, 0);
```

Once we have generated the mesh data, we can draw it using the `ID3DXMesh::DrawSubset` method. This method takes one parameter, which identifies a subset of the mesh. The meshes generated by the above `D3DXCreate*` functions create a mesh with only one subset, so zero can be specified for this parameter. An example of rendering the mesh:

```
_device->BeginScene();
    mesh->DrawSubset(0);
_device->EndScene();
```

When you are done with the mesh, you must release it:

```
_mesh->Release();
_mesh = 0;
```

3.6 Sample Applications: Triangle, Cube, Teapot, D3DXCreate*

There are four samples located in this chapter's directory in the book's companion files, which can be downloaded from the book's web site.

- Triangle—This very simple application demonstrates how to create and render a triangle in the wireframe mode.

- Cube—A little more advanced than the triangle sample, this application renders a spinning wireframe cube.

- Teapot—This application uses the `D3DXCreateTeapot` function to create and render a spinning teapot.

- D3DXCreate—This application creates and renders several different kinds of 3D objects that can be created with the `D3DXCreate*` functions.

Let's briefly discuss the implementation of the Cube sample. You can study the others on your own.

The sample application draws and renders a cube, as shown in Figure 3.4. The project and complete source code for this sample can be found in this chapter's directory.

Part II

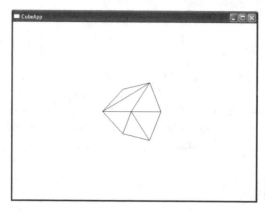

Figure 3.4 A screen shot from the CubeApp sample

First we instantiate the following two global variables to hold the vertex and index data of our cube:

```
IDirect3DVertexBuffer9* VB = 0;
IDirect3DIndexBuffer9*  IB = 0;
```

In addition, we instantiate two constant global variables that define the resolution of our screen:

```
const int Width  = 800;
const int Height = 600;
```

We then define our vertex structure and the flexible vertex format of that structure. The vertex structure in this sample holds only vertex position information:

```
struct Vertex
{
    Vertex(){}
    Vertex(float x, float y, float z)
    {
        _x = x;  _y = y;  _z = z;
    }
    float _x, _y, _z;
    static const DWORD FVF;
};
const DWORD Vertex::FVF = D3DFVF_XYZ;
```

Let's move on to the framework functions. The `Setup` function creates the vertex and index buffers, locks them, writes the vertices that make up the cube to the vertex buffer, and writes the indices that define the triangles of the cube. It then moves the camera a few units back so that it can see the cube that will be rendered at the origin of the world. Then it sets the projection transform. Finally, it sets the fill mode render state to wireframe mode:

```
bool Setup()
{
```

```
// create vertex and index buffers
Device->CreateVertexBuffer(
    8 * sizeof(Vertex),
    D3DUSAGE_WRITEONLY,
    Vertex::FVF,
    D3DPOOL_MANAGED,
    &VB,
    0);

Device->CreateIndexBuffer(
    36 * sizeof(WORD),
    D3DUSAGE_WRITEONLY,
    D3DFMT_INDEX16,
    D3DPOOL_MANAGED,
    &IB,
    0);

// fill the buffers with the cube data
Vertex* vertices;
VB->Lock(0, 0, (void**)&vertices, 0);

// vertices of a unit cube
vertices[0] = Vertex(-1.0f, -1.0f, -1.0f);
vertices[1] = Vertex(-1.0f,  1.0f, -1.0f);
vertices[2] = Vertex( 1.0f,  1.0f, -1.0f);
vertices[3] = Vertex( 1.0f, -1.0f, -1.0f);
vertices[4] = Vertex(-1.0f, -1.0f,  1.0f);
vertices[5] = Vertex(-1.0f,  1.0f,  1.0f);
vertices[6] = Vertex( 1.0f,  1.0f,  1.0f);
vertices[7] = Vertex( 1.0f, -1.0f,  1.0f);

VB->Unlock();

// define the triangles of the cube:
WORD* indices = 0;
IB->Lock(0, 0, (void**)&indices, 0);

// front side
indices[0]  = 0; indices[1]  = 1; indices[2]  = 2;
indices[3]  = 0; indices[4]  = 2; indices[5]  = 3;

// back side
indices[6]  = 4; indices[7]  = 6; indices[8]  = 5;
indices[9]  = 4; indices[10] = 7; indices[11] = 6;

// left side
indices[12] = 4; indices[13] = 5; indices[14] = 1;
indices[15] = 4; indices[16] = 1; indices[17] = 0;

// right side
indices[18] = 3; indices[19] = 2; indices[20] = 6;
indices[21] = 3; indices[22] = 6; indices[23] = 7;

// top
indices[24] = 1; indices[25] = 5; indices[26] = 6;
indices[27] = 1; indices[28] = 6; indices[29] = 2;
```

```
// bottom
indices[30] = 4; indices[31] = 0; indices[32] = 3;
indices[33] = 4; indices[34] = 3; indices[35] = 7;

IB->Unlock();

// position and aim the camera
D3DXVECTOR3 position(0.0f, 0.0f, -5.0f);
D3DXVECTOR3 target(0.0f, 0.0f, 0.0f);
D3DXVECTOR3 up(0.0f, 1.0f, 0.0f);
D3DXMATRIX V;
D3DXMatrixLookAtLH(&V, &position, &target, &up);

Device->SetTransform(D3DTS_VIEW, &V);

// set projection matrix
D3DXMATRIX proj;
D3DXMatrixPerspectiveFovLH(
    &proj,
    D3DX_PI * 0.5f, // 90 - degree
    (float)Width / (float)Height,
    1.0f,
    1000.0f);
Device->SetTransform(D3DTS_PROJECTION, &proj);

// set the render states
Device->SetRenderState(D3DRS_FILLMODE, D3DFILL_WIREFRAME);

return true;
}
```

The `Display` method has two tasks: It must update the scene and then render it. Since we want to spin the cube, we are going to increment an angle every frame that specifies how much the cube is to rotate that frame. By incrementing it every frame, the cube will be slightly more rotated every frame, making it look like it is spinning. Notice that we use the world transformation to actually orient the cube. Then we draw the cube using the `IDirect3DDevice9::DrawIndexedPrimitive` method.

```
bool Display(float timeDelta)
{
    if( Device )
    {
        //
        // spin the cube:
        //
        D3DXMATRIX Rx, Ry;

        // rotate 45 degrees on x-axis
        D3DXMatrixRotationX(&Rx, 3.14f / 4.0f);

        // incremenent y-rotation angle each frame
        static float y = 0.0f;
        D3DXMatrixRotationY(&Ry, y);
```

```
          y += timeDelta;

          // reset angle to zero when angle reaches 2*PI
          if( y >= 6.28f )
                y = 0.0f;

          // combine rotations
          D3DXMATRIX p = Rx * Ry;

          Device->SetTransform(D3DTS_WORLD, &p);

          //
          // draw the scene:
          //
          Device->Clear(0, 0,
                    D3DCLEAR_TARGET | D3DCLEAR_ZBUFFER,
                    0xffffffff, 1.0f, 0);
          Device->BeginScene();

          Device->SetStreamSource(0, VB, 0, sizeof(Vertex));
          Device->SetIndices(IB);
          Device->SetFVF(Vertex::FVF);
          Device->DrawIndexedPrimitive(D3DPT_TRIANGLELIST,
                                       0, 0, 8, 0, 12);

          Device->EndScene();
          Device->Present(0, 0, 0, 0);
     }
     return true;
}
```

Finally, we clean up any memory that we have allocated. This means
releasing the vertex and index buffer interfaces:

```
void Cleanup()
{
     d3d::Release<IDirect3DVertexBuffer9*>(VB);
     d3d::Release<IDirect3DIndexBuffer9*>(IB);
}
```

3.7 Summary

- Vertex data is stored in the `IDirect3DVertexBuffer9` interface. Similarly, index data is stored in the `IDirect3DIndex-
  Buffer9` interface. The reason for using vertex/index buffers is
  that the data can be stored in video memory.

- Geometry that is static (that is, does not need to be updated every
  frame) should be stored in a static vertex/index buffer. On the other
  hand, geometry that is dynamic (that is, does need to get updated
  every frame) should be stored in a dynamic vertex/index buffer.

■ Render states are states that the device maintains that affect how geometry is rendered. Render states remain in effect until changed, and the current values are applied to the geometry of any subsequent drawing operations. All render states have initial default values.

■ To draw the contents of a vertex buffer and an index buffer you must:

   □ Call `IDirect3DDevice9::SetStreamSource` and hook the vertex buffer that you wish to draw from to a stream.

   □ Call `IDirect3DDevice9::SetFVF` to set the vertex format of the vertices to render.

   □ If you are using an index buffer, call `IDirect3DDevice9::SetIndices` to set the index buffer.

   □ Call either `IDirect3DDevice9::DrawPrimitive` or `IDirect3DDevice9::DrawIndexedPrimitive` in between an `IDirect3DDevice9::BeginScene` and `IDirect3DDevice9::EndScene` pair.

■ Using the `D3DXCreate*` functions, we can create the geometry of more complex 3D objects, such as spheres, cylinders, and teapots.

Chapter 4

Color

In the last chapter we rendered the objects in the scene using lines to form wireframe meshes. In this chapter we learn how to render solid objects with color.

Objectives

- To learn how color is described in Direct3D
- To understand how colors are shaded across a triangle

4.1 Color Representation

In Direct3D, colors are described with an RGB triplet. That is, we specify the amount of red, green, and blue color. The additive mixing of these three components determines the final color. By using a combination of red, green, and blue, we can represent millions of colors.

We use two different types of structures to hold the RGB data. The first is the D3DCOLOR type, which is actually `typedef`ed as a DWORD and is 32 bits. The bits in the D3DCOLOR type are divided into four 8-bit sections, where each section stores the intensity of a color component. Figure 4.1 shows the distribution.

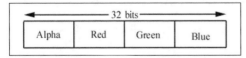

Figure 4.1: A 32-bit color, where a byte is allocated for each primary color component red, green, and blue. A fourth byte is allocated for the alpha component.

Since each color component gets a byte of memory, the intensity of the color can range from 0-255. Values near 0 specify a low intensity, and values near 255 specify a strong intensity.

> **Note:** Do not worry about the alpha component now; it is used for alpha blending—the topic of Chapter 7.

Specifying each component and then inserting it into the proper position in the D3DCOLOR type will require some bit operations. Direct3D provides a macro that performs this for us called D3DCOLOR_ARGB. There is one parameter for each color component and the alpha component. Each parameter must be in the range 0-255 and is used like so:

```
D3DCOLOR brightRed = D3DCOLOR_ARGB(255, 255, 0, 0);
D3DCOLOR someColor = D3DCOLOR_ARGB(255, 144, 87, 201);
```

Alternatively, we can use the D3DCOLOR_XRGB macro, which is similar but does not take the alpha parameter; rather, it sets the alpha to 0xff (255).

```
#define D3DCOLOR_XRGB(r,g,b) D3DCOLOR_ARGB(0xff,r,g,b)
```

Another way to store a color in Direct3D is with the D3DCOLORVALUE structure. With this structure we use a floating-point value to measure the intensity of each component. The range measures from 0 to 1—0 being no intensity and 1 being full intensity.

```
typedef struct _D3DCOLORVALUE {
    float r; // the red component, range 0.0-1.0
    float g; // the green component, range 0.0-1.0
    float b; // the blue component, range 0.0-1.0
    float a; // the alpha component, range 0.0-1.0
} D3DCOLORVALUE;
```

Alternatively, we can use the D3DXCOLOR structure, which contains the same data members as D3DCOLORVALUE but provides useful constructors and overloaded operators, making color manipulations easy. In addition, since they can contain the same data members, we can cast back and fourth between the two. D3DXCOLOR is defined as:

```
typedef struct D3DXCOLOR
{
#ifdef __cplusplus
public:
    D3DXCOLOR() {}
    D3DXCOLOR( DWORD argb );
    D3DXCOLOR( CONST FLOAT * );
    D3DXCOLOR( CONST D3DXFLOAT16 * );
    D3DXCOLOR( CONST D3DCOLORVALUE& );
    D3DXCOLOR( FLOAT r, FLOAT g, FLOAT b, FLOAT a );

    // casting
    operator DWORD () const;

    operator FLOAT* ();
    operator CONST FLOAT* () const;
```

```
    operator D3DCOLORVALUE* ();
    operator CONST D3DCOLORVALUE* () const;


    operator D3DCOLORVALUE& ();
    operator CONST D3DCOLORVALUE& () const;

    // assignment operators
    D3DXCOLOR& operator += ( CONST D3DXCOLOR& );
    D3DXCOLOR& operator -= ( CONST D3DXCOLOR& );
    D3DXCOLOR& operator *= ( FLOAT );
    D3DXCOLOR& operator /= ( FLOAT );

    // unary operators
    D3DXCOLOR operator + () const;
    D3DXCOLOR operator - () const;

    // binary operators
    D3DXCOLOR operator + ( CONST D3DXCOLOR& ) const;
    D3DXCOLOR operator - ( CONST D3DXCOLOR& ) const;
    D3DXCOLOR operator * ( FLOAT ) const;
    D3DXCOLOR operator / ( FLOAT ) const;

    friend D3DXCOLOR operator * (FLOAT, CONST D3DXCOLOR& );

    BOOL operator == ( CONST D3DXCOLOR& ) const;
    BOOL operator != ( CONST D3DXCOLOR& ) const;

#endif //__cplusplus
    FLOAT r, g, b, a;
} D3DXCOLOR, *LPD3DXCOLOR;
```

Note: Observe that the `D3DCOLORVALUE` and the `D3DXCOLOR` structure both have four floating-point components. This leads to the common notation of treating a color as a 4D vector (r, g, b, a). Color vectors are added, subtracted, and scaled just like regular vectors. On the other hand, dot and cross products do *not* make sense for color vectors, but component-wise multiplication does make sense for colors. Thus, the color-color multiplication operator in the `D3DXCOLOR` class performs component-wise multiplication. The symbol $\otimes$ denotes component-wise multiplication, and it is defined as:
$(c_1, c_2, c_3, c_4) \otimes (k_1, k_2, k_3, k_4) = (c_1 k_1, c_2 k_2, c_3 k_3, c_4 k_4)$.

We now update our d3dUtility.h file with the following global color constants:

```
namespace d3d
{
    .
    .
    .
    const D3DXCOLOR       WHITE( D3DCOLOR_XRGB(255, 255, 255) );
    const D3DXCOLOR       BLACK( D3DCOLOR_XRGB(  0,   0,   0) );
    const D3DXCOLOR         RED( D3DCOLOR_XRGB(255,   0,   0) );
    const D3DXCOLOR       GREEN( D3DCOLOR_XRGB(  0, 255,   0) );
    const D3DXCOLOR        BLUE( D3DCOLOR_XRGB(  0,   0, 255) );
```

```
    const D3DXCOLOR      YELLOW( D3DCOLOR_XRGB(255, 255,   0) );
    const D3DXCOLOR        CYAN( D3DCOLOR_XRGB(  0, 255, 255) );
    const D3DXCOLOR     MAGENTA( D3DCOLOR_XRGB(255,   0, 255) );
}
```

4.2 Vertex Colors

The color of a primitive is determined by the color of the vertices that make it up. Therefore, we must add a color member to our vertex data structure. Note that a D3DCOLORVALUE type cannot be used here because Direct3D expects a 32-bit value to describe the color of a vertex. (Actually, by using a vertex shader we could use 4D color vectors for the vertex color, and thereby gain 128-bit color, but that is getting ahead of ourselves for now. Vertex shaders are covered in Chapter 17.)

```
struct ColorVertex
{
    float _x, _y, _z;
    D3DCOLOR _color;
    static const DWORD FVF;
}
const DWORD ColorVertex::FVF = D3DFVF_XYZ | D3DFVF_DIFFUSE;
```

4.3 Shading

Shading occurs during rasterization and specifies how the vertex colors are used to compute the pixel colors that make up the primitive. There are two shading modes that are presently used: flat shading and Gouraud shading.

With flat shading, the pixels of a primitive are uniformly colored by the color specified in the *first* vertex of the primitive. So the triangle formed by the following three vertices would be red, since the first vertex color is red. The colors of the second and third vertices are ignored with flat shading.

```
ColorVertex t[3];
t[0]._color = D3DCOLOR_XRGB(255, 0, 0);
t[1]._color = D3DCOLOR_XRGB(0, 255, 0);
t[2]._color = D3DCOLOR_XRGB(0, 0, 255);
```

Flat shading tends to make objects appear blocky because there is no smooth transition from one color to the next. A much better form of shading is called Gouraud shading (also called smooth shading). With Gouraud shading, the colors at each vertex are interpolated linearly across the face of the primitive. Figure 4.2 shows a red flat shaded triangle and a triangle colored using Gouraud shading.

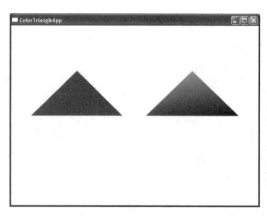

Figure 4.2: On the left is a triangle colored red with flat shading. On the right is a triangle with vertex colors red, green, and blue; notice that with Gouraud shading, the vertex colors are interpolated across the triangle.

Like many things in Direct3D, the shading mode is controlled through the Direct3D state machine.

```
// set flat shading
Device->SetRenderState(D3DRS_SHADEMODE, D3DSHADE_FLAT);

// set Gouraud shading
Device->SetRenderState(D3DRS_SHADEMODE, D3DSHADE_GOURAUD);
```

4.4 Sample Application: Colored Triangle

The sample program for this chapter demonstrates a triangle colored using flat shading and a triangle colored using Gouraud shading. It renders the image shown in Figure 4.2. First we add the following global variables:

```
D3DXMATRIX                 World;
IDirect3DVertexBuffer9* Triangle = 0;
```

We include a D3DXMATRIX that is used to store the world transformation of the triangles that we are going to draw. The Triangle variable is the vertex buffer that stores the vertex data of a triangle. Notice that we only have to store the geometry of one triangle because we can draw it multiple times at different positions in the world using the world matrix.

The Setup method creates the vertex buffer and fills it with the data of a triangle with colored vertices. The first vertex in the triangle is full-intensity red (255), the second is full-intensity green (255), and the third is full-intensity blue (255). Finally, we disable lighting for this sample. Notice that this sample uses the new ColorVertex structure, as explained in section 4.2.

```
bool Setup()
{
    // create vertex buffer
    Device->CreateVertexBuffer(
        3 * sizeof(ColorVertex),
        D3DUSAGE_WRITEONLY,
        ColorVertex::FVF,
        D3DPOOL_MANAGED,
        &Triangle,
        0);

    // fill the buffers with the triangle data
    ColorVertex* v;
    Triangle->Lock(0, 0, (void**)&v, 0);

    v[0] = ColorVertex(-1.0f, 0.0f, 2.0f, D3DCOLOR_XRGB(255, 0, 0));
    v[1] = ColorVertex( 0.0f, 1.0f, 2.0f, D3DCOLOR_XRGB(0, 255, 0));
    v[2] = ColorVertex( 1.0f, 0.0f, 2.0f, D3DCOLOR_XRGB(0, 0, 255));

    Triangle->Unlock();

    // set projection matrix
    D3DXMATRIX proj;
    D3DXMatrixPerspectiveFovLH(
        &proj,
        D3DX_PI * 0.5f, // 90 - degree
        (float)Width / (float)Height,
        1.0f,
        1000.0f);
    Device->SetTransform(D3DTS_PROJECTION, &proj);

    // set the render states
    Device->SetRenderState(D3DRS_LIGHTING, false);

    return true;
}
```

Then, the `Display` function draws `Triangle` twice in two different positions and with different shade modes. The position of each triangle is controlled with the world matrix—`World`.

```
bool Display(float timeDelta)
{
    if( Device )
    {
        Device->Clear(0, 0, D3DCLEAR_TARGET | D3DCLEAR_ZBUFFER,
                    0xffffffff, 1.0f, 0);
        Device->BeginScene();

        Device->SetFVF(ColorVertex::FVF);
        Device->SetStreamSource(0, Triangle, 0, sizeof(ColorVertex));
```

```
// draw the triangle to the left with flat shading
D3DXMatrixTranslation(&World, -1.25f, 0.0f, 0.0f);
Device->SetTransform(D3DTS_WORLD, &World);

Device->SetRenderState(D3DRS_SHADEMODE, D3DSHADE_FLAT);
Device->DrawPrimitive(D3DPT_TRIANGLELIST, 0, 1);

// draw the triangle to the right with gouraud shading
D3DXMatrixTranslation(&World, 1.25f, 0.0f, 0.0f);
Device->SetTransform(D3DTS_WORLD, &World);

Device->SetRenderState(D3DRS_SHADEMODE, D3DSHADE_GOURAUD);
Device->DrawPrimitive(D3DPT_TRIANGLELIST, 0, 1);

Device->EndScene();
Device->Present(0, 0, 0, 0);
}
return true;
}
```

4.5 Summary

- Colors are described by specifying an intensity of red, green, and blue. The additive mixing of these three colors at different intensities allows us to describe millions of colors. In Direct3D, we can use the D3DCOLOR, the D3DCOLORVALUE, or the D3DXCOLOR type to describe a color in code.

- We sometimes treat a color as a 4D vector (r, g, b, a). Color vectors are added, subtracted, and scaled just like regular vectors. On the other hand, dot and cross products do *not* make sense for color vectors, but component-wise multiplication does make sense for colors. The symbol $\otimes$ denotes component-wise multiplication, and it is defined as: $(c_1, c_2, c_3, c_4) \otimes (k_1, k_2, k_3, k_4) = (c_1k_1, c_2k_2, c_3k_3, c_4k_4)$.

- We specify the color of each vertex, and then Direct3D uses the current shade mode to determine how these vertex colors are used to compute the pixel colors of the triangle during rasterization.

- With flat shading, the pixels of a primitive are uniformly colored by the color specified in the *first* vertex of the primitive. With Gouraud shading, the colors at each vertex are interpolated linearly across the face of the primitive.

Part II

Chapter 5

Lighting

To enhance the realism of our scenes, we can add lighting. Lighting also helps to depict the solid form and volume of objects. When using lighting, we no longer specify vertex colors ourselves; rather, Direct3D runs each vertex through its lighting engine and computes a vertex color based on defined light sources, materials, and the orientation of the surface with regard to the light sources. Computing the vertex colors based on a lighting model results in a more natural scene.

Objectives

- To learn the light sources that Direct3D supports and types of light that these sources emit
- To understand how we define light to interact with the surface that it strikes
- To find out how we can mathematically describe the direction a triangle is facing so that we can determine the angle at which a light ray strikes the triangle

5.1 Light Components

In the Direct3D lighting model, the light emitted by a light source consists of three components, or three kinds of light.

- **Ambient light**—This kind of light models light that has reflected off other surfaces and is used to brighten up the overall scene. For example, parts of objects are often lit, to a degree, even though they are not in direct sight of a light source. These parts get lit from light that has bounced off other surfaces. Ambient light is a hack used to roughly, and cheaply, model this reflected light.

- **Diffuse light**—This type of light travels in a particular direction. When it strikes a surface, it reflects equally in all directions. Because diffuse light reflects equally in all directions, the reflected light will reach the eye no matter the viewpoint, and therefore we do not need to take the viewer into consideration. Thus, the diffuse lighting equation needs only to consider the light direction and the attitude of the surface. This kind of light will be your general light that emits from a source.

■ **Specular light**—This type of light travels in a particular direction. When it strikes a surface, it reflects harshly in one direction, causing a bright shine that can only be seen from some angles. Since the light reflects in one direction, clearly the viewpoint, in addition to the light direction and surface attitude, must be taken into consideration in the specular lighting equation. Specular light is used to model light that produces highlights on objects, such as the bright shine created when light strikes a polished surface.

Specular lighting requires more computations than the other types of light; therefore, Direct3D provides the option to turn it off. In fact, by default it is turned off; to enable specular lighting you must set the `D3DRS_SPECULARENABLE` render state.

```
Device->SetRenderState(D3DRS_SPECULARENABLE, true);
```

Each type of light is represented by a `D3DCOLORVALUE` structure or `D3DXCOLOR`, which describes the color of the light. Here are some examples of several light colors:

```
D3DXCOLOR redAmbient(1.0f, 0.0f, 0.0f, 1.0f);
D3DXCOLOR blueDiffuse(0.0f, 0.0f, 1.0f, 1.0f);
D3DXCOLOR whiteSpecular(1.0f, 1.0f, 1.0f, 1.0f);
```

Note: The alpha values in the `D3DXCOLOR` class are ignored when used for describing light colors.

5.2 Materials

The color of an object we see in the real world is determined by the color of light that the object reflects. For instance, a red ball is red because it absorbs all colors of light except red light. The red light is reflected from the ball and makes it into our eyes, and we therefore see the ball as red. Direct3D models this same phenomenon by having us define a material for an object. The material allows us to define the percentage at which light is reflected from the surface. In code a material is represented with the `D3DMATERIAL9` structure.

```
typedef struct _D3DMATERIAL9 {
    D3DCOLORVALUE  Diffuse, Ambient, Specular, Emissive;
    float   Power;
} D3DMATERIAL9;
```

■ `Diffuse`—Specifies the amount of diffuse light this surface reflects

- Ambient—Specifies the amount of ambient light this surface reflects
- Specular—Specifies the amount of specular light this surface reflects
- Emissive—This component is used to add to the overall color of the surface, making it appear brighter like it's giving off its own light.
- Power—Specifies the sharpness of specular highlights; the higher this value, the sharper the highlights

As an example, suppose we want a red ball. We would define the ball's material to reflect only red light and absorb all other colors of light:

```
D3DMATERIAL9 red;
::ZeroMemory(&red, sizeof(red));
red.Diffuse  = D3DXCOLOR(1.0f, 0.0f, 0.0f, 1.0f); // red
red.Ambient  = D3DXCOLOR(1.0f, 0.0f, 0.0f, 1.0f); // red
red.Specular = D3DXCOLOR(1.0f, 0.0f, 0.0f, 1.0f); // red
red.Emissive = D3DXCOLOR(0.0f, 0.0f, 0.0f, 1.0f); // no emission
red.Power    = 5.0f;
```

Here we set the green and blue components to 0, indicating that the material reflects 0% of these colored lights. We set the red component to 1, indicating that the material reflects 100% red light. Notice that we have the ability to control the color of light reflected for each type of light (ambient, diffuse, and specular light).

Also notice that if we define a light source that emits only blue-colored light, it would fail to light the ball because the blue light would be completely absorbed and zero red light would be reflected. An object appears black when it absorbs all light. Similarly, an object is white when it reflects 100% red, green, and blue light.

Because it is somewhat tedious to manually fill out a material structure, we add the following utility function and global material constants to the d3dUtility.h/cpp files:

```
D3DMATERIAL9 d3d::InitMtrl(D3DXCOLOR a, D3DXCOLOR d,
                           D3DXCOLOR s, D3DXCOLOR e, float p)
{
    D3DMATERIAL9 mtrl;
    mtrl.Ambient  = a;
    mtrl.Diffuse  = d;
    mtrl.Specular = s;
    mtrl.Emissive = e;
    mtrl.Power    = p;
    return mtrl;
}

namespace d3d
{
```

```
.
.
.
D3DMATERIAL9 InitMtrl(D3DXCOLOR a, D3DXCOLOR d,
                      D3DXCOLOR s, D3DXCOLOR e, float p);

const D3DMATERIAL9 WHITE_MTRL  = InitMtrl(WHITE, WHITE,
                                 WHITE, BLACK, 8.0f);

const D3DMATERIAL9 RED_MTRL    = InitMtrl(RED, RED,
                                 RED, BLACK, 8.0f);

const D3DMATERIAL9 GREEN_MTRL  = InitMtrl(GREEN, GREEN,
                                 GREEN, BLACK, 8.0f);

const D3DMATERIAL9 BLUE_MTRL   = InitMtrl(BLUE, BLUE,
                                 BLUE, BLACK, 8.0f);

const D3DMATERIAL9 YELLOW_MTRL = InitMtrl(YELLOW, YELLOW,
                                 YELLOW, BLACK, 8.0f);
}
```

Note: An excellent paper on color theory, lighting, and how the human eye perceives color is available at http://www.adobe.com/support/techguides/color/colortheory/main.html.

A vertex structure does not have a material property; rather, a current material must be set. To set the current material, we use the `IDirect3DDevice9::SetMaterial(CONST D3DMATERIAL9* pMaterial)` method.

Suppose that we want to render several objects with different materials; we would write the following:

```
D3DMATERIAL9 blueMaterial, redMaterial;

...// set up material structures

Device->SetMaterial(&blueMaterial);
drawSphere(); // blue sphere

Device->SetMaterial(&redMaterial);
drawSphere(); // red sphere
```

5.3 Vertex Normals

A *face normal* is a vector that describes the direction a polygon is facing (see Figure 5.1).

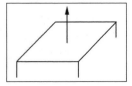

Figure 5.1: The face normal of a surface

Vertex normals are based on the same idea, but rather than specifying the normal per polygon, we specify them for each vertex that forms the polygon (see Figure 5.2).

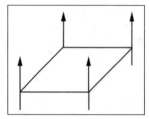

Figure 5.2: The vertex normals of a surface

Direct3D needs to know the vertex normals so that it can determine the angle at which light strikes a surface, and since lighting calculations are done per vertex, Direct3D needs to know the surface orientation (normal) per vertex. Note that the vertex normal isn't necessarily the same as the face normal. Sphere/circle approximations are good examples of objects where the vertex normals are not the same as the triangle normals (see Figure 5.3).

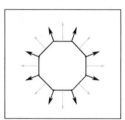

Figure 5.3: An example where vertex normals are different from the face normal. The bolder vectors denote the vertex normals, while the lighter vectors denote the face normals.

To describe the vertex normal of a vertex, we must update our vertex structure:

```
struct Vertex
{
    float _x,  _y,  _z;
    float _nx, _ny, _nz;
    static const DWORD FVF;
}
const DWORD Vertex::FVF = D3DFVF_XYZ | D3DFVF_NORMAL;
```

Notice that we have removed the color member that was used in the last chapter. This is because we are using lighting to compute the colors of our vertices.

For simple objects such as cubes and spheres, we can see the vertex normals by inspection. For more complex meshes, we need a more mechanical method. Suppose a triangle is formed by the vertices p_0, p_1, and $\mathbf{p}_2$, and we need to compute the vertex normal for each of the vertices $\mathbf{n}_0$, $\mathbf{n}_1$, and $\mathbf{n}_2$.

The simplest approach, and the approach we illustrate, is to find the face normal of the triangle that the three vertices form and use the face normal as the vertex normals. First compute two vectors that lie on the triangle:

$$\mathbf{P}_1 - \mathbf{P}_0 = \mathbf{u}$$
$$\mathbf{P}_2 - \mathbf{P}_0 = \mathbf{v}$$

Then the face normal is:

$$\mathbf{n} = \mathbf{u} \times \mathbf{v}$$

Since each vertex normal is the same as the face normal:

$$\mathbf{n}_0 = \mathbf{n}_1 = \mathbf{n}_2 = \mathbf{n}$$

Below is a C function that computes the face normal of a triangle from three vertex points on the triangle. Note that this function assumes that the vertices are specified in a clockwise winding order. If they are not, the normal will point in the opposite direction.

```
void ComputeNormal(D3DXVECTOR3* p0,
                   D3DXVECTOR3* p1,
                   D3DXVECTOR3* p2,
                   D3DXVECTOR3* out)
{
    D3DXVECTOR3 u = *p1 - *p0;
    D3DXVECTOR3 v = *p2 - *p0;

    D3DXVec3Cross(out, &u, &v);
    D3DXVec3Normalize(out, out);
}
```

Using face normals as vertex normals does not produce smooth results when approximating curved surfaces with triangles. A better method for finding a vertex normal is *normal averaging*. To find the vertex normal $\mathbf{v}_n$ of a vertex $\mathbf{v}$, we find the face normals for all the triangles in the mesh that share vertex $\mathbf{v}$. Then $\mathbf{v}_n$ is given by averaging all of these face normals. Here's an example to illustrate. Suppose three triangles, whose face normals are given by $\mathbf{n}_0$, $\mathbf{n}_1$, and $\mathbf{n}_2$, share the vertex $\mathbf{v}$. Then $\mathbf{v}_n$ is given by averaging the face normals:

$$\mathbf{v}_n = \frac{1}{3}\left(\mathbf{n}_0 + \mathbf{n}_1 + \mathbf{n}_2\right)$$

During the transformation stages, it is possible for vertex normals to become non-normal. Therefore, it is best to be safe and have Direct3D

Part II

renormalize all of your normals after the transformation stages by enabling the `D3DRS_NORMALIZENORMALS` render state:

```
Device->SetRenderState(D3DRS_NORMALIZENORMALS, true);
```

5.4 Light Sources

Direct3D supports three types of light sources.

- **Point lights**—This light source has a position in world space and emits light in all directions.

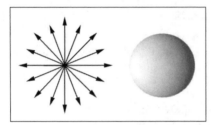

Figure 5.4: A point light

- **Directional lights**—This light source has no position but shoots parallel rays of light in the specified direction.

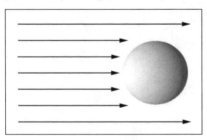

Figure 5.5: Directional light

- **Spotlights**—This type of light source is similar to a flashlight; it has a position and shines light through a conical shape in a particular direction. The cone is characterized by two angles, ϑ and ϕ. The angle ϑ describes an inner cone, and ϕ describes the outer cone.

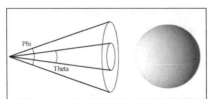

Figure 5.6: A spotlight

In code a light source is represented with the D3DLIGHT9 structure.

```
typedef struct _D3DLIGHT9 {
    D3DLIGHTTYPE  Type;
    D3DCOLORVALUE  Diffuse;
    D3DCOLORVALUE  Specular;
    D3DCOLORVALUE  Ambient;
    D3DVECTOR  Position;
    D3DVECTOR  Direction;
    float  Range;
    float  Falloff;
    float  Attenuation0;
    float  Attenuation1;
    float  Attenuation2;
    float  Theta;
    float  Phi;
} D3DLIGHT9;
```

- Type—Defines the type of light that we are making and can be one of the following three types: D3DLIGHT_POINT, D3DLIGHT_SPOT, D3DLIGHT_DIRECTIONAL
- Diffuse—The color of diffuse light that this source emits
- Specular—The color of specular light that this source emits
- Ambient—The color of ambient light that this source emits
- Position—A vector describing the world position of the light source. This value is meaningless for directional lights.
- Direction—A vector describing the world direction that the light is traveling. This value is not used for point lights.
- Range—The maximum range that the light can travel before it "dies." This value cannot be greater than $\sqrt{FLT\_MAX}$ and has no effect on directional lights.
- Falloff—This value is used only for spotlights. It defines how the light's intensity weakens from the inner cone to the outer cone. This value is generally set to 1.0f.
- Attenuation0, Attenuation1, Attenuation2—The attenuation variables are used to define how the intensity of light weakens over distance. These variables are only used for point and spotlights. The attenuation0 variable defines a constant falloff, attenuation1 defines the linear falloff, and attenuation2 defines the quadratic falloff. Calculated using this formula, where D is distance from light source and A_0, A_1, A_2 correspond to Attenuation 0, 1, and 2. $$Attenuation = \frac{1}{A_0 + A_1 \cdot D + A_2 \cdot D^2}$$
- Theta—Used for spotlights only; specifies inner cone angle in radians
- Phi—Used for spotlights only; specifies outer cone angle in radians

Part II

Like initializing a D3DMATERIAL9 structure, initializing a D3DLIGHT9 structure can also be tedious when you only want a simple light. We add the following functions to the d3dUtility.h/cpp files to initialize simple lights:

```
namespace d3d
{
    .
    .
    .
D3DLIGHT9 InitDirectionalLight(D3DXVECTOR3* direction,
                               D3DXCOLOR* color);

D3DLIGHT9 InitPointLight(D3DXVECTOR3* position,
                         D3DXCOLOR* color);

D3DLIGHT9 InitSpotLight(D3DXVECTOR3* position,
                        D3DXVECTOR3* direction,
                        D3DXCOLOR* color);
}
```

The implementation of these functions is straightforward. We will only show the implementation of InitDirectionalLight. The others are similar:

```
D3DLIGHT9 d3d::InitDirectionalLight(D3DXVECTOR3* direction,
                                    D3DXCOLOR* color)
{
    D3DLIGHT9 light;
    ::ZeroMemory(&light, sizeof(light));

    light.Type      = D3DLIGHT_DIRECTIONAL;
    light.Ambient   = *color * 0.4f;
    light.Diffuse   = *color;
    light.Specular  = *color * 0.6f;
    light.Direction = *direction;

    return light;
}
```

Then to create a directional light that runs parallel with the x-axis in the positive direction and emits white light, we would write:

```
D3DXVECTOR3 dir(1.0f, 0.0f, 0.0f);
D3DXCOLOR   c = d3d::WHITE;
D3DLIGHT9 dirLight = d3d::InitDirectionalLight(&dir, &c);
```

After we have initialized a D3DLIGHT9 instance, we need to register it with an internal list of lights that Direct3D maintains. We do this like so:

```
Device->SetLight(
    0, // element in the light list to set, range is 0-maxlights
    &light);// address of the D3DLIGHT9 structure to set
```

Once a light is registered, we can turn it on and off using what this next example illustrates:

```
Device->LightEnable(
    0,     // the element in the light list to enable/disable
    true); // true = enable, false = disable
```

5.5 Sample Application: Lighting

The sample for this chapter creates the scene shown in Figure 5.7. It demonstrates how to specify vertex normals, how to create a material, and how to create and activate a directional light. Note that in this sample program we do not make use of the d3dUtility.h/cpp material and light functionality code because we want to show how it is done manually first. However, the rest of the samples in this book do use the material and light utility code.

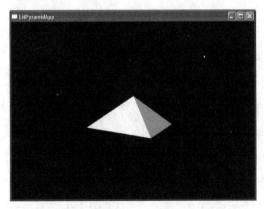

Figure 5.7: Screen shot from the LitPyramid sample

The steps for adding light to a scene are:

1. Enable lighting.

2. Create a material for each object and set the material before rendering the corresponding object.

3. Create one or more light sources, set the light sources, and enable them.

4. Enable any additional lighting states, such as specular highlights.

First we instantiate a global vertex buffer that stores the pyramid's vertices:

```
IDirect3DVertexBuffer9* Pyramid = 0;
```

The Setup function contains all the code relevant to this chapter, so we omit the other functions to save space. It implements the previously discussed steps to add lighting to a scene. The Setup method starts by enabling lighting, which isn't necessary because it's enabled by default (but it doesn't hurt either).

```
bool Setup()
{
    Device->SetRenderState(D3DRS_LIGHTING, true);
```

Next, we create the vertex buffer, lock it, and specify the vertices that form triangles of the pyramid. The vertex normals were precomputed using the algorithm covered in section 5.3. Notice that while the triangles share vertices, they do not share normals; thus it is not very advantageous to use an index list for this object. For example, all the triangles share the peak point (0, 1, 0); however, for each triangle, the peak vertex normal points in a different direction.

```
Device->CreateVertexBuffer(
        12 * sizeof(Vertex),
        D3DUSAGE_WRITEONLY,
        Vertex::FVF,
        D3DPOOL_MANAGED,
        &Pyramid,
        0);

// fill the vertex buffer with pyramid data
Vertex* v;
Pyramid->Lock(0, 0, (void**)&v, 0);

// front face
v[0] = Vertex(-1.0f, 0.0f, -1.0f, 0.0f, 0.707f, -0.707f);
v[1] = Vertex( 0.0f, 1.0f,  0.0f, 0.0f, 0.707f, -0.707f);
v[2] = Vertex( 1.0f, 0.0f, -1.0f, 0.0f, 0.707f, -0.707f);

// left face
v[3] = Vertex(-1.0f, 0.0f,  1.0f, -0.707f, 0.707f, 0.0f);
v[4] = Vertex( 0.0f, 1.0f,  0.0f, -0.707f, 0.707f, 0.0f);
v[5] = Vertex(-1.0f, 0.0f, -1.0f, -0.707f, 0.707f, 0.0f);

// right face
v[6] = Vertex( 1.0f, 0.0f, -1.0f, 0.707f, 0.707f, 0.0f);
v[7] = Vertex( 0.0f, 1.0f,  0.0f, 0.707f, 0.707f, 0.0f);
v[8] = Vertex( 1.0f, 0.0f,  1.0f, 0.707f, 0.707f, 0.0f);

// back face
v[9]  = Vertex( 1.0f, 0.0f,  1.0f, 0.0f, 0.707f, 0.707f);
v[10] = Vertex( 0.0f, 1.0f,  0.0f, 0.0f, 0.707f, 0.707f);
v[11] = Vertex(-1.0f, 0.0f,  1.0f, 0.0f, 0.707f, 0.707f);

Pyramid->Unlock();
```

After we have generated the vertex data of our object, we describe how the object interacts with light by describing its materials. In this sample, the pyramid reflects white lights, emits no light, and produces some highlights.

```
D3DMATERIAL9 mtrl;
    mtrl.Ambient  = d3d::WHITE;
    mtrl.Diffuse  = d3d::WHITE;
    mtrl.Specular = d3d::WHITE;
    mtrl.Emissive = d3d::BLACK;
    mtrl.Power    = 5.0f;

    Device->SetMaterial(&mtrl);
```

Second to last, we create and enable a directional light. The directional light rays run parallel to the x-axis in the positive direction. The light emits strong white diffuse light (`dir.Diffuse = WHITE`), weak white specular light (`dir.Specular = WHITE * 0.3f`), and a medium amount of white ambient light (`dir.Ambient = WHITE * 0.6f`).

```
D3DLIGHT9 dir;
    ::ZeroMemory(&dir, sizeof(dir));
    dir.Type      = D3DLIGHT_DIRECTIONAL;
    dir.Diffuse   = d3d::WHITE;
    dir.Specular  = d3d::WHITE * 0.3f;
    dir.Ambient   = d3d::WHITE * 0.6f;
    dir.Direction = D3DXVECTOR3(1.0f, 0.0f, 0.0f);

    Device->SetLight(0, &dir);
    Device->LightEnable(0, true);
```

Finally, we set the state to renormalize normals and enable specular highlights.

```
    Device->SetRenderState(D3DRS_NORMALIZENORMALS, true);
    Device->SetRenderState(D3DRS_SPECULARENABLE, true);

    // ... code to set up the view matrix and projection matrix
    // omitted

    return true;
}
```

5.6 Additional Samples

Three additional samples are included for this chapter in the companion files. They use the `D3DXCreate*` functions to create the 3D objects that compose the scene. The `D3DXCreate*` functions create vertex data with the format `D3DFVF_XYZ | D3DFVF_NORMAL`. In addition, these functions compute the vertex normals of each mesh for us. The additional samples demonstrate how to use directional lights, point lights, and spotlights. Figure 5.8 shows a screen shot from the directional light sample.

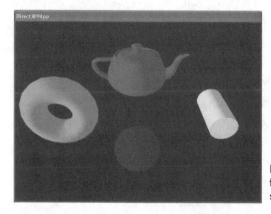

Figure 5.8: A screen shot from the DirectionalLight sample

5.7 Summary

■ Direct3D supports three light source models: directional lights, point lights, and spotlights. Light sources emit three types of light: ambient light, diffuse light, and specular light.

■ The material of a surface defines how light interacts with the surface that it strikes (that is, how much light is reflected and absorbed, thus determining the color of the surface).

■ Vertex normals are used to define the orientation of a vertex. They are used so that Direct3D can determine the angle at which a ray of light strikes the vertex. In some cases, the vertex normal is equal to the normal of the triangle that it forms, but this is not usually the case when approximating smooth surfaces (e.g., spheres, cylinders).

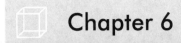

Chapter 6

Texturing

Texture mapping is a technique that allows us to map image data onto a triangle; this capability allows us to increase the details and realism of our scene significantly. For example, we can build a cube and turn it into a crate by mapping a crate texture to each side (see Figure 6.1).

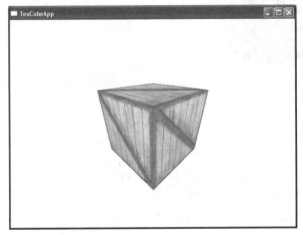

Figure 6.1:
A cube with a crate
texture

In Direct3D a texture is represented with the `IDirect3DTexture9` interface. A texture is a matrix of pixels similar to a surface, but it can be mapped onto triangles.

Objectives

- To learn how to specify the part of a texture that gets mapped to the triangle
- To find out how to create textures
- To learn how textures can be filtered to create a smoother image

6.1 Texture Coordinates

Direct3D uses a texture coordinate system that consists of a u-axis that runs horizontally and a v-axis that runs vertically. A pair of u, v coordinates identifies an element on the texture called a *texel*. Notice that the v-axis is positive in the "down" direction (see Figure 6.2).

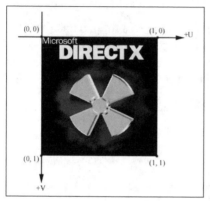

Figure 6.2: The texture coordinate system, sometimes called texture space

Also, notice the normalized coordinate interval, [0, 1], which is used because it gives Direct3D a fixed range to work with textures of various dimensions.

For each 3D triangle, we want to define a corresponding triangle on the texture that is to be mapped to the 3D triangle (see Figure 6.3).

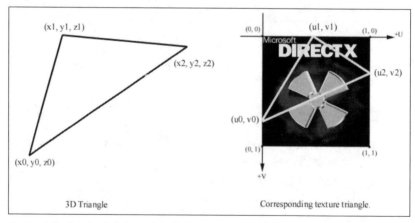

Figure 6.3: On the left is a triangle in 3D space, and on the right we define a 2D triangle on the texture that is going to be mapped onto the 3D triangle.

To do this, we modify our vertex structure once again and add a pair of texture coordinates that identifies a vertex on the texture.

```
struct Vertex
{
    float _x, _y, _z;
    float _nx, _ny, _nz;
    float _u, _v; // texture coordinates

    static const DWORD FVF;
};
const DWORD Vertex::FVF = D3DFVF_XYZ | D3DFVF_NORMAL | D3DFVF_TEX1;
```

Observe that we have added D3DFVF_TEX1 to our vertex format description, which says that our vertex structure contains one pair of texture coordinates.

Now every triangle built from three Vertex objects also defines a corresponding texture triangle from the texture coordinates.

Note: Although we specify a corresponding texture triangle to a 3D triangle, the texture isn't mapped until the rasterization stage where the 3D triangle has been transformed to screen space.

6.2 Creating and Enabling a Texture

Texture data is usually read from an image file stored on disk and loaded into an IDirect3DTexture9 object. To do this, we can use the following D3DX function:

```
HRESULT D3DXCreateTextureFromFile(
    LPDIRECT3DDEVICE9 pDevice,     // device to create the texture
    LPCSTR pSrcFile,               // filename of image to load
    LPDIRECT3DTEXTURE9* ppTexture  // ptr to receive the created texture
);
```

This function can load any of the following image formats: BMP, DDS, DIB, JPG, PNG, and TGA.

For example, to create a texture from an image called stone-wall.bmp, we would write the following:

```
IDirect3Dtexture9* _stonewall;
D3DXCreateTextureFromFile(_device, "stonewall.bmp", &_stonewall);
```

To set the current texture, we use the following method:

```
HRESULT IDirect3DDevice9::SetTexture(
    DWORD Stage, // A value in the range 0-7 identifying the texture
                 // stage - see note on Texture Stages
    IDirect3DBaseTexture9* pTexture // ptr to the texture to set
);
```

Example:

```
Device->SetTexture(0, _stonewall);
```

Note: In Direct3D, you can set up to eight textures that can be combined to create a more detailed image. This is called multitexturing. We do not use multitexturing in this book until Part IV; therefore we always set the texture's stage to 0, for now.

To disable a texture at a particular texturing stage, set `pTexture` to 0. For instance, if we don't want to render an object with a texture, we would write:

```
Device->SetTexture(0, 0);
renderObjectWithoutTexture();
```

If our scene has triangles that use different textures, we would have to do something similar to the following code:

```
Device->SetTexture(0, _tex0);
drawTrisUsingTex0();

Device->SetTexture(0, _tex1);
drawTrisUsingTex1();
```

6.3 Filters

As mentioned previously, textures are mapped to triangles in screen space. Usually, the texture triangle is not the same size as the screen triangle. When the texture triangle is smaller than the screen triangle, the texture triangle is *magnified* to fit. When the texture triangle is larger than the screen triangle, the texture triangle is *minified* to fit. In both cases, distortion will occur. *Filtering* is a technique Direct3D uses to help smooth out these distortions.

Direct3D provides three different types of filters; each one provides a different level of quality. The better the quality, the slower it is, so you must make the trade-off between quality and speed. Texture filters are set with the `IDirect3DDevice9::SetSamplerState` method.

- **Nearest point sampling**—This is the default filtering method and produces the worst-looking results, but it is also the fastest to compute. The following code sets nearest point sampling as the minification and magnification filter:

  ```
  Device->SetSamplerState(0, D3DSAMP_MAGFILTER, D3DTEXF_POINT);
  Device->SetSamplerState(0, D3DSAMP_MINFILTER, D3DTEXF_POINT);
  ```

- **Linear filtering**—This type of filtering produces fairly good results and can be done very fast on today's hardware. It is recommended that you use linear filtering as a minimum. The following code sets linear filtering as the minification and magnification filter:

```
Device->SetSamplerState(0, D3DSAMP_MAGFILTER, D3DTEXF_LINEAR);
Device->SetSamplerState(0, D3DSAMP_MINFILTER, D3DTEXF_LINEAR);
```

- **Anisotropic filtering**—This type of filtering produces the best results but also takes the longest to compute. The following code sets anisotropic filtering as the minification and magnification filter:

```
Device->SetSamplerState(0, D3DSAMP_MAGFILTER, D3DTEXF_
    ANISOTROPIC);
Device->SetSamplerState(0, D3DSAMP_MINFILTER, D3DTEXF_
    ANISOTROPIC);
```

When using anisotropic filtering, we must also set the `D3DSAMP_MAXANISOTROPY` level, which determines the quality of the anisotropic filtering. The higher this value, the better the results. Check the `D3DCAPS9` structure for the valid range that your device supports. The following code sets this value to 4:

```
Device->SetSamplerState(0, D3DSAMP_MAXANISOTROPY, 4);
```

Part II

6.4 Mipmaps

As said in section 6.3, the triangle on the screen is usually not the same size as the texture triangle. In an effort to make the size difference less drastic, we can create a chain of *mipmaps* for a texture. The idea is to take a texture and create a series of smaller, lower resolution textures but customize the filtering for each of these levels so it preserves the detail that is important to us (see Figure 6.4).

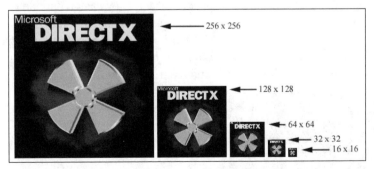

Figure 6.4: A chain of mipmaps; notice that each successive mipmap is half the size of the previous mipmap.

6.4.1 Mipmap Filter

The mipmap filter is used to control how Direct3D uses the mipmaps. You can set the mipmap filter by writing:

```
Device->SetSamplerState(0, D3DSAMP_MIPFILTER, Filter);
```

where `Filter` is one of the following three options:

- `D3DTEXF_NONE`—Disables mipmapping
- `D3DTEXF_POINT`—By using this filter, Direct3D will choose the mipmap level that is closest in size to the screen triangle. Once that level is chosen, Direct3D will filter that level based on the specified min and mag filters.
- `D3DTEXF_LINEAR`—By using this filter, Direct3D will take the two closest mipmap levels, filter each level with the min and mag filters, and linearly combine these two levels to form the final color values.

6.4.2 Using Mipmaps with Direct3D

Using mipmaps with Direct3D is easy. If the device supports mipmaps, `D3DXCreateTextureFromFile` will generate a mipmap chain for you. In addition, Direct3D automatically selects the mipmap that matches the screen triangle the best. So mipmapping is pretty much used and set up automatically.

6.5 Address Modes

Previously, we stated that texture coordinates must be specified in the range [0, 1]. Technically, that is not correct; they can go outside that range. The behavior for texture coordinates that go outside the [0, 1] range is defined by the Direct3D address mode. There are four types of address modes: *wrap*, *border color*, *clamp*, and *mirror*, which are illustrated in Figures 6.5, 6.6, 6.7, and 6.8, respectively.

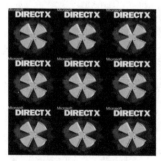

Figure 6.5:
Wrap mode

Figure 6.6:
Border
color mode

Figure 6.7:
Clamp
mode

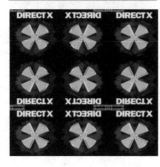

Figure 6.8:
Mirror mode

In these figures, the texture coordinates for the four unique quad vertices are defined as (0, 0), (0, 3), (3, 0), and (3, 3). From the three in both the u-axis and v-axis direction, the quad is subdivided into a 3 × 3 area matrix. If, for instance, you wanted the texture to be tiled 5 × 5 across the quad, you would specify the wrap address mode and texture coordinates (0, 0), (0, 5), (5, 0), and (5, 5).

The following code snippet taken from the AddressModes sample illustrates how the four address modes are set:

```
// set wrap address mode
if( ::GetAsyncKeyState('W') & 0x8000f )
{
    Device->SetSamplerState(0, D3DSAMP_ADDRESSU, D3DTADDRESS_WRAP);
    Device->SetSamplerState(0, D3DSAMP_ADDRESSV, D3DTADDRESS_WRAP);
}

// set border color address mode
if( ::GetAsyncKeyState('B') & 0x8000f )
{
    Device->SetSamplerState(0, D3DSAMP_ADDRESSU, D3DTADDRESS_BORDER);
    Device->SetSamplerState(0, D3DSAMP_ADDRESSV, D3DTADDRESS_BORDER);
    Device->SetSamplerState(0, D3DSAMP_BORDERCOLOR, 0x000000ff);
}

// set clamp address mode
if( ::GetAsyncKeyState('C') & 0x8000f )
{
    Device->SetSamplerState(0, D3DSAMP_ADDRESSU, D3DTADDRESS_CLAMP);
```

```
        Device->SetSamplerState(0, D3DSAMP_ADDRESSV, D3DTADDRESS_CLAMP);
}

// set mirror address mode
if( ::GetAsyncKeyState('M') & 0x8000f )
{
        Device->SetSamplerState(0, D3DSAMP_ADDRESSU, D3DTADDRESS_MIRROR);
        Device->SetSamplerState(0, D3DSAMP_ADDRESSV, D3DTADDRESS_MIRROR);
}
```

6.6 Sample Application: Textured Quad

The sample for this chapter demonstrates how to texture a quad and set a texture filter (see Figure 6.9). A mipmap chain is created automatically with the `D3DXCreateTextureFromFile` function if the device supports mipmapping.

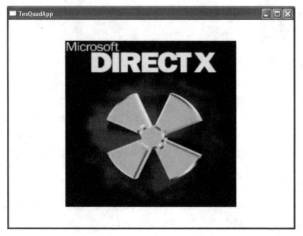

Figure 6.9:
A screen shot of a textured quad taken from the TexQuad sample

Note: There are two additional samples on the web page for this chapter. One sample textures a cube with the crate texture, as shown in Figure 6.1. The second demonstrates texture address modes.

The tasks required for adding textures to a scene are:

1. Construct the vertices of the objects with the texture coordinates specified.

2. Load a texture into an `IDirect3DTexture9` interface using the `D3DXCreateTextureFromFile` function.

3. Set the minification, magnification, and mipmap filters.

4. Before you draw an object, set the texture that is associated with the object with `IDirect3DDevice9::SetTexture`.

We begin by instantiating several global variables; one is the vertex buffer that stores the vertices of the quad and the other is the texture that we map to the quad:

```
IDirect3DVertexBuffer9* Quad = 0;
IDirect3DTexture9*       Tex = 0;
```

The `Setup` routine is fairly straightforward; we construct a quad from two triangles with texture coordinates defined. We then load the bitmap file dx5_logo.bmp into an `IDirect3DTexture9` interface. Next we enable the texture using the `SetTexture` method. Finally, we set the minification and magnification filters to linear filtering, and we also set the mipmap filter to `D3DTEXF_POINT`:

```
bool Setup()
{
    Device->CreateVertexBuffer(
        6 * sizeof(Vertex),
        D3DUSAGE_WRITEONLY,
        Vertex::FVF,
        D3DPOOL_MANAGED,
        &Quad,
        0);

    Vertex* v;
    Quad->Lock(0, 0, (void**)&v, 0);

    // quad built from two triangles, note texture coordinates:
    v[0] = Vertex(-1.0f, -1.0f, 1.25f, 0.0f, 0.0f, -1.0f, 0.0f, 1.0f);
    v[1] = Vertex(-1.0f,  1.0f, 1.25f, 0.0f, 0.0f, -1.0f, 0.0f, 0.0f);
    v[2] = Vertex( 1.0f,  1.0f, 1.25f, 0.0f, 0.0f, -1.0f, 1.0f, 0.0f);

    v[3] = Vertex(-1.0f, -1.0f, 1.25f, 0.0f, 0.0f, -1.0f, 0.0f, 1.0f);
    v[4] = Vertex( 1.0f,  1.0f, 1.25f, 0.0f, 0.0f, -1.0f, 1.0f, 0.0f);
    v[5] = Vertex( 1.0f, -1.0f, 1.25f, 0.0f, 0.0f, -1.0f, 1.0f, 1.0f);

    Quad->Unlock();

    // Load texture data.
    D3DXCreateTextureFromFile(
        Device,
        "dx5_logo.bmp",
        &Tex);

    // Enable the texture.
    Device->SetTexture(0, Tex);

    // Set texture filters.
    Device->SetSamplerState(0, D3DSAMP_MAGFILTER, D3DTEXF_LINEAR);
    Device->SetSamplerState(0, D3DSAMP_MINFILTER, D3DTEXF_LINEAR);
    Device->SetSamplerState(0, D3DSAMP_MIPFILTER, D3DTEXF_POINT);

    // set projection matrix
    D3DXMATRIX proj;
    D3DXMatrixPerspectiveFovLH(
```

Part II

```
                &proj,
                D3DX_PI * 0.5f, // 90 - degree
                (float)Width / (float)Height,
                1.0f,
                1000.0f);
    Device->SetTransform(D3DTS_PROJECTION, &proj);

    // don't use lighting for this sample
    Device->SetRenderState(D3DRS_LIGHTING, false);

    return true;
}
```

We can now render our quad as normal, and the currently set texture is mapped to it:

```
bool Display(float timeDelta)
{
    if( Device )
    {
        Device->Clear(0, 0, D3DCLEAR_TARGET | D3DCLEAR_ZBUFFER,
                    0xffffffff, 1.0f, 0);
        Device->BeginScene();

        Device->SetStreamSource(0, Quad, 0, sizeof(Vertex));
        Device->SetFVF(Vertex::FVF);

        // Draw primitives using presently enabled texture.
        Device->DrawPrimitive(D3DPT_TRIANGLELIST, 0, 2);

        Device->EndScene();
        Device->Present(0, 0, 0, 0);
    }
    return true;
}
```

6.7 Summary

- Texture coordinates are used to define a triangle on the texture that gets mapped to the 3D triangle.
- We can create textures from image files stored on disk using the `D3DXCreateTextureFromFile` function.
- We can filter textures by using the minification, magnification, and mipmap filter sampler states.
- Address modes define what Direct3D is supposed to do with texture coordinates outside the [0, 1] range. For example, should the texture be tiled, mirrored, clamped, etc.?

Chapter 7

Blending

In this chapter we examine a technique called *blending* that allows us to blend (combine) pixels that we are currently rasterizing with pixels that have been previously rasterized to the same pixel locations. In other words, we blend primitives over previously drawn primitives. This technique allows us to achieve a variety of effects (in particular, transparency).

Objectives

- To understand how blending works and how to use it
- To learn about the different blend modes that Direct3D supports
- To find out how the alpha component can be used to control the transparency of a primitive

7.1 The Blending Equation

Consider Figure 7.1, where we have a red teapot drawn in front of a wooden crate background.

Figure 7.1: An opaque teapot

Suppose that we want to draw the teapot with a level of transparency so that we could see the background crate through the teapot (see Figure 7.2).

Figure 7.2: A transparent teapot

How would we accomplish this? As we are rasterizing the teapot's triangles on top of the crate, we need to combine the pixel colors being computed for the teapot with the pixel colors of the crate in such a way that the crate shows through the teapot. The idea of combining the pixel values that are currently being computed (source pixel) with the pixel values previously written (destination pixel) is called *blending*. Note that the effect of blending is not limited to ordinary glass-like transparency. We have a variety of options that specify how the colors are combined, as seen in section 7.2.

It is important to realize that the triangles currently being rasterized are blended with the pixels that were previously written to the back buffer. In the example figures, the crate image is drawn first so that the crate's pixels are on the back buffer. We then draw the teapot so that the teapot's pixels are blended with the crate's pixels. Thus, the following rule should be followed when using blending:

Rule: Draw objects that do not use blending first. Then sort the objects that use blending by their distance from the camera; this is most efficiently done if the objects are in view space so that you can sort simply by the z-component. Finally, draw the objects that use blending in a back-to-front order.

The following formula is used to blend two pixel values:

$$OutputPixel = SourcePixel \otimes SourceBlendFactor + DestPixel \otimes DestBlendFactor$$

Each of the above variables is a 4D color vector (*r, g, b, a*), and the ⊗ symbol denotes component-wise multiplication.

- *OutputPixel*—The resulting blended pixel
- *SourcePixel*—The pixel currently being computed that is to be blended with the pixel on the back buffer
- *SourceBlendFactor*—A value in the interval [0, 1] that specifies the percent of the source pixel to use in the blend
- *DestPixel*—The pixel currently on the back buffer
- *DestBlendFactor*—A value in the interval [0, 1] that specifies the percent of the destination pixel to use in the blend

The *source and destination blend factors* let us modify the original source and destination pixels in a variety of ways, allowing for different effects to be achieved. Section 7.2 covers the predefined values that can be used.

Blending is disabled by default; you can enable it by setting the D3DRS_ALPHABLENDENABLE render state to true:

```
Device->SetRenderState(D3DRS_ALPHABLENDENABLE, true);
```

Tip: Blending is not a cheap operation and should only be enabled for the geometry that needs it. When you are done rendering that geometry, you should disable alpha blending. Also try to batch triangles that use blending and render them at once so that you can avoid turning blending on and off multiple times per frame.

7.2 Blend Factors

By setting different combinations of source and destination blend factors, you can create dozens of different blending effects. Experiment with different combinations to see what they do. You can set the source blend factor and the destination blend factor by setting the D3DRS_SRCBLEND and D3DRS_DESTBLEND render states, respectively. For example, we can write:

```
Device->SetRenderState(D3DRS_SRCBLEND, Source);
Device->SetRenderState(D3DRS_DESTBLEND, Destination);
```

where Source and Destination can be one of the following blend factors:

- D3DBLEND_ZERO—*blendFactor* = (0, 0, 0, 0)
- D3DBLEND_ONE—*blendFactor* = (1, 1, 1, 1)
- D3DBLEND_SRCCOLOR—*blendFactor* = (r_s, g_s, b_s, a_s)

- D3DBLEND_INVSRCCOLOR—*blendFactor*$=(1 - r_s, 1 - g_s, 1 - b_s, 1 - a_s)$
- D3DBLEND_SRCALPHA—*blendFactor*$=(a_s, a_s, a_s, a_s)$
- D3DBLEND_INVSRCALPHA—*blendFactor*$=(1 - a_s, 1 - a_s, 1 - a_s, 1 - a_s)$
- D3DBLEND_DESTALPHA—*blendFactor*$=(a_d, a_d, a_d, a_d)$
- D3DBLEND_INVDESTALPHA—*blendFactor*$=(1 - a_d, 1 - a_d, 1 - a_d, 1 - a_d)$
- D3DBLEND_DESTCOLOR—*blendFactor*$=(r_d, g_d, b_d, a_d)$
- D3DBLEND_INVDESTCOLOR—*blendFactor*$=(1 - r_d, 1 - g_d, 1 - b_d, 1 - a_d)$
- D3DBLEND_SRCALPHASAT—*blendFactor*$=(f, f, f, 1)$, where $f=\min(a_s, 1 - a_d)$
- D3DBLEND_BOTHINVSRCALPHA—This blend mode sets the source blend factor to $(1 - a_s, 1 - a_s, 1 - a_s, 1 - a_s)$ and the destination blend factor to (a_s, a_s, a_s, a_s). This blend mode is only valid for D3DRS_SRCBLEND.

The default values for the source blend factor and destination blend factor are D3DBLEND_SRCALPHA and D3DBLEND_INVSRCALPHA, respectively.

7.3 **Transparency**

In previous chapters we ignored the alpha component of a vertex color and material because it was not needed then, as it is primarily used in blending. However, the alpha components from each vertex color are shaded across the face of the triangle just as the colors are, but rather than determining the pixels' colors, it determines the pixels' alpha component.

The alpha component is mainly used to specify the level of transparency of a pixel. Assuming that we have reserved 8 bits for the alpha component for each pixel, the valid interval of values for the alpha component would be [0, 255], where [0, 255] corresponds to [0%, 100%] opacity. Thus, pixels with a black (0) alpha value are completely transparent, pixels with a gray alpha value of (128) are 50% transparent, and pixels with a white alpha value of (255) are completely opaque.

In order to make the alpha component describe the level of transparency of the pixels, we must set the source blend factor to D3DBLEND_SRCALPHA and the destination blend factor to

D3DBLEND_INVSRCALPHA. These values also happen to be the default blend factors.

7.3.1 Alpha Channels

Instead of using the alpha components computed from shading, we can obtain alpha info from a texture's *alpha channel*. The alpha channel is an extra set of bits reserved for each texel that stores an alpha component. When the texture is mapped to a primitive, the alpha components in the alpha channel are also mapped, and they become the alpha components for the pixels of the textured primitive. Figure 7.3 shows an image representation of an 8-bit alpha channel.

Figure 7.3: An 8-bit grayscale map representing the alpha channel of a texture

Figure 7.4 shows the result of rendering a textured quad with an alpha channel specifying the parts that are transparent.

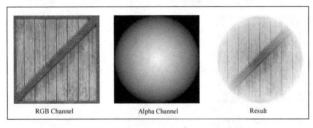

RGB Channel   Alpha Channel   Result

Figure 7.4: A textured quad, where the alpha channel specifies the transparency of the quad

7.3.2 Specifying the Source of Alpha

By default, if the currently set texture has an alpha channel, the alpha is taken from the alpha channel. If no alpha channel is present, the alpha is obtained from the vertex color. However, you can specify which source to use (diffuse color or alpha channel) with the following render states:

```
// compute alpha from diffuse colors during shading
Device->SetTextureStageState(0, D3DTSS_ALPHAARG1, D3DTA_DIFFUSE);
Device->SetTextureStageState(0, D3DTSS_ALPHAOP, D3DTOP_SELECTARG1);

// take alpha from alpha channel
```

Part II

```
Device->SetTextureStageState(0, D3DTSS_ALPHAARG1, D3DTA_TEXTURE);
Device->SetTextureStageState(0, D3DTSS_ALPHAOP, D3DTOP_SELECTARG1);
```

7.4 Creating an Alpha Channel Using the DirectX Texture Tool

The most common image file formats do not store alpha information. In this section we show you how to create a DDS file with an alpha channel using the DirectX Texture tool. A DDS file is an image format specifically designed for DirectX applications and textures. DDS files can be loaded into textures using `D3DXCreateTextureFromFile` just as BMP and JPG files can be. The DirectX Texture tool is located in the \Bin\DXUtils folder of your root DXSDK directory.

Open the DirectX Texture tool and the crate.jpg file located in this chapter's sample folder. The crate is automatically loaded in as a 24-bit RGB texture with 8 bits of red, 8 bits of green, and 8 bits of blue per pixel. We need to augment this texture to a 32-bit ARGB texture, reserving an extra 8-bit slot for the alpha channel. Select **Format** from the menu and choose **Change Surface Format**. A dialog box pops up, as shown in Figure 7.5. Select the **A8 R8 G8 B8** format and press **OK**.

Figure 7.5: Changing the format of the texture

This creates an image with a 32-bit color depth for each pixel with 8 bits for the alpha channel, 8 bits for red, 8 bits for green, and 8 bits for blue. Our next task is to load data into the alpha channel. We load the 8-bit grayscale map shown in Figure 7.3 into the alpha channel. Select **File** from the menu, and then choose **Open Onto Alpha Channel Of This Texture**. A dialog box pops up asking you to locate the image file that contains the data you want to load into the alpha channel. Select the **alphachannel.bmp** file that is located in this chapter's texAlpha sample folder. Figure 7.6 shows the program after the alpha channel data has been inserted.

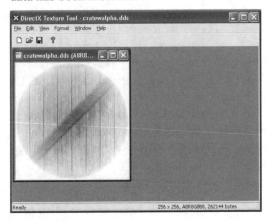

Figure 7.6: Resulting texture with an alpha channel

Now save the texture with the name of your choice; we used the name cratewalpha.dds.

7.5 Sample Application: Transparency

The sample application draws a transparent teapot on top of a crate background—the same one shown in Figure 7.2. The alpha is taken from the material in this example. The application allows you to increase/decrease the alpha component interactively by pressing the A and S keys. The A key increases the alpha component; the S key decreases it.

The steps required to use blending are:

1. Set the blend factors D3DRS_SRCBLEND and D3DRS_DESTBLEND.

2. If using the alpha component, specify the source (material or alpha channel).

3. Enable the alpha blending render state.

For this sample, we instantiate the following self-explanatory global variables:

```
ID3DXMesh*   Teapot = 0; // the teapot
D3DMATERIAL9 TeapotMtrl; // the teapot's material

IDirect3DVertexBuffer9* BkGndQuad = 0; // background quad - crate
IDirect3DTexture9*      BkGndTex  = 0; // crate texture
D3DMATERIAL9            BkGndMtrl;     // background material
```

The `Setup` method sets up many things; we have omitted most of the code that is not relevant to this chapter. With regard to blending, the `Setup` method specifies the source that the alpha should be taken from. In this example we instruct the alpha to be taken from the diffuse component of the material. Notice that we set the teapot material's diffuse alpha component to 0.5, indicating that the teapot should be rendered at 50% transparency. We also set the blend factors here as well. Take note that we do not enable alpha blending in this method. The reason is that the alpha blending stage takes up additional processing and should only be used on the geometry that needs it. For instance, in this sample only the teapot needs to be rendered with alpha blending enabled—the quad does not. Therefore, we enable alpha blending in the `Display` function.

```
bool Setup()
{
        TeapotMtrl = d3d::RED_MTRL;
        TeapotMtrl.Diffuse.a = 0.5f; // set alpha to 50% opacity
        BkGndMtrl = d3d::WHITE_MTRL;

        D3DXCreateTeapot(Device, &Teapot, 0);

        ...// Create background quad snipped

        ...// Light and texture setup snipped

        // use alpha in material's diffuse component for alpha
        Device->SetTextureStageState(0, D3DTSS_ALPHAARG1, D3DTA_DIFFUSE);
        Device->SetTextureStageState(0, D3DTSS_ALPHAOP,
                                    D3DTOP_SELECTARG1);

        // set blending factors so that alpha
        // component determines transparency
        Device->SetRenderState(D3DRS_SRCBLEND, D3DBLEND_SRCALPHA);
        Device->SetRenderState(D3DRS_DESTBLEND, D3DBLEND_INVSRCALPHA);

        ...// view/projection matrix setup snipped

        return true;
}
```

In the `Display` function, we check to see if the A or S key was pressed and respond by increasing or decreasing the material's alpha value. Notice that the method ensures that the alpha value does not go outside the interval [0, 1]. We then render the background quad. Finally, we enable alpha blending, render the teapot with alpha blending enabled, and then disable alpha blending.

```
bool Display(float timeDelta)
{
        if( Device )
```

```
{
    //
    // Update
    //

    // increase/decrease alpha via keyboard input
    if( ::GetAsyncKeyState('A') & 0x8000f )
        TeapotMtrl.Diffuse.a += 0.01f;
    if( ::GetAsyncKeyState('S') & 0x8000f )
        TeapotMtrl.Diffuse.a -= 0.01f;

    // force alpha to [0, 1] interval
    if(TeapotMtrl.Diffuse.a > 1.0f)
        TeapotMtrl.Diffuse.a = 1.0f;
    if(TeapotMtrl.Diffuse.a < 0.0f)
        TeapotMtrl.Diffuse.a = 0.0f;


    //
    // Render
    //

    Device->Clear(0, 0, D3DCLEAR_TARGET | D3DCLEAR_ZBUFFER,
                  0xffffffff, 1.0f, 0);
    Device->BeginScene();

    // Draw the background
    D3DXMATRIX W;
    D3DXMatrixIdentity(&W);
    Device->SetTransform(D3DTS_WORLD, &W);
    Device->SetFVF(Vertex::FVF);
    Device->SetStreamSource(0, BkGndQuad, 0, sizeof(Vertex));
    Device->SetMaterial(&BkGndMtrl);
    Device->SetTexture(0, BkGndTex);
    Device->DrawPrimitive(D3DPT_TRIANGLELIST, 0, 2);

    // Draw the teapot
    Device->SetRenderState(D3DRS_ALPHABLENDENABLE, true);

    D3DXMatrixScaling(&W, 1.5f, 1.5f, 1.5f);
    Device->SetTransform(D3DTS_WORLD, &W);
    Device->SetMaterial(&TeapotMtrl);
    Device->SetTexture(0, 0);
    Teapot->DrawSubset(0);

    Device->SetRenderState(D3DRS_ALPHABLENDENABLE, false);

    Device->EndScene();
    Device->Present(0, 0, 0, 0);
}
    return true;
}
```

Part II

Note: On the web page for this chapter, there is another sample called texAlpha that demonstrates alpha blending using a texture's alpha channel. Code-wise, the only difference is that we specify to take the alpha component from the texture rather than the material.

```
// use alpha channel in texture for alpha
Device->SetTextureStageState(0, D3DTSS_ALPHAARG1, D3DTA_TEXTURE);
Device->SetTextureStageState(0, D3DTSS_ALPHAOP, D3DTOP_SELECTARG1);
```

The application loads a DDS file that contains an alpha channel and was created using the DirectX Texure tool, as explained in section 7.4.

7.6 Summary

- Alpha blending allows combining the pixels of the primitive currently being rasterized with the pixel values previously written at the same locations on the back buffer.

- The blend factors allow us to control how the source and destination pixels are blended together.

- Alpha information can come from the diffuse component of the primitive's material alpha channel or from the alpha channel of the primitive's set texture.

Chapter 8

Stenciling

This chapter brings us to the study of the stencil buffer and is the conclusion of Part II of this text. The stencil buffer is an off-screen buffer that we can use to achieve special effects. The stencil buffer has the same resolution as the back buffer and depth buffer so that the ij^{th} pixel in the stencil buffer corresponds with the ij^{th} pixel in the back buffer and depth buffer. As the name suggests, the stencil buffer works as a stencil and allows us to block rendering to certain parts of the back buffer.

For instance, when implementing a mirror, we simply need to reflect a particular object across the plane of the mirror; however, we only want to draw the reflection into a mirror. We can use the stencil buffer to block the rendering of the reflection unless it is in a mirror. Figure 8.1 should make this clear.

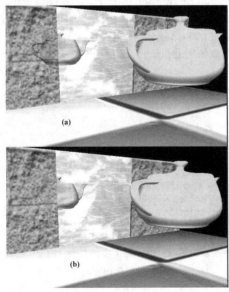

Figure 8.1: Here we have a teapot being reflected without using the stencil buffer (a). We see that the reflected teapot is always rendered no matter if it is in front of the mirror or a wall. Using the stencil buffer, we can block the reflected teapot from being rendered unless it is being drawn in the mirror (b).

The stencil buffer is a small part of Direct3D and is controlled through a simple interface. Like blending, the simple interface offers a flexible and powerful set of capabilities. Learning to use the stencil buffer

131

effectively is best done by studying existing applications. Once you understand a few applications of the stencil buffer, you will have a better idea of how it can be applied for your own specific needs. For this reason, this chapter puts a special emphasis on the study of two specific applications using stencils (in particular, implementing mirrors and planar shadows).

Objectives

- To gain an understanding of how the stencil buffer works, how to create a stencil buffer, and how we can control the stencil buffer
- To learn how to implement mirrors and use the stencil buffer to prevent reflections from being drawn to non-mirror surfaces
- To discover how to render shadows and prevent "double blending" by using the stencil buffer

8.1 Using the Stencil Buffer

To use the stencil buffer, we must first request one when we initialize Direct3D and then we must enable it. We describe requesting a stencil buffer in section 8.1.1. To enable the stencil buffer, we must set the D3DRS_STENCILENABLE render state and specify true. To disable the stencil buffer, we specify false for the D3DRS_STENCILENABLE render state. The following code snippet enables the stencil buffer and then disables it:

```
Device->SetRenderState(D3DRS_STENCILENABLE,    true);

... // do stencil work

Device->SetRenderState(D3DRS_STENCILENABLE,    false);
```

Aside: Although not used in this book, DirectX 9.0 has added a *two-sided stencil* feature that speeds up shadow volume rendering by reducing the number of rendering passes required to draw the shadow volume. See the SDK documentation for details.

We can clear the stencil buffer to a default value using the IDirect3DDevice9::Clear method. Recall that this is the same method used to clear the back buffer and depth buffer as well.

```
Device->Clear(0, 0,
    D3DCLEAR_TARGET | D3DCLEAR_ZBUFFER | D3DCLEAR_STENCIL,
    0xff000000, 1.0f, 0 );
```

Note that we have added D3DCLEAR_STENCIL to the third argument, indicating that we want to clear the stencil buffer as well as the target (back buffer) and depth buffer. Argument six is used to specify the value to clear the stencil buffer to; in this example we clear it to 0.

> **Note:** Using the stencil buffer can be considered a "free" operation in modern hardware if you are already using depth buffering, according to the NVIDIA presentation *Creating Reflections and Shadows Using Stencil Buffers* by Mark J. Kilgard.

8.1.1 Requesting a Stencil Buffer

A stencil buffer can be created at the time that we create the depth buffer. When specifying the format of the depth buffer, we can specify the format of the stencil buffer at the same time. In actuality, the stencil buffer and depth buffer share the same off-screen surface buffer, but a segment of memory in each pixel is designated to each particular buffer. For instance, consider the following three depth/stencil formats:

■ `D3DFMT_D24S8`—This format says to create a 32-bit depth/stencil buffer and designate 24 bits per pixel to the depth buffer and 8 bits per pixel to the stencil buffer.

■ `D3DFMT_D24X4S4`—This format says to create a 32-bit depth/stencil buffer and designate 24 bits per pixel to the depth buffer and 4 bits per pixel to the stencil buffer. Four of the bits will not be used.

■ `D3DFMT_D15S1`—This format says to create a 16-bit depth/stencil buffer and designate 15 bits per pixel to the depth buffer and 1 bit per pixel to the stencil buffer.

Note that there are formats that do not allocate any bits to the stencil buffer. For example, the `D3DFMT_D32` format says to create a 32-bit depth buffer only.

Also, the support for stenciling varies among the various graphics cards. Some cards may not support an 8-bit stencil buffer, for example.

8.1.2 The Stencil Test

As previously stated, we can use the stencil buffer to block rendering to certain areas of the back buffer. The decision to block a particular pixel from being written is decided by the *stencil test*, which is given by the following expression:

```
(ref & mask) ComparisonOperation (value & mask)
```

The stencil test is performed for every pixel, assuming stenciling is enabled, and takes two operands:

- A left-hand side operand (*LHS=ref&mask*) that is determined by ANDing an application-defined stencil reference value (`ref`) with an application-defined masking value (`mask`).

- A right-hand side (*RHS = value&mask*) that is determined by ANDing the entry in the stencil buffer for the particular pixel that we are testing (`value`) with an application-defined masking value (`mask`).

The stencil test then compares the LHS with the RHS, as specified by the *comparison operation*. The entire expression evaluates to a Boolean (true or false) value. We write the pixel to the back buffer if the test evaluates to true (passes). If the test evaluates to false (fails), we block the pixel from being written to the back buffer. And of course, if a pixel isn't written to the back buffer, it isn't written to the depth buffer either.

8.1.3 Controlling the Stencil Test

To give us flexibility, Direct3D allows us to control the variables used in the stencil test. In other words, we get to specify the stencil reference value, the mask value, and even the comparison operation. Though we do not get to explicitly set the stencil value, we do have some control over what values get written to the stencil buffer (in addition to clearing the stencil buffer).

8.1.3.1 Stencil Reference Value

The stencil reference value `ref` is zero by default, but we can change it with the `D3DRS_STENCILREF` render state. For example, the following code sets the stencil reference value to one:

```
Device->SetRenderState(D3DRS_STENCILREF, 0x1);
```

Note that we tend to use hexadecimal because it makes it easier to see the bit alignment of an integer, and this is useful to see when doing bit-wise operations, such as ANDing.

8.1.3.2 Stencil Mask

The stencil masking value `mask` is used to mask (hide) bits in both the `ref` and `value` variables. The default mask is `0xffffffff`, which doesn't mask any bits. We can change the mask by setting the `D3DRS_STENCILMASK` render state. The following example masks the 16 high bits:

```
Device->SetRenderState(D3DRS_STENCILMASK, 0x0000ffff);
```

Note: If you do not understand this talk of bits and masking, it most likely means that you need to brush up on your binary, hexadecimal, and bit-wise operations.

8.1.3.3 Stencil Value

As stated previously, this is the value in the stencil buffer for the current pixel that we are stencil testing. For example, if we are performing the stencil test on the ij^{th} pixel, then `value` will be the value in the ij^{th} entry of the stencil buffer. We cannot explicitly set individual stencil values, but recall that we can clear the stencil buffer. In addition we can use the stencil render states to control what gets written to the stencil buffer. The stencil-related render states are covered shortly.

8.1.3.4 Comparison Operation

We can set the comparison operation by setting the D3DRS_STENCIL-FUNC render state. The comparison operation can be any member of the D3DCMPFUNC enumerated type:

```
typedef enum _D3DCMPFUNC {
    D3DCMP_NEVER = 1,
    D3DCMP_LESS = 2,
    D3DCMP_EQUAL = 3,
    D3DCMP_LESSEQUAL = 4,
    D3DCMP_GREATER = 5,
    D3DCMP_NOTEQUAL = 6,
    D3DCMP_GREATEREQUAL = 7,
    D3DCMP_ALWAYS = 8,
    D3DCMP_FORCE_DWORD = 0x7fffffff
} D3DCMPFUNC;
```

- D3DCMP_NEVER—The stencil test never succeeds.
- D3DCMP_LESS—The stencil test succeeds if $LHS < RHS$.
- D3DCMP_EQUAL—The stencil test succeeds if $LHS = RHS$.
- D3DCMP_LESSEQUAL—The stencil test succeeds if $LHS \leq RHS$.
- D3DCMP_GREATER—The stencil test succeeds if $LHS > RHS$.
- D3DCMP_NOTEQUAL—The stencil test succeeds if $LHS \neq RHS$.
- D3DCMP_GREATEREQUAL—The stencil test succeeds if $LHS \geq RHS$.
- D3DCMP_ALWAYS—The stencil test always succeeds.

8.1.4 Updating the Stencil Buffer

In addition to deciding whether to write or block a particular pixel from being written to the back buffer, we can define how the stencil buffer entry should be updated based on three possible cases:

Part II

- The stencil test fails for the ij^{th} pixel. We can define how to update the ij^{th} entry in the stencil buffer in response to this case by setting the D3DRS_STENCILFAIL render state:

```
Device->SetRenderState(D3DRS_STENCILFAIL, StencilOperation);
```

- The depth test fails for the ij^{th} pixel. We can define how to update the ij^{th} entry in response to this case by setting the D3DRS_STENCILZFAIL render state:

```
Device->SetRenderState(D3DRS_STENCILZFAIL, StencilOperation);
```

- The depth test and stencil test succeed for the ij^{th} pixel. We can define how to update the ij^{th} entry in response to this case by setting the D3DRS_STENCILPASS render state:

```
Device->SetRenderState(D3DRS_STENCILPASS, StencilOperation);
```

where StencilOperation can be one of the following predefined constants:

☐ D3DSTENCILOP_KEEP—Specifies to not change the stencil buffer (that is, keep the value currently there)

☐ D3DSTENCILOP_ZERO—Specifies to set the stencil buffer entry to zero

☐ D3DSTENCILOP_REPLACE—Specifies to replace the stencil buffer entry with the stencil reference value

☐ D3DSTENCILOP_INCRSAT—Specifies to increment the stencil buffer entry. If the incremented value exceeds the maximum allowed value, we clamp the entry to that maximum.

☐ D3DSTENCILOP_DECRSAT—Specifies to decrement the stencil buffer entry. If the decremented value is less than zero, we clamp the entry to zero.

☐ D3DSTENCILOP_INVERT—Specifies to invert the bits of the stencil buffer entry

☐ D3DSTENCILOP_INCR—Specifies to increment the stencil buffer entry. If the incremented value exceeds the maximum allowed value, we wrap to zero.

☐ D3DSTENCILOP_DECR—Specifies to decrement the stencil buffer entry. If the decremented value is less than zero, we wrap to the maximum allowed value.

8.1.5 Stencil Write Mask

In addition to the mentioned stencil render states, we can set a *write mask* that will mask off bits of any value that we write to the stencil buffer. We can set the write mask with the D3DRS_STENCILWRITE-MASK render state. The default value is 0xffffffff. The following example masks the top 16 bits:

```
Device->SetRenderState(D3DRS_STENCILWRITEMASK, 0x0000ffff);
```

8.2 Sample Application: Mirrors

Many surfaces in nature serve as mirrors and allow us to see object reflections in those mirrors. This section describes how we can simulate mirrors for our 3D applications. Note that for simplicity we reduce the task of implementing mirrors to planar surfaces only. For instance, a shiny car can display a reflection; however, a car's body is smooth and round, not planar. Instead, we render reflections such as those that are displayed in a shiny marble floor or in a mirror hanging on a wall—in other words, mirrors that lie on a plane.

Implementing mirrors programmatically requires us to solve two problems. First, we must learn how to reflect an object about an arbitrary plane so that we can draw the reflection correctly. Second, we must only display the reflection in a mirror. That is, we must somehow "mark" a surface as a mirror, and then as we are rendering we only draw the reflected object if it is in a mirror. Refer to Figure 8.1, which first introduced this concept.

The first problem is easily solved with some vector geometry. We can solve the second problem with the stencil buffer. The next two subsections explain the solutions to these problems individually. The third subsection ties them together and reviews the relevant code for the first sample application for this chapter—Mirrors.

8.2.1 The Mathematics of Reflection

We now show how to compute the reflection point $\mathbf{v}' = (v'_x, v'_y, v'_z)$ of a point $\mathbf{v} = (v_x, v_y, v_z)$ about an arbitrary plane $\hat{\mathbf{n}} \cdot \mathbf{p} + d = 0$. Refer to Figure 8.2 throughout this discussion.

Part II

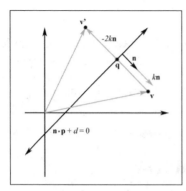

Figure 8.2: Reflection about an arbitrary plane. Note that k is the shortest signed distance from $\mathbf{v}$ to the plane and k is positive in this figure since $\mathbf{v}$ lies in the positive half-space of the plane.

From the "Planes" section in Part I, we know that $\mathbf{q} = \mathbf{v} - k\hat{\mathbf{n}}$, where k is the shortest signed distance from $\mathbf{v}$ and the plane. It follows then that the reflection of $\mathbf{v}$ about the plane $(\hat{\mathbf{n}}, d)$ is given by:

$$\mathbf{v}' = \mathbf{v} - 2k\hat{\mathbf{n}}$$
$$= \mathbf{v} - 2(\hat{\mathbf{n}} \cdot \mathbf{v} + d)\hat{\mathbf{n}}$$
$$= \mathbf{v} - 2[(\hat{\mathbf{n}} \cdot \mathbf{v})\hat{\mathbf{n}} + d\hat{\mathbf{n}}]$$

We can represent this transformation from $\mathbf{v}$ to $\mathbf{v}'$ with the following matrix:

$$\mathbf{R} = \begin{bmatrix} -2n_x n_x + 1 & -2n_y n_x & -2n_z n_x & 0 \\ -2n_x n_y & -2n_y n_y + 1 & -2n_z n_y & 0 \\ -2n_x n_z & -2n_y n_z & -2n_z n_z + 1 & 0 \\ -2n_x d & -2n_y d & -2n_z d & 1 \end{bmatrix}$$

The D3DX library provides the following function to create the reflection matrix as shown by $\mathbf{R}$ about an arbitrary plane:

```
D3DXMATRIX *D3DXMatrixReflect(
    D3DXMATRIX *pOut,        // The resulting reflection matrix.
    CONST D3DXPLANE *pPlane  // The plane to reflect about.
);
```

Since we are on the topic of reflection transformations, let's present the matrices representing three other special case reflection transformations. They are the reflections about the three standard coordinate planes—the yz plane, xz plane, and xy plane—and are represented by the following three matrices, respectively:

$$\mathbf{R}_{yz} = \begin{bmatrix} -1 & 0 & 0 & 0 \\ 0 & 1 & 0 & 0 \\ 0 & 0 & 1 & 0 \\ 0 & 0 & 0 & 1 \end{bmatrix} \quad \mathbf{R}_{xz} = \begin{bmatrix} 1 & 0 & 0 & 0 \\ 0 & -1 & 0 & 0 \\ 0 & 0 & 1 & 0 \\ 0 & 0 & 0 & 1 \end{bmatrix} \quad \mathbf{R}_{xy} = \begin{bmatrix} 1 & 0 & 0 & 0 \\ 0 & 1 & 0 & 0 \\ 0 & 0 & -1 & 0 \\ 0 & 0 & 0 & 1 \end{bmatrix}$$

To reflect a point across the yz plane, we simply take the opposite of the x-component. Similarly, to reflect a point across the xz plane, we take the opposite of the y-component. Finally, to reflect a point across the xy plane, we take the opposite of the z-component. These reflections are readily seen by observing the symmetry on each of the standard coordinate planes.

8.2.2 Mirror Implementation Overview

When implementing a mirror, an object is only reflected if it is in front of a mirror. However, we don't want to test spatially if an object is in front of a mirror, as it could get complicated. Therefore, to simplify things, we always reflect the object and render it no matter where it is. But this introduces problems seen in Figure 8.1 at the beginning of this chapter. Namely, the object's (a teapot in this case) reflection is rendered into surfaces that are not mirrors (like the walls for example). We can solve this problem using the stencil buffer because the stencil buffer allows us to block rendering to certain areas on the back buffer. Thus, we can use the stencil buffer to block the rendering of the reflected teapot if it is not being rendered into the mirror. The following outline briefly explains the steps of how this can be accomplished:

1. Render the entire scene as normal—the floor, walls, mirror, and teapot—but *not* the teapot's reflection. Note that this step does not modify the stencil buffer.

2. Clear the stencil buffer to 0. Figure 8.3 shows the back buffer and stencil buffer up to this point.

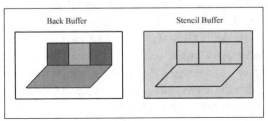

Figure 8.3: The scene rendered to the back buffer and the stencil buffer cleared to zero. The light gray on the stencil buffer denotes pixels cleared to zero.

Part II

3. Render the primitives that make up the mirror into the *stencil buffer only*. Set the stencil test to always succeed, and specify that the stencil buffer entry should be replaced with 1 if the test passes. Since we are only rendering the mirror, all the pixels in the stencil buffer will be 0 except for the pixels that correspond to the mirror—they will have a 1. Figure 8.4 shows the updated stencil buffer. Essentially, we are marking the pixels of the mirror in the stencil buffer.

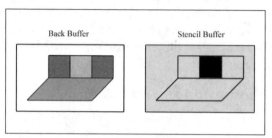

Figure 8.4: Rendering the mirror to the stencil buffer, essentially marking the pixels in the stencil buffer that correspond to the mirror. The black on the stencil buffer denotes pixels set to 1.

4. Now we render the reflected teapot to the back buffer and stencil buffer. But recall that we only render to the back buffer if the stencil test passes. This time we set the stencil test to only succeed if the value in the stencil buffer is a 1. In this way, the teapot is only rendered to areas that have a 1 in their corresponding stencil buffer entry. Since the areas in the stencil buffer that correspond to the mirror are the only entries that have a 1, the reflected teapot is only rendered into the mirror.

8.2.3 Code and Explanation

The code relevant to this sample lies in the `RenderMirror` function, which first renders the mirror primitives to the stencil buffer and then renders the reflected teapot only if it is being rendered into the mirror. We walk through the `RenderMirror` function almost line by line and explain what is occurring and, more importantly, why.

If you are using the steps outlined in section 8.2.2 to serve as an overall guide to the code, note that we are starting at step 3 since steps 1 and 2 have nothing to do with the stencil buffer. Also be aware that we are discussing the rendering of the mirror through this explanation.

Note that we divide this explanation up into parts for no other reason than to offer a more modular discussion.

8.2.3.1 **Part I**

We begin by enabling the stencil buffer and setting the related render states:

```
void RenderMirror()
{
Device->SetRenderState(D3DRS_STENCILENABLE,    true);
Device->SetRenderState(D3DRS_STENCILFUNC,      D3DCMP_ALWAYS);
Device->SetRenderState(D3DRS_STENCILREF,       0x1);
Device->SetRenderState(D3DRS_STENCILMASK,      0xffffffff);
Device->SetRenderState(D3DRS_STENCILWRITEMASK, 0xffffffff);
Device->SetRenderState(D3DRS_STENCILZFAIL,     D3DSTENCILOP_KEEP);
Device->SetRenderState(D3DRS_STENCILFAIL,      D3DSTENCILOP_KEEP);
Device->SetRenderState(D3DRS_STENCILPASS,      D3DSTENCILOP_REPLACE);
```

This is fairly straightforward. We set the stencil comparison operation to D3DCMP_ALWAYS, which specifies that the stencil test will always pass.

If the depth test fails, we specify D3DSTENCILOP_KEEP, which indicates to not update the stencil buffer entry. That is, we keep its current value. We do this because if the depth test fails, it means the pixel is obscured. Therefore, we do not want to render part of the reflection to a pixel that is obscured.

We also specify D3DSTENCILOP_KEEP if the stencil test fails. But this isn't really necessary here, since the test never fails because we specified D3DCMP_ALWAYS. However, we change the comparison operation in just a bit, so setting the stencil fail render state is required eventually; we just do it now.

If the depth and stencil tests pass, we specify D3DSTENCILOP_ REPLACE, which replaces the stencil buffer entry with the stencil reference value—0x1.

8.2.3.2 **Part II**

This next block of code renders the mirror, but only to the stencil buffer. We can stop writes to the depth buffer by setting the D3DRS_ ZWRITEENABLE and specifying false. We can prevent updating the back buffer with blending and setting the source blend factor to D3DBLEND_ ZERO and the destination blend factor to D3DBLEND_ONE. Plugging these blend factors into the blending equation, we show that the back buffer is left unchanged:

$$FinalPixel = sourcePixel \otimes (0, \quad 0, \quad 0, \quad 0) + DestPixel \otimes (I, \quad I, \quad I, \quad I)$$

$$= (0, \quad 0, \quad 0, \quad 0) + DestPixel$$

$$= DestPixel$$

Part II

```
// disable writes to the depth and back buffers
Device->SetRenderState(D3DRS_ZWRITEENABLE, false);
Device->SetRenderState(D3DRS_ALPHABLENDENABLE, true);
Device->SetRenderState(D3DRS_SRCBLEND,  D3DBLEND_ZERO);
Device->SetRenderState(D3DRS_DESTBLEND, D3DBLEND_ONE);

// draw the mirror to the stencil buffer
Device->SetStreamSource(0, VB, 0, sizeof(Vertex));
Device->SetFVF(Vertex::FVF);
Device->SetMaterial(&MirrorMtrl);
Device->SetTexture(0, MirrorTex);
D3DXMATRIX I;
D3DXMatrixIdentity(&I);
Device->SetTransform(D3DTS_WORLD, &I);
Device->DrawPrimitive(D3DPT_TRIANGLELIST, 18, 2);

// re-enable depth writes
Device->SetRenderState(D3DRS_ZWRITEENABLE, true);
```

8.2.3.3 Part III

At this point, the pixels in the stencil buffer that correspond to the visible pixels of the mirror have an entry of `0x1`, thus marking the area where the mirror has been rendered. We now prepare to render the reflected teapot. Recall that we only want to render the reflection into pixels that correspond to the mirror. We can do this easily now that we have marked those pixels in the stencil buffer.

We set the following render states:

```
Device->SetRenderState(D3DRS_STENCILFUNC, D3DCMP_EQUAL);
Device->SetRenderState(D3DRS_STENCILPASS, D3DSTENCILOP_KEEP);
```

With a new comparison operation set, we get the following stencil test:

```
        (ref & mask == (value & mask)
(0x1 & 0xffffffff) == (value & 0xffffffff)
        (0x1)== (value & 0xffffffff)
```

This shows that the stencil test only succeeds if `value = 0x1`. Since `value` is only `0x1` in areas of the stencil buffer that correspond to the mirror, the test only succeeds if we are rendering to those areas. Thus, the reflected teapot is only drawn into the mirror and is *not* drawn into other surfaces.

Note that we have changed the `D3DRS_STENCILPASS` render state to `D3DSTENCILOP_KEEP`, which simply says to keep the value in the stencil buffer if the test passed. Therefore, in this next rendering pass, we do not change the values in the stencil buffer (all controls are `D3DSTENCILOP_KEEP`). We are only using the stencil buffer to mark the pixels that correspond to the mirror.

8.2.3.4 **Part IV**

The next part of the `RenderMirror` function computes the matrix that positions the reflection in the scene:

```
// position reflection
D3DXMATRIX W, T, R;
D3DXPLANE plane(0.0f, 0.0f, 1.0f, 0.0f); // xy plane
D3DXMatrixReflect(&R, &plane);

D3DXMatrixTranslation(&T,
     TeapotPosition.x,
     TeapotPosition.y,
     TeapotPosition.z);

W = T * R;
```

Notice that we first translate to where the non-reflection teapot is positioned. Then, once positioned there, we reflect across the xy plane. This order of transformation is specified by the order in which we multiply the matrices.

8.2.3.5 **Part V**

We are almost ready to render the reflected teapot. However, if we render it now, it will not be displayed. Why? Because the reflected teapot's depth is greater than the mirror's depth, and thus the mirror primitives technically obscure the reflected teapot. To get around this, we clear the depth buffer:

```
Device->Clear(0, 0, D3DCLEAR_ZBUFFER, 0, 1.0f, 0);
```

Not all problems are solved, however. If we simply clear the depth buffer, the reflected teapot is drawn in front of the mirror and things do not look right. What we want to do is clear the depth buffer in addition to blending the reflected teapot with the mirror. In this way, the reflected teapot looks like it is "in" the mirror. We can blend the reflected teapot with the mirror with the following blending equation:

$$FinalPixel = sourcePixel \otimes destPixel + DestPixel \otimes (0, \quad 0, \quad 0, \quad 0)$$

$$= sourcePixel \otimes destPixel$$

Since the source pixel will be from the reflected teapot and the destination pixel will be from the mirror, we can see from this equation how they will be blended together. In code we have:

```
Device->SetRenderState(D3DRS_SRCBLEND, D3DBLEND_DESTCOLOR);
Device->SetRenderState(D3DRS_DESTBLEND, D3DBLEND_ZERO);
```

Part II

Finally, we are ready to draw the reflected teapot:

```
Device->SetTransform(D3DTS_WORLD, &W);
Device->SetMaterial(&TeapotMtrl);
Device->SetTexture(0, 0);

Device->SetRenderState(D3DRS_CULLMODE, D3DCULL_CW);
Teapot->DrawSubset(0);
```

Recall from section 8.2.3.4 that W correctly transforms the reflected teapot into its appropriate position in the scene. Also, observe that we change the backface cull mode. We must do this because when an object is reflected, its front faces will be swapped with its back faces; however, the winding order will not be changed. Thus, the "new" front faces will have a winding order that indicates to Direct3D that they are back facing. Similarly, the "new" back-facing triangles will have a winding order that indicates to Direct3D that they are front facing. Therefore, to correct this, we must change our backface culling condition.

Cleaning up, we disable blending and stenciling and restore the usual cull mode:

```
Device->SetRenderState(D3DRS_ALPHABLENDENABLE, false);
Device->SetRenderState( D3DRS_STENCILENABLE, false);
Device->SetRenderState(D3DRS_CULLMODE, D3DCULL_CCW);

} // end RenderMirror()
```

8.3 Sample Application: Planar Shadows

Shadows aid in our perception of where light is being emitted in a scene and ultimately makes the scene more realistic. In this section we show how to implement planar shadows—that is, shadows that lie on a plane (see Figure 8.5).

Figure 8.5: A screen shot taken from this chapter's sample application. Notice the teapot's shadow on the floor.

Note that these types of shadows are a quick hack, and although they enhance the scene, they aren't as realistic as shadow volumes. Shadow volumes are an advanced concept that we feel is best left out of an introductory book. However, it is worth mentioning that the DirectX SDK has a sample program that demonstrates shadow volumes.

To implement planar shadows, we must first find the shadow that an object casts to a plane and model it geometrically so that we can render it. This can easily be done with some 3D math. We then render the polygons that describe the shadow with a black material at 50% transparency. Rendering the shadow like this can introduce some artifacts, namely "double blending," which we explain a little later. We employ the stencil buffer to prevent double blending from occurring.

8.3.1 Parallel Light Shadows

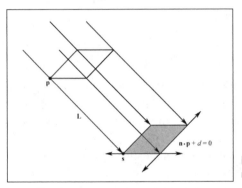

Figure 8.6: The shadow cast with respect to a parallel light source

Figure 8.6 shows the shadow that an object casts with respect to a parallel light source. The light ray from a parallel light, with direction **L**, through any vertex **p** is given by $\mathbf{r}(t) = \mathbf{p} + t\mathbf{L}$. The intersection of the ray $\mathbf{r}(t)$ with the plane $\mathbf{n} \cdot \mathbf{p} + d = 0$ gives **s**. The set of intersection points found by shooting $\mathbf{r}(t)$ through each of the object's vertices with the plane defines the geometry of the shadow. An intersection point **s** is easily found with a ray/plane intersection test:

$\mathbf{n} \cdot (\mathbf{p} + t\mathbf{L}) + d = 0$ Plugging $\mathbf{r}(t)$ into the plane equation $\mathbf{n} \cdot \mathbf{p} + d = 0$

$\mathbf{n} \cdot \mathbf{p} + t(\mathbf{n} \cdot \mathbf{L}) = -d$

$t(\mathbf{n} \cdot \mathbf{L}) = -d - \mathbf{n} \cdot \mathbf{p}$ Solving for t

$t = \dfrac{-d - \mathbf{n} \cdot \mathbf{p}}{\mathbf{n} \cdot \mathbf{L}}$

Then:

$$s = p + \left[\frac{-d - n \cdot p}{n \cdot L} \right] L$$

8.3.2 Point Light Shadows

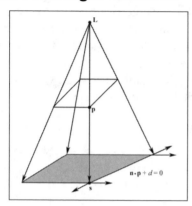

Figure 8.7: The shadow cast with respect to a point light source

Figure 8.7 shows the shadow that an object casts with respect to a point light source whose position is described by the point **L**. The light ray from a point light through any vertex **p** is given by $r(t) = p + t(p - L)$. The intersection point of the ray $r(t)$ with the plane $n \cdot p + d = 0$ gives **s**. The set of intersection points found by shooting $r(t)$ through each of the object's vertices with the plane defines the geometry of the shadow. **s** can be solved for using the same technique (plane/ray intersection) used in section 8.3.1.

Note: Notice that **L** serves different purposes for point and parallel lights. For point lights we use **L** to define the position of the point light. For parallel lights we use **L** to define the direction of the parallel light rays.

8.3.3 The Shadow Matrix

Notice from Figure 8.6 that for a parallel light, the shadow is essentially a *parallel* projection of the object onto the plane $n \cdot p + d = 0$ in the specified light direction. Similarly, Figure 8.7 shows that for a point light, the shadow is essentially a *perspective* projection of the object onto the plane $n \cdot p + d = 0$ from the viewpoint of the light source.

We can represent the transformation from a vertex **p** to its projection **s** with the plane $n \cdot p + d = 0$ with a matrix. Moreover, we can represent both an orthogonal projection and a perspective projection with the same matrix using some ingenuity.

Let (n_x, n_y, n_z, d) be a 4D vector representing the coefficients of the general plane equation describing the plane that we wish to cast the shadow onto. Let $\mathbf{L} = (L_x, L_y, L_z, L_w)$ be a 4D vector describing either the direction of a parallel light or the location of a point light. We use the w coordinate to denote which:

1. If $w = 0$, then $\mathbf{L}$ describes the direction of the parallel light.
2. If $w = 1$, then $\mathbf{L}$ describes the location of the point light.

Assuming the normal of the plane is normalized, we let $k = (n_x, n_y, n_z, d) \cdot (L_x, L_y, L_z, L_w) = n_x L_x + n_y L_y + n_z L_z + dL_w$.

Then we represent the transformation from a vertex $\mathbf{p}$ to its projection $\mathbf{s}$ with the following *shadow matrix*:

$$
\mathbf{S} = \begin{bmatrix}
n_x L_x + k & n_x L_y & n_x L_z & n_x L_w \\
n_y L_x & n_y L_y + k & n_y L_z & n_y L_w \\
n_y L_x & n_z L_y & n_z L_z + k & n_z L_w \\
dL_x & dL_y & dL_z & dL_w + k
\end{bmatrix}
$$

Because it's been done elsewhere and not of significant importance to us, we do not show how to derive this matrix. However, for the interested reader, we refer you to Chapter 6, "Me and My (Fake) Shadow," of *Jim Blinn's Corner: A Trip Down the Graphics Pipeline*, which shows how this matrix can be derived.

The D3DX library provides the following function to build the shadow matrix given the plane that we wish to project the shadow to and a vector describing a parallel light if $w = 0$ or a point light if $w = 1$:

```
D3DXMATRIX *D3DXMatrixShadow(
    D3DXMATRIX *pOut,
    CONST D3DXVECTOR4 *pLight,  // L
    CONST D3DXPLANE *pPlane     // plane to cast shadow onto
);
```

8.3.4 Using the Stencil Buffer to Prevent Double Blending

When we flatten out the geometry of an object onto the plane to describe its shadow, it is possible that two or more of the flattened triangles will overlap. When we render the shadow with transparency (using blending), these areas that have overlapping triangles will get blended multiple times and thus appear darker. Figure 8.8 shows this.

Part II

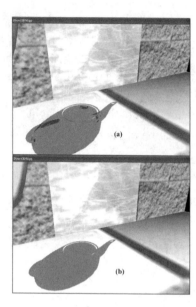

Figure 8.8: Notice the "black" areas of the shadow in (a). These correspond to areas where parts of the flattened teapot overlap, causing a "double blend." Image (b) shows the shadow rendered correctly without double blending.

We can solve this problem by using the stencil buffer. We set the stencil test to only accept pixels the first time they are rendered. That is, as we render the shadow's pixels to the back buffer, we mark the corresponding stencil buffer entries. Then, if we attempt to write a pixel to an area that has already been rendered to (marked in the stencil buffer), the stencil test will fail. In this way, we prevent writing overlapping pixels and therefore avoid double blending artifacts.

8.3.5 Code and Explanation

The following code explanation is taken from the Shadow sample in the companion files. The code relevant to this sample lies in the RenderShadow function. Note that we assume the stencil buffer has already been cleared to zero.

We begin by setting the stencil render states. We set the stencil comparison function to D3DCMP_EQUAL and the D3DRS_STENCILREF render state to 0x0, thereby specifying to render the shadow to the back buffer if the corresponding entry in the stencil buffer equals 0x0.

Since the stencil buffer is cleared to zero (0x0), this will always be true the first time we write a particular pixel of the shadow; but because we set D3DRS_STENCILPASS to D3DSTENCILOP_INCR, the test will fail if we try to write to a pixel that we have already written to. The pixel's stencil entry will have been incremented to 0x1 the first time it was written to, and thus the stencil test will fail if we try to write to it again. Hence, we avoid overwriting a pixel and thus avoid double blending.

```
void RenderShadow()
{
Device->SetRenderState(D3DRS_STENCILENABLE,    true);
Device->SetRenderState(D3DRS_STENCILFUNC,      D3DCMP_EQUAL);
Device->SetRenderState(D3DRS_STENCILREF,       0x0);
Device->SetRenderState(D3DRS_STENCILMASK,      0xffffffff);
Device->SetRenderState(D3DRS_STENCILWRITEMASK, 0xffffffff);
Device->SetRenderState(D3DRS_STENCILZFAIL,     D3DSTENCILOP_KEEP);
Device->SetRenderState(D3DRS_STENCILFAIL,      D3DSTENCILOP_KEEP);
Device->SetRenderState(D3DRS_STENCILPASS,      D3DSTENCILOP_INCR);
```

Next, we compute the shadow transformation and translate the shadow into the appropriate place in the scene.

```
// compute the transformation to flatten the teapot into
// a shadow.
D3DXVECTOR4 lightDirection(0.707f, -0.707f, 0.707f, 0.0f);
D3DXPLANE groundPlane(0.0f, -1.0f, 0.0f, 0.0f);

D3DXMATRIX S;
D3DXMatrixShadow(&S, &lightDirection, &groundPlane);

D3DXMATRIX T;
D3DXMatrixTranslation(&T, TeapotPosition.x, TeapotPosition.y,
                      TeapotPosition.z);

D3DXMATRIX W = T * S;
Device->SetTransform(D3DTS_WORLD, &W);
```

Lastly, we set a black material at 50% transparency, disable depth testing, render the shadow, and then clean up by re-enabling the depth buffer and disabling alpha blending and stencil testing. We disable the depth buffer to prevent *z-fighting*, which is a visual artifact that occurs when two different surfaces have the same depth values in the depth buffer; the depth buffer doesn't know which should be in front of the other, and an annoying flicker occurs. Because the shadow and floor lie on the same plane, z-fighting between them will most likely occur. By rendering the floor first and the shadow after with depth testing disabled, we guarantee our shadow will be drawn over the floor.

Note: An alternative method for preventing z-fighting is to use the Direct3D *depth bias* mechanism. See the `D3DRS_DEPTHBIAS` and `D3DRS_SLOPESCALEDEPTHBIAS` render states in the SDK documentation for details.

```
Device->SetRenderState(D3DRS_ALPHABLENDENABLE, true);
Device->SetRenderState(D3DRS_SRCBLEND, D3DBLEND_SRCALPHA);
Device->SetRenderState(D3DRS_DESTBLEND, D3DBLEND_INVSRCALPHA);
```

Part II

```
D3DMATERIAL9 mtrl = d3d::InitMtrl(d3d::BLACK, d3d::BLACK,
                                  d3d::BLACK, d3d::BLACK, 0.0f);
mtrl.Diffuse.a = 0.5f; // 50% transparency.

// Disable depth buffer so that z-fighting doesn't occur when we
// render the shadow on top of the floor.
Device->SetRenderState(D3DRS_ZENABLE, false);

Device->SetMaterial(&mtrl);
Device->SetTexture(0, 0);
Teapot->DrawSubset(0);

Device->SetRenderState(D3DRS_ZENABLE, true);

Device->SetRenderState(D3DRS_ALPHABLENDENABLE, false);
Device->SetRenderState(D3DRS_STENCILENABLE,    false);

}//end RenderShadow()
```

8.4 Summary

- The stencil buffer and depth buffer share the same surface and are therefore created at the same time. We specify the format of the depth/stencil surface using the D3DFORMAT types.

- Stenciling is used to block certain pixels from being rasterized. As we have seen in this chapter, this ability is useful for implementing mirrors and shadows among other applications.

- We can control stenciling operations and how the stencil buffer is updated through the D3DRS_STENCIL* render states.

- Some other applications that can be implemented with the stencil buffer:
  - ☐ Shadow volumes
  - ☐ Dissolves and fades
  - ☐ Visualizing depth complexity
  - ☐ Outlines and silhouettes
  - ☐ Constructive solid geometry
  - ☐ Fixing z-fighting caused by coplanar geometry

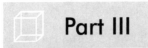

Part III

Applied Direct3D

In this part, we focus on applying Direct3D to implement several 3D applications, demonstrating techniques such as terrain rendering, particle systems, picking, and building a flexible 3D camera. In addition, we spend some time further exploring the D3DX library (in particular, the mesh-related components). A brief description of the chapters in this part follows.

Chapter 9, "Fonts"—During a game we often need to display textual information to the user. This chapter discusses three ways that we can generate and output text in Direct3D.

Chapter 10, "Meshes Part I"—This chapter thoroughly explains the data and methods of the D3DX mesh interface ID3DXMesh.

Chapter 11, "Meshes Part II"—In this chapter, we continue our study of the D3DX mesh-related interfaces and functions. We learn about .X files and how to load and render them. In addition, we examine the progressive mesh interface ID3DXPMesh. The chapter also shows how to compute the bounding box and bounding sphere of a mesh.

Chapter 12, "Building a Flexible Camera Class"—In this chapter, we design and implement a flexible camera class that has six degrees of freedom. This camera is suited for flight simulators and first-person shooters.

Chapter 13, "Basic Terrain Rendering"—This chapter shows how to create, texture, light, and render 3D terrains. Furthermore, we show how to smoothly "walk" the camera over the terrain so that it looks like we are walking on the terrain.

Chapter 14, "Particle Systems"—In this chapter, we learn how to model systems that consist of many small particles that all behave in a similar manner. For example, particle systems can be used to model falling snow and rain, the sparks of an explosion, puffs of smoke, rocket trails, and even the bullets of a gun.

Chapter 15, "Picking"—This chapter shows how to determine the particular 3D object that the user has selected with the mouse. Picking is often a necessity in 3D games and applications where the user interacts with the 3D world using the mouse.

Chapter 9

Fonts

During a game we often need to display textual information to the user. This chapter discusses three ways that we can generate and output text in Direct3D. Each way has a corresponding sample application on the web page for this chapter and in the companion files.

Objectives

- To learn how to render text using the ID3DXFont interface
- To learn how to render text using the CD3DFont class
- To learn how to calculate the number of frames rendered per second
- To learn how to create and render 3D text using the D3DXCreateText function

9.1 ID3DXFont

The D3DX library provides the ID3DXFont interface that can be used to draw text in a Direct3D application. This interface uses GDI internally to draw the text, and so we take a performance hit using this interface. However, ID3DXFont can handle complex fonts and formatting because it uses GDI.

9.1.1 Creating an ID3DXFont Interface

We can create an ID3DXFont interface using the D3DXCreateFontIndirect function.

```
HRESULT D3DXCreateFontIndirect(
        LPDIRECT3DDEVICE9 pDevice,  // device to be associated with
                                    // the font
        CONST LOGFONT* pLogFont,    // LOGFONT structure describing
                                    // the font
        LPD3DXFONT* ppFont          // return the created font
);
```

The following code snippet shows how to use this function:

```
LOGFONT lf;
ZeroMemory(&lf, sizeof(LOGFONT));
lf.lfHeight        = 25;   // in logical units
lf.lfWidth         = 12;   // in logical units
lf.lfWeight        = 500;  // boldness, range 0(light) - 1000(bold)
lf.lfItalic        = false;
lf.lfUnderline     = false;
lf.lfStrikeOut     = false;
lf.lfCharSet       = DEFAULT_CHARSET;
strcpy(lf.lfFaceName, "Times New Roman"); // font style

ID3DXFont* font = 0;
D3DXCreateFontIndirect(Device, &lf, &font);
```

Observe that first we must fill out a LOGFONT structure to describe the kind of font we want to create.

Note: Alternatively, you can use the D3DXCreateFont function to obtain a pointer to an ID3DXFont interface.

9.1.2 Drawing Text

Once we have obtained a pointer to an ID3DXFont interface, drawing text is a simple matter of calling the ID3DXFont::DrawText method.

```
INT ID3DXFont::DrawText(
    LPCSTR pString,
    INT Count,
    LPRECT pRect,
    DWORD Format,
    D3DCOLOR Color
);
```

- pString—Pointer to the string to draw
- Count—Number of characters in the string. We can specify –1 if the string is null terminating.
- pRect—Pointer to a RECT structure that defines the area on the screen to which the text is to be drawn
- Format—Optional flags that specify how the text should be formatted; see the SDK documentation for details.
- Color—The text color

Example:

```
Font->DrawText(
    "Hello World",     // String to draw.
    -1,                // Null terminating string.
    &rect,             // Rectangle to draw the string in.
    DT_TOP | DT_LEFT,  // Draw in top-left corner of rect.
    0xff000000);       // Black.
```

9.1.3 **Computing the Frames Rendered Per Second**

The ID3DXFont and CFont samples for this chapter compute and display the frames rendered per second (FPS). This section explains how to compute the FPS.

First we instantiate the following three global variables:

```
DWORD FrameCnt;      // The number of frames that have occurred.
float TimeElapsed;   // The time that has elapsed so far.
float FPS;           // The frames rendered per second.
```

We compute the FPS every one second; this gives us a good average. In addition, it keeps the FPS the same for one second, giving us enough time to read it before it changes again.

So every frame we increment `FrameCnt` and add the time elapsed from the last frame to `TimeElapsed`:

```
FrameCnt++;
TimeElapsed += timeDelta;
```

where `timeDelta` is the time it took between frames.

After one second has passed, we can compute the FPS with the following formula:

```
FPS = (float)FrameCnt / TimeElapsed;
```

We then reset `FrameCnt` and `TimeElapsed` and begin averaging the FPS for the next second. Here is the code put together:

```
void CalcFPS(float timeDelta)
{
    FrameCnt++;
    TimeElapsed += timeDelta;

    if(TimeElapsed >= 1.0f)
    {
        FPS = (float)FrameCnt / TimeElapsed;

        TimeElapsed = 0.0f;
        FrameCnt    = 0;
    }
}
```

9.2 **CD3DFont**

The DirectX SDK provides some useful utility code located in the \Samples\C++\Common folder of your DXSDK root directory. Among that code is the CD3DFont class, which renders text using textured triangles and Direct3D. Since CD3DFont uses Direct3D for rendering instead of GDI, it is much faster than ID3DXFont. However, CD3DFont does not support the complex fonts and formatting that

ID3DXFont does. If you're after speed and only need a simple font, the CD3DFont class is the way to go.

To use the CD3DFont class, you need to add the following files to your application: d3dfont.h, d3dfont.cpp, d3dutil.h, d3dutil.cpp, dxutil.h, and dxutil.cpp. These files can be found in the Include and Src folders located in the previously mentioned Common folder.

9.2.1 Constructing a CD3DFont Instance

To create a CD3DFont instance, we simply instantiate it like a normal C++ object; below is the constructor prototype:

```
CD3DFont(const TCHAR* strFontName, DWORD dwHeight, DWORD
        dwFlags=0L);
```

- strFontName—A null-terminated string that specifies the typeface name of the font

- dwHeight—The height of the font

- dwFlags—Optional creation flags; you can set this parameter to zero or use a combination of the following flags: D3DFONT_BOLD, D3DFONT_ITALIC, D3DFONT_ZENABLE.

After we have instantiated a CD3DFont object, we must call the following methods (in the order shown) that initialize the font:

```
Font = new CD3DFont("Times New Roman", 16, 0); // instantiate
Font->InitDeviceObjects( Device );
Font->RestoreDeviceObjects();
```

9.2.2 Drawing Text

Now that we have constructed and initialized a CD3DFont object, we are ready to draw some text. Text drawing is done with the following method:

```
HRESULT CD3DFont::DrawText(FLOAT x, FLOAT y, DWORD dwColor,
                    const TCHAR* strText, DWORD dwFlags=0L);
```

- x—The x-coordinate in screen space at which to begin drawing the text

- y—The y-coordinate in screen space at which to begin drawing the text

- dwColor—The color of the text

- strText—Pointer to the string to draw

- dwFlags—Optional rendering flags; you can set this parameter to 0 or use a combination of the following: D3DFONT_CENTERED, D3DFONT_TWOSIDED, D3DFONT_FILTERED.

Example:
```
Font->DrawText(20, 20, 0xff000000, "Hello, World");
```

9.2.3 Cleanup

Before deleting a `CD3DFont` object, we must call some cleanup routines first, as the following code snippet illustrates:
```
Font->InvalidateDeviceObjects();
Font->DeleteDeviceObjects();
delete Font;
```

9.3 D3DXCreateText

This last function is used for creating 3D meshes of text. Figure 9.1 shows the 3D text mesh that the FontMesh3D sample of this chapter renders.

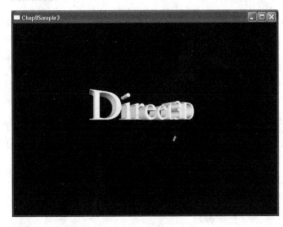

Figure 9.1: 3D text created with the D3DXCreateText function

The function is prototyped as:
```
HRESULT D3DXCreateText(
    LPDIRECT3DDEVICE9 pDevice,
    HDC hDC,
    LPCTSTR pText,
    FLOAT Deviation,
    FLOAT Extrusion,
    LPD3DXMESH* ppMesh,
    LPD3DXBUFFER* ppAdjacency,
    LPGLYPHMETRICSFLOAT pGlyphMetrics
);
```

This function returns `D3D_OK` on success.

■ `pDevice`—The device to be associated with the mesh

■ `hDC`—A handle to a device context that contains a description of the font that we are going to use to generate the mesh

- `pText`—Pointer to a null-terminating string specifying the text to create a mesh of

- `Deviation`—Maximum chordal deviation from TrueType font outlines. This value must be greater than or equal to 0. When this value is 0, the chordal deviation is equal to one design unit of the original font.

- `Extrusion`—The depth of the font measured in the negative z-axis direction

- `ppMesh`—Returns the created mesh

- `ppAdjacency`—Returns the created mesh's adjacency info. Specify null if you don't need this.

- `pGlyphMetrics`—A pointer to an array of `LPGLYPHMETRICS-FLOAT` structures that contain the glyph metric data. You can set this to 0 if you are not concerned with glyph metric data.

The following example code shows how to create a 3D mesh of text using this function.

```
// Obtain a handle to a device context.
HDC hdc = CreateCompatibleDC( 0 );

// Fill out a LOGFONT structure that describes the font's properties.
LOGFONT lf;
ZeroMemory(&lf, sizeof(LOGFONT));

lf.lfHeight     = 25;    // in logical units
lf.lfWidth      = 12;    // in logical units
lf.lfWeight     = 500;   // boldness, range 0(light) - 1000(bold)
lf.lfItalic     = false;
lf.lfUnderline  = false;
lf.lfStrikeOut  = false;
lf.lfCharSet    = DEFAULT_CHARSET;
strcpy(lf.lfFaceName, "Times New Roman"); // font style

// Create a font and select that font with the device context.
HFONT hFont;
HFONT hFontOld;
hFont = CreateFontIndirect(&lf);
hFontOld = (HFONT)SelectObject(hdc, hFont);

// Create the 3D mesh of text.
ID3DXMesh* Text = 0;
D3DXCreateText(_device, hdc, "Direct3D", 0.001f, 0.4f, &Text, 0, 0);

// Reselect the old font, and free resources.
SelectObject(hdc, hFontOld);
DeleteObject( hFont );
DeleteDC( hdc );
```

Then you can render the 3D text mesh by simply calling the mesh's `DrawSubset` method:

```
Text->DrawSubset( 0 );
```

9.4 Summary

- Use the `ID3DXFont` interface to render text when you need to support complex fonts and formatting. This interface uses GDI internally to render text and therefore takes a performance hit.

- Use `CD3DFont` to render simple text quickly. This class uses textured triangles and Direct3D to render text and is therefore much faster than `ID3DXFont`.

- Use `D3DXCreateText` to create a 3D mesh of a string of text.

Part III

Chapter 10

Meshes Part I

We have already worked with the `ID3DXMesh` interface using the `D3DXCreate*` routines; in this chapter we examine this interface in more detail. This chapter is largely a survey of the data and methods related to the `ID3DXMesh` interface.

Take note that the `ID3DXMesh` interface inherits the majority of its functionality from its parent, `ID3DXBaseMesh`. This is important to know because other mesh interfaces such as `ID3DXPMesh` (progressive mesh) also inherit from `ID3DXBaseMesh`. Therefore the topics covered in this chapter are also relevant when working with other mesh types.

Objectives

- To learn the internal data organization of an `ID3DXMesh` object
- To learn how to create an `ID3DXMesh`
- To learn how to optimize an `ID3DXMesh`
- To learn how to render an `ID3DXMesh`

10.1 Geometry Info

The `ID3DXBaseMesh` interface contains a vertex buffer that stores the vertices of the mesh and an index buffer that defines how these vertices are put together to form the triangles of the mesh. We can get a pointer to these buffers using the following methods:

```
HRESULT ID3DXMesh::GetVertexBuffer(LPDIRECT3DVERTEXBUFFER9* ppVB);
HRESULT ID3DXMesh::GetIndexBuffer(LPDIRECT3DINDEXBUFFER9* ppIB);
```

Here is an example of how these methods are used:

```
IDirect3DVertexBuffer9* vb = 0;
Mesh->GetVertexBuffer( &vb );

IDirect3DIndexBuffer9* ib = 0;
Mesh->GetIndexBuffer( &ib );
```

Note: The only primitive type the `ID3DXMesh` interface supports is indexed triangle lists.

Alternatively, if we just want to lock the buffers to read or write to them, we can use this next pair of methods. Note that these methods lock the entire vertex/index buffer.

```
HRESULT ID3DXMesh::LockVertexBuffer(DWORD Flags, BYTE** ppData);
HRESULT ID3DXMesh::LockIndexBuffer(DWORD Flags, BYTE** ppData);
```

The `Flags` parameter describes how the lock is done. Locking flags for a vertex/index buffer is explained in Chapter 3, where we first introduced buffers. The `ppData` argument is the address of a pointer that is to point to the locked memory when the function returns.

Remember to call the appropriate unlock method when you are done with the lock:

```
HRESULT ID3DXMesh::UnlockVertexBuffer();
HRESULT ID3DXMesh::UnlockIndexBuffer();
```

Below is a list of additional `ID3DXMesh` methods used to obtain geometry-related information:

- `DWORD GetFVF();`—Returns a `DWORD` describing the vertex format of the vertices

- `DWORD GetNumVertices();`—Returns the number of vertices in the vertex buffer

- `DWORD GetNumBytesPerVertex();`—Returns the number of bytes per vertex

- `DWORD GetNumFaces();`—Returns the number of faces (triangles) in the mesh

10.2 Subsets and the Attribute Buffer

A mesh consists of one or more subsets. A *subset* is a group of triangles in the mesh that can all be rendered using the same attribute. By *attribute* we mean material, texture, and render states. Figure 10.1 illustrates how a mesh representing a house may be divided into several subsets.

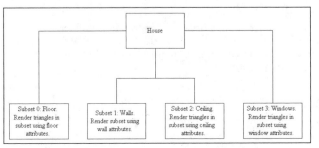

Figure 10.1: A house broken up into subsets

We label each subset by specifying a unique positive integer value for that subset. This value can be any number that can be stored in a DWORD. For instance, in Figure 10.1 we labeled the subsets 0, 1, 2, and 3.

Each triangle in the mesh is given an *attribute ID* that specifies the subset in which the triangle lives. For example, from Figure 10.1, the triangles that make up the floor of the house would have an attribute ID of 0 to indicate that they live in subset 0. Similarly, the triangles that make up the walls of the house have an attribute ID equal to 1 to indicate that they live in subset 1.

The attribute IDs for the triangles are stored in the mesh's *attribute buffer*, which is a DWORD array. Since each face has an entry in the attribute buffer, the number of elements in the attribute buffer is equal to the number of faces in the mesh. The entries in the attribute buffer and the triangles defined in the index buffer have a one-to-one correspondence; that is, entry i in the attribute buffer corresponds with triangle i in the index buffer. Triangle i is defined by the following three indices in the index buffer:

$$A = i \cdot 3$$
$$B = i \cdot 3 + 1$$
$$C = i \cdot 3 + 2$$

Figure 10.2 shows this correspondence:

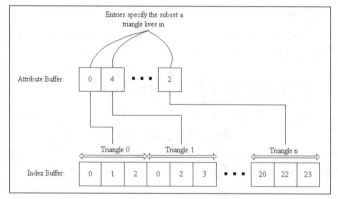

Figure 10.2: The correspondence between the triangles defined in the index buffer and the entries in the attribute buffer. We see that triangle 0 exists in subset 0, triangle 1 exists in subset 4, and triangle n exists in subset 2.

We can access the attribute buffer by locking it, as this next code snippet illustrates:

```
DWORD* buffer = 0;
Mesh->LockAttributeBuffer(lockingFlags, &buffer);

// Read or write to attribute buffer...

Mesh->UnlockAttributeBuffer();
```

10.3 Drawing

The `ID3DXMesh` interface provides the `DrawSubset(DWORD AttribId)` method to draw the triangles of a particular subset specified by the `AttribId` argument. For instance, to draw all the triangles that live in subset 0, we would write:

```
Mesh->DrawSubset(0);
```

To draw the entire mesh, we must draw all the subsets of the mesh. It is convenient to label subsets in the order 0, 1, 2, ..., $n - 1$, where n is the number of subsets, and have a corresponding material and texture array, such that index i refers to the material and texture associated with subset i. This allows us to render the entire mesh using a simple loop:

```
for(int i = 0; i < numSubsets; i++)
{
    Device->SetMaterial( mtrls[i] );
    Device->SetTexture( 0, textures[i] );
    Mesh->DrawSubset(i);
}
```

10.4 Optimizing

The vertices and indices of a mesh can be reorganized to render the mesh more efficiently. When we do this, we say that we are optimizing a mesh, and we use the following method to do this:

```
HRESULT ID3DXMesh::OptimizeInplace(
    DWORD Flags,
    CONST DWORD* pAdjacencyIn,
    DWORD* pAdjacencyOut,
    DWORD* pFaceRemap,
    LPD3DXBUFFER* ppVertexRemap
);
```

Part III

- ■ `Flags`—Optimization flags that tell the method what kind of optimizations to perform. These can be one or more of the following:

  - ☐ `D3DXMESHOPT_COMPACT`—Removes unused indices and vertices from the mesh

  - ☐ `D3DXMESHOPT_ATTRSORT`—Sorts the triangles by attribute and generates an attribute table. This allows `DrawSubset` to be more efficient (see section 10.5).

  - ☐ `D3DXMESHOPT_VERTEXCACHE`—Increases vertex cache rate hits

  - ☐ `D3DXMESHOPT_STRIPREORDER`—Reorganizes the indices so that triangle strips can be as long as possible

  - ☐ `D3DXMESHOPT_IGNOREVERTS`—Optimizes index info only, ignoring vertices

Note: The `D3DXMESHOPT_VERTEXCACHE` and `D3DXMESHOPT_STRIPREORDER` **flags cannot be used together.**

- ■ `pAdjacencyIn`—Pointer to the adjacency array of the non-optimized mesh

- ■ `pAdjacencyOut`—Pointer to a `DWORD` array to be filled with the adjacency info of the optimized mesh. The array must have `ID3DXMesh::GetNumFaces()` * 3 elements. If you do not need this info, pass 0.

- ■ `pFaceRemap`—Pointer to a `DWORD` array to be filled with the face remap info. The array should be of size `ID3DXMesh::GetNumFaces()`. When a mesh is optimized, its faces may be moved around in the index buffer. The face remap info tells where the original faces have moved to; that is, the ith entry in `pFaceRemap` holds the face index identifying where the ith original face has moved. If you do not need this info, pass 0.

- ■ `ppVertexRemap`—Address of a pointer to an `ID3DXBuffer` (see section 11.1) that will be filled with the vertex remap info. This buffer should contain `ID3DXMesh::GetNumVertices()` vertices. When a mesh is optimized, its vertices may be moved around in the vertex buffer. The vertex remap info tells where the original vertices have moved; that is, the ith entry in `ppVertexRemap` holds the vertex index identifying where the ith original vertex has moved. If you do not need this info, pass 0.

Example call:

```
// Get the adjacency info of the non-optimized mesh.
DWORD adjacencyInfo[Mesh->GetNumFaces() * 3];
Mesh->GenerateAdjacency(0.0f, adjacencyInfo);

// Array to hold optimized adjacency info.
DWORD optimizedAdjacencyInfo[Mesh->GetNumFaces() * 3];

Mesh->OptimizeInplace(
    D3DXMESHOPT_ATTRSORT   |
    D3DXMESHOPT_COMPACT    |
    D3DXMESHOPT_VERTEXCACHE,
    adjacencyInfo,
    optimizedAdjacencyInfo,
    0,
    0);
```

A similar method is the `Optimize` method, which outputs an optimized version of the calling mesh object rather than actually optimizing the calling mesh object.

```
HRESULT ID3DXMesh::Optimize(
    DWORD Flags,
    CONST DWORD* pAdjacencyIn,
    DWORD* pAdjacencyOut,
    DWORD* pFaceRemap,
    LPD3DXBUFFER* ppVertexRemap,
    LPD3DXMESH* ppOptMesh // the optimized mesh to be output
);
```

10.5 The Attribute Table

When a mesh is optimized with the D3DXMESHOPT_ATTRSORT flag, the geometry of the mesh is sorted by its attribute so that the geometry of a particular subset exists as a contiguous block in the vertex/index buffers (see Figure 10.3).

Part III

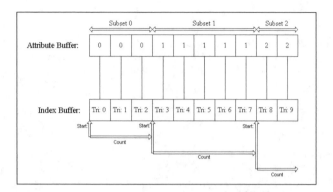

Figure 10.3: Notice that the geometry and attribute buffer are sorted by attribute such that the geometry of a particular subset is contiguous. We can now easily mark where the geometry of one subset begins and ends. Note that every "Tri" block in the index buffer represents three indices.

In addition to sorting the geometry, the D3DXMESHOPT_ATTRSORT optimization builds an attribute table. The attribute table is an array of D3DXATTRIBUTERANGE structures. Each entry in the attribute table corresponds to a subset of the mesh and specifies the block of memory in the vertex/index buffers, where the geometry for the subset resides. The D3DXATTRIBUTERANGE structure is defined as:

```
typedef struct _D3DXATTRIBUTERANGE {
    DWORD   AttribId;
    DWORD   FaceStart;
    DWORD   FaceCount;
    DWORD   VertexStart;
    DWORD   VertexCount;
} D3DXATTRIBUTERANGE;
```

- ■ AttribId—The subset ID
- ■ FaceStart—An offset into the index buffer (FaceStart * 3) identifying the start of the triangles that are associated with this subset
- ■ FaceCount—The number of faces (triangles) in this subset
- ■ VertexStart—An offset into the vertex buffer identifying the start of the vertices that are associated with this subset
- ■ VertexCount—The number of vertices in this subset

We can easily see the members of the D3DXATTRIBUTERANGE structure at work graphically in Figure 10.3. The attribute table for the mesh in Figure 10.3 would have three entries—one to correspond with each subset.

With the attribute table built, rendering a subset can be done very efficiently, for only a quick lookup in the attribute table is required to find all the geometry of a particular subset. Note that without an attribute table, rendering a subset requires a linear search of the entire attribute buffer to find the geometry that exists in the particular subset that we are drawing.

To access the attribute table of a mesh, we use the following method:

```
HRESULT ID3DXMesh::GetAttributeTable(
    D3DXATTRIBUTERANGE* pAttribTable,
    DWORD* pAttribTableSize
);
```

This method can do two things: It can return the number of attributes in the attribute table or it can fill an array of D3DXATTRIBUTERANGE structures with the attribute data.

To get the number of elements in the attribute table, we pass in 0 for the first argument:

```
DWORD numSubsets = 0;
Mesh->GetAttributeTable(0, &numSubsets);
```

Once we know the number of elements, we can fill a D3DXATTRI-BUTERANGE array with the actual attribute table by writing:

```
D3DXATTRIBUTERANGE table = new D3DXATTRIBUTERANGE [numSubsets];
Mesh->GetAttributeTable( table, &numSubsets );
```

We can directly set the attribute table using the ID3DXMesh::Set-AttributeTable method. The following example sets an attribute table with 12 subsets:

```
D3DXATTRIBUTERANGE attributeTable[12];

// ...fill attributeTable array with data

Mesh->SetAttributeTable( attributeTable, 12);
```

Part III

10.6 Adjacency Info

For certain mesh operations, such as optimizing, it is necessary to know the triangles that are adjacent to a given triangle. A mesh's *adjacency array* stores this information.

The adjacency array is a DWORD array, where each entry contains an index identifying a triangle in the mesh. For example, an entry *i* refers to the triangle formed by indices:

$$A = i \cdot 3$$
$$B = i \cdot 3 + 1$$
$$C = i \cdot 3 + 2$$

Note that an entry of `ULONG_MAX` = `4294967295` as its value indicates that the particular edge does not have an adjacent triangle. We can also use –1 to denote this because assigning –1 to a `DWORD` results in `ULONG_MAX`. To see this, recall that a `DWORD` is an *unsigned* 32-bit integer.

Since each triangle has three edges, it can have up to three adjacent triangles (see Figure 10.4).

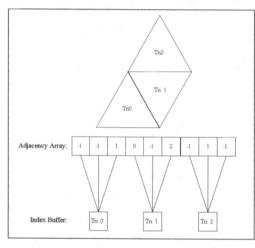

Figure 10.4: We see that each triangle has three entries in the adjacency array that identify the triangles adjacent to it. For instance, `Tri: 1` has two adjacent triangles (`Tri: 0` and `Tri: 2`). Thus for `Tri: 1` there is a 0, 2, and –1 in its corresponding adjacency entries specifying that `Tri: 0` and `Tri: 2` are adjacent. The –1 indicates that one edge of `Tri: 1` doesn't have an adjacent triangle.

Therefore, the adjacency array must have (`ID3DXBaseMesh::GetNumFaces() * 3`) elements—three possible adjacent triangles for every triangle in the mesh.

Many of the D3DX mesh creation functions can output the adjacency info, but the following method can also be used:

```
HRESULT ID3DXMesh::GenerateAdjacency(
    FLOAT fEpsilon,
    DWORD* pAdjacency
);
```

- `fEpsilon`—An epsilon value specifying when two points are close enough in distance that they should be treated as the same. For instance, if the distance between two points is less than epsilon, we treat them as the same.

- `pAdjacency`—A pointer to an array of `DWORD`s that is to be filled with the adjacency info

Example:

```
DWORD adjacencyInfo[Mesh->GetNumFaces() * 3];
Mesh->GenerateAdjacency(0.001f, adjacencyInfo);
```

10.7 Cloning

Sometimes we need to copy the data from one mesh to another. This is accomplished with the `ID3DXBaseMesh::CloneMeshFVF` method.

```
HRESULT ID3DXMesh::CloneMeshFVF(
    DWORD Options,
    DWORD FVF,
    LPDIRECT3DDEVICE9 pDevice,
    LPD3DXMESH* ppCloneMesh
);
```

- `Options`—One or more creation flags that are used to create the cloned mesh. See the `D3DXMESH` enumerated type in the SDK documentation for a complete list of option flags. Some common flags are:

  - `D3DXMESH_32BIT`—The mesh will use 32-bit indices.

  - `D3DXMESH_MANAGED`—The mesh will be placed in the managed memory pool.

  - `D3DXMESH_WRITEONLY`—The mesh's data will only be written to and not read from.

  - `D3DXMESH_DYNAMIC`—The mesh's buffers will be made dynamic.

- `FVF`—The flexible vertex format with which to create the cloned mesh

- `pDevice`—The device to be associated with the cloned mesh

- `ppCloneMesh`—Outputs the cloned mesh

Notice that this method allows the creation options and flexible vertex format of the destination mesh to be different from those of the source mesh. For example, suppose we have a mesh that has the flexible vertex format `D3DFVF_XYZ` and we would like to create a clone but with a vertex format of `D3DFVF_XYZ | D3DFVF_NORMAL`. We would write:

```
// assume _mesh and device are valid
ID3DXMesh* clone = 0;
Mesh->CloneMeshFVF(
    Mesh->GetOptions(),          // use same options as source mesh
    D3DFVF_XYZ | D3DFVF_NORMAL, // specify clones FVF
    Device,
    &clone);
```

Part III

10.8 Creating a Mesh (D3DXCreateMeshFVF)

Thus far, we have created mesh objects using the `D3DXCreate*` functions. However, we can also create an "empty" mesh using the `D3DXCreateMeshFVF` function. By empty mesh, we mean that we specify the number of faces and vertices that we want the mesh to be able to hold; then `D3DXCreateMeshFVF` allocates the appropriately sized vertex, index, and attribute buffers. Once we have the mesh's buffers allocated, we manually fill in the mesh's data contents (that is, we must write the vertices, indices, and attributes to the vertex buffer, index buffer, and attribute buffer, respectively).

As said, to create an empty mesh we use the `D3DXCreateMeshFVF` function:

```
HRESULT D3DXCreateMeshFVF(
    DWORD NumFaces,
    DWORD NumVertices,
    DWORD Options,
    DWORD FVF,
    LPDIRECT3DDEVICE9 pDevice,
    LPD3DXMESH* ppMesh
);
```

- `NumFaces`—The number of faces the mesh will have. This must be greater than zero.

- `NumVertices`—The number of vertices the mesh will have. This must be greater than zero.

- `Options`—One or more creation flags that will be used to create the mesh. See the `D3DXMESH` enumerated type in the SDK documentation for a complete list of option flags. Some common flags are:

  - `D3DXMESH_32BIT`—The mesh will use 32-bit indices.

  - `D3DXMESH_MANAGED`—The mesh will be placed in the managed memory pool.

  - `D3DXMESH_WRITEONLY`—The mesh's data will only be written to and not read from.

  - `D3DXMESH_DYNAMIC`—The mesh's buffers will be made dynamic.

- `FVF`—The flexible vertex format of the vertices stored in this mesh

- `pDevice`—The device associated with the mesh

- `ppMesh`—Outputs the created mesh

The sample application, reviewed in the next section, gives a concrete example of how to create a mesh using this function and manually fill in the mesh's data contents.

Alternatively, you can create an empty mesh with the `D3DX-CreateMesh` function. Its prototype is:

```
HRESULT D3DXCreateMesh(
    DWORD NumFaces,
    DWORD NumVertices,
    DWORD Options,
    CONST LPD3DVERTEXELEMENT9* pDeclaration,
    LPDIRECT3DDEVICE9 pDevice,
    LPD3DXMESH* ppMesh
);
```

The parameters are similar to `D3DXCreateMeshFVF`, except for the fourth. Instead of specifying the FVF, we specify an array of `D3DVER-TEXELEMENT9` structures that describe the format of the vertices. For now, we leave it to the reader to investigate the `D3DVERTEXELEMENT9` structure; however, the following related function is worth mentioning:

```
HRESULT D3DXDeclaratorFromFVF(
    DWORD FVF, // input format
    D3DVERTEXELEMENT9 Declaration[MAX_FVF_DECL_SIZE]//output format
);
```

 Note: `D3DVERTEXELEMENT9` is discussed in Chapter 17.

This function outputs an array of `D3DVERTEXELEMENT9` structures given an FVF as input. Note that `MAX_FVF_DECL_SIZE` is defined as:

```
typedef enum {
    MAX_FVF_DECL_SIZE = 18
} MAX_FVF_DECL_SIZE;
```

Part III

10.9 **Sample Application: Creating and Rendering a Mesh**

The sample application for this chapter renders a mesh of a box (see Figure 10.5).

It demonstrates most of the functionality that we have discussed in this chapter, including the following operations:

- Creating an empty mesh
- Filling the mesh with the geometry of a cube
- Specifying the subset in which each face of the mesh exists
- Generating the adjacency info of the mesh

- Optimizing the mesh
- Drawing the mesh

Figure 10.5: Screen shot of a cube created and rendered as an `ID3DXMesh` object

Note that we omit irrelevant code from the discussion of the sample. You can find the complete source code in the companion files. This sample is called D3DXCreateMeshFVF.

In addition, to facilitate debugging and investigating the components of a mesh, we implement the following functions that dump its internal contents to file:

```
void dumpVertices(std::ofstream& outFile, ID3DXMesh* mesh);
void dumpIndices(std::ofstream& outFile, ID3DXMesh* mesh);
void dumpAttributeBuffer(std::ofstream& outFile, ID3DXMesh* mesh);
void dumpAdjacencyBuffer(std::ofstream& outFile, ID3DXMesh* mesh);
void dumpAttributeTable(std::ofstream& outFile, ID3DXMesh* mesh);
```

The names of these functions describe their actions. Since the implementations of these functions are straightforward, we omit a discussion of them here (see the source code in the companion files). However, we do show an example of `dumpAttributeTable` later in this section.

To begin our review of the sample, we instantiate the following global variables:

```
ID3DXMesh*        Mesh = 0;
const DWORD       NumSubsets = 3;

IDirect3DTexture9* Textures[3] = {0, 0, 0};// texture for each subset

std::ofstream OutFile; // used to dump mesh data to file
```

Here we have instantiated a pointer to a mesh that we create later. We also define the number of subsets that the mesh will have—three. In this example, each subset is rendered with a different texture; the array Textures contains a texture for each subset, such that the ith index in the texture array is associated with the ith subset of the mesh. Finally, the variable OutFile is used to output the contents of the mesh to a text file. We pass this object to the dump* functions.

The majority of the work for this sample takes place in the Setup function. We first create an empty mesh:

```
bool Setup()
{
HRESULT hr = 0;

hr = D3DXCreateMeshFVF(
    12,
    24,
    D3DXMESH_MANAGED,
    Vertex::FVF,
    Device,
    &Mesh);
```

Here we allocate a mesh with 12 faces and 24 vertices, the amount needed to describe a box.

At this point, the mesh is empty, so we need to write the vertices and indices that describe a box to the vertex buffer and index buffer, respectively. Locking the vertex/index buffer and manually writing the data easily accomplishes this:

```
// Fill in vertices of a box
Vertex* v = 0;
Mesh->LockVertexBuffer(0, (void**)&v);

// fill in the front face vertex data
v[0] = Vertex(-1.0f, -1.0f, -1.0f, 0.0f, 0.0f, -1.0f, 0.0f, 0.0f);
v[1] = Vertex(-1.0f,  1.0f, -1.0f, 0.0f, 0.0f, -1.0f, 0.0f, 1.0f);
.
.
.
v[22] = Vertex( 1.0f,  1.0f,  1.0f, 1.0f, 0.0f, 0.0f, 1.0f, 1.0f);
v[23] = Vertex( 1.0f, -1.0f,  1.0f, 1.0f, 0.0f, 0.0f, 1.0f, 0.0f);

Mesh->UnlockVertexBuffer();
```

```
// Define the triangles of the box
WORD* i = 0;
Mesh->LockIndexBuffer(0, (void**)&i);

// fill in the front face index data
i[0] = 0; i[1] = 1; i[2] = 2;
i[3] = 0; i[4] = 2; i[5] = 3;
.

.

.
// fill in the right face index data
i[30] = 20; i[31] = 21; i[32] = 22;
i[33] = 20; i[34] = 22; i[35] = 23;

Mesh->UnlockIndexBuffer();
```

Once the geometry of the mesh has been written, we must not forget to specify the subset in which each triangle exists. Recall that the attribute buffer stores the subset to which each triangle in the mesh belongs. In this sample, we specify that the first four triangles defined in the index buffer exist in subset 0, the next four triangles exist in subset 1, and the last four triangles (12 total) exist in subset 2. We express this in code as follows:

```
DWORD* attributeBuffer = 0;
Mesh->LockAttributeBuffer(0, &attributeBuffer);

for(int a = 0; a < 4; a++)    // triangles 1-4
    attributeBuffer[a] = 0; // subset 0

for(int b = 4; b < 8; b++)    // triangles 5-8
    attributeBuffer[b] = 1; // subset 1

for(int c = 8; c < 12; c++)   // triangles 9-12
    attributeBuffer[c] = 2; // subset 2

Mesh->UnlockAttributeBuffer();
```

Now we have a created mesh that contains valid data. We could render the mesh at this point, but let's optimize it first. Note that for a trivial box mesh, nothing is really gained by optimizing the mesh data, but nonetheless we get practice using the ID3DXMesh interface methods. In order to optimize a mesh, we first need to compute the adjacency info of the mesh:

```
std::vector<DWORD> adjacencyBuffer(Mesh->GetNumFaces() * 3);
Mesh->GenerateAdjacency(0.0f, &adjacencyBuffer[0]);
```

Then we can optimize the mesh, as shown here:

```
hr = Mesh->OptimizeInplace(
    D3DXMESHOPT_ATTRSORT |
    D3DXMESHOPT_COMPACT  |
    D3DXMESHOPT_VERTEXCACHE,
```

```
&adjacencyBuffer[0],
0, 0, 0);
```

At this point, setting up the mesh is complete and we are ready to render it. But there is one last block of code in the `Setup` function that is relevant. It uses the previously mentioned `dump*` functions to output the internal data contents of the mesh to file. Being able to examine the data of a mesh helps for debugging and learning the structure of the mesh.

```
OutFile.open("Mesh Dump.txt");

dumpVertices(OutFile, Mesh);
dumpIndices(OutFile, Mesh);
dumpAttributeTable(OutFile, Mesh);
dumpAttributeBuffer(OutFile, Mesh);
dumpAdjacencyBuffer(OutFile, Mesh);

OutFile.close();

...Texturing loading, setting render states, etc., snipped

return true;
} // end Setup()
```

For example, the `dumpAttributeTable` function writes the attribute table's data to file. It is implemented as follows:

```
void dumpAttributeTable(std::ofstream& outFile, ID3DXMesh* mesh)
{
  outFile << "Attribute Table:" << std::endl;
  outFile << "----------------" << std::endl << std::endl;

  // number of entries in the attribute table
  DWORD numEntries = 0;

  mesh->GetAttributeTable(0, &numEntries);

  std::vector<D3DXATTRIBUTERANGE> table(numEntries);

  mesh->GetAttributeTable(&table[0], &numEntries);

  for(int i = 0; i < numEntries; i++)
    {
    outFile << "Entry " << i << std::endl;
    outFile << "------" << std::endl;

    outFile << "Subset ID:    " << table[i].AttribId     << std::endl;
    outFile << "Face Start:   " << table[i].FaceStart     << std::endl;
    outFile << "Face Count:   " << table[i].FaceCount     << std::endl;
    outFile << "Vertex Start: " << table[i].VertexStart << std::endl;
    outFile << "Vertex Count: " << table[i].VertexCount << std::endl;
    outFile << std::endl;
    }
```

```
    outFile << std::endl << std::endl;
}
```

The following text comes from the Mesh Dump.txt file for this sample application and corresponds to the data written by `dumpAttribute-Table`.

```
Attribute Table:
-----------------

Entry 0
-----------
Subset ID:    0
Face Start:   0
Face Count:   4
Vertex Start: 0
Vertex Count: 8

Entry 1
-----------
Subset ID:    1
Face Start:   4
Face Count:   4
Vertex Start: 8
Vertex Count: 8

Entry 2
-----------
Subset ID:    2
Face Start:   8
Face Count:   4
Vertex Start: 16
Vertex Count: 8
```

We can see that this matches the data that we specified for the mesh—three subsets with four triangles per subset. We advise you to examine the entire output Mesh Dump.txt file for this sample. It can be found in this sample's folder in the companion files.

Finally, we can easily render the mesh using the following code; essentially we just loop through each subset, set the associated texture, and then draw the subset. This is easy since we specified the subsets in the order 0, 1, 2, ..., $n - 1$, where n is the number of subsets.

```
bool Display(float timeDelta)
{
    if( Device )
    {
        //...update frame code snipped

        Device->Clear(0, 0, D3DCLEAR_TARGET | D3DCLEAR_ZBUFFER,
                      0x00000000, 1.0f, 0);
        Device->BeginScene();


        for(int i = 0; i < NumSubsets; i++)
```

```
        {
                Device->SetTexture( 0, Textures[i] );
                Mesh->DrawSubset( i );
        }


        Device->EndScene();
        Device->Present(0, 0, 0, 0);
    }
    return true;
}
```

10.10 Summary

- A mesh contains vertex, index, and attribute buffers. The vertex and index buffers hold the geometry of the mesh (vertices and triangles). The attribute buffer contains a corresponding entry for each triangle and specifies the subset to which a triangle belongs.

- A mesh can be optimized with the `OptimizeInplace` or `Optimize` method. Optimization reorganizes the geometry of the mesh to make rendering more efficient. Optimizing a mesh with `D3DXMESHOPT_ATTRSORT` generates an attribute table. An attribute table allows the mesh to render an entire subset using a simple lookup into the attribute table.

- The adjacency info of a mesh is a `DWORD` array that contains three entries for every triangle in the mesh. The three entries corresponding to a particular triangle specify the triangles that are adjacent to that triangle.

- We can create an empty mesh using the `D3DXCreateMeshFVF` function. We can then write valid data to the mesh using the appropriate locking methods (`LockVertexBuffer`, `LockIndexBuffer`, and `LockAttributeBuffer`).

Part III

Chapter 11

Meshes Part II

In this chapter we continue our study of the mesh-related interfaces, structures, and functions provided by the D3DX library. With the foundation built in the last chapter, we can move on to more interesting techniques, such as loading and rendering complex 3D models stored on disk and controlling the level of detail of our meshes through the progressive mesh interface.

Objectives

- To learn how to load the data of an XFile into an `ID3DXMesh` object
- To gain an understanding of the benefits of using progressive meshes and how to use the progressive mesh interface— `ID3DXPMesh`
- To learn about bounding volumes, why they are useful, and how to create them using the D3DX functions

11.1 ID3DXBuffer

A brief reference to the `ID3DXBuffer` interface was made in the last chapter, but we didn't elaborate on it. We see this interface throughout our utilization of the D3DX library, and therefore a brief overview of this interface is called for.

The `ID3DXBuffer` interface is a generic data structure that D3DX uses to store data in a contiguous block of memory. It has only two methods:

- `LPVOID GetBufferPointer();`—Returns a pointer to the start of the data
- `DWORD GetBufferSize();`—Returns the size of the buffer in bytes

To keep the structure generic, it uses a void pointer. This means that it is up to us to realize the type of data being stored. For example, `D3DXLoadMeshFromX` uses an `ID3DXBuffer` to return the adjacency info of a mesh. Since adjacency info is stored as a DWORD array, we have to cast the buffer to a DWORD array when we wish to use the adjacency info from the buffer.

Examples:

```
DWORD* info =(DWORD*)adjacencyInfo->GetBufferPointer();
D3DXMATERIAL* mtrls  = (D3DXMATERIAL*)mtrlBuffer->GetBufferPointer();
```

Since an ID3DXBuffer is a COM object, it must be released when you are done with it to avoid a memory leak:

```
adjacencyInfo->Release();
mtrlBuffer->Release();
```

We can create an empty ID3DXBuffer using the following function:

```
HRESULT D3DXCreateBuffer(
    DWORD NumBytes,        // Size of the buffer, in bytes.
    LPD3DXBUFFER *ppBuffer // Returns the created buffer.
);
```

The following example creates a buffer that can hold four integers:

```
ID3DXBuffer* buffer = 0;
D3DXCreateBuffer( 4 * sizeof(int), &buffer );
```

11.2 XFiles

Thus far, we have worked with simple geometric objects, such as spheres, cylinders, cubes, etc., using the D3DXCreate* functions. If you have attempted to construct your own 3D object by manually specifying the vertices, you have, no doubt, found it quite tedious. To alleviate this tiresome task of constructing the data of 3D objects, special applications called 3D *modelers* have been developed. These modelers allow the user to build complex and realistic meshes in a visual and interactive environment with a rich tool set, making the entire modeling process much easier. Examples of popular modelers used for game development are 3ds max (www.discreet.com), LightWave 3D (www.newtek.com), and Maya (www.aliaswave-front.com).

These modelers, of course, can export the created mesh data (geometry, materials, animations, and other possible useful data) to a file. Thus, we could write a file reader to extract the mesh data and use it in our 3D applications. This is certainly a viable solution. However, an even more convenient solution exists. There is a particular mesh file format called the XFile format (with the extension .x). Many 3D modelers can export to this format and there exist converters that can

Part III

convert other popular mesh file formats to .x. What makes XFiles convenient is that they are a DirectX defined format, and therefore the D3DX library readily supports XFiles. That is, the D3DX library provides functions for loading and saving XFiles. Thus, we avoid having to write our own file loading/saving routines if we use this format.

Note: You can download the DirectX9 SDK Extra—Direct3D Tools package from MSDN at http://www.msdn.microsoft.com/ to get some already made .x exporters for popular 3D modelers like 3ds max, LightWave, and Maya.

11.2.1 Loading an XFile

We use the following function to load the mesh data stored in an XFile. Note that this method creates an `ID3DXMesh` object and loads the geometric data of the XFile into it.

```
HRESULT D3DXLoadMeshFromX(
    LPCSTR pFilename,
    DWORD Options,
    LPDIRECT3DDEVICE9 pDevice,
    LPD3DXBUFFER *ppAdjacency,
    LPD3DXBUFFER *ppMaterials,
    LPD3DXBUFFER* ppEffectInstances,
    PDWORD pNumMaterials,
    LPD3DXMESH *ppMesh
);
```

- `pFilename`—The filename of the XFile to load
- `Options`—One or more creation flags that are used to create the mesh. See the `D3DXMESH` enumerated type in the SDK documentation for a complete list of option flags. Some common flags are:
  - □ `D3DXMESH_32BIT`—The mesh will use 32-bit indices.
  - □ `D3DXMESH_MANAGED`—The mesh will be placed in the managed memory pool.
  - □ `D3DXMESH_WRITEONLY`—The mesh's data will only be written to and not read from.
  - □ `D3DXMESH_DYNAMIC`—The mesh's buffers will be made dynamic.
- `pDevice`—The device to be associated with the mesh
- `ppAdjacency`—Returns an `ID3DXBuffer` containing a `DWORD` array that describes the adjacency info of the mesh
- `ppMaterials`—Returns an `ID3DXBuffer` containing an array of `D3DXMATERIAL` structures that contains the material data for this mesh. We cover the mesh materials in the following section.

- ppEffectInstances—Returns an ID3DXBuffer containing an array of D3DXEFFECTINSTANCE structures. We ignore this parameter for now by specifying 0.

- pNumMaterials—Returns the number of materials for the mesh (that is, the number of elements in the D3DXMATERIAL array output by ppMaterials)

- ppMesh—Returns the created ID3DXMesh object filled with the XFile geometry

11.2.2 XFile Materials

Argument seven of D3DXLoadMeshFromX returns the number of materials that the mesh contains, and argument five returns an array of D3DXMATERIAL structures containing the material data. The D3DX-MATERIAL structure is defined as follows:

```
typedef struct D3DXMATERIAL {
    D3DMATERIAL9 MatD3D;
    LPSTR pTextureFilename;
} D3DXMATERIAL;
```

It is a simple structure; it contains the basic D3DMATERIAL9 structure and a pointer to a null-terminating string that specifies the associative texture filename. An XFile doesn't embed the texture data; rather it embeds the filename, which is then used as a reference to the image file that contains the actual texture data. Thus, after we load an XFile with D3DXLoadMeshFromX, we must load the texture data given the texture filenames. We show how to do this in the next section.

It is worth noting that the D3DXLoadMeshFromX function loads the XFile data so that the ith entry in the returned D3DXMATERIAL array corresponds with the ith subset. Thus, the subsets are labeled in the order 0, 1, 2, ..., $n - 1$, where n is the number of subsets and materials. This allows the mesh to be rendered as a simple loop that iterates through each subset and renders it.

11.2.3 Sample Application: XFile

We now show the relevant code to the first sample of this chapter called XFile. The sample loads an .x file called bigship1.x that was taken from the media folder of the DirectX SDK. The complete source code can be found in the companion files. Figure 11.1 shows a screen shot of the sample.

Part III

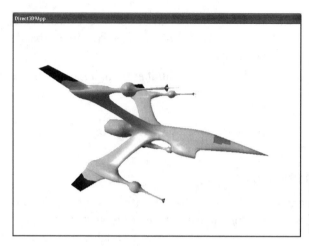

Figure 11.1: A screen shot taken from the XFile sample

This sample uses the following global variables:

```
ID3DXMesh*                         Mesh = 0;
std::vector<D3DMATERIAL9>          Mtrls(0);
std::vector<IDirect3DTexture9*> Textures(0);
```

Here we have an `ID3DXMesh` object that is used to store the mesh data that we load from the XFile. We also have a vector of materials and textures that we use to hold the mesh's materials and textures.

We begin by implementing our standard `Setup` function. First, we load the XFile:

```
bool Setup()
{
HRESULT hr = 0;

//
// Load the XFile data.
//
ID3DXBuffer* adjBuffer  = 0;
ID3DXBuffer* mtrlBuffer = 0;
DWORD        numMtrls   = 0;

hr = D3DXLoadMeshFromX(
     "bigship1.x",
     D3DXMESH_MANAGED,
     Device,
     &adjBuffer,
     &mtrlBuffer,
     0,
     &numMtrls,
     &Mesh);

if(FAILED(hr))
{
```

```
            ::MessageBox(0, "D3DXLoadMeshFromX() - FAILED", 0, 0);
        return false;
}
```

After we have loaded the XFile data, we must iterate through the
D3DXMATERIAL array and load any textures that the mesh references:

```
//
// Extract the materials, load textures.
//

if( mtrlBuffer != 0 && numMtrls != 0 )
{
    D3DXMATERIAL* mtrls=(D3DXMATERIAL*)mtrlBuffer->
      GetBufferPointer();

        for(int i = 0; i < numMtrls; i++)
        {
            // the MatD3D property doesn't have an ambient value
            // set when it's loaded, so set it now:
            mtrls[i].MatD3D.Ambient = mtrls[i].MatD3D.Diffuse;

            // save the ith material
            Mtrls.push_back( mtrls[i].MatD3D );

            // check if the ith material has an associative
            // texture
            if( mtrls[i].pTextureFilename != 0 )
            {
                // yes, load the texture for the ith subset
                IDirect3DTexture9* tex = 0;
                D3DXCreateTextureFromFile(
                    Device,
                    mtrls[i].pTextureFilename,
                    &tex);

                // save the loaded texture
                Textures.push_back( tex );
            }
            else
            {
                // no texture for the ith subset
                Textures.push_back( 0 );
            }
        }
    }
}
d3d::Release<ID3DXBuffer*>(mtrlBuffer); // done w/ buffer

.
. // Snipped irrelevant code to this chapter (e.g., setting up lights,
. // view and projection matrices, etc.)
.

return true;
} // end Setup()
```

In the `Display` function we rotate the mesh slightly every frame so that it spins. The mesh can be rendered trivially using a simple loop since the subsets are labeled in the order 0, 1, 2, ..., $n - 1$, where n is the number of subsets:

```
bool Display(float timeDelta)
{
    if( Device )
    {
        //
        // Update: Rotate the mesh.
        //

        static float y = 0.0f;
        D3DXMATRIX yRot;
        D3DXMatrixRotationY(&yRot, y);
        y += timeDelta;

        if( y >= 6.28f )
            y = 0.0f;

        D3DXMATRIX World = yRot;

        Device->SetTransform(D3DTS_WORLD, &World);

        //
        // Render
        //

        Device->Clear(0, 0, D3DCLEAR_TARGET | D3DCLEAR_ZBUFFER,
                      0xffffffff, 1.0f, 0);

        Device->BeginScene();

        for(int i = 0; i < Mtrls.size(); i++)
        {
            Device->SetMaterial( &Mtrls[i] );
            Device->SetTexture(0, Textures[i]);
            Mesh->DrawSubset(i);
        }

        Device->EndScene();
        Device->Present(0, 0, 0, 0);
    }
    return true;
}
```

11.2.4 Generating Vertex Normals

It is possible that an XFile does not contain vertex normal data. If this is the case, it may be necessary to compute the vertex normals manually so that we can use lighting. We briefly outlined how to do this way back in Chapter 5. However, now that we know about the `ID3DXMesh` interface and its parent `ID3DXBaseMesh`, we can use the following function to generate vertex normals for any mesh:

```
HRESULT D3DXComputeNormals(
    LPD3DXBASEMESH pMesh,      // Mesh to compute normals of.
    const DWORD *pAdjacency // Input adjacency info.
);
```

This function generates the vertex normals by using normal averaging. If adjacency info is provided, then duplicated vertices are disregarded. If adjacency info is *not* provided, then duplicated vertices have normals averaged from the faces that reference them. It is important to realize that the mesh we pass in for `pMesh` must have a vertex format that contains the `D3DFVF_NORMAL` flag.

Note that if an XFile does not contain vertex normal data, the `ID3DXMesh` object created from `D3DXLoadMeshFromX` does not have the `D3DFVF_NORMAL` flag specified in its vertex format. Therefore, before we can use `D3DXComputeNormals`, we have to clone the mesh and specify a vertex format for the cloned mesh that includes `D3DFVF_NORMAL`. The following example demonstrates this:

```
// does the mesh have a D3DFVF_NORMAL in its vertex format?
if ( !(pMesh->GetFVF() & D3DFVF_NORMAL) )
{
    // no, so clone a new mesh and add D3DFVF_NORMAL to its format:
    ID3DXMesh* pTempMesh = 0;
    pMesh->CloneMeshFVF(
        D3DXMESH_MANAGED,
        pMesh->GetFVF() | D3DFVF_NORMAL, // add it here
        Device,
        &pTempMesh );

    // compute the normals:
    D3DXComputeNormals( pTempMesh, 0 );

    pMesh->Release();   // get rid of the old mesh
    pMesh = pTempMesh; // save the new mesh with normals
}
```

11.3 Progressive Meshes

Progressive meshes, represented by the `ID3DXPMesh` interface, allow us to simplify a mesh by applying a sequence of *edge collapse transformations* (ECT). Each ECT removes one vertex and one or two faces. Because each ECT is invertible (its inverse is called a *vertex split*), we can reverse the simplification process and restore the mesh to its exact original state. This, of course, means that we cannot obtain a mesh more detailed than the original; we can only simplify and then reverse those simplification operations. Figure 11.2 shows a mesh at three different levels of detail (LOD): high, medium, and low.

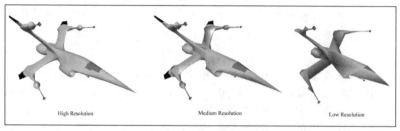

High Resolution   Medium Resolution   Low Resolution

Figure 11.2: A mesh shown at three different resolutions

The idea of progressive meshes is analogous to using mipmaps for textures. When texturing, we noticed that it was wasteful to use a high-resolution texture for a small, far-away primitive where the extra detail would go unnoticed. The same goes for meshes; a small, far-away mesh does not need as high a triangle count as a large, close-up mesh because the extra triangle detail for the small mesh would go unnoticed. Thus, we would end up spending time rendering a high triangle count model when a simpler low triangle count model would suffice.

One way that we can use progressive meshes is to adjust the LOD of a mesh based on its distance from the camera. That is, as the distance decreases, we would add detail (triangles) to the mesh, and as the distance increases, we would remove detail.

Note that we do not discuss how progressive meshes can be implemented; rather we show how to use the ID3DXPMesh interface. For those readers interested in the implementation details, you can find the original progressive mesh papers at Hugues Hoppe's web site: http://research.microsoft.com/~hoppe/.

11.3.1 Generating a Progressive Mesh

We can create an ID3DXPMesh object using the following function:

```
HRESULT D3DXGeneratePMesh(
    LPD3DXMESH pMesh,
    CONST DWORD *pAdjacency,
    CONST LPD3DXATTRIBUTEWEIGHTS pVertexAttributeWeights,
    CONST FLOAT *pVertexWeights,
    DWORD MinValue,
    DWORD Options,
    LPD3DXPMESH *ppPMesh
);
```

■ pMesh—An input mesh that contains the data of the mesh from which we want to generate a progressive mesh

- pAdjacency—Pointer to a `DWORD` array that contains the adjacency info of `pMesh`

- pVertexAttributeWeights—Pointer to a `D3DXATTRIBUTE-WEIGHTS` array of size `pMesh->GetNumVertices()`, where the ith entry corresponds with the ith vertex in `pMesh` and specifies its attribute weight. The attribute weights are used to determine the chance that a vertex is removed during simplification. You can pass in null for this parameter and a default vertex attribute weight will be used for each vertex. See section 11.3.2 for more information on attribute weights and the `D3DXATTRIBUTEWEIGHTS` structure.

- pVertexWeights—Pointer to a `float` array of size `pMesh->GetNumVertices()`, where the ith entry corresponds to the ith vertex in `pMesh` and specifies its vertex weight. The higher a vertex weight, the less chance it has of being removed during simplification. You can pass in null for this parameter and a default vertex weight of 1.0 will be used for each vertex.

- MinValue—The minimum vertices or faces (determined by the next parameter—`Options`) we want to simplify down to. Note that this value is a request, and depending on vertex/attribute weights the resulting mesh might not match this value.

- Options—Exactly one member of the `D3DXMESHSIMP` enumerated type:
  - ☐ D3DXMESHSIMP_VERTEX—Specifies that the previous parameter `MinValue` refers to vertices
  - ☐ D3DXMESHSIMP_FACE—Specifies that the previous parameter `MinValue` refers to faces

- ppPMesh—Returns the generated progressive mesh

11.3.2 Vertex Attribute Weights

```
typedef struct _D3DXATTRIBUTEWEIGHTS {
    FLOAT Position;
    FLOAT Boundary;
    FLOAT Normal;
    FLOAT Diffuse;
    FLOAT Specular;
    FLOAT Texcoord[8];
    FLOAT Tangent;
    FLOAT Binormal;
} D3DXATTRIBUTEWEIGHTS;
```

The vertex weight structure allows us to specify a weight for each possible component of a vertex. A value of 0.0 would indicate that the component carries no weight. The higher the weights for the vertex

Part III

components, the less likely the vertex will be removed in simplification. The default weights are as follows:

```
D3DXATTRIBUTEWEIGHTS AttributeWeights;
AttributeWeights.Position = 1.0;
AttributeWeights.Boundary = 1.0;
AttributeWeights.Normal   = 1.0;
AttributeWeights.Diffuse  = 0.0;
AttributeWeights.Specular = 0.0;
AttributeWeights.Tex[8]   = {0.0, 0.0, 0.0, 0.0, 0.0, 0.0, 0.0, 0.0};
```

The default weights are recommended, unless the application has a significant reason not to use them.

11.3.3 ID3DXPMesh Methods

The `ID3DXPMesh` interface inherits from the `ID3DXBaseMesh` interface. It therefore has all the functionality of the previously studied `ID3DXMesh`, as well as the following (but not limited to) additional methods:

- `DWORD GetMaxFaces(VOID);`—Returns the maximum number of faces that the progressive mesh can be set to have

- `DWORD GetMaxVertices(VOID);`—Returns the maximum number of vertices that the progressive mesh can be set to have

- `DWORD GetMinFaces(VOID);`—Returns the minimum number of faces that the progressive mesh can be set to have

- `DWORD GetMinVertices(VOID);`—Returns the minimum number of vertices that the progressive mesh can be set to have

- `HRESULT SetNumFaces(DWORD Faces);`—This method allows us to set the number of faces that we want the mesh to be simplified/*complexified* to. For example, suppose that the mesh presently has 50 faces and we want to simplify it to 30 faces; we would write:

  ```
  pmesh->SetNumFaces(30);
  ```

  Note that after the adjustment the number of faces of the mesh may differ by one from the number desired. If `Faces` is less than `GetMinFaces()`, it is clamped to `GetMinFaces()`. Similarly, if `Faces` is greater than `GetMaxFaces()`, it is clamped to `GetMaxFaces()`.

- `HRESULT SetNumVertices(DWORD Vertices);`—This method allows us to set the number of vertices that we want the mesh to be simplified/*complexified* to. For example, suppose the mesh presently has 20 vertices and we want to add detail to it by increasing the vertex count to 40 vertices; we would write:

```
pmesh->SetNumVertices(40);
```

Note that the number of vertices of the mesh, after the adjustment, may differ by one from the number desired. If `Vertices` is less than `GetMinVertices()`, it is clamped to `GetMinVertices()`. Similarly, if `Vertices` is greater than `GetMaxVertices()`, it is clamped to `GetMaxVertices()`.

■ HRESULT TrimByFaces(
       DWORD NewFacesMin,
       DWORD NewFacesMax,
       DWORD *rgiFaceRemap, // Face remap info.
       DWORD *rgiVertRemap // Vertex remap info.
   );

This method allows us to set a new face count minimum and maximum, as specified by the arguments `NewFacesMin` and `NewFacesMax`, respectively. Note that the new minimum and maximum must be in the present face minimum and maximum interval; that is, it must be in [`GetMinFaces()`, `GetMaxFaces()`]. The function also returns face and vertex remap information. See section 10.4 for a description of remap information.

■ HRESULT TrimByVertices(
       DWORD NewVerticesMin,
       DWORD NewVerticesMax,
       DWORD *rgiFaceRemap, // Face remap info.
       DWORD *rgiVertRemap // Vertex remap info.
   );

This method allows us to set a new vertex count minimum and maximum as specified by the arguments `NewVerticesMin` and `NewVerticesMax`, respectively. Note that the new minimum and maximum must be in the present vertex minimum and maximum interval; that is, it must be in [`GetMinVertices()`, `GetMax-Vertices()`]. The function also returns face and vertex remap information. See section 10.4 for a description of remap information.

Part III

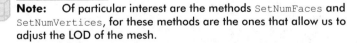

Note: Of particular interest are the methods `SetNumFaces` and `SetNumVertices`, for these methods are the ones that allow us to adjust the LOD of the mesh.

11.3.4 **Sample Application: Progressive Mesh**

The Progressive Mesh sample is similar to the XFile sample, except for the fact that the mesh we create and render is a progressive mesh and thus represented by the `ID3DXPMesh` interface. We allow the user to change the resolution of the progressive mesh interactively via keyboard input. You can add faces to the mesh by pressing the A key, and you can remove faces from the mesh by pressing the S key.

The global variables used in the sample are almost the same as those used in the XFile sample, but we add an additional variable to store the progressive mesh:

```
ID3DXMesh*                          SourceMesh = 0;
ID3DXPMesh*                         PMesh      = 0; // progressive mesh
std::vector<D3DMATERIAL9>           Mtrls(0);
std::vector<IDirect3DTexture9*>     Textures(0);
```

Recall that to generate a progressive mesh we must pass in a "source" mesh that contains the data we want to create a progressive mesh of. Thus, we first load the XFile data into an `ID3DXMesh` object `SourceMesh` and then generate the progressive mesh:

```
bool Setup()
{
HRESULT hr = 0;

// ...Load XFile data into SourceMesh snipped.
//
// ...Extracting materials and textures snipped.
```

Since the code to do this is exactly the same as it was in the XFile sample, we have omitted it. Once we have a source mesh, we can generate the progressive mesh as follows:

```
//
// Generate the progressive mesh.
//

hr = D3DXGeneratePMesh(
    SourceMesh,
    (DWORD*)adjBuffer->GetBufferPointer(), // adjacency
    0,                     // default vertex attribute weights
    0,                     // default vertex weights
    1,                     // simplify as low as possible
    D3DXMESHSIMP_FACE,     // simplify by face count
    &PMesh);

d3d::Release<ID3DXMesh*>(SourceMesh);   // done w/ source mesh
d3d::Release<ID3DXBuffer*>(adjBuffer);  // done w/ buffer

if(FAILED(hr))
{
```

```
    ::MessageBox(0, "D3DXGeneratePMesh() - FAILED", 0, 0);
    return false;
}
```

Note that while we request to simplify the mesh down to one face, this will usually not occur due to vertex/attribute weights; however, specifying 1 will reduce the mesh to its lowest resolution.

At this point, the progressive mesh has been generated but if we render it now, it will be rendered at its lowest resolution. Because we want to initially render the mesh at full resolution, we set it to:

```
// set to original (full) detail
DWORD maxFaces = PMesh->GetMaxFaces();
PMesh->SetNumFaces(maxFaces);
```

In the `Display` function, we test for an A keypress and an S keypress and handle the input accordingly:

```
bool Display(float timeDelta)
{
if( Device )
{
    //
    // Update: Mesh resolution.
    //

    // Get the current number of faces the pmesh has.
    int numFaces = PMesh->GetNumFaces();

    // Add a face, note the SetNumFaces() will automatically
    // clamp the specified value if it goes out of bounds.
    if( ::GetAsyncKeyState('A') & 0x8000f )
    {
        // Sometimes we must add more than one face to invert
        // an edge collapse transformation because of the internal
        // implementation details of the ID3DXPMesh interface. In
        // other words, adding one face may possibly result in a
        // mesh with the same number of faces as before. Thus to
        // increase the face count we may sometimes have to add
        // two faces at once.
        PMesh->SetNumFaces(numFaces + 1);
        if(PMesh->GetNumFaces() == numFaces)
            PMesh->SetNumFaces(numFaces + 2);
    }

    // Remove a face, note the SetNumFaces() will automatically
    // clamp the specified value if it goes out of bounds.
    if(::GetAsyncKeyState('S') & 0x8000f)
        PMesh->SetNumFaces(numFaces - 1);
```

This is straightforward, but notice that when adding a face we must sometimes add two faces in order to invert an edge collapse transformation.

To conclude, we can render an `ID3DXPMesh` object the same way that we render an `ID3DXMesh` object. In addition, we also outline the mesh's triangles in yellow by drawing the mesh in wireframe mode with a yellow material. We do this so that we can see the individual triangles being added and removed by the progressive mesh when we adjust the LOD.

```
Device->Clear(0, 0, D3DCLEAR_TARGET | D3DCLEAR_ZBUFFER,
              0xffffffff, 1.0f, 0);
Device->BeginScene();

for(int i = 0; i < Mtrls.size(); i++)
{
    Device->SetMaterial( &Mtrls[i] );
    Device->SetTexture(0, Textures[i]);
    PMesh->DrawSubset(i);

    // draw wireframe outline
    Device->SetMaterial(&d3d::YELLOW_MTRL);
    Device->SetRenderState(D3DRS_FILLMODE, D3DFILL_WIREFRAME);
    PMesh->DrawSubset(i);
    Device->SetRenderState(D3DRS_FILLMODE, D3DFILL_SOLID);
}

Device->EndScene();
Device->Present(0, 0, 0, 0);
}
return true;
} // end Display
```

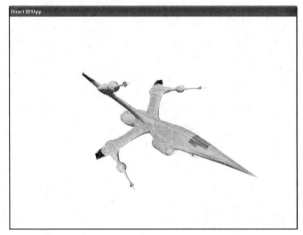

Figure 11.3: A screen shot of the Progressive Mesh sample

11.4 Bounding Volumes

Sometimes we want to compute a bounding volume of a mesh. Two common examples of the bounding volumes used are spheres and boxes. Other examples are cylinders, ellipsoids, lozenges, and capsules. Figure 11.4 shows a mesh with a bounding sphere and the same mesh with a bounding box. For this section we work only with bounding boxes and bounding spheres.

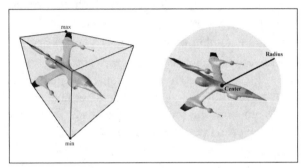

Figure 11.4: A mesh rendered with its bounding sphere and bounding box. A sphere can be defined by its center point and radius. A box can be defined by its minimum and maximum points.

Bounding boxes/spheres are often used to speed up visibility tests and collision tests, among other things. For example, we can say that a mesh is not visible if its bounding box/sphere is not visible. A box/sphere visibility test is much cheaper than individually testing the visibility of each triangle in the mesh. For a collision example, suppose that a missile is fired in the scene and we want to determine if the missile hit an object in the scene. Since the objects are made up of triangles, we could iterate through each triangle of each object and test if the missile (modeled mathematically by a ray) hit a triangle of the object. This approach would require many ray/triangle intersection tests—one for each triangle of each object in the scene. A more efficient approach would be to compute the bounding box/sphere of each mesh and then do one ray/box or ray/sphere intersection test per object. We can then say that the object is hit if the ray intersected its bounding volume. This is a fair approximation; if more precision is necessary, we can use the ray/box or ray/sphere to quickly reject objects that are obviously not going to be hit and then apply a more precise test to objects that have a good chance of being hit. Objects that have a good chance of being hit are objects whose bounding volumes were hit.

The D3DX library provides functions to calculate the bounding sphere of a mesh and the bounding box of a mesh. These functions take an array of vertices as input to compute the bounding sphere or box.

These functions are designed to be flexible and can work with various vertex formats.

```
HRESULT D3DXComputeBoundingSphere(
    LPD3DXVECTOR3 pFirstPosition,
    DWORD NumVertices,
    DWORD dwStride,
    D3DXVECTOR3* pCenter,
    FLOAT* pRadius
);
```

■ `pFirstPosition`—A pointer to a vector in the first vertex of an array of vertices that describes the position of the vertex

■ `NumVertices`—The number of vertices in the vertex array

■ `dwStride`—The size of each vertex in bytes. This is needed because a vertex structure may have additional information such as a normal vector and texture coordinates that is not needed for the bounding sphere function, and the function needs to know how much data to skip over to get to the next vertex position.

■ `pCenter`—Returns the center of the bounding sphere

■ `pRadius`—Returns the radius of the bounding sphere

```
HRESULT D3DXComputeBoundingBox(
    LPD3DXVECTOR3 pFirstPosition,
    DWORD NumVertices,
    DWORD dwStride,
    D3DXVECTOR3* pMin,
    D3DXVECTOR3* pMax
);
```

The first three parameters are exactly the same as the first three in `D3DXComputeBoundingSphere`. The last two parameters are used to return the bounding box's minimum and maximum point, respectively.

11.4.1 Some New Special Constants

Let's introduce two constants that will prove useful throughout the rest of this book. We add these to the `d3d` namespace:

```
namespace d3d
{

...

const float INFINITY = FLT_MAX;
const float EPSILON  = 0.001f;
```

The `INFINITY` constant is simply used to represent the largest number that we can store in a `float`. Since we can't have a `float` bigger than `FLT_MAX`, we can conceptualize it as infinity, which makes for more readable code that signifies ideas of infinity. The `EPSILON` constant is a small value we define such that we consider any number smaller than it equal to zero. This is necessary because due to floating-point imprecision, a number that should really be zero may be off slightly. Thus, comparing it to zero would fail. We therefore test if a floating-point variable is zero by testing if it's less than EPSILON. The following function illustrates how EPSILON can be used to test if two floating-point values are equal:

```
bool Equals(float lhs, float rhs)
{
    // if lhs == rhs their difference should be zero
    return fabs(lhs - rhs) < EPSILON ? true : false;
}
```

11.4.2 Bounding Volume Types

To facilitate work with bounding spheres and bounding volumes, it is natural to implement classes representing each. We implement such classes now in the d3d namespace:

```
struct BoundingBox
{
    BoundingBox();

    bool isPointInside(D3DXVECTOR3& p);

    D3DXVECTOR3 _min;
    D3DXVECTOR3 _max;
};

struct BoundingSphere
{
    BoundingSphere();

    D3DXVECTOR3 _center;
    float       _radius;
};

d3d::BoundingBox::BoundingBox()
{
    // infinite small bounding box
    _min.x = d3d::INFINITY;
    _min.y = d3d::INFINITY;
    _min.z = d3d::INFINITY;

    _max.x = -d3d::INFINITY;
    _max.y = -d3d::INFINITY;
    _max.z = -d3d::INFINITY;
}

bool d3d::BoundingBox::isPointInside(D3DXVECTOR3& p)
{
    // is the point inside the bounding box?
    if(p.x >= _min.x && p.y >= _min.y && p.z >= _min.z &&
```

```
                p.x <= _max.x && p.y <= _max.y && p.z <= _max.z)
        {
                return true;
        }
        else
        {
                return false;
        }
}

d3d::BoundingSphere::BoundingSphere()
{
        _radius = 0.0f;
}
```

11.4.3 Sample Application: Bounding Volumes

The Bounding Volumes sample located in this chapter's folder in the companion files demonstrates using `D3DXComputeBoundingSphere` and `D3DXComputeBoundingBox`. The program loads an XFile and computes its bounding sphere and mesh. It then creates two `ID3DXMesh` objects, one to model the bounding sphere and one to model the bounding box. The mesh corresponding to the XFile is then rendered with either the bounding sphere or bounding box displayed (see Figure 11.5). The user can switch between displaying the bounding sphere and bounding box mesh by pressing the Spacebar.

Figure 11.5: A screen shot of the Bounding Volumes sample. Note that transparency using alpha blending is used to make the bounding sphere transparent.

The sample is pretty straightforward, and we will leave it to you to study the source code. The two functions we implement that are of interest to this discussion compute the bounding sphere and bounding box of a specific mesh:

```
bool ComputeBoundingSphere(
    ID3DXMesh* mesh, // mesh to compute bounding sphere for
    d3d::BoundingSphere* sphere) // return bounding sphere
{
    HRESULT hr = 0;

    BYTE* v = 0;
    mesh->LockVertexBuffer(0, (void**)&v);

    hr = D3DXComputeBoundingSphere(
            (D3DXVECTOR3*)v,
            mesh->GetNumVertices(),
            D3DXGetFVFVertexSize(mesh->GetFVF()),
            &sphere->_center,
            &sphere->_radius);

    mesh->UnlockVertexBuffer();

    if( FAILED(hr) )
        return false;

    return true;
}
bool ComputeBoundingBox(
    ID3DXMesh* mesh, // mesh to compute bounding box for
    d3d::BoundingBox* box) // return bounding box
{
    HRESULT hr = 0;

    BYTE* v = 0;
    mesh->LockVertexBuffer(0, (void**)&v);

    hr = D3DXComputeBoundingBox(
            (D3DXVECTOR3*)v,
            mesh->GetNumVertices(),
            D3DXGetFVFVertexSize(mesh->GetFVF()),
            &box->_min,
            &box->_max);

    mesh->UnlockVertexBuffer();

    if( FAILED(hr) )
        return false;

    return true;
}
```

Part III

Notice that the cast `(D3DXVECTOR3*)v` assumes the vertex position
component is stored first in the vertex structure that we are using.
Also notice that we can use the `D3DXGetFVFVertexSize` function to
get the size of a vertex structure given the flexible vertex format
description.

11.5 **Summary**

- We can construct complex triangle meshes using 3D modeling programs and either export or convert them to XFiles. Then, using the D3DXLoadMeshFromX function, we can load the mesh data in an XFile into an ID3DXMesh object that we can use in our applications.

- Progressive meshes, represented by the ID3DXPMesh interface, can be used to control the level of detail of a mesh; that is, we can adjust the detail of the mesh dynamically. This is useful because we will often want to adjust the detail of the mesh based on how prominent it is in the scene. For example, a mesh closer to the viewer should be rendered with more detail than a mesh far away from the viewer.

- We can compute the bounding sphere and bounding box using the D3DXComputeBoundingSphere and D3DXComputeBounding-Box functions, respectively. Bounding volumes are useful because they approximate the volume of a mesh and can therefore be used to speed up calculations related to the volume of space that a mesh occupies.

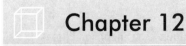
Building a Flexible Camera Class

Thus far, we have used the `D3DXMatrixLookAtLH` function to compute a view space transformation matrix. This function is particularly useful for positioning and aiming a camera in a fixed position, but its user interface is not so useful for a moving camera that reacts to user input. This motivates us to develop our own solution. In this chapter we show how to implement a `Camera` class that gives us better control of the camera than the `D3DXMatrixLookAtLH` function and is particularly suitable for flight simulators and games played from the first-person perspective.

Objective

- To learn how to implement a flexible `Camera` class that can be used for flight simulators and games played from the first-person perspective

12.1 Camera Design

We define the position and orientation of the camera relative to the world coordinate system using four *camera vectors*: a *right vector, up vector, look vector,* and *position vector,* as Figure 12.1 illustrates. These vectors essentially define a local coordinate system for the camera described relative to the world coordinate system. Since the right, up, and look vectors define the camera's orientation in the world, we sometimes refer to all three as the *orientation vectors*. The orientation vectors must be *orthonormal*. A set of vectors is orthonormal if they are mutually perpendicular to each other and of unit length. The reason we make this restriction is because later we insert the orientation vectors into the rows of a matrix, and a matrix where the row vectors are orthonormal means the matrix is orthogonal. Recall that an orthogonal

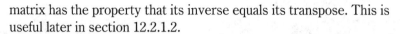

matrix has the property that its inverse equals its transpose. This is useful later in section 12.2.1.2.

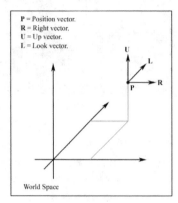

P = Position vector.
R = Right vector.
U = Up vector.
L = Look vector.

World Space

Figure 12.1: The camera vectors defining the position and orientation of the camera relative to the world

With these four vectors describing the camera, we would like our camera to be able to perform the following six operations:

■ Rotate around the right vector (pitch)
■ Rotate around the up vector (yaw)
■ Rotate around the look vector (roll)
■ Strafe along the right vector
■ Fly along the up vector
■ Move along the look vector

Through these six operations, we are able to move along three axes and rotate around three axes, giving us a flexible six degrees of freedom. The following `Camera` class definition reflects our description of data and desired methods:

```
class Camera
{
public:
      enum CameraType { LANDOBJECT, AIRCRAFT };

      Camera();
      Camera(CameraType cameraType);
      ~Camera();

      void strafe(float units);   // left/right
      void fly(float units);      // up/down
      void walk(float units);     // forward/backward

      void pitch(float angle);    // rotate on right vector
      void yaw(float angle);      // rotate on up vector
      void roll(float angle);     // rotate on look vector
```

```
        void getViewMatrix(D3DXMATRIX* V);
        void setCameraType(CameraType cameraType);
        void getPosition(D3DXVECTOR3* pos);
        void setPosition(D3DXVECTOR3* pos);
        void getRight(D3DXVECTOR3* right);
        void getUp(D3DXVECTOR3* up);
        void getLook(D3DXVECTOR3* look);

private:
        CameraType   _cameraType;
        D3DXVECTOR3  _right;
        D3DXVECTOR3  _up;
        D3DXVECTOR3  _look;
        D3DXVECTOR3  _pos;
};
```

One thing shown in this class definition that we haven't discussed is the `CameraType` enumerated type. Presently, our camera supports two types of camera models, a `LANDOBJECT` model and an `AIRCRAFT` model. The `AIRCRAFT` model allows us to move freely through space and gives us six degrees of freedom. However, in some games, such as a first-person shooter, people can't fly; therefore we must restrict movement on certain axes. Specifying `LANDOBJECT` for the camera type has these restrictions carried out, as you can see in the following section.

12.2 Implementation Details

12.2.1 Computing the View Matrix

We now show how the view matrix transformation can be computed given the camera vectors. Let $\mathbf{p} = (p_x, p_y, p_z)$, $\mathbf{r} = (r_x, r_y, r_z)$, $\mathbf{u} = (u_x, u_y, u_z)$, and $\mathbf{d} = (d_x, d_y, d_z)$ be the position, right, up, and look vectors, respectively.

Recall that in Chapter 2 we said that the view space transformation transforms the geometry in the world so that the camera is centered at the origin and axis aligned with the major coordinate axes (see Figure 12.2).

Part III

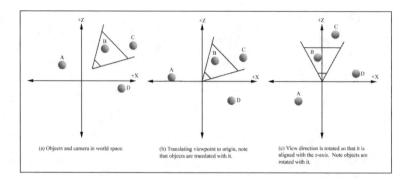

(a) Objects and camera in world space.

(b) Translating viewpoint to origin, note that objects are translated with it.

(c) View direction is rotated so that it is aligned with the z-axis. Note objects are rotated with it.

Figure 12.2: The transformation from world space to view space. This transformation transforms the camera to the origin of the system looking down the positive z-axis. Notice that the objects in space are transformed along with the camera so that the camera's view of the world remains the same.

Therefore, we want a transformation matrix $\mathbf{V}$ such that:

- $\mathbf{p}\mathbf{V} = (0, 0, 0)$—The matrix $\mathbf{V}$ transforms the camera to the origin.
- $\mathbf{r}\mathbf{V} = (1, 0, 0)$—The matrix $\mathbf{V}$ aligns the right vector with the world x-axis.
- $\mathbf{u}\mathbf{V} = (0, 1, 0)$—The matrix $\mathbf{V}$ aligns the up vector with the world y-axis.
- $\mathbf{d}\mathbf{V} = (0, 0, 1)$—The matrix $\mathbf{V}$ aligns the look vector with the world z-axis.

We can divide the task of finding such a matrix into two parts: 1) a translation part that takes the camera's position to the origin and 2) a rotation part that aligns the camera vectors with the world's axes.

12.2.1.1 **Part 1: Translation**

The translation that takes $\mathbf{p}$ to the origin is easily given by $-\mathbf{p}$, since $\mathbf{p} - \mathbf{p} = \mathbf{0}$. So we can describe the translation part of the view transformation with the following matrix:

$$\mathbf{T} = \begin{bmatrix} 1 & 0 & 0 & 0 \\ 0 & 1 & 0 & 0 \\ 0 & 0 & 1 & 0 \\ -p_x & -p_y & -p_z & 1 \end{bmatrix}$$

12.2.1.2 **Part 2: Rotation**

Aligning all three of the camera vectors with the world's axes requires a little more work. We need a 3×3 rotation matrix $\mathbf{A}$ that aligns the right, up, and look vectors with the world's x-, y-, and z-axes, respectively. Such a matrix would satisfy the following three systems of equations:

$$\mathbf{rA} = \begin{bmatrix} r_x, & r_y, & r_z \end{bmatrix} \begin{bmatrix} a_{00} & a_{01} & a_{02} \\ a_{10} & a_{11} & a_{12} \\ a_{20} & a_{21} & a_{22} \end{bmatrix} = \begin{bmatrix} 1, & 0, & 0 \end{bmatrix}$$

$$\mathbf{uA} = \begin{bmatrix} u_x, & u_y, & u_z \end{bmatrix} \begin{bmatrix} a_{00} & a_{01} & a_{02} \\ a_{10} & a_{11} & a_{12} \\ a_{20} & a_{21} & a_{22} \end{bmatrix} = \begin{bmatrix} 0, & 1, & 0 \end{bmatrix}$$

$$\mathbf{dA} = \begin{bmatrix} d_x, & d_y, & d_z \end{bmatrix} \begin{bmatrix} a_{00} & a_{01} & a_{02} \\ a_{10} & a_{11} & a_{12} \\ a_{20} & a_{21} & a_{22} \end{bmatrix} = \begin{bmatrix} 0, & 0, & 1 \end{bmatrix}$$

Note: We work with 3×3 matrices here because we do not need homogeneous coordinates to represent rotations. Later we augment back to our usual 4×4 matrix.

Since these three systems have the same coefficient matrix $\mathbf{A}$, we can solve them all at once. We rewrite them together as:

$$\mathbf{BA} = \begin{bmatrix} r_x & r_y & r_z \\ u_x & u_y & u_z \\ d_x & d_y & d_z \end{bmatrix} \begin{bmatrix} a_{00} & a_{01} & a_{02} \\ a_{10} & a_{11} & a_{12} \\ a_{20} & a_{21} & a_{22} \end{bmatrix} = \begin{bmatrix} 1 & 0 & 0 \\ 0 & 1 & 0 \\ 0 & 0 & 1 \end{bmatrix}$$

We can solve for $\mathbf{A}$ in a variety of ways, but we immediately see that $\mathbf{A}$ is the inverse of $\mathbf{B}$ because $\mathbf{BA} = \mathbf{BB}^{-1} = \mathbf{I}$. Because $\mathbf{B}$ is an orthogonal matrix (its row vectors are an orthonormal basis), we know that its inverse is its transpose. Thus, the transformation that aligns the orientation vectors with the world's axes is:

$$\mathbf{B}^{-1} = \mathbf{B}^{\mathsf{T}} = \mathbf{A} = \begin{bmatrix} r_x & u_x & d_x \\ r_y & u_y & d_y \\ r_z & u_z & d_z \end{bmatrix}$$

12.2.1.3 **Combining Both Parts**

Finally, augmenting **A** to a 4 × 4 matrix and combining the translation part with the rotation part yields the view transformation matrix **V**:

$$
\mathbf{TA} =
\begin{bmatrix}
1 & 0 & 0 & 0 \\
0 & 1 & 0 & 0 \\
0 & 0 & 1 & 0 \\
-p_x & -p_y & -p_z & 1
\end{bmatrix}
\begin{bmatrix}
r_x & u_x & d_x & 0 \\
r_y & u_y & d_y & 0 \\
r_z & u_z & d_z & 0 \\
0 & 0 & 0 & 1
\end{bmatrix}
=
\begin{bmatrix}
r_x & u_x & d_x & 0 \\
r_y & u_y & d_y & 0 \\
r_z & u_z & d_z & 0 \\
-\mathbf{p}\cdot\mathbf{r} & -\mathbf{p}\cdot\mathbf{u} & -\mathbf{p}\cdot\mathbf{d} & 1
\end{bmatrix}
= \mathbf{V}
$$

We build this matrix in the `Camera::getViewMatrix` method:

```
void Camera::getViewMatrix(D3DXMATRIX* V)
{
    // Keep camera's axes orthogonal to each other:
    D3DXVec3Normalize(&_look, &_look);

    D3DXVec3Cross(&_up, &_look, &_right);
    D3DXVec3Normalize(&_up, &_up);

    D3DXVec3Cross(&_right, &_up, &_look);
    D3DXVec3Normalize(&_right, &_right);

    // Build the view matrix:
    float x = -D3DXVec3Dot(&_right, &_pos);
    float y = -D3DXVec3Dot(&_up, &_pos);
    float z = -D3DXVec3Dot(&_look, &_pos);

    (*V)(0, 0) = _right.x;
    (*V)(0, 1) = _up.x;
    (*V)(0, 2) = _look.x;
    (*V)(0, 3) = 0.0f;

    (*V)(1, 0) = _right.y;
    (*V)(1, 1) = _up.y;
    (*V)(1, 2) = _look.y;
    (*V)(1, 3) = 0.0f;

    (*V)(2, 0) = _right.z;
    (*V)(2, 1) = _up.z;
    (*V)(2, 2) = _look.z;
    (*V)(2, 3) = 0.0f;

    (*V)(3, 0) = x;
    (*V)(3, 1) = y;
    (*V)(3, 2) = z;
    (*V)(3, 3) = 1.0f;
}
```

You may wonder what the first few lines of the method are for. After several rotations, the camera's axes can become non-orthogonal to each other due to floating-point errors. Therefore, every time this function is called, we recompute the up and right vectors with respect to the look vector to ensure that they are all mutually orthogonal to each other. A new orthogonal up vector is found by up = look × right. Then a new orthogonal right vector is found with right = up × look.

12.2.2 **Rotation about an Arbitrary Axis**

To implement our camera rotation methods, we need to be able to rotate around an arbitrary axis. The D3DX library provides the following function for just that purpose:

```
D3DXMATRIX *D3DXMatrixRotationAxis(
    D3DXMATRIX *pOut,         // returns rotation matrix
    CONST D3DXVECTOR3 *pV,    // axis to rotate around
    FLOAT Angle               // angle, in radians, to rotate
);
```

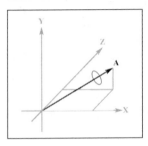

Figure 12.3: Rotations about an arbitrary axis defined by the vector **A**

For example, suppose we want to rotate $\pi/2$ radians around the axis defined by the vector (0.707, 0.707, 0). We would write:

```
D3DXMATRIX R;
D3DXVECTOR3 axis(0.707f, 0.707f, 0.0f);
D3DXMatrixRotationAxis(&R, &axis, D3DX_PI / 2.0f);
```

A derivation of the matrix `D3DXMatrixRotationAxis` builds can be found in Eric Lengyel's *Mathematics for 3D Game Programming & Computer Graphics*.

12.2.3 **Pitch, Yaw, and Roll**

Because the orientation vectors describe the orientation of the camera relative to the world coordinate system, we must figure out how we update them when we pitch, yaw, and roll. This is actually very easy. Consider Figures 12.4, 12.5, and 12.6, which show the camera pitching, yawing, and rolling, respectively.

Part III

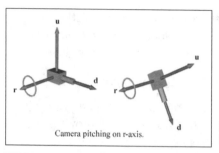

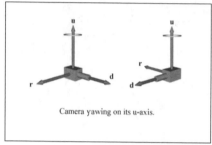

Figure 12.4: Pitch, or rotation about the camera's right vector

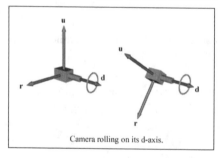

Figure 12.5: Yaw, or rotation about the camera's up vector

Figure 12.6: Roll, or rotation about the camera's look vector

We see that when we pitch, we need to rotate the up and look vectors around the right vector by the specified rotation angle. Similarly, we see that when we yaw, we need to rotate the look and right vectors around the up vector by the specified rotation angle. Finally, we see that when we roll, we need to rotate the up and right vectors around the look vector by the specified rotation angle.

We now see why the D3DXMatrixRotationAxis function is necessary, as any of these three vectors that we rotate around may have an arbitrary orientation in the world.

The implementations for the pitch, yaw, and roll methods follow what we have just discussed. However, there are some restrictions that we make for LANDOBJECTs. In particular, it doesn't look and feel right for a land object to yaw when tilted or for it to roll. Therefore, for LANDOBJECTs we rotate around the world's y-axis rather than the camera's up vector in the yaw method, and we disable rolling for land objects completely. Keep in mind that you can alter the `Camera` class to suit your application; we offer only an example.

The code for the pitch, yaw, and roll methods is implemented as follows:

```
void Camera::pitch(float angle)
{
    D3DXMATRIX T;
    D3DXMatrixRotationAxis(&T, &_right, angle);

    // rotate _up and _look around _right vector
    D3DXVec3TransformCoord(&_up,&_up, &T);
    D3DXVec3TransformCoord(&_look,&_look, &T);
}

void Camera::yaw(float angle)
{
    D3DXMATRIX T;

    // rotate around world y (0, 1, 0) always for land object
    if( _cameraType == LANDOBJECT )
        D3DXMatrixRotationY(&T, angle);

    // rotate around own up vector for aircraft
    if( _cameraType == AIRCRAFT )
        D3DXMatrixRotationAxis(&T, &_up, angle);

    // rotate _right and _look around _up or y-axis
    D3DXVec3TransformCoord(&_right,&_right, &T);
    D3DXVec3TransformCoord(&_look,&_look, &T);
}

void Camera::roll(float angle)
{
    // only roll for aircraft type
    if( _cameraType == AIRCRAFT )
    {
        D3DXMATRIX T;
        D3DXMatrixRotationAxis(&T, &_look, angle);

        // rotate _up and _right around _look vector
        D3DXVec3TransformCoord(&_right,&_right, &T);
        D3DXVec3TransformCoord(&_up,&_up, &T);
    }
}
```

12.2.4 **Walking, Strafing, and Flying**

When we refer to walking, we mean moving in the direction that we are looking (that is, along the look vector). Strafing is moving side to side from the direction we are looking, which is of course moving along the right vector. Finally, we say that flying is moving along the up vector. To move along any of these axes, we simply add a vector that points in the same direction as the axis that we want to move along to our position vector (see Figure 12.7).

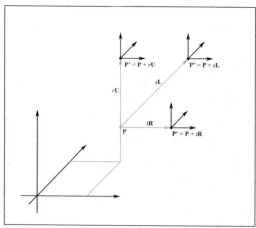

Figure 12.7: Moving along the camera's orientation vectors

As with the rotations, we need to set some restrictions on moving for land objects. For example, LANDOBJECTs shouldn't be able to get airborne by flying on their up vector, moving forward if they're looking up, or strafing at a tilt. Therefore, we restrict movement to the xz plane. However, because LANDOBJECTs can change their elevation by climbing stairs or a hill, for example, we expose the Camera::setPosition method, which allows you to manually position your camera to a desired height and position.

The code that implements the walk, strafe, and fly methods follows:

```
void Camera::walk(float units)
{
    // move only on xz plane for land object
    if( _cameraType == LANDOBJECT )
        _pos += D3DXVECTOR3(_look.x, 0.0f, _look.z) * units;

    if( _cameraType == AIRCRAFT )
        _pos += _look * units;
}

void Camera::strafe(float units)
{
    // move only on xz plane for land object
    if( _cameraType == LANDOBJECT )
        _pos += D3DXVECTOR3(_right.x, 0.0f, _right.z) * units;

    if( _cameraType == AIRCRAFT )
        _pos += _right * units;
}
```

```
void Camera::fly(float units)
{
    if( _cameraType == AIRCRAFT )
        _pos += _up * units;
}
```

12.3 Sample Application: Camera

This chapter's sample program creates and renders the scene shown in Figure 12.8. You are free to fly around this scene using input from the keyboard. The following keys are implemented:

- W/S—Walk forward/backward
- A/D—Strafe left/right
- R/F—Fly up/down
- Up/Down arrow keys—Pitch
- Left/Right arrow keys—Yaw
- N/M—Roll

Figure 12.8: A screen shot of the camera sample program for this chapter

The implementation of the sample is trivial, since all the work is inside the Camera class, which we have already discussed. We handle user input in the Display function accordingly. Keep in mind that we have instantiated the camera object TheCamera at the global scope. Also notice that we move the camera with respect to the time change (timeDelta); this keeps us moving at a steady speed independent of the frame rate.

```
bool Display(float timeDelta)
{
    if( Device )
    {
```

```
//
// Update: Update the camera.
//

if( ::GetAsyncKeyState('W') & 0x8000f )
    TheCamera.walk(4.0f * timeDelta);

if( ::GetAsyncKeyState('S') & 0x8000f )
    TheCamera.walk(-4.0f * timeDelta);

if( ::GetAsyncKeyState('A') & 0x8000f )
    TheCamera.strafe(-4.0f * timeDelta);

if( ::GetAsyncKeyState('D') & 0x8000f )
    TheCamera.strafe(4.0f * timeDelta);

if( ::GetAsyncKeyState('R') & 0x8000f )
    TheCamera.fly(4.0f * timeDelta);

if( ::GetAsyncKeyState('F') & 0x8000f )
    TheCamera.fly(-4.0f * timeDelta);

if( ::GetAsyncKeyState(VK_UP) & 0x8000f )
    TheCamera.pitch(1.0f * timeDelta);

if( ::GetAsyncKeyState(VK_DOWN) & 0x8000f )
    TheCamera.pitch(-1.0f * timeDelta);

if( ::GetAsyncKeyState(VK_LEFT) & 0x8000f )
    TheCamera.yaw(-1.0f * timeDelta);

if( ::GetAsyncKeyState(VK_RIGHT) & 0x8000f )
    TheCamera.yaw(1.0f * timeDelta);

if( ::GetAsyncKeyState('N') & 0x8000f )
    TheCamera.roll(1.0f * timeDelta);

if( ::GetAsyncKeyState('M') & 0x8000f )
    TheCamera.roll(-1.0f * timeDelta);

// Update the view matrix representing the cameras
// new position/orientation.
D3DXMATRIX V;
TheCamera.getViewMatrix(&V);
Device->SetTransform(D3DTS_VIEW, &V);

//
// Render
//

Device->Clear(0, 0,
    D3DCLEAR_TARGET | D3DCLEAR_ZBUFFER,
    0x00000000, 1.0f, 0);
Device->BeginScene();

d3d::DrawBasicScene(Device, 1.0f);
```

```
        Device->EndScene();
        Device->Present(0, 0, 0, 0);
    }
    return true;
}
```

> **Note:** We have updated the d3d namespace with a new function called DrawBasicScene. The function draws the scene in Figure 12.8. We have added it to the d3d namespace because it is convenient to have one function that sets up a basic scene so that in later samples we can concentrate on the code that the sample illustrates rather than irrelevant drawing code. Its declaration in d3dUtility.h is as follows:

```
// Function references "desert.bmp" internally.  This file must
// be in the working directory.
bool DrawBasicScene(
    IDirect3DDevice9* device,   // Pass in 0 for cleanup.
    float scale);               // uniform scale
```

The first time the function is called with a valid device pointer it sets up the geometry internally; therefore it is recommended that you call this function first in the Setup function. To clean up the internal geometry, call the function in the Cleanup routine, but pass null for the device pointer. Since this function doesn't implement anything that we haven't seen, we leave it to you to examine the code, which can be found in this chapter's folder in the companion files. Make a note that the function loads the image desert.bmp as a texture. This file can be found in this sample's folder.

12.4 Summary

- We describe the position and orientation of our camera in the world coordinate system by maintaining four vectors: a right vector, an up vector, a look vector, and a position vector. With this description, we can easily implement a camera with six degrees of freedom, giving a flexible camera interface that works well for flight simulators and games played from the first-person perspective.

Part III

 **Chapter 13**

Basic Terrain Rendering

A terrain mesh is really nothing more than a triangle grid, as Figure 13.1.a shows, but with the heights of each vertex in the grid specified in such a way that the grid models a smooth transition from mountain to valley, simulating a natural terrain (Figure 13.1.b). And of course, we apply a nice texture showing sandy beaches, grassy hills, and snowy mountains (Figure 13.1.c).

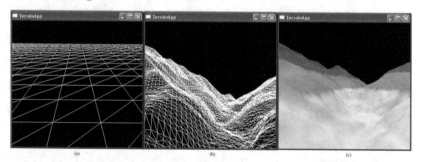

Figure 13.1: (a) A triangle grid. (b) A triangle grid with smooth height transitions. (c) A lit and textured terrain that is a screen shot from the sample we create in this chapter.

This chapter walks you through implementing the `Terrain` class. This class uses a brute force approach. By that we mean it simply stores the entire terrain vertex/index data and then renders it. For games requiring a small terrain, this approach is workable with modern graphics cards that support hardware vertex processing. However, for games requiring larger terrains, you have to do some kind of level of detail or culling because the enormous amount of geometry data needed to model such huge terrains is overwhelming for a brute force approach.

Objectives

- To learn how to generate height info for the terrain that results in smooth transitions of mountains and valleys, simulating a natural terrain
- To understand how to generate the vertex and triangle data for a terrain
- To learn a technique that we can use to texture and light the terrain
- To discover a way to keep the camera planted on the terrain so that walking or running on the terrain is simulated

13.1 Heightmaps

We use a heightmap to describe the hills and valleys of our terrain. A *heightmap* is an array where each element specifies the height of a particular vertex in the terrain grid. (An alternate implementation might have a heightmap entry for each square world unit.) We usually think of a heightmap as a matrix so that each element has a one-to-one correspondence with each vertex in the terrain grid.

When we store our heightmaps on disk, we usually allocate a byte of memory for each element in heightmap, so the height can range from 0 to 255. The range 0 to 255 is enough to preserve the transition between heights of our terrain, but in our application we may need to scale out of the 0 to 255 range in order to match the scale of our 3D world. For example, if our unit of measure in the 3D world is feet, then 0 to 255 does not give us enough values to represent anything interesting. For this reason, when we load the data into our applications we allocate an integer (or float) for each height element. This allows us to scale well outside the 0 to 255 range to match any scale necessary.

One of the possible graphical representations of a heightmap is a grayscale map, where darker values reflect portions of the terrain with low altitudes and whiter values reflect portions of the terrain with higher altitudes. Figure 13.2 shows a grayscale map.

Part III

Figure 13.2: A heightmap as a grayscale

13.1.1 **Creating a Heightmap**

Heightmaps can be generated either procedurally or in an image editor such as Adobe Photoshop. Using an image editor is probably the easiest way to go, and it allows you to create the terrain interactively and visually as you want it. In addition, you can take advantage of your image editor features, such as filters, to create interesting heightmaps. Figure 13.3 shows a pyramid-type heightmap created in Adobe Photoshop using the editing tools. Note that we specify a grayscale map when creating the image.

Figure 13.3: A grayscale image created in Adobe Photoshop

Once you have finished drawing your heightmap, you need to save it as an 8-bit RAW file. RAW files simply contain the bytes of the image one after another. This makes it very easy to read the image into our applications. Your software may ask you to save the RAW file with a header. Specify no header.

Note: You do not have to use the RAW format to store your height information; you can use any format that meets your needs. The RAW format is just one example of a format that we can use. We decided to use the RAW format because many popular image editors can export to that format and it is very easy to read the data in a RAW file into the application. The samples in this chapter use 8-bit RAW files.

13.1.2 Loading a RAW File

Since a RAW file is nothing more than a contiguous block of bytes, we can easily read in the block with this next method. Note that the variable `_heightmap` is a member of the `Terrain` class and defined as:

```cpp
std::vector<int> _heightmap;

bool Terrain::readRawFile(std::string fileName)
{
    // A height for each vertex
    std::vector<BYTE> in( _numVertices );

    std::ifstream inFile(fileName.c_str(), std::ios_base::binary);

    if( inFile == 0 )
        return false;

    inFile.read(
        (char*)&in[0], // buffer
        in.size());// number of bytes to read into buffer

    inFile.close();

    // copy BYTE vector to int vector
    _heightmap.resize( _numVertices );
    for(int i = 0; i < in.size(); i++)
        _heightmap[i] = in[i];

    return true;
}
```

Observe that we copy the vector of bytes to a vector of integers; we do this so that we can scale the height values outside the [0, 255] interval.

The only restriction of this method is that the RAW file being read in must have at least as many bytes as there are vertices in the terrain. Therefore, if you are reading in a 256x256 RAW file, you must construct the terrain with, at most, 256x256 vertices.

13.1.3 Accessing and Modifying the Heightmap

The `Terrain` class provides the following two methods to access and modify an entry in the heightmap:

```cpp
int Terrain::getHeightmapEntry(int row, int col)
{
    return _heightmap[row * _numVertsPerRow + col];
```

```
}

void Terrain::setHeightmapEntry(int row, int col, int value)
{
        _heightmap[row * _numVertsPerRow + col] = value;
}
```

These methods allow us to refer to an entry by row and column and hide the way we must index a linear array when using it to describe a matrix.

13.2 Generating the Terrain Geometry

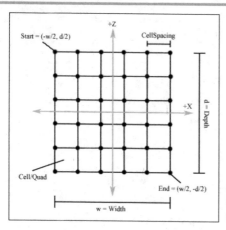

Figure 13.4: Properties of the triangle grid labeled. The dots along the grid lines are vertices.

Figure 13.4 shows some properties of a terrain, vocabulary, and special points that we refer to. We define the size of our terrain by specifying the number of vertices per row, the number of vertices per column, and the cell spacing. We pass these values into the constructor of the `Terrain` class. In addition, we also pass the device associated with the terrain, a string identifying the filename that the heightmap data is contained in, and a height scale value that is used to scale the heightmap elements.

```
class Terrain
{
public:
        Terrain(
                IDirect3DDevice9* device,
                std::string heightmapFileName,
                int numVertsPerRow,
                int numVertsPerCol,
                int cellSpacing,    // space between cells
                float heightScale); // value to scale heights by

        ... methods snipped
```

```
private:
        ...device/vertex buffer etc snipped

        int _numVertsPerRow;
        int _numVertsPerCol;
        int _cellSpacing;

        int _numCellsPerRow;
        int _numCellsPerCol;
        int _width;
        int _depth;
        int _numVertices;
        int _numTriangles;

        float _heightScale;
};
```

See the source code in the companion files for the complete class definition of `Terrain`; it is too big to include here.

From the values passed into the constructor, we can compute these other variables of the terrain as:

```
_numCellsPerRow = _numVertsPerRow - 1;
_numCellsPerCol = _numVertsPerCol - 1;
_width          = _numCellsPerRow * _cellSpacing;
_depth          = _numCellsPerCol * _cellSpacing;
_numVertices    = _numVertsPerRow * _numVertsPerCol;
_numTriangles   = _numCellsPerRow * _numCellsPerCol * 2;
```

Also, the vertex structure of our terrain is defined as:

```
struct TerrainVertex
{
        TerrainVertex(){}
        TerrainVertex(float x, float y, float z, float u, float v)
        {
                _x = x; _y = y; _z = z; _u = u; _v = v;
        }
        float _x, _y, _z;
        float _u, _v;

        static const DWORD FVF;
};
const DWORD Terrain::TerrainVertex::FVF = D3DFVF_XYZ | D3DFVF_TEX1;
```

Note that `TerrainVertex` is a nested class inside the `Terrain` class. This was done because `TerrainVertex` is not needed outside the `Terrain` class.

13.2.1 Computing the Vertices

Refer to Figure 13.4 during this discussion. To compute the vertices of our triangle grid, we are simply going to begin generating vertices at *start* and then go row by row generating vertices until we reach *end*, leaving a gap defined by the *cell spacing* between the vertices. This will give us our x- and z-coordinate, but what about the y-coordinate? The y-coordinate is easily obtained by finding the corresponding entry in the loaded heightmap data structure.

> **Note:** This implementation uses one large vertex buffer to hold all of the vertices for the entire terrain. This can be problematic due to hardware limitations. For example, there is a maximum primitive count limit and maximum vertex index limit that is set for the 3D device. Check the `MaxPrimitiveCount` and `MaxVertexIndex` members of the `D3DCAPS9` structure to see what your particular device's limits are. Section 13.7 discusses a solution to the problems of using one vertex buffer.

To compute the texture coordinates, consider Figure 13.5, which gives us a simple scenario allowing us to see that the (u, v) texture coordinate that corresponds to the terrain vertex at (i, j) is given by:

$u = j \cdot uCoordIncrementSize$

$v = i \cdot vCoordIncrementSize$

And where:

$$uCoordIncrementSize = \frac{1}{numCellCols}$$

$$vCoordIncrementSize = \frac{1}{numCellRows}$$

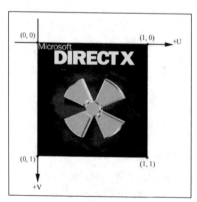

Figure 13.5: The correspondence between the terrain vertices and the texture vertices

Finally, the code to generate the vertices:

```
bool Terrain::computeVertices()
{
    HRESULT hr = 0;

    hr = _device->CreateVertexBuffer(
        _numVertices * sizeof(TerrainVertex),
```

```
        D3DUSAGE_WRITEONLY,
        TerrainVertex::FVF,
        D3DPOOL_MANAGED,
        &_vb,
        0);

    if(FAILED(hr))
        return false;

    // coordinates to start generating vertices at
    int startX = -_width / 2;
    int startZ =  _depth / 2;

    // coordinates to end generating vertices at
    int endX =  _width / 2;
    int endZ = -_depth / 2;

    // compute the increment size of the texture coordinates
    // from one vertex to the next.
    float uCoordIncrementSize = 1.0f / (float)_numCellsPerRow;
    float vCoordIncrementSize = 1.0f / (float)_numCellsPerCol;

    TerrainVertex* v = 0;
    _vb->Lock(0, 0, (void**)&v, 0);

    int i = 0;
    for(int z = startZ; z >= endZ; z -= _cellSpacing)
    {
        int j = 0;
        for(int x = startX; x <= endX; x += _cellSpacing)
        {
            // compute the correct index into the vertex buffer
            // and heightmap based on where we are in the nested
            // loop.
            int index = i * _numVertsPerRow + j;

            v[index] = TerrainVertex(
                (float)x,
                (float)_heightmap[index],
                (float)z,
                (float)j * uCoordIncrementSize,
                (float)i * vCoordIncrementSize);

            j++; // next column
        }
        i++; // next row
    }

    _vb->Unlock();

    return true;
}
```

13.2.2 **Computing the Indices—Defining the Triangles**

To compute the indices of the triangle grid, we simply iterate through each quad, starting in the upper left and ending in the lower right of Figure 13.4, and compute the two triangles that make up that quad.

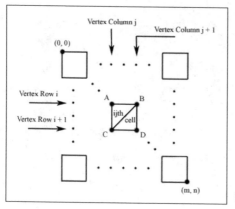

Figure 13.6: A quad's vertices

The trick is to come up with the general formulas to compute the two triangles of the ij^{th} quad. Using Figure 13.6 to develop our general formulas, we find that for quad (i, j):

$$\Delta ABC = \left\{ i \cdot numVertsPerRow + j \quad i \cdot numVertsPerRow + j + 1 \quad (i+1) \cdot numVertsPerRow + j \right\}$$

$$\Delta CBD = \left\{ (i+1) \cdot numVertsPerRow + j \quad i \cdot numVertsPerRow + j + 1 \quad (i+1) \cdot numVertsPerRow + j + 1 \right\}$$

The code to generate the indices:

```
bool Terrain::computeIndices()
{
    HRESULT hr = 0;

    hr = _device->CreateIndexBuffer(
        _numTriangles * 3 * sizeof(WORD), // 3 indices per triangle
        D3DUSAGE_WRITEONLY,
        D3DFMT_INDEX16,
        D3DPOOL_MANAGED,
        &_ib,
        0);

    if (FAILED(hr))
        return false;

    WORD* indices = 0;
    _ib->Lock(0, 0, (void**)&indices, 0);

    // index to start of a group of 6 indices that describe the
    // two triangles that make up a quad
```

```
    int baseIndex = 0;

    // loop through and compute the triangles of each quad
    for(int i = 0; i < _numCellsPerCol; i++)
    {
        for(int j = 0; j < _numCellsPerRow; j++)
        {
            indices[baseIndex]     =   i   * _numVertsPerRow + j;
            indices[baseIndex + 1] =   i   * _numVertsPerRow +
                                                       j + 1;
            indices[baseIndex + 2] = (i+1) * _numVertsPerRow + j;

            indices[baseIndex + 3] = (i+1) * _numVertsPerRow + j;
            indices[baseIndex + 4] =   i   * _numVertsPerRow +
                                                       j + 1;
            indices[baseIndex + 5] = (i+1) * _numVertsPerRow +
                                                       j + 1;

            // next quad
            baseIndex += 6;
        }
    }

    _ib->Unlock();

    return true;
}
```

13.3 Texturing

The `Terrain` class provides two ways to texture the terrain. The obvious way is to simply load a previously made texture file and use that. The following method implemented by the `Terrain` class loads a texture from the file into the `_tex` data member, which is a pointer to an `IDirect3DTexture9` interface. Internally, the `Terrain::draw` method sets `_tex` before rendering the terrain.

```
bool  loadTexture(std::string fileName);
```

At this point in the book its implementation should be straightforward to you. It is:

```
bool Terrain::loadTexture(std::string fileName)
{
    HRESULT hr = 0;

    hr = D3DXCreateTextureFromFile(
        _device,
        fileName.c_str(),
        &_tex);

    if(FAILED(hr))
        return false;
```

Part III

```
        return true;
}
```

13.3.1 A Procedural Approach

An alternative way to texture the terrain is to compute the texture procedurally; that is, we create an "empty" texture and compute the color of each texel in code based on some defined parameter(s). In our example, the parameter will be the height of the terrain.

We generate the texture procedurally in the `Terrain::genTexture` method. It first creates an empty texture using the `D3DXCreateTexture` method. Then we lock the top level (remember a texture has mipmaps and can have multiple levels). From there we iterate through each texel and color it. We color the texel based on the approximate height of the quad to which it corresponds. The idea is to have lower altitudes of the terrain colored a sandy beach color, medium altitudes colored as grassy hills, and the high altitudes colored as snowy mountains. We define the approximate height of the quad as the height of the upper-left vertex of the quad.

Once we have a color for each texel, we want to darken or brighten each texel based on the angle at which sunlight (modeled by a directional light) strikes the cell to which the texel corresponds. This is done in the `Terrain::lightTerrain` method, whose implementation is covered in the next section.

The `Terrain::genTexture` method concludes by computing the texels of the lower mipmap levels. This is done using the `D3DXFilterTexture` function. The code to generate the texture:

```
bool Terrain::genTexture(D3DXVECTOR3* directionToLight)
{
    // Method fills the top surface of a texture procedurally. Then
    // lights the top surface. Finally, it fills the other mipmap
    // surfaces based on the top surface data using
    // D3DXFilterTexture.

    HRESULT hr = 0;

    // texel for each quad cell
    int texWidth  = _numCellsPerRow;
    int texHeight = _numCellsPerCol;

    // create an empty texture
    hr = D3DXCreateTexture(
        _device,
        texWidth, texHeight,    // dimensions
        0,                      // create a complete mipmap chain
        0,                      // usage - none
        D3DFMT_X8R8G8B8,        // 32-bit XRGB format
        D3DPOOL_MANAGED,        // memory pool
```

```
                &_tex);

if(FAILED(hr))
      return false;

D3DSURFACE_DESC textureDesc;
_tex->GetLevelDesc(0 /*level*/, &textureDesc);

// make sure we got the requested format because our code
// that fills the texture is hard coded to a 32-bit pixel depth.
if( textureDesc.Format != D3DFMT_X8R8G8B8 )
      return false;

D3DLOCKED_RECT lockedRect;
_tex->LockRect(0/*lock top surface*/, &lockedRect,
      0 /* lock entire tex*/, 0/*flags*/);

// fill the texture
DWORD* imageData = (DWORD*)lockedRect.pBits;
for(int i = 0; i < texHeight; i++)
{
      for(int j = 0; j < texWidth; j++)
      {
      D3DXCOLOR c;

      // get height of upper-left vertex of quad.
      float height = (float)getHeightmapEntry(i, j)/_heightScale;

      // set the color of the texel based on the height
      // of the quad it corresponds to.
      if( (height) < 42.5f )        c = d3d::BEACH_SAND;
      else if( (height) < 85.0f )   c = d3d::LIGHT_YELLOW_GREEN;
      else if( (height) < 127.5f )  c = d3d::PUREGREEN;
      else if( (height) < 170.0f )  c = d3d::DARK_YELLOW_GREEN;
      else if( (height) < 212.5f )  c = d3d::DARKBROWN;
      else                          c = d3d::WHITE;

      // fill locked data, note we divide the pitch by four
      // because the pitch is given in bytes and there are
      // 4 bytes per DWORD.
      imageData[i * lockedRect.Pitch / 4 + j] = (D3DCOLOR)c;
      }
}

_tex->UnlockRect(0);

// light the terrain
if(!lightTerrain(directionToLight))
{
      ::MessageBox(0, "lightTerrain() - FAILED", 0, 0);
      return false;
}

// fill mipmaps
hr = D3DXFilterTexture(
      _tex,// texture to fill mipmap levels
      0,   // default palette
```

```
     0,   // use top level as source for lower levels
     D3DX_DEFAULT); // default filter

if(FAILED(hr))
{
     ::MessageBox(0, "D3DXFilterTexture() - FAILED", 0, 0);
     return false;
}

return true;
}
```

Note that the color constant variables BEACH_SAND, etc., are defined in
d3dUtility.h.

13.4 **Lighting**

The `Terrain::genTexture` method makes a call to `Terrain::`
`lightTerrain` that, as the name implies, lights the terrain to enhance
the realism. Since we already computed the colors of the terrain texture, we only need to compute a shade factor that brightens or darkens
areas of the terrain with respect to a defined light source. In this section we examine such a technique. You may wonder why we are
lighting the terrain and not letting Direct3D do it. There are three benefits to doing the calculations ourselves:

- We save memory by not having to store vertex normals.

- Since terrains are static and we won't be moving the light either,
  we can precalculate the lighting, thus eliminating the processing
  time it would take for Direct3D to light the terrain in real time.

- We get some math practice, familiarity with a basic lighting concept, and practice using Direct3D functions.

13.4.1 **Overview**

The lighting technique we use to compute the shade of the terrain is
one of the most basic and is commonly known as *diffuse lighting*. We
define a parallel light source that we described by specifying the direction to the light, which is in the opposite direction of the light rays
being emitted by the parallel light source. So, for example, if we wanted
the light rays to fall straight down from the sky in the direction
lightRaysDirection = (0, –1, 0), then the direction to the parallel light is
given as the opposite direction: *directionToLight* = (0, 1, 0). Note that
we make the light vector a unit vector.

Note: Although specifying the direction the light rays are emitted from a light source is perhaps more intuitive, specifying the direction to the light is better suited for the diffuse lighting calculation.

Then for each quad in the terrain, we calculate the angle between the light vector $\hat{L}$ and the quad's surface normal $\hat{N}$.

In Figure 13.7 we see that as angles get larger, the quad faces more and more away from the light source, thus receiving less light. On the other hand, as angles get smaller, the quad faces more and more toward the light source, thus receiving more light. Also, notice that once the angle between the light vector and the normal is greater than 90 degrees, the surface receives no light.

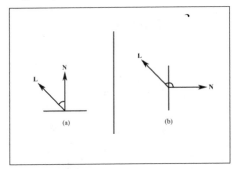

Figure 13.7: Angles between the light vector $\hat{L}$ and the surface normal $\hat{N}$ determine how much light the surface is receiving. In (a) we see an angle less than 90 degrees. In (b) we see an angle greater than 90 degrees. Observe that the surface receives zero light because the light rays (emitting in the opposite direction of $\hat{L}$) strike the back of the surface.

Using the angular relationships between the light vector and the surface normal, we can construct a shading scalar in the interval [0, 1] that determines how much light a surface receives. Using this shading scalar, a large angle is represented by a scalar close to zero. When a color is multiplied by this shading scalar that is close to zero, it is darkened, which is the desired result. On the other hand, a small angle is represented by a scalar close to one. When a color is multiplied by a shading scalar close to one, the color is kept close to its original brightness, which again is the desired result.

13.4.2 Computing the Shade of a Quad

The direction to the light source is given as a normalized vector that we call $\hat{L}$ in this discussion. In order to calculate the angle between $\hat{L}$ and the quad's normal vector $\hat{N}$, we first need to find $\hat{N}$. This is a trivial application of the cross product. But first we must find two non-zero and non-parallel vectors that are coplanar with the quad. There are two such vectors, **u** and **v**, in Figure 13.8:

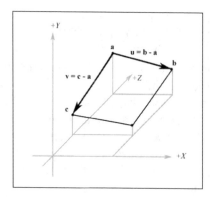

Figure 13.8: Computing two vectors coplanar with a quad

$$u = \begin{pmatrix} cellSpacing & b_y - a_y & 0 \end{pmatrix}$$

$$v = \begin{pmatrix} 0 & c_y - a_y & -cellSpacing \end{pmatrix}$$

With **u** and **v**, the quad's normal **N** is found by $\mathbf{N} = \mathbf{u} \times \mathbf{v}$. Of course we want **N** to be normalized:

$$\hat{\mathbf{N}} = \frac{\mathbf{N}}{\|\mathbf{N}\|}$$

To find the angle between $\hat{\mathbf{L}}$ and $\hat{\mathbf{N}}$, recall that the dot product of two unit vectors in 3-space is the cosine of the angle between the two vectors:

$$\hat{\mathbf{L}} \cdot \hat{\mathbf{N}} = s$$

The scalar s is in the interval $[-1, 1]$. Because values for s in $[-1, 0)$ correspond to angles between $\hat{\mathbf{L}}$ and $\hat{\mathbf{N}}$ greater than 90 degrees, which in Figure 13.7 receive no light, we clamp s to 0 if it's in $[-1, 0)$:

```
float cosine = D3DXVec3Dot(&n, directionToLight);

if(cosine < 0.0f)
        cosine = 0.0f;
```

Now, with s clamped for angles greater than 90 degrees, s becomes our shading scalar from $[0, 1]$ exactly because as the angle between $\hat{\mathbf{L}}$ and $\hat{\mathbf{N}}$ increases from 0 degrees to 90 degrees, s goes from 1 to 0. This gives us the desired functionality described in section 13.4.1.

The shade factor for a particular quad is computed by the `Terrain::computeShade` method. It takes as parameters the row and column identifying the quad and the direction of our parallel light source.

```
float Terrain::computeShade(int cellRow, int cellCol,
                            D3DXVECTOR3* directionToLight)
{
    // get heights of three vertices on the quad
    float heightA = getHeightmapEntry(cellRow,   cellCol);
    float heightB = getHeightmapEntry(cellRow,   cellCol+1);
    float heightC = getHeightmapEntry(cellRow+1, cellCol);

    // build two vectors on the quad
    D3DXVECTOR3 u(_cellSpacing, heightB - heightA, 0.0f);
    D3DXVECTOR3 v(0.0f, heightC - heightA, -_cellSpacing);

    // find the normal by taking the cross product of two
    // vectors on the quad.
    D3DXVECTOR3 n;
    D3DXVec3Cross(&n, &u, &v);
    D3DXVec3Normalize(&n, &n);

    float cosine = D3DXVec3Dot(&n, directionToLight);

    if(cosine < 0.0f)
        cosine = 0.0f;

    return cosine;
}
```

13.4.3 Shading the Terrain

Once we know how to shade a particular quad, we can shade all the
quads in the terrain. We simply iterate through each quad, compute the
shade value of that quad, and then scale the quad's corresponding texel
color by that shade. This darkens quads that receive less light. The following snippet of code shows the important part of the `Terrain::`
`lightTerrain` method:

```
DWORD* imageData = (DWORD*)lockedRect.pBits;
for(int i = 0; i < textureDesc.Height; i++)
{
    for(int j = 0; j < textureDesc.Width; j++)
    {
        int index = i * lockedRect.Pitch / 4 + j;

        // get current color of cell
        D3DXCOLOR c( imageData[index] );

        // shade current cell
        c *= computeShade(i, j, lightDirection);;

        // save shaded color
        imageData[index] = (D3DCOLOR)c;
    }
}
```

Part III

13.5 "Walking" on the Terrain

After we have constructed a terrain, we would like the ability to move the camera so that it simulates us walking on the terrain. That is, we need to adjust the camera's height (y-coordinate) depending on the part of the terrain that we are standing on. In order to do this we first need to find the cell we are in given the x- and z-coordinates of the camera's position. The `Terrain::getHeight` function does this; it takes the camera's x- and z-coordinates as parameters and returns the height the camera needs to be set to in order for it to be on the terrain. Let's now walk through its implementation.

```
float Terrain::getHeight(float x, float z)
{
    // Translate on xz-plane by the transformation that takes
    // the terrain START point to the origin.
    x = ((float)_width / 2.0f) + x;
    z = ((float)_depth / 2.0f) - z;

    // Scale down by the transformation that makes the
    // cellspacing equal to one. This is given by
    // 1 / cellspacing since cellspacing * 1 / cellspacing = 1.
    x /= (float)_cellSpacing;
    z /= (float)_cellSpacing;
```

We first translate by the transformation that takes the *start* point of the terrain to the origin. Next, we scale by the inverse of the cell spacing variable; this scaling sets the cell spacing to 1. Then we switch to a new frame of reference where the positive z-axis points "down." Of course, there is no code that changes the frame of reference, but it is now understood that +z goes down. Figure 13.9 shows these steps graphically.

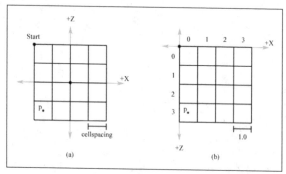

Figure 13.9: The terrain grid before and after translating start to the origin, making the cell spacing equal to 1 and flipping the z-axis

We see that our changed coordinate system matches the ordering of a matrix. That is, the upper-left corner is at the origin, the column count increases in the right direction, and the row count increases in the down direction. Thus, by Figure 13.9 and knowing the cell spacing is equal to 1, we can immediately see that the row and column of the cell we are in is given by:

```
float col = ::floorf(x);
float row = ::floorf(z);
```

In other words, column equals the integer part of x, and row equals the integer part of z. Also recall that the *floor(t)* function gives the greatest integer $\leq t$.

Now that we know the cell we are in, we can grab the heights of its four vertices:

```
//  A   B
//  *—*
//  | / |
//  *—*
//  C   D

float A = getHeightmapEntry(row,   col);
float B = getHeightmapEntry(row,   col+1);
float C = getHeightmapEntry(row+1, col);
float D = getHeightmapEntry(row+1, col+1);
```

At this point, we know the cell we are in and we know the heights of the four vertices of that cell. Now we need to find the height (y-coordinate) of the cell at the particular x- and z-coordinates at which the camera is located. This is a little tricky since the cell can be slanted in a couple of directions; see Figure 13.10.

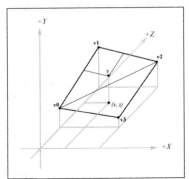

Figure 13.10: The height y-coordinate of the cell at the particular x- and z-coordinates of the camera's position

In order to find the height, we need to know which triangle of the cell we are in. Recall that our cells are rendered as two triangles. To find the triangle we are in, we are going to take the cell we are in and translate it so that its upper-left vertex is at the origin.

Since `col` and `row` describe the position of the upper-left vertex of the cell we are in, we must translate by `-col` on the x-axis and `-row` on the z-axis. Translating our x- and z-coordinates gives:

Part III

```
float dx = x - col;
float dz = z - row;
```

Figure 13.11 shows our cell after this translation.

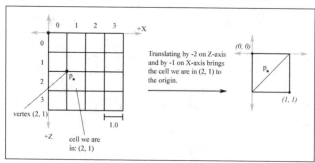

Figure 13.11: The cell we are in before and after we translate by the translation that takes the cell's upper-left vertex to the origin

Then, if $dz < 1.0 - dx$ we are in the "upper" triangle $\Delta v0v1v2$. Otherwise, we are in the "lower" triangle $\Delta v0v2v3$ (see Figure 13.10).

Now we explain how to find the height if we are in the "upper" triangle. The process is similar for the "lower" triangle, and of course the code for both follows shortly. To find the height if we are in the "upper" triangle, we construct two vectors, $\mathbf{u} = (cellSpacing,\ B - A,\ 0)$ and $\mathbf{v} = (0,\ C - A,\ -cellSpacing)$, on the sides of the triangle and originating at the terminal point of the vector $\mathbf{q} = (q_x,\ A,\ q_z)$ as Figure 13.12.a shows. Then we linearly interpolate along $\mathbf{u}$ by dx, and we linearly interpolate along $\mathbf{v}$ by dz. Figure 13.12.b illustrates these interpolations. The y-coordinate of the vector $(\mathbf{q} + dx\mathbf{u} + dz\mathbf{v})$ gives the height based on the given x- and z-coordinates; recall the geometric interpretation of vector addition to see this.

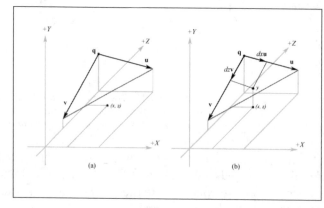

Figure 13.12: (a) Computing two vectors on the adjacent and opposite sides of the triangle. (b) The height is found by linearly interpolating down $\mathbf{u}$ by dx and then by linearly interpolating down $\mathbf{v}$ by dz.

Note that since we are only concerned about the interpolated height value, we can just interpolate the y-components and ignore the other components. Thus, the height is obtained by the sum $A + dx u_y + dz v_y$.

Thus, the conclusion of the `Terrian::getHeight` code is:

```
    if(dz < 1.0f - dx)  // upper triangle ABC
    {
        float uy = B - A;  // A->B
        float vy = C - A;  // A->C

        height = A + d3d::Lerp(0.0f, uy, dx) +
                     d3d::Lerp(0.0f, vy, dz);
    }
    else // lower triangle DCB
    {
        float uy = C - D;  // D->C
        float vy = B - D;  // D->B

        height = D + d3d::Lerp(0.0f, uy, 1.0f - dx) +
                     d3d::Lerp(0.0f, vy, 1.0f - dz);
    }    return height;
}
```

The `Lerp` function is basic linear interpolation along a 1D line and is implemented as:

```
float d3d::Lerp(float a, float b, float t)
{
    return a - (a*t) + (b*t);
}
```

13.6 Sample Application: Terrain

The sample for this chapter creates a terrain given a RAW file containing the heightmap data, textures the terrain, and lights it. In addition, we can walk on the terrain using the arrow keys. Note that in the following functions, non-relevant code has been omitted; a place where code has been omitted is denoted by ellipses (...). Also, depending on your hardware, the sample may run slow; try using a smaller terrain.

First we add the following global variables representing our terrain, camera, and frames per second counter:

```
Terrain* TheTerrain = 0;
Camera   TheCamera(Camera::LANDOBJECT);

FPSCounter* FPS = 0;
```

Then the framework functions:

```
bool Setup()
{
    D3DXVECTOR3 lightDirection(0.0f, -1.0f, 0.0f);
    TheTerrain = new Terrain(Device, "coastMountain256.raw",
                         256, 256, 10, 1.0f);
    TheTerrain->genTexture();
    TheTerrain->lightTerrain(&directionToLight);
```

Part III

```
      ...

      return true;
}

void Cleanup()
{
      d3d::Delete<Terrain*>(TheTerrain);
      d3d::Delete<FPSCounter*>(FPS);
}

bool Display(float timeDelta)
{
      if( Device )
      {
      //
          // Update the scene:
          //
          ...[snipped input checking]

          // Walking on the terrain: Adjust camera's height so we
          // are standing 5 units above the cell point we are
          // standing on.
          D3DXVECTOR3 pos;
          TheCamera.getPosition(&pos);

          float height = TheTerrain->getHeight( pos.x, pos.z );

          pos.y = height + 5.0f;

          TheCamera.setPosition(&pos);

          D3DXMATRIX V;
          TheCamera.getViewMatrix(&V);
          Device->SetTransform(D3DTS_VIEW, &V);

          //
          // Draw the scene:
          //
          Device->Clear(0, 0, D3DCLEAR_TARGET | D3DCLEAR_ZBUFFER,
                        0xff000000, 1.0f, 0);
          Device->BeginScene();

          D3DXMATRIX I;
          D3DXMatrixIdentity(&I);

          if( TheTerrain )
              TheTerrain->draw(&I, false);

          if( FPS )
              FPS->render(0xffffffff, timeDelta);

          Device->EndScene();
          Device->Present(0, 0, 0, 0);
      }
      return true;
}
```

13.7 **Some Improvements**

The implementation of the `Terrain` class loaded all the vertex data into one huge vertex buffer. It can be advantageous in both speed and scalability to divide the geometry of the terrain among multiple vertex buffers. This brings us to the question: "What size vertex buffer is best?" The answer depends on the target hardware. Therefore, you must experiment!

Because dividing up the terrain geometry into many smaller vertex buffers is largely an exercise in indexing into matrix-like data structures and data management and doesn't introduce any new concepts, we omit a detailed discussion of it. Briefly, you basically break your terrain into a matrix of what we will call "blocks." Each block covers a rectangular area of the terrain. In addition, each block contains the geometry (in its own vertex/index buffers) of the terrain that falls inside the block's area. Then each block is responsible for drawing its portion of the terrain that it contains.

Alternatively, you can load the terrain geometry into one big `ID3DXMesh` interface. Then use the D3DX function `D3DXSplitMesh` to divide the terrain mesh into multiple smaller ones. `D3DXSplitMesh` is prototyped as:

```
void D3DXSplitMesh(
    const LPD3DXMESH pMeshIn,
    const DWORD *pAdjacencyIn,
    const DWORD MaxSize,
    const DWORD Options,
    DWORD *pMeshesOut,
    LPD3DXBUFFER *ppMeshArrayOut,
    LPD3DXBUFFER *ppAdjacencyArrayOut,
    LPD3DXBUFFER *ppFaceRemapArrayOut,
    LPD3DXBUFFER *ppVertRemapArrayOut
);
```

This function takes an input source mesh and splits it into multiple smaller meshes. The `pMeshIn` parameter is a pointer to the mesh that we want to divide up, and `pAdjacencyIn` is a pointer to its adjacency array. The `MaxSize` parameter is used to specify the maximum vertex count allowed for the resulting meshes. The `Options` flag is used to specify the creation options/flags of the resulting meshes. The `pMeshesOut` parameter returns the number of created meshes being returned in the `ppMeshArrayOut` array buffer. The last three parameters are optional (specify null to ignore them) and return arrays of adjacency information, face remap info, and vertex remap info for each of the created meshes.

Part III

13.8 Summary

- We can model terrains using triangle grids with different height values that create mountains and valleys, simulating a terrain.

- A heightmap is the data set that contains the height values for the vertices of the terrain.

- We can texture the terrain using an image on disk as the texture or by generating a texture procedurally.

- We light the terrain by computing a shade factor for each quad that specifies how bright/dark it should be. The shade factor is determined by the angle at which the light strikes the quad.

- To have the camera "walk" over the terrain, we need to find the triangle that we are standing on. Then we compute two vectors on the adjacent and opposite sides of the triangle. The height is then found by linearly interpolating on each of these vectors using the x- and z-coordinates in a normalized cell with an upper-left vertex at the origin as parameters.

Chapter 14

Particle Systems

Many natural phenomena consist of many small particles that all behave in a similar manner (for example, flakes of snow falling, sparks from a firework, and the "bullets" a futuristic space gun emits). Particle systems are used to model such phenomena.

Objectives

- To learn the attributes that we give to a particle and how we describe a particle in Direct3D
- To design a flexible particle system base class that includes attributes and methods general to all particle systems
- To model three concrete particle systems, namely snow, an explosion, and a particle gun

14.1 Particles and Point Sprites

A particle is a very small object that is usually modeled as a point mathematically. It follows then that a point primitive (`D3DPT_POINTLIST` of `D3DPRIMITIVETYPE`) would be a good candidate to display particles. However, point primitives are rasterized as a single pixel. This does not give us much flexibility, as we would like to have particles of various sizes and even map entire textures to these particles. Before Direct3D 8.0, the way to get around the limitations of point primitives was to not use them at all. Instead, programmers would use a *billboard* to display a particle. A billboard is a quad whose world matrix orients it so that it always faces the camera.

Direct3D 8.0 introduced a special point primitive called a *point sprite* that is most applicable to particle systems. Unlike ordinary point primitives, point sprites can have textures mapped to them and can change size. Unlike billboards, we can describe a point sprite by a single point; this saves memory and processing time because we only have to store and process one vertex rather than the four needed to store a billboard (quad).

14.1.1 **Structure Format**

We use the following vertex structure to describe the location and color of our particles:

```
struct Particle
{
    D3DXVECTOR3 _position;
    D3DCOLOR    _color;
    static const DWORD FVF;
};
const DWORD Particle::FVF = D3DFVF_XYZ | D3DFVF_DIFFUSE;
```

The structure simply stores the position of the particle and its color. Depending on your application needs, you could also store a set of texture coordinates. We discuss texturing the point sprites in the next section.

It is possible to add a floating-point variable to the `Particle` structure to specify the size of the particle. We must add the `D3DFVF_PSIZE` flag to our flexible vertex format to reflect this addition. Having each particle maintain its own size is useful because it allows us to specify and change the size of a particle on an individual basis. However, most graphics cards do not support controlling the size of the particle this way so we avoid it. (Check the `D3DFVFCAPS_PSIZE` bit in the `FVFCaps` member of the `D3DCAPS9` structure to verify.) Instead, we control the particle size with render states, as you soon see. An example of a vertex structure with a size member:

```
struct Particle
{
    D3DXVECTOR3 _position;
    D3DCOLOR    _color;
    float       _size;
    static const DWORD FVF;
};
const DWORD Particle::FVF = D3DFVF_XYZ | D3DFVF_DIFFUSE |
  D3DFVF_PSIZE;
```

We note that it is possible to obtain per-particle size manipulation through a vertex shader, even if `D3DFVFCAPS_PSIZE` is not supported. Vertex shaders are covered in Part IV of this text.

14.1.2 **Point Sprite Render States**

The behavior of point sprites is largely controlled through render states. Let's review these render states now.

- `D3DRS_POINTSPRITEENABLE`—A Boolean value. The default value is false.

☐ True specifies that the entire currently set texture should be mapped to the point sprite.

☐ False specifies that the texel specified by the texture coordinate of the point sprite (if it has a texture coordinate in the vertex structure) should be used to texture the point sprite.

```
_device->SetRenderState(D3DRS_POINTSPRITEENABLE, true);
```

■ D3DRS_POINTSCALEENABLE—A Boolean value. The default value is false.

☐ True specifies that the point size will be interpreted as view space units. View space units simply refer to 3D points in camera space. The point sprite's size will then be scaled accordingly, depending on how far away it is, like other objects so that particles farther away will appear smaller than particles close to the camera.

☐ False specifies that the point size will be interpreted as screen space units. Screen space units are pixel units on the screen. So if you specify false and, for example, set the size of the point sprite to 3, the point sprite will be 3x3 pixels in area on the screen.

```
_device->SetRenderState(D3DRS_POINTSCALEENABLE, true);
```

■ D3DRS_POINTSIZE—Used to specify the size of the point sprites. This value is either interpreted as the point sprite's size in view space or in screen space, depending on how the D3DRS_POINT-SCALEENABLE state is set. The following code snippet sets the point size to 2.5 units:

```
_device->SetRenderState( D3DRS_POINTSIZE, d3d::FtoDw(2.5f) );
```

The function d3d::FtoDw is a function that we have added to the d3dUtility.h/cpp files that casts a float to a DWORD. We must do this because the general call to IDirect3DDevice9::SetRenderState expects a DWORD value and not a float.

```
DWORD d3d::FtoDw(float f)
{
    return *((DWORD*)&f);
}
```

■ D3DRS_POINTSIZE_MIN—Specifies the minimum size that a point sprite can be. Here is an example of setting the minimum to 0.2:

```
_device->SetRenderState(D3DRS_POINTSIZE_MIN, d3d::FtoDw(0.2f));
```

Part III

- D3DRS_POINTSIZE_MAX—Specifies the maximum size that a point sprite can be. Here is an example of setting the maximum to 5.0:

```
_device->SetRenderState(D3DRS_POINTSIZE_MAX, d3d::FtoDw(5.0f));
```

- D3DRS_POINTSCALE_A, D3DRS_POINTSCALE_B, D3DRS_POINTSCALE_C—These three constants control how a point sprite's size changes with distance—the distance being the distance from the point sprite to the camera.

Direct3D uses the following formula to calculate the final size of a point sprite based on distance and these constants:

$$FinalSize = ViewportHeight \cdot Size \cdot \sqrt{\frac{1}{A + B(D) + C(D^2)}}$$

where:

- *FinalSize*: The final size of the point sprite after the distance calculations
- *ViewportHeight*: The height of the viewport
- *Size*: Corresponds to the value specified by the D3DRS_POINTSIZE render state
- *A, B, C*: Correspond to the values specified by D3DRS_POINTSCALE_A, D3DRS_POINTSCALE_B, and D3DRS_POINTSCALE_C, respectively
- *D*: The distance of the point sprite in view space to the camera's position. Since the camera is positioned at the origin in view space, this value is $D = \sqrt{x^2 + y^2 + z^2}$, where (x, y, z) is the position of the point sprite in view space.

The following code sets the point sprite distance constants so that the point sprites will get smaller with distance:

```
_device->SetRenderState(D3DRS_POINTSCALE_A, d3d::FtoDw(0.0f));
_device->SetRenderState(D3DRS_POINTSCALE_B, d3d::FtoDw(0.0f));
_device->SetRenderState(D3DRS_POINTSCALE_C, d3d::FtoDw(1.0f));
```

14.1.3 Particles and Their Attributes

A particle consists of many more attributes than its position and color; for instance, a particle has a certain velocity. However, these additional attributes are not needed to render the particle. Therefore, we keep the data needed to render a particle and particle attributes in separate structures. When we are creating, destroying, and updating particles, we work with the attributes; then when we are ready to render, we copy the position and color over to the `Particle` structure.

The attributes of a particle are specific to the particular kind of particle system that we are modeling. However, we can generalize a bit and come up with common attributes. The following example structure contains some common particle attributes. Most systems won't need all of these, and some systems may need additional attributes not listed.

```
struct Attribute
{
    D3DXVECTOR3  _position;
    D3DXVECTOR3  _velocity;
    D3DXVECTOR3  _acceleration;
    float        _lifeTime;
    float        _age;
    D3DXCOLOR    _color;
    D3DXCOLOR    _colorFade;
    bool         _isAlive;
};
```

- `_position`—The position of the particle in world space
- `_velocity`—The velocity of the particle, which we usually measure in units per second
- `_acceleration`—The acceleration of the particle, which we usually measure in units per second
- `_lifeTime`—How long the particle can live before it dies. For instance, we might kill a laser beam particle after a certain period of time.
- `_age`—The current age of the particle
- `_color`—The color of the particle
- `_colorFade`—How the color of the particle fades over time
- `_isAlive`—True if the particle is alive, false if it has died

14.2 Particle System Components

A particle system is a collection of particles and is responsible for maintaining and displaying these particles. The particle system keeps track of global properties that affect all particles in the system, such as the size of the particles, the location that the particles originate from, the texture to apply to the particles, etc. Functionality-wise, the particle system is responsible for updating, displaying, killing, and creating particles.

Part III

Although different concrete particle systems have different behavior, we can generalize and find some basic properties that all particle systems share. We put these common properties into an abstract PSystem base class, which is the parent to all of our concrete particle systems. Let's review the PSystem class now:

```cpp
class PSystem
{
public:
    PSystem();
    virtual ~PSystem();

    virtual bool init(IDirect3DDevice9* device, char* texFileName);
    virtual void reset();
    virtual void resetParticle(Attribute* attribute) = 0;
    virtual void addParticle();
    virtual void update(float timeDelta) = 0;

    virtual void preRender();
    virtual void render();
    virtual void postRender();

    bool isEmpty();
    bool isDead();
protected:
    virtual void removeDeadParticles();

protected:
    IDirect3DDevice9*       _device;
    D3DXVECTOR3             _origin;
    d3d::BoundingBox        _boundingBox;
    float                   _emitRate;
    float                   _size;
    IDirect3DTexture9*      _tex;
    IDirect3DVertexBuffer9* _vb;
    std::list<Attribute>    _particles;
    int                     _maxParticles;

    DWORD _vbSize;
    DWORD _vbOffset;
    DWORD _vbBatchSize;
};
```

Selected data members:

- _origin—The origin of the system. This is where particles in the system originate.

- _boundingBox—The bounding box is used for systems in which we want to limit the volume where the particles can go. For example, suppose we want a snow system to only fall in the volume surrounding a high mountain peak; we would define the bounding box to cover this volume, and particles going outside this volume would be killed.

- ■ `_emitRate`—The rate at which new particles are added to the system. This is usually measured in particles per second.

- ■ `_size`—The size of all the particles in the system

- ■ `_particles`—A list of particle attributes in the system. We work with this list to create, destroy, and update particles. When we are ready to draw the particles, we copy a portion of the list nodes to the vertex buffer and draw the particles. Then we copy another batch and draw the particles, and we repeat this process until all the particles have been drawn. This is an oversimplification; we explain the drawing process in detail in section 14.2.1.

- ■ `_maxParticles`—The maximum number of particles that the system is allowed to have at a given time. For instance, if particles are being created faster than they are being destroyed, we end up with a huge amount of particles over time. This member helps us avoid that scenario.

- ■ `_vbSize`—The number of particles that our vertex buffer can hold at a given time. This value is independent of the number of particles in the actual particle system.

Note: The data members `_vbOffset` and `_vbBatchSize` are used to render the particle system. We defer a discussion of them until section 14.2.1.

Methods:

- ■ `PSystem`/`~PSystem`—The constructor initializes default values and the destructor releases device interfaces (vertex buffer, texture).

- ■ `init`—This method does Direct3D device-dependent initialization work, such as creating the vertex buffer to store the point sprites and creating the texture. The vertex buffer creation contains some flags that we have discussed but haven't used until now:

```
hr = device->CreateVertexBuffer(
    _vbSize * sizeof(Particle),
    D3DUSAGE_DYNAMIC | D3DUSAGE_POINTS | D3DUSAGE_WRITEONLY,
    Particle::FVF,
    D3DPOOL_DEFAULT,
    &_vb,
    0);
```

- ☐ Notice that we are using a dynamic vertex buffer. This is because we will need to update our particles every frame, which means we will need to access the vertex buffer's memory. Recall that accessing a static vertex buffer is unacceptably slow; we therefore use a dynamic vertex buffer.

Part III

☐ Observe that we use the `D3DUSAGE_POINTS` flag, which specifies that the vertex buffer will hold point sprites.

☐ Take note that the vertex buffer size is predefined by `_vbSize` and has nothing to do with the number of particles in the system. That is, `_vbSize` will rarely equal the number of particles in the system. This is because we render the particle system in batches and not all at once. We explain the rendering process in section 14.2.1.

☐ We use the default memory pool instead of the usual managed memory pool because dynamic vertex buffers cannot be placed in the managed memory pool.

■ `reset`—This method resets the attributes of every particle in the system:

```
void PSystem::reset()
{
    std::list<Attribute>::iterator i;
    for(i = particles.begin(); i != particles.end(); i++)
    {
        resetParticle( &(*i) );
    }
}
```

■ `resetParticle`—This method resets the attributes of a particle. How a particle's attributes should be reset is dependent upon the specifics of a particular particle system. Therefore, we make this method abstract to force the subclass to implement it.

■ `addParticle`—This method adds a particle to the system. It uses the `resetParticle` method to initialize the particle before adding it to the list:

```
void PSystem::addParticle()
{
    Attribute attribute;

    resetParticle(&attribute);

    particles.push_back(attribute);
}
```

■ `update`—This method updates all the particles in the system. Since the implementation of such a method is dependent upon the specifics of a particular particle system, we declare this method abstract to force the subclass to implement it.

■ `render`—This method displays all the particles in the system. The implementation is quite involved, and we devote section 14.2.1 to a discussion of it.

■ preRender—Used to set initial render states that must be set before rendering. Since this can vary from system to system, we make it virtual. The default implementation is as follows:

```
void PSystem::preRender()
{
  device->SetRenderState(D3DRS LIGHTING, false);
  device->SetRenderState(D3DRS POINTSPRITEENABLE, true);
  device->SetRenderState(D3DRS POINTSCALEENABLE, true);
  device->SetRenderState(D3DRS POINTSIZE, d3d::FtoDw( size));
  device->SetRenderState(D3DRS POINTSIZE MIN, d3d::FtoDw(0.0f));

  // control the size of the particle relative to distance
  device->SetRenderState(D3DRS POINTSCALE A, d3d::FtoDw(0.0f));
  device->SetRenderState(D3DRS POINTSCALE B, d3d::FtoDw(0.0f));
  device->SetRenderState(D3DRS POINTSCALE C, d3d::FtoDw(1.0f));

  // use alpha from texture
  device->SetTextureStageState(0, D3DTSS ALPHAARG1, D3DTA
    TEXTURE);
  device->SetTextureStageState(0, D3DTSS ALPHAOP, D3DTOP
    SELECTARG1);

  device->SetRenderState(D3DRS ALPHABLENDENABLE, true);
  device->SetRenderState(D3DRS SRCBLEND, D3DBLEND SRCALPHA);
  device->SetRenderState(D3DRS DESTBLEND, D3DBLEND INVSRCALPHA);
}
```

Note that we have enabled alpha blending so that the currently set texture's alpha channel specifies the transparency of the texture's pixels. We use this for a variety of effects; one in particular is to obtain particles that are not rectangular shaped, as the texture is. For instance, to obtain a round "snowball-looking" particle, we use a plain white texture with an alpha channel that is black with a white circle. Thus, only a round white circle will be displayed rather than a rectangular white texture.

■ postRender—Used to restore any render states that a particular particle system might have set. Since this can vary from system to system, we make it virtual. The default implementation is as follows:

```
void PSystem::postRender()
{
  device->SetRenderState(D3DRS LIGHTING,          true);
  device->SetRenderState(D3DRS POINTSPRITEENABLE, false);
  device->SetRenderState(D3DRS POINTSCALEENABLE,  false);
  device->SetRenderState(D3DRS ALPHABLENDENABLE,  false);
}
```

■ isEmpty—True if there are no particles in the current system, and false otherwise

Part III

- isDead—True if every particle in the system is dead, and false otherwise. Note that every particle being dead doesn't imply that the system is empty. Empty means that we have no particles in the system. Dead means that we have particles in the system, but they are all marked dead.

- removeDeadParticles—Searches the attribute list _particle and removes any dead particles from the list:

```
void PSystem::removeDeadParticles()
{
    std::list<Attribute>::iterator i;

    i = particles.begin();

    while( i != particles.end() )
    {
        if( i-> isAlive == false )
        {
            // erase returns the next iterator, so no need
            // to incrememnt to the next one ourselves.
            i = particles.erase(i);
        }
        else
        {
            i++; // next in list
        }
    }
}
```

Remark: This method is usually called in a subclass's update method to remove any particles that have been killed (marked as dead). However, for some particle systems, it may be advantageous to recycle dead particles rather than remove them. That is, instead of allocating and deallocating particles from the list as they are born and killed, we simply reset a dead particle to create a new one. The snow system we implement in section 14.3 demonstrates this technique.

14.2.1 Drawing a Particle System

Since the particle system is dynamic, we need to update the particle in the system every frame. An intuitive but inefficient approach to rendering the particle system is as follows:

- Create a vertex buffer large enough to hold the maximum number of particles.

For each frame:
A. Update all particles.
B. Copy *all* living particles to the vertex buffer.
C. Draw the vertex buffer.

This approach works, but it is not the most efficient. For one, the vertex buffer must be big enough to hold all the particles in the system. But more significant is that the graphics card is idling while we copy all the particles from the list to the vertex buffer (step B). For example, suppose our system has 10,000 particles; first we need a vertex buffer that can hold 10,000 particles, which is quite a bit of memory. In addition the graphics card will sit and do nothing until all 10,000 particles in the list are copied to the vertex buffer and we call `DrawPrimitive`. This scenario is a good example of the CPU and graphics card *not* working together.

A better approach (and the approach that the Point Sprite sample on the SDK uses) goes something like this:

Note: This is a simplified description, but it illustrates the idea. It assumes that we will always have 500 particles to fill an entire segment, which in reality doesn't happen because we are constantly killing and creating particles so the number of particles existing varies from frame to frame. For example, suppose we only have 200 particles left to copy over and render in the current frame. Because 200 particles won't fill an entire segment, we handle this scenario as a special case in the code. This scenario can only happen on the last segment being filled for the current frame because if it's not the last segment, that implies there must be at least 500 particles to move onto the next segment.

■ Create a fair-sized vertex buffer (say, one that can hold 2,000 particles). We then divide the vertex buffer into segments; as an example, we set the segment size to 500 particles.

Vertex Buffer: 2000 particle capacity.			
Segment 0: 500 particle capacity.	Segment 1: 500 particle capacity.	Segment 2: 500 particle capacity.	Segment 3: 500 particle capacity.

Figure 14.1: Vertex buffer with segments labeled

Then create the global variable $i = 0$ to keep track of the segment that we're in.

For each frame:

A. Update all particles.

B. Until all living particles have been rendered:

    1. If the vertex buffer is not full, then:

        a. Lock segment i with the `D3DLOCK_NOOVER-WRITE` flag.

        b. Copy 500 particles to segment i.

    2. If the vertex buffer is full, then:

a. Start at the beginning of the vertex buffer: $i = 0$.

b. Lock segment i with the `D3DLOCK_DISCARD` flag.

c. Copy 500 particles to segment i.

3. Render segment i.

4. Next segment: $i++$

Remark: Recall that our vertex buffer is dynamic, and therefore we can take advantage of the dynamic locking flags `D3DLOCK_NOOVER-WRITE` and `D3DLOCK_DISCARD`. These flags allow us to lock parts of the vertex buffer that are not being rendered while other parts of the vertex buffer are being rendered. For instance, suppose that we are rendering segment 0; using the `D3DLOCK_NOOVERWRITE` flag, we can lock and fill segment 1 while we are rendering segment 0. This prevents a rendering stall that otherwise would incur.

This approach is more efficient. First, we have reduced the size of the vertex buffer needed. Secondly, the CPU and graphics card are now working in unison; that is, we copy a small batch of particles to the vertex buffer (CPU work), and then we draw the small batch (graphics card work). Then we copy the next batch of particles to the vertex buffer and draw that batch. This continues until all the particles have been rendered. As you can see, the graphics card is no longer sitting idle waiting for the entire vertex buffer to be filled.

We now turn our attention to the implementation of this rendering scheme. To facilitate the rendering of a particle system using this scheme, we use the following data members of the `PSystem` class:

■ `_vbSize`—The number of particles that our vertex buffer can hold at a given time. This value is independent of the number of particles in the actual particle system.

■ `_vbOffset`—This variable marks the offset (measured in particles, *not* bytes) into the vertex buffer into which we should begin copying the next batch of particles. For instance, if batch one resides in entries 0 to 499 of the vertex buffer, the offset to start copying batch two would be 500.

■ `_vbBatchSize`—The number of particles that we define to be in a batch

We now present the code for the rendering method:

```
void PSystem::render()
{
  if( !_particles.empty() )
  {
      // set render states
      preRender();
```

```
_device->SetTexture(0, _tex);
_device->SetFVF(Particle::FVF);
_device->SetStreamSource(0, _vb, 0, sizeof(Particle));

// start at beginning if we're at the end of the vb
if(_vbOffset >= _vbSize)
    _vbOffset = 0;

Particle* v = 0;

_vb->Lock(
    _vbOffset    * sizeof( Particle ),
    _vbBatchSize * sizeof( Particle ),
    (void**)&v,
    _vbOffset ? D3DLOCK_NOOVERWRITE : D3DLOCK_DISCARD);

DWORD numParticlesInBatch = 0;

//
// Until all particles have been rendered.
//
std::list<Attribute>::iterator i;
for(i = _particles.begin(); i != _particles.end(); i++)
{
    if( i->_isAlive )
    {
        //
        // Copy a batch of the living particles to the
        // next vertex buffer segment
        //
        v->_position = i->_position;
        v->_color    = (D3DCOLOR)i->_color;
        v++; // next element;

        numParticlesInBatch++; //increase batch counter

        // is this batch full?
        if(numParticlesInBatch == _vbBatchSize)
        {
            //
            // Draw the last batch of particles that was
            // copied to the vertex buffer.
            //
            _vb->Unlock();

            _device->DrawPrimitive(
                D3DPT_POINTLIST,
                _vbOffset,
                _vbBatchSize);

            //
            // While that batch is drawing, start filling the
            // next batch with particles.
            //

            // move the offset to the start of the next batch
```

```
              _vbOffset += _vbBatchSize;

              // don't offset into memory thats outside the vb's
              // range. If we're at the end, start at the beginning.
              if(_vbOffset >= _vbSize)
                  _vbOffset = 0;

              _vb->Lock(
                  _vbOffset    * sizeof( Particle ),
                  _vbBatchSize * sizeof( Particle ),
                  (void**)&v,
                  _vbOffset ? D3DLOCK_NOOVERWRITE :
                      D3DLOCK_DISCARD);

              numParticlesInBatch = 0; // reset for new batch
        }//end if
      }//end if
    }//end for

    _vb->Unlock();

    // it's possible that the LAST batch being filled never
    // got rendered because the condition
    // (numParticlesInBatch == _vbBatchSize) would not have
    // been satisfied.  We draw the last partially filled batch now.

    if( numParticlesInBatch )
    {
        _device->DrawPrimitive(
            D3DPT_POINTLIST,
            _vbOffset,
            numParticlesInBatch);
    }

    // next block
    _vbOffset += _vbBatchSize;

    postRender();

    }//end if
}// end render()
```

14.2.2 Randomness

There is a sort of randomness to the particles of a system. For example, if we are modeling snow, we do not want all the snowflakes to fall in exactly the same way. We want them to fall in a similar way but not exactly the same way. To facilitate the randomness functionality required for particle systems, we add the following two functions to the d3dUtility.h/cpp files.

This first function returns a random float in the interval [lowBound, highBound]:

```
float d3d::GetRandomFloat(float lowBound, float highBound)
{
    if( lowBound >= highBound ) // bad input
        return lowBound;

    // get random float in [0, 1] interval
    float f = (rand() % 10000) * 0.0001f;

    // return float in [lowBound, highBound] interval.
    return (f * (highBound - lowBound)) + lowBound;
}
```

This next function outputs a random vector in the box defined by its minimum point `min` and maximum point `max`.

```
void d3d::GetRandomVector(
        D3DXVECTOR3* out,
        D3DXVECTOR3* min,
        D3DXVECTOR3* max)
{
    out->x = GetRandomFloat(min->x, max->x);
    out->y = GetRandomFloat(min->y, max->y);
    out->z = GetRandomFloat(min->z, max->z);
}
```

Note: Remember to seed the random number generator using `srand()`.

14.3 Concrete Particle Systems: Snow, Firework, Particle Gun

Now let's derive several concrete particle systems from `PSystem`. These systems have been kept simple by design for illustration purposes and do not take advantage of all the flexibility that the `PSystem` class provides. We implement Snow, Firework, and Particle Gun systems. These systems' names pretty much sum up the system that they model. The Snow system models falling snowflakes. The Firework system models an explosion that looks like a firework. The Particle Gun system fires particles out from the camera's position in the direction that the camera is looking based on a keypress; this makes it look like we are firing "particle bullets" and could be used as a foundation for a gun system in a game.

Note: As usual, the complete code projects illustrating these systems can be found in the companion files for this chapter.

14.3.1 Sample Application: Snow

Figure 14.2: A screen shot of the Snow sample

The Snow system's class is defined as:

```
class Snow : public PSystem
{
public:
    Snow(d3d::BoundingBox* boundingBox, int numParticles);
    void resetParticle(Attribute* attribute);
    void update(float timeDelta);
};
```

Remark: Notice how simple the interface is for the Snow system because the parent class takes care of most of the work. In fact, all three of the particle systems that we implement in this section have simple interfaces and are relatively easy to implement.

The constructor takes a pointer to a bounding box structure and the number of particles the system will have. The bounding box describes the volume that the snowflakes will fall in. If the snowflakes go outside this volume, they are killed and respawned. This way, the Snow system always has the same amount of particles active. The constructor is implemented as follows:

```
Snow::Snow(d3d::BoundingBox* boundingBox, int numParticles)
{
    _boundingBox   = *boundingBox;
    _size          = 0.8f;
    _vbSize        = 2048;
    _vbOffset      = 0;
    _vbBatchSize   = 512;
```

```
for(int i = 0; i < numParticles; i++)
    addParticle();
}
```

Also notice that we specify the size of the vertex buffer, the batch size, and the starting offset.

The `resetParticle` method creates a snowflake with a random x- and z-coordinate position inside the bounding box and sets the y-coordinate to be equal to the top of the bounding box. It then gives the snowflakes a velocity so that the snowflakes fall downward and slightly toward the left. The snowflakes are colored white:

```
void Snow::resetParticle(Attribute* attribute)
{
    attribute->_isAlive  = true;

    // get random x, z coordinate for the position of the snowflake.
    d3d::GetRandomVector(
        &attribute->_position,
        &_boundingBox._min,
        &_boundingBox._max);

    // no randomness for height (y-coordinate). Snowflake
    // always starts at the top of bounding box.
    attribute->_position.y = _boundingBox._max.y;

    // snowflakes fall downward and slightly to the left
    attribute->_velocity.x = d3d::GetRandomFloat(0.0f, 1.0f)*-3.0f;
    attribute->_velocity.y = d3d::GetRandomFloat(0.0f, 1.0f)*-10.0f;
    attribute->_velocity.z = 0.0f;

    // white snowflake
    attribute->_color = d3d::WHITE;
}
```

The `update` method updates the position of the particle and then tests if the particle has gone outside the system's bounding box. If it has gone outside the bounding box, we respawn it.

```
void Snow::update(float timeDelta)
{
    std::list<Attribute>::iterator i;
    for(i = _particles.begin(); i != _particles.end(); i++)
    {
        i->_position += i->_velocity * timeDelta;

        // is the point outside bounds?
        if( _boundingBox.isPointInside( i->_position ) == false )
        {
            // nope so kill it, but we want to recycle dead
            // particles, so respawn it instead.
            resetParticle( &(*i) );
        }
    }
}
```

14.3.2 Sample Application: Firework

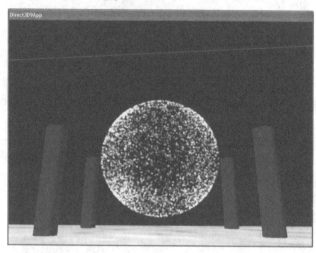

Figure 14.3: A screen shot of the Firework sample

The Firework system's class is defined as:

```
class Firework : public PSystem
{
public:
    Firework(D3DXVECTOR3* origin, int numParticles);
    void resetParticle(Attribute* attribute);
    void update(float timeDelta);
    void preRender();
    void postRender();
};
```

The constructor takes a pointer to the origin of the system and the number of particles that the system has. In this case, the origin of the system refers to where the firework will explode.

The `resetParticle` method initializes a particle at the origin of the system and creates a random velocity in a sphere. Each particle in the Firework system is given a random color. Finally, we define that the particle will live for two seconds.

```
void Firework::resetParticle(Attribute* attribute)
{
    attribute->_isAlive  = true;
    attribute->_position = _origin;

    D3DXVECTOR3 min = D3DXVECTOR3(-1.0f, -1.0f, -1.0f);
    D3DXVECTOR3 max = D3DXVECTOR3( 1.0f,  1.0f,  1.0f);

    d3d::GetRandomVector(
        &attribute->_velocity,
        &min,
        &max);
```

```
    // normalize to make spherical
    D3DXVec3Normalize(
         &attribute->_velocity,
         &attribute->_velocity);

    attribute->_velocity *= 100.0f;

    attribute->_color = D3DXCOLOR(
         d3d::GetRandomFloat(0.0f, 1.0f),
         d3d::GetRandomFloat(0.0f, 1.0f),
         d3d::GetRandomFloat(0.0f, 1.0f),
         1.0f);

    attribute->_age      = 0.0f;
    attribute->_lifeTime = 2.0f; // lives for 2 seconds
}
```

The `update` method updates the position of each particle and kills particles that have aged past their specified lifetime. Notice that the system doesn't remove dead particles. We do this because when we want to create a new firework particle system, we can simply reset an existing firework particle system. This saves us from having to create and destroy particles frequently.

```
void Firework::update(float timeDelta)
{
    std::list<Attribute>::iterator i;

    for(i = _particles.begin(); i != _particles.end(); i++)
    {
        // only update living particles
        if( i->_isAlive )
        {
            i->_position += i->_velocity * timeDelta;

            i->_age += timeDelta;

            if(i->_age > i->_lifeTime) // kill
                i->_isAlive = false;
        }
    }
}
```

The Firework system uses different blend factors when rendering. Further, it disables writes to the depth buffer. We can easily change the blend factors and depth write from the default by overriding the `PSystem::preRender` and `PSystem::postRender` methods. The overridden implementations:

```
void Firework::preRender()
{
    PSystem::preRender();

    _device->SetRenderState(D3DRS_SRCBLEND, D3DBLEND_ONE);
    _device->SetRenderState(D3DRS_DESTBLEND, D3DBLEND_ONE);
```

Part III

```
        // read, but don't write particles to z-buffer
        _device->SetRenderState(D3DRS_ZWRITEENABLE, false);
}

void Firework::postRender()
{
        PSystem::postRender();

        _device->SetRenderState(D3DRS_ZWRITEENABLE, true);
}
```

Notice that both of the methods call the parent version. In this way, we can still reuse some of the functionality of the parent while making minimal specific changes to the Firework system.

14.3.3 Sample Application: Particle Gun

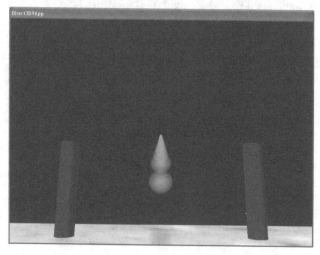

Figure 14.4: A screen shot of the Laser (Particle Gun) sample

The Particle Gun system's class is defined as:

```
class ParticleGun : public PSystem
{
public:
        ParticleGun(Camera* camera);
        void resetParticle(Attribute* attribute);
        void update(float timeDelta);

private:
        Camera* _camera;
};
```

The constructor takes a pointer to the camera. This is because the system needs to know the position and direction of the camera whenever it creates a new particle.

The `resetParticle` method sets the position of the particle to the current camera position and sets the velocity of the particle to the direction that the camera is looking times 100 units. In this way, the "bullets" will fire in the direction we are looking. We color the particles green.

```
void ParticleGun::resetParticle(Attribute* attribute)
{
    attribute->_isAlive  = true;

    D3DXVECTOR3 cameraPos;
    _camera->getPosition(&cameraPos);

    D3DXVECTOR3 cameraDir;
    _camera->getLook(&cameraDir);

    // change to camera position
    attribute->_position = cameraPos;
    attribute->_position.y -= 1.0f; // slightly below camera so it's
                                    // like we're carrying a gun

    // travels in the direction the camera is looking
    attribute->_velocity = cameraDir * 100.0f;

    // green
    attribute->_color = D3DXCOLOR(0.0f, 1.0f, 0.0f, 1.0f);

    attribute->_age      = 0.0f;
    attribute->_lifeTime = 1.0f; // lives for 1 second
}
```

The `update` method updates the position of the particle and kills the particle if it has aged to death. Afterward, we search the particle list and remove any dead particles.

```
void ParticleGun::update(float timeDelta)
{
    std::list<Attribute>::iterator i;

    for(i = _particles.begin(); i != _particles.end(); i++)
    {
        i->_position += i->_velocity * timeDelta;

        i->_age += timeDelta;

        if(i->_age > i->_lifeTime) // kill
            i->_isAlive = false;
    }
    removeDeadParticles();
}
```

Part III

14.4 **Summary**

■ Point sprites are a convenient and flexible way to display particles. They can change size and be textured. Furthermore, a single vertex can describe them.

■ A particle system maintains a collection of particles and is responsible for creating, destroying, updating, and displaying particles.

■ Some other particle system ideas that you can implement are: smoke, rocket trail, fountain/sprinkler, fire, lightning, explosion, and rain.

Chapter 15

Picking

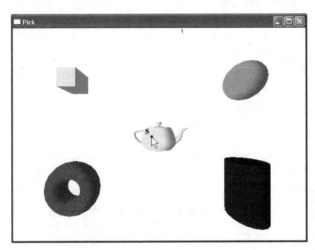

Figure 15.1:
The user picking
the teapot

Suppose that the user clicked the screen point **s** = (x, y). From Figure 15.1 we can see that the user has *picked* the teapot. However, the application cannot immediately determine that the teapot was picked given just **s**. Therefore, we must come up with a technique to calculate this. We call this technique *picking*.

One thing that we know about the teapot and its relationship with **s** is that the teapot was projected to the area surrounding **s**. More correctly, it was projected to the area surrounding the point **p** on the projection window that corresponds to the screen point **s**. Since this problem relies on the relationship between a 3D object and its projection, we gain some insights by examining Figure 15.2.

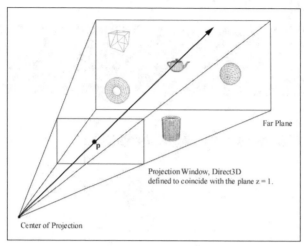

Far Plane

Projection Window, Direct3D
defined to coincide with the plane z = 1.

p

Center of Projection

Figure 15.2:
A ray shooting
through **p** will
intersect the object
whose projection
surrounds **p**. Note
that the point **p** on
the projection win-
dow corresponds to
the clicked screen
point **s**.

In Figure 15.2 we see that if we shoot a *picking ray*, originating at the origin, through **p**, we will intersect the object whose projection surrounds **p**, namely the teapot. Therefore, once we compute the picking ray, we can iterate through each object in the scene and test if the ray intersects it. The object that the ray intersects is the object that was picked by the user, which again is the teapot in this example.

The above example is specific to **s** and the teapot. Generally, we have an arbitrary clicked screen point. We then compute the picking ray and iterate through each object in the scene, testing if the ray intersects it. The object that the ray intersects is the object that was picked by the user. However, it is possible that the ray would not intersect any objects. For instance, in Figure 15.1, if the user doesn't pick one of the five objects but clicks the white background, the picking ray would not intersect any of the objects. Thus, we conclude that if the ray doesn't intersect any of the objects in the scene, then we, the user, didn't pick an object, but rather the background of the screen or something we are not interested in.

Picking is applicable to all sorts of games and 3D applications. For example, players often interact with various objects in the world by clicking on them with the mouse. The player may click on an enemy to fire a projectile at the enemy or click on an item to pick it up. In order for the game to respond appropriately, it needs to know the object that was picked (was it an enemy or item?) and its location in 3D space (where should the projectile be fired or where should the player move to pick up the item?). Picking allows us to answer these questions.

Objectives

- To learn how to implement the picking algorithm and understand how it works. We break picking down into the following four steps:
  - ☐ Given the clicked screen point **s**, find its corresponding point on the projection window, namely **p**.
  - ☐ Compute the picking ray, that is, the ray originating at the origin that shoots through **p**.
  - ☐ Transform the picking ray and the models into the same space.
  - ☐ Determine the object that the picking ray intersects. The intersected object corresponds to the picked screen object.

15.1 Screen to Projection Window Transform

The first task is to transform the screen point to the projection window. The viewport transformation matrix is:

$$\begin{bmatrix} \dfrac{Width}{2} & 0 & 0 & 0 \\ 0 & -\dfrac{Height}{2} & 0 & 0 \\ 0 & 0 & MaxZ - MinZ & 0 \\ X + \dfrac{Width}{2} & Y + \dfrac{Height}{2} & MinZ & 1 \end{bmatrix}$$

Transforming a point $\mathbf{p} = (p_x, p_y, p_z)$ on the projection window by the viewport transformation yields the screen point $\mathbf{s} = (s_x, s_y)$:

$$s_x = p_x \left(\frac{Width}{2} \right) + X + \frac{Width}{2}$$

$$s_y = -p_y \left(\frac{Height}{2} \right) + Y + \frac{Height}{2}$$

Recall that the z-coordinate after the viewport transformation is not stored as part of the 2D image but is stored in the depth buffer.

In our situation we are initially given the screen point **s**, and we need to find **p**. Solving for **p**, we obtain:

$$p_x = \frac{2s_x - 2X - Width}{Width}$$

$$p_y = \frac{-2s_y + 2Y + Height}{Height}$$

Assuming the X and Y members of the viewport are 0, which is usually the case, we can simply go a step further and get:

$$p_x = \frac{2 \cdot s_x}{Width} - 1$$

$$p_y = \frac{-2 \cdot s_y}{Height} + 1$$

$$p_z = 1$$

By definition, the projection window coincides with the $z = 1$ plane; therefore $p_z = 1$.

However, we are not done. The projection matrix scales the points on the projection window to simulate different fields of view. To reclaim the point values before this scaling, we must transform the points by the inverse of the scaling operations. Let **P** be the projection matrix, and since entries P_{00} and P_{11} of a transformation matrix scale the x and y coordinates of a point, we get:

$$p_x = \left(\frac{2x}{viewportWidth} - 1 \right) \left(\frac{1}{P_{00}} \right)$$

$$p_y = \left(\frac{-2y}{viewPortHeight} + 1 \right) \left(\frac{1}{P_{11}} \right)$$

$$p_z = 1$$

15.2 Computing the Picking Ray

Recall that a ray can be represented by the parametric equation $\mathbf{p}(t) = \mathbf{p}_0 + t\mathbf{u}$, where $\mathbf{p}_0$ is the origin of the ray describing its position and $\mathbf{u}$ is a vector describing its direction.

From Figure 15.2 we can see that the origin of the ray is also the origin of the view space, so $\mathbf{p}_0 = (0, 0, 0)$. If $\mathbf{p}$ is the point on the projection window to shoot the ray through, the direction vector $\mathbf{u}$ is given by: $\mathbf{u} = \mathbf{p} - \mathbf{p}_0 = (p_x, p_y, 1) - (0, 0, 0) = \mathbf{p}$.

The following method computes the picking ray in view space given the x and y coordinates of the clicked point from screen space:

```
d3d::Ray CalcPickingRay(int x, int y)
{
        float px = 0.0f;
        float py = 0.0f;

        D3DVIEWPORT9 vp;
        Device->GetViewport(&vp);
```

```
D3DXMATRIX proj;
Device->GetTransform(D3DTS_PROJECTION, &proj);

px = ((( 2.0f*x) / vp.Width)  - 1.0f) / proj(0, 0);
py = (((-2.0f*y) / vp.Height) + 1.0f) / proj(1, 1);

d3d::Ray ray;
ray._origin    = D3DXVECTOR3(0.0f, 0.0f, 0.0f);
ray._direction = D3DXVECTOR3(px, py, 1.0f);

return ray;
}
```

where `Ray` is defined as:

```
struct Ray
{
    D3DXVECTOR3 _origin;
    D3DXVECTOR3 _direction;
};
```

We update the d3dUtility.h file and `d3d` namespace by adding `Ray` to it.

15.3 Transforming Rays

The picking ray we computed in the previous section is described in view space. In order to perform a ray-object intersection test, the ray and the objects must be in the same coordinate system. Rather than transform all the objects into view space, it is often easier to transform the picking ray into world space or even an object's local space.

We can transform a ray $\mathbf{r}(t) = \mathbf{p}_0 + t\mathbf{u}$ by transforming its origin $\mathbf{p}_0$ and direction $\mathbf{u}$ by a transformation matrix. Note that the origin is transformed as a point and the direction is treated as a vector. The picking sample for this chapter implements the following function to transform a ray:

Part III

```
void TransformRay(d3d::Ray* ray, D3DXMATRIX* T)
{
    // transform the ray's origin, w = 1.
    D3DXVec3TransformCoord(
        &ray->_origin,
        &ray->_origin,
        T);

    // transform the ray's direction, w = 0.
    D3DXVec3TransformNormal(
        &ray->_direction,
        &ray->_direction,
        T);

    // normalize the direction
    D3DXVec3Normalize(&ray->_direction, &ray->_direction);
}
```

The `D3DXVec3TransformCoord` and `D3DXVec3TransformNormal` functions take 3D vectors as parameters, but observe that with the `D3DXVec3TransformCoord` function there is an understood $w = 1$ for the fourth component. Conversely, with the `D3DXVec3Trans-formNormal` function there is an understood $w = 0$ for the fourth component. Thus, we can use `D3DXVec3TransformCoord` to transform points, and we can use `D3DXVec3TransformNormal` to transform vectors.

15.4 Ray-Object Intersections

After we have the picking ray and the objects in the same coordinate system, we are ready to test which object the ray will hit. Since we represent objects as triangle meshes, one approach would be the following. For each object in the scene, iterate through its triangle list and test if the ray intersects one of the triangles. If it does, it must have hit the object that the triangle belongs to.

However, performing a ray intersection test for every triangle in the scene adds up in computation time. A faster method, albeit less accurate, is to approximate each object with a bounding sphere. Then we can perform a ray intersection test with each bounding sphere, and the sphere that gets intersected specifies the object that got picked.

> **Note:** The picking ray may intersect multiple objects. However, the object closest to the camera is the object that was picked, since the closer object would have obscured the object behind it.

Given the center point $\mathbf{c}$ and the radius r of a sphere, we can test if a point $\mathbf{p}$ is on the sphere using the following implicit equation:

$$\|\mathbf{p} - \mathbf{c}\| - r = 0$$

where $\mathbf{p}$ is a point on the sphere if the equation is satisfied. See Figure 15.3.

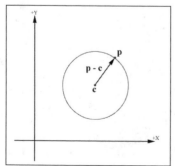

Figure 15.3: The length of the vector formed by $\mathbf{p} - \mathbf{c}$, denoted by $\|\mathbf{p} - \mathbf{c}\|$, is equal to the radius of the sphere if $\mathbf{p}$ lies on the sphere. Note that we use a circle in the figure for simplicity, but the idea extends to three dimensions.

To determine if and where a ray $\mathbf{p}(t) = \mathbf{p}_0 + t\mathbf{u}$ intersects a sphere, we plug the ray into an implicit sphere equation and solve for the parameter t that satisfies the sphere equation, giving us the parameter that yields the intersection point(s).

Plugging the ray into the sphere equation:

$$\|\mathbf{p}(t) - \mathbf{c}\| - r = 0$$

$$\|\mathbf{p}_0 + t\mathbf{u} - \mathbf{c}\| - r = 0$$

...from which we obtain the quadratic equation:

$$At^2 + Bt + C = 0$$

where $A = \mathbf{u} \cdot \mathbf{u}$, $B = 2(\mathbf{u} \cdot (\mathbf{p}_0 - \mathbf{c}))$, and $C = (\mathbf{p}_0 - \mathbf{c}) \cdot (\mathbf{p}_0 - \mathbf{c}) - r^2$. If $\mathbf{u}$ is normalized, then $A = 1$.

Assuming $\mathbf{u}$ is normalized, we solve for t_0 and t_1:

$$t_0 = \frac{-B + \sqrt{B^2 - 4C}}{2} \qquad t_1 = \frac{-B - \sqrt{B^2 - 4C}}{2}$$

Figure 15.4 shows the possible results for t_0 and t_1 and shows what these results mean geometrically.

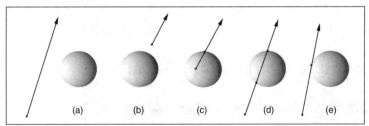

Figure 15.4: a) The ray misses the sphere; both t_0 and t_1 will result in imaginary solutions. b) The ray is in front of the sphere; both t_0 and t_1 will be negative. c) The ray is inside the sphere; one of the solutions will be positive and one will be negative. The positive solution yields the single intersection point. d) The ray intersects the sphere; both t_0 and t_1 are positive. e) The ray is tangent to the sphere, in which case the solutions are positive and $t_0 = t_1$.

The following method returns true if the ray passed in intersects the sphere passed in. It returns false if the ray misses the sphere:

```
bool PickApp::raySphereIntersectionTest(Ray* ray,
                                        BoundingSphere* sphere)
{
    D3DXVECTOR3 v = ray->_origin - sphere->_center;
```

```
    float b = 2.0f * D3DXVec3Dot(&ray->_direction, &v);
    float c = D3DXVec3Dot(&v, &v) - (sphere->_radius * sphere->
                                      _radius);

    // find the discriminant
    float discriminant = (b * b) - (4.0f * c);

    // test for imaginary number
    if( discriminant < 0.0f )
        return false;

    discriminant = sqrtf(discriminant);

    float s0 = (-b + discriminant) / 2.0f;
    float s1 = (-b - discriminant) / 2.0f;

    // if a solution is >= 0, then we intersected the sphere
    if( s0 >= 0.0f || s1 >= 0.0f )
        return true;

    return false;
}
```

Of course, we have seen BoundingSphere already, but for convenience we show its definition again here:

```
struct BoundingSphere
{
    BoundingSphere();

    D3DXVECTOR3 _center;
    float       _radius;
};
```

15.5 Sample Application: Picking

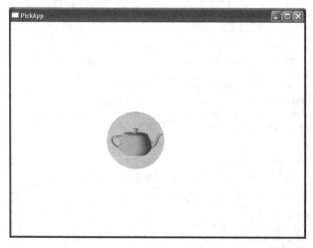

Figure 15.5:
Screen shot of this
chapter's sample

Figure 15.5 shows a screen shot of the sample application for this chapter. The teapot moves around the screen, and you can try to click on it with the mouse. If you click on the bounding sphere of the teapot, a message box will pop up indicating that you hit it. We handle the mouse click event by testing for a WM_LBUTTONDOWN message:

```
case WM_LBUTTONDOWN:

// compute the ray in view space given the clicked screen point
d3d::Ray ray = CalcPickingRay(LOWORD(lParam), HIWORD(lParam));

// transform the ray to world space
D3DXMATRIX view;
Device->GetTransform(D3DTS_VIEW, &view);

D3DXMATRIX viewInverse;
D3DXMatrixInverse(&viewInverse, 0, &view);

TransformRay(&ray, &viewInverse);

// test for a hit
if( RaySphereIntTest(&ray, &BSphere) )
    ::MessageBox(0, "Hit!", "HIT", 0);

break;
```

15.6 Summary

- Picking is the technique used to determine the 3D object that corresponds to the 2D projected object displayed on the screen that the user clicked on with the mouse.

- The picking ray is found by shooting a ray, originating at the origin of the view space, through the point on the projection window that corresponds to the clicked screen point.

- We can transform a ray $\mathbf{r}(t) = \mathbf{p}_0 + t\mathbf{u}$ by transforming its origin $\mathbf{p}_0$ and direction $\mathbf{u}$ by a transformation matrix. Note that the origin is transformed as a point ($w = 1$) and the direction is treated as a vector ($w = 0$).

- To test if the ray has intersected an object, we can test if the ray intersected a triangle that composes the object or test if the ray intersected a bounding volume of the object, such as a bounding sphere.

Part III

Shaders and Effects

Thus far, we have achieved a desired effect by altering the configuration of device states such as transforms, lights, textures, and render states. Although the various supported configurations provide us with some flexibility, we are still limited to predefined fixed operations (hence the name "fixed function pipeline").

The primary theme of this part is vertex and pixel shaders, which replace sections of the fixed function pipeline with a custom program that we implement, called a *shader*. Shaders are completely programmable and allow us to implement techniques that are not defined in the fixed function pipeline. Consequently, the number of techniques that we have available at our disposal has greatly increased. The programmable sections of the rendering pipeline are commonly referred to as the *programmable pipeline*. A brief description of the chapters in this part follows.

Chapter 16, "Introduction to the High-Level Shading Language"— In this chapter we explore the High-Level Shading Language (HLSL), which is the language we use to write vertex and pixel shader programs in this book.

Chapter 17, "Introduction to Vertex Shaders"—This chapter explains what vertex shaders are and how to create and use them in Direct3D. The chapter illustrates vertex shaders by explaining the implementation of a cartoon-style shading technique.

Chapter 18, "Introduction to Pixel Shaders"—This chapter explains what pixel shaders are and how to create and use them in Direct3D. The chapter concludes by showing how to implement multitexturing using a pixel shader.

Chapter 19, "The Effects Framework"—In this chapter, we discuss the Direct3D effects framework. The chapter describes the purpose of the effects framework, the structure and syntax of effect files, how to create effect files, and how to use effect files in Direct3D applications.

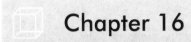

Chapter 16

Introduction to the High-Level Shading Language

In this chapter we describe the High-Level Shading Language (HLSL), which we use to program vertex and pixel shaders over the next three chapters. Briefly, vertex and pixel shaders are small custom programs we write, executed on the graphics card's GPU (graphics processing unit), that replace a portion of the fixed function pipeline. By replacing a section of the fixed function pipeline with our own custom shader program, we obtain a huge amount of flexibility in the graphical effects that we can achieve. We are no longer limited to predefined "fixed" operations.

In order to write shader programs, we need a language to write them in. In DirectX 8.x, shaders were written in a low-level shader assembly language. Fortunately, we no longer have to write shaders in assembly language, as DirectX 9 has supplied a High-Level Shading Language that we can use to write shaders. Using HLSL over assembly language to write shader programs has the same advantages as using a high-level language, like C++, over assembly language to write applications, namely:

- Increased productivity—Writing programs in a high-level language is faster and easier than writing them in a low-level language. We can spend more time focusing on algorithms rather than coding.

- Improved readability—Programs in a high-level language are easier to read, which implies programs written in a high-level language are easier to debug and maintain.

- The compilers, more often than not, generate more efficient assembly code than hand-written assembly code.

■ Using the HLSL compiler, we can compile our code to any available shader version. Using the assembly language, we would have to port the code for each desired version.

HLSL is also very similar to C and C++ syntax, thus there is a very short learning curve.

Finally, you will need to switch to the REF device for the shader samples if your graphics card does not support vertex and pixel shaders. Using the REF device means the shader samples run very slowly, but they still display the correct results, allowing us to verify that our code is correct.

Note: Vertex shaders can be emulated in software with software vertex processing—D3DCREATE_SOFTWARE_VERTEX-PROCESSING.

Objectives

■ To learn how to write and compile an HLSL shader program
■ To learn how to communicate data from the application to the shader program
■ To become familiar with the syntax, types, and built-in functions of HLSL

16.1 Writing an HLSL Shader

We can write the code to our HLSL shaders directly into our application source files as a long character string. However, it is more convenient and modular to separate the shader code from the application code. For this reason, we write our shaders in Notepad and save them as regular ASCII text files. Then we use the `D3DXCompileShaderFromFile` function (section 16.2.2) to compile our shaders.

As an introduction, the following is a simple vertex shader written in HLSL that was saved to a text file generated in Notepad called Transform.txt. The complete project can be found in the companion files under the title Transform. This vertex shader transforms the vertices by a combined view and projection matrix and sets the diffuse color component of the vertex to blue.

Note: This sample uses a vertex shader as an example, but do not worry about what a vertex shader is supposed to do yet, as they are covered in the next chapter. For now, the objective is to familiarize yourself with the syntax and format of an HLSL program.

```
//////////////////////////////////////////////////////////////
//
// File: transform.txt
//
// Author: Frank D. Luna (C) All Rights Reserved
//
// System: AMD Athlon 1800+ XP, 512 DDR, Geforce 3, Windows XP,
//         MSVC++ 7.0
//
// Desc: Vertex shader that transforms a vertex by the view and
//       projection transformation, and sets the vertex color to blue.
//
//////////////////////////////////////////////////////////////


//
// Globals
//

// Global variable to store a combined view and projection
// transformation matrix.  We initialize this variable
// from the application.
matrix ViewProjMatrix;

// Initialize a global blue color vector.
vector Blue = {0.0f, 0.0f, 1.0f, 1.0f};


//
// Structures
//

// Input structure describes the vertex that is input
// into the shader.  Here the input vertex contains
// a position component only.
struct VS_INPUT
{
    vector position  : POSITION;
};

// Output structure describes the vertex that is
// output from the shader.  Here the output
// vertex contains a position and color component.
struct VS_OUTPUT
{
    vector position : POSITION;
    vector diffuse  : COLOR;
};

//
// Main Entry Point, observe the main function
// receives a copy of the input vertex through
// its parameter and returns a copy of the output
// vertex it computes.
//

VS_OUTPUT Main(VS_INPUT input)
{
    // zero out members of output
```

```
VS_OUTPUT output = (VS_OUTPUT)0;

// transform to view space and project
output.position  = mul(input.position, ViewProjMatrix);

// set vertex diffuse color to blue
output.diffuse = Blue;

//Output the projected and colored vertex.
return output;
}
```

16.1.1 Globals

First we instantiate two global variables:

```
matrix ViewProjMatrix;
vector Blue = {0.0f, 0.0f, 1.0f, 1.0f};
```

The first variable, `ViewProjMatrix`, is of the type `matrix`, which is a 4 × 4 matrix type that is built into the HLSL. This variable stores a combined view and projection matrix, such that it describes both transformations. This way we only have to do one vector-matrix multiplication instead of two. Notice that nowhere in the shader source code do we initialize this variable. That is because we set it through the application source code—not the shader. Communication from the application to the shader program is a frequently required operation and is explained in section 16.2.1.

The second variable, `Blue`, is of the built-in type `vector`, which is a 4D vector. We simply initialize its components to the color blue, treating it as an RGBA color vector.

16.1.2 Input and Output Structures

After the global variables are declared, we define two special structures, which we call the *input* and *output* structures. For vertex shaders, these structures define the vertex data that our shader inputs and outputs, respectively.

```
struct VS_INPUT
{
    vector position : POSITION;
};

struct VS_OUTPUT
{
    vector position : POSITION;
    vector diffuse  : COLOR;
};
```

Note: The input and output structures for pixel shaders define pixel data.

In this sample, the vertex that we input into our vertex shader contains only a position component. The vertex that our shader outputs contains a position component and a color component.

The special colon syntax denotes a *semantic*, which is used to specify the usage of the variable. This is similar to the flexible vertex format (FVF) of a vertex structure. For example, in `VS_INPUT`, we have the member:

```
vector position : POSITION;
```

The syntax ": `POSITION`" says that the vector `position` is used to describe the position of the input vertex. As another example, in `VS_OUTPUT` we have:

```
vector diffuse  : COLOR;
```

Here ": `COLOR`" says that the vector `diffuse` is used to describe the color of the output vertex. We talk more about the available usage identifiers in the next two chapters on vertex and pixel shaders.

> **Note:** From a low-level perspective, the semantic syntax associates a variable in the shader with a hardware register. That is, the input variables are associated with the input registers, and the output variables are associated with the output registers. For example, the `position` member of `VS_INPUT` is connected to the vertex input position register. Similarly, `diffuse` is connected with a particular vertex output color register.

16.1.3 Entry Point Function

As with a C++ program, every HLSL program has an entry point. In our sample shader, we call our entry point function `Main`; however, that name is not mandatory. The shader's entry point function name can be any valid function name. The entry point function must have an input structure parameter, which is used to pass the input vertex into our shader. The entry point function must also return an output structure instance, which is used to output the manipulated vertex from our shader.

```
VS_OUTPUT Main(VS_INPUT input)
{
```

> **Note:** In actuality, it isn't mandatory to use input and output structures. For example, you will sometimes see syntax similar to the following used, particularly with pixel shaders:

```
float4 Main(in float2 base : TEXCOORD0,
            in float2 spot : TEXCOORD1,
            in float2 text : TEXCOORD2) : COLOR
{
```

```
...
}
```

The parameters are inputs into the shader; in this example we are inputting three texture coordinates. The shader returns a single color as output, which is denoted by the : COLOR syntax following the function signature. This definition is equivalent to:

```
struct INPUT
{
    float2 base : TEXCOORD0;
    float2 spot : TEXCOORD1;
    float2 text : TEXCOORD2;
};

struct OUTPUT
{
    float4 c : COLOR;
};

OUTPUT Main(INPUT input)
{
    ...
}
```

The body of the entry point function is responsible for computing the output vertex given the input vertex. The shader in this example simply transforms the input vertex to view space and projection space, sets the vertex color to blue, and returns the resulting vertex. First we instantiate a VS_OUTPUT instance and set all of its members to 0.

```
VS_OUTPUT output = (VS_OUTPUT)0; // zero out all members
```

Then our shader transforms the input vertex position by the ViewProjMatrix variable using the mul function, which is a built-in function that can do both vector-matrix multiplication and matrix-matrix multiplication. We save the resulting transformed vector in the position member of the output instance:

```
// transform and project
output.position  = mul(input.position, ViewProjMatrix);
```

Next we set the diffuse color member of output to Blue:

```
// set vertex diffuse color to blue
output.diffuse = Blue;
```

Finally, we return our resulting vertex:

```
return output;
}
```

16.2 Compiling an HLSL Shader

16.2.1 The Constant Table

Every shader has a constant table that is used to store its variables. The D3DX library provides our application access to a shader's constant table through the `ID3DXConstantTable` interface. Via this interface we can set variables in the shader source code from our application's code.

We now describe an abridged list of the methods that `ID3DXConstantTable` implements. For a complete list, see the Direct3D documentation.

16.2.1.1 Getting a Handle to a Constant

In order to set a particular variable in a shader from our application code, we need a way to refer to it. We can refer to a variable in the shader from our application with a `D3DXHANDLE`. The following method returns a `D3DXHANDLE` to a variable in the shader when given its name:

```
D3DXHANDLE ID3DXConstantTable::GetConstantByName(
    D3DXHANDLE hConstant, // scope of constant
    LPCSTR pName          // name of constant
);
```

- `hConstant`—A `D3DXHANDLE` that identifies the parent structure in which the variable that we want a handle to lives. For example, if we wanted to get a handle to a single data member of a particular structure instance, we would pass in the handle to the structure instance here. If we are obtaining a handle to a top-level variable, we can pass 0 for this parameter.

- `pName`—The name of the variable in the shader source code that we want to obtain a handle to

For example, if the name of the variable in the shader is `ViewProj-Matrix` and it was a top-level parameter, we would write:

```
// Get a handle to the ViewProjMatrix variable in the shader.
D3DXHANDLE h0;
h0 = ConstTable->GetConstantByName(0, "ViewProjMatrix");
```

16.2.1.2 Setting Constants

Once our application has a `D3DXHANDLE` that refers to a particular variable in the shader code, we can set that variable from our application using the `ID3DXConstantTable::SetXXX` methods, where the XXX is replaced by a type name to indicate the type of variable being set. For example, if the variable that we wish to set is a `vector` array, the method name would be `SetVectorArray`.

The general syntax of the `ID3DXConstantTable::SetXXX` methods is of the form:

```
HRESULT ID3DXConstantTable::SetXXX(
    LPDIRECT3DDEVICE9 pDevice,
    D3DXHANDLE hConstant,
    XXX value
);
```

- `pDevice`—Pointer to the device that is associated with the constant table

- `hConstant`—A handle that refers to the variable that we are setting

- `value`—The value that we are setting the variable to, where XXX is replaced with the variable type name we are setting. For some types (`bool`, `int`, `float`), we pass a copy of the value, and for other types (`vectors`, `matrices`, `structures`), we pass a pointer to the value.

When we set arrays, the `SetXXX` method takes an additional fourth parameter that specifies the number of elements in the array. For example, the method to set an array of 4D vectors is prototyped as:

```
HRESULT ID3DXConstantTable::SetVectorArray(
    LPDIRECT3DDEVICE9 pDevice,     // associated device
    D3DXHANDLE hConstant,          // handle to shader variable
    CONST D3DXVECTOR4* pVector,    // pointer to array
    UINT Count                     // number of elements in array
);
```

The following list describes the types that we can set with the `ID3DXConstantTable` interface. Assume that we have a valid device (`Device`) and a valid handle to the variable that we are setting (`handle`).

- `SetBool`—Used to set a Boolean value. Sample call:

    ```
    bool b = true;
    ConstTable->SetBool(Device, handle, b);
    ```

- `SetBoolArray`—Used to set a Boolean array. Sample call:

    ```
    bool b[3] = {true, false, true};
    ConstTable->SetBoolArray(Device, handle, b, 3);
    ```

- `SetFloat`—Used to set a float. Sample call:

    ```
    float f = 3.14f;
    ConstTable->SetFloat(Device, handle, f);
    ```

■ `SetFloatArray`—Used to set a float array. Sample call:

```
float f[2] = {1.0f, 2.0f};
ConstTable->SetFloatArray(Device, handle, f, 2);
```

■ `SetInt`—Used to set an integer. Sample call:

```
int x = 4;
ConstTable->SetInt(Device, handle, x);
```

■ `SetIntArray`—Used to set an integer array. Sample call:

```
int x[4] = {1, 2, 3, 4};
ConstTable->SetIntArray(Device, handle, x, 4);
```

■ `SetMatrix`—Used to set a 4 × 4 matrix. Sample call:

```
D3DXMATRIX  M(…);
ConstTable->SetMatrix(Device, handle, &M);
```

■ `SetMatrixArray`—Used to set a 4 × 4 matrix array. Sample call:

```
D3DXMATRIX M[4];

// ...Initialize matrices

ConstTable->SetMatrixArray(Device, handle, M, 4);
```

■ `SetMatrixPointerArray`—Used to set an array of 4 × 4 matrix pointers. Sample call:

```
D3DXMATRIX* M[4];

// ...Allocate and initialize matrix pointers

ConstTable->SetMatrixPointerArray(Device, handle, M, 4);
```

■ `SetMatrixTranspose`—Used to set a transposed 4 × 4 matrix. Sample call:

```
D3DXMATRIX  M(…);
D3DXMatrixTranspose(&M, &M);
ConstTable->SetMatrixTranspose(Device, handle, &M);
```

■ `SetMatrixTransposeArray`—Used to set an array of 4 × 4 transposed matrices. Sample call:

```
D3DXMATRIX M[4];

// ...Initialize matrices and transpose them.

ConstTable->SetMatrixTransposeArray(Device, handle, M, 4);
```

■ `SetMatrixTransposePointerArray`—Used to set an array of pointers to 4 × 4 transposed matrices. Sample call:

```
D3DXMATRIX* M[4];

// ...Allocate, initialize matrix pointers and transpose them.

ConstTable->SetMatrixTransposePointerArray(Device, handle, M, 4);
```

- `SetVector`—Used to set a variable of type `D3DXVECTOR4`. Sample call:

```
D3DXVECTOR4 v(1.0f, 2.0f, 3.0f, 4.0f);
ConstTable->SetVector(Device, handle, &v);
```

- `SetVectorArray`—Used to set a variable that is a vector array. Sample call:

```
D3DXVECTOR4 v[3];

// ...Initialize vectors

ConstTable->SetVectorArray(Device, handle, v, 3);
```

- `SetValue`—Used to set an arbitrarily sized type, such as a structure. In the sample call, we use `SetValue` to set a `D3DXMATRIX`:

```
D3DXMATRIX M(...);
ConstTable->SetValue(Device, handle, (void*)&M, sizeof(M));
```

16.2.1.3 Setting the Constant Default Values

This next method simply sets the constants to their default values, which are the values they are initialized with when they are declared. This method should be called once during application setup.

```
HRESULT ID3DXConstantTable::SetDefaults(
    LPDIRECT3DDEVICE9 pDevice
);
```

- `pDevice`—Pointer to the device that is associated with the constant table

16.2.2 Compiling an HLSL Shader

We can compile a shader, which we have saved to a text file, using the following function:

```
HRESULT D3DXCompileShaderFromFile(
    LPCSTR               pSrcFile,
    CONST D3DXMACRO*     pDefines,
    LPD3DXINCLUDE        pInclude,
    LPCSTR               pFunctionName,
    LPCSTR               pTarget,
    DWORD                Flags,
    LPD3DXBUFFER*        ppShader,
    LPD3DXBUFFER*        ppErrorMsgs,
    LPD3DXCONSTANTTABLE* ppConstantTable
);
```

- `pSrcFile`—Name of the text file that contains the shader source code that we want to compile

- `pDefines`—This parameter is optional, and we specify null for it in this book.

- `pInclude`—Pointer to an `ID3DXInclude` interface. This interface is designed to be implemented by the application so that we can override default include behavior. In general, the default behavior is fine and we can ignore this parameter by specifying null.

- `pFunctionName`—A string specifying the name of the entry point function. For example, if the shader's entry point function were called `Main`, we would pass "Main" for this parameter.

- `pTarget`—A string specifying the shader version to compile the HLSL source code to. Valid vertex shader versions are: vs_1_1, vs_2_0, vs_2_sw. Valid pixel shader versions are: ps_1_1, ps_1_2, ps_1_3, ps_1_4, ps_2_0, ps_2_sw. For example, if we wanted to compile our vertex shader to version 2.0, we would pass vs_2_0 for this parameter.

> **Remark:** The ability to compile to different shader versions is one of the major benefits of using HLSL over assembly language. With HLSL we can almost instantly port a shader to a different version by simply recompiling to the desired target. Using assembly, we would have to port the code by hand.

- `Flags`—Optional compiling flags; specify 0 for no flags. Valid options are:
  - `D3DXSHADER_DEBUG`—Instructs the compiler to write debug information
  - `D3DXSHADER_SKIPVALIDATION`—Instructs the compiler not to do any code validation. This should only be used when you are using a shader that is known to work.
  - `D3DXSHADER_SKIPOPTIMIZATION`—Instructs the compiler not to perform any code optimization. In practice this would only be used in debugging, where you would not want the compiler to alter the code in any way.

- `ppShader`—Returns a pointer to an `ID3DXBuffer` that contains the compiled shader code. This compiled shader code is then used as a parameter to another function to actually create the vertex/pixel shader.

- `ppErrorMsgs`—Returns a pointer to an `ID3DXBuffer` that contains a string of error codes and messages

- `ppConstantTable`—Returns a pointer to an `ID3DXConstant-Table` that contains the constant table data for this shader

Here is an example call of `D3DXCompileShaderFromFile`:

```
//
// Compile shader
//

ID3DXConstantTable* TransformConstantTable = 0;
ID3DXBuffer* shader       = 0;
ID3DXBuffer* errorBuffer = 0;

hr = D3DXCompileShaderFromFile(
    "transform.txt",        // shader filename
    0,
    0,
    "Main",                 // entry point function name
    "vs_2_0",               // shader version to compile to
    D3DXSHADER_DEBUG,       // debug compile
    &shader,
    &errorBuffer,
    &TransformConstantTable);

// output any error messages
if( errorBuffer )
{
    ::MessageBox(0, (char*)errorBuffer->GetBufferPointer(), 0, 0);
    d3d::Release<ID3DXBuffer*>(errorBuffer);
}

if(FAILED(hr))
{
    ::MessageBox(0, "D3DXCreateEffectFromFile() - FAILED", 0, 0);
    return false;
}
```

16.3 Variable Types

 Note: In addition to the types that are described in the following sections, HLSL also has some built-in object types (e.g., texture object). However, since these object types are primarily used only in the effects framework, we defer a discussion of them until Chapter 19.

16.3.1 Scalar Types

HLSL supports the following scalar types:

- `bool`—True or false value. Note that HLSL provides the `true` and `false` keywords.
- `int`—32-bit signed integer
- `half`—16-bit floating-point number

- `float`—32-bit floating-point number
- `double`—64-bit floating-point number

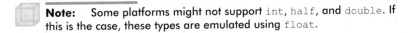

Note: Some platforms might not support `int`, `half`, and `double`. If this is the case, these types are emulated using `float`.

16.3.2 Vector Types

HLSL has the following built-in vector types:

- `vector`—A 4D vector where each component is of type `float`
- `vector<T, n>`—An n-dimensional vector, where each component is of *scalar* type `T`. The dimension n must be between 1 and 4. Here is an example of a 2D double vector:

```
vector<double, 2> vec2;
```

We can access a component of a vector using an array subscript syntax. For example, to set the ith component of a vector `vec`, we would write:

```
vec[i] = 2.0f;
```

In addition, we can access the components of a vector `vec` as we would access the members of a structure, using the defined component names x, y, z, w, r, g, b, and a.

```
vec.x = vec.r = 1.0f;
vec.y = vec.g = 2.0f;
vec.z = vec.b = 3.0f;
vec.w = vec.a = 4.0f;
```

The names r, g, b, and a refer to exactly the same component as the names x, y, z, and w, respectively. When using vectors to represent colors, the RGBA notation is more desirable since it reinforces the fact that the vector is representing a color.

Alternatively, we can use these other predefined types that represent a 2D, 3D, and 4D vector, respectively:

```
float2 vec2;
float3 vec3;
float4 vec4;
```

Consider the vector $\mathbf{u} = (u_x, u_y, u_z, u_w)$ and suppose we want to copy the components of $\mathbf{u}$ to a vector $\mathbf{v}$ such that $\mathbf{v} = (u_x, u_y, u_y, u_w)$. The most immediate solution would be to individually copy each component of $\mathbf{u}$ over to $\mathbf{v}$ as necessary. However, HLSL provides a special syntax for doing these kinds of out-of-order copies called *swizzles*:

```
vector u = {1.0f, 2.0f, 3.0f, 4.0f};
vector v = {0.0f, 0.0f, 5.0f, 6.0f};

v = u.xyyw; // v = {1.0f, 2.0f, 2.0f, 4.0f}
```

Part IV

When copying vectors, we do not have to copy every component over. For example, we can copy over only the x- and y-components, as this code snippet illustrates:

```
vector u = {1.0f, 2.0f, 3.0f, 4.0f};
vector v = {0.0f, 0.0f, 5.0f, 6.0f};

v.xy = u; // v = {1.0f, 2.0f, 5.0f, 6.0f}
```

16.3.3 Matrix Types

HLSL has the following built-in matrix types:

- `matrix`—A 4×4 matrix, where each entry is of type `float`
- `matrix<T, m, n>`—An $m \times n$ matrix, where each entry is of scalar type `T`. The matrix dimensions m and n must be between 1 and 4. Here is an example of an 2×2 integer matrix:

```
matrix<int, 2, 2> m2x2;
```

Alternatively, we can define an $m \times n$ matrix, where m and n are between 1 and 4, using the following syntax:

```
floatmxn matmxn;
```

Examples:

```
float2x2 mat2x2;
float3x3 mat3x3;
float4x4 mat4x4;
float2x4 mat2x4;
```

Note: The types need not be only `float`—we can use other types. For instance we can use integers and write:

```
int2x2 i2x2;
int2x2 i3x3;
int2x2 i2x4;
```

We can access an entry in a matrix using a double array subscript syntax. For example, to set the ij^{th} entry of a matrix M, we would write:

```
M[i][j] = value;
```

In addition, we can refer to the entries of a matrix M as we would access the members of a structure. The following entry names are defined:

One-based:

```
M._11 = M._12 = M._13 = M._14 = 0.0f;
M._21 = M._22 = M._23 = M._24 = 0.0f;
M._31 = M._32 = M._33 = M._34 = 0.0f;
M._41 = M._42 = M._43 = M._44 = 0.0f;
```

Zero-based:

```
M._m00 = M._m01 = M._m02 = M._m03 = 0.0f;
M._m10 = M._m11 = M._m12 = M._m13 = 0.0f;
M._m20 = M._m21 = M._m22 = M._m23 = 0.0f;
M._m30 = M._m31 = M._m32 = M._m33 = 0.0f;
```

Sometimes we want to refer to a particular row vector in a matrix. We can do so using a single array subscript syntax. For example, to refer to the ith row vector in a matrix M, we would write:

```
vector ithRow = M[i]; // get the ith row vector in M
```

Note: We can initialize variables in HLSL using the following two types of syntax:

```
vector u = {0.6f, 0.3f, 1.0f, 1.0f};
vector v = {1.0f, 5.0f, 0.2f, 1.0f};
```

Or, equivalently, using a constructor style syntax:

```
vector u = vector(0.6f, 0.3f, 1.0f, 1.0f);
vector v = vector(1.0f, 5.0f, 0.2f, 1.0f);
```

Some other examples:

```
float2x2 f2x2 = float2x2(1.0f, 2.0f, 3.0f, 4.0f);
int2x2 m = {1, 2, 3, 4};
int n = int(5);
int a = {5};
float3 x = float3(0, 0, 0);
```

16.3.4 Arrays

We can declare an array of a particular type using familiar C++ syntax. For example:

```
float   M[4][4];
half    p[4];
vector v[12];
```

16.3.5 Structures

Structures are defined exactly as they are in C++. However, structures in HLSL cannot have member functions. Here is an example of a structure in HLSL:

```
struct MyStruct
{
    matrix T;
    vector n;
    float  f;
    int    x;
    bool   b;
};
```

Part IV

```
MyStruct s; // instantiate
s.f = 5.0f; // member access
```

16.3.6 The typedef Keyword

The HLSL `typedef` keyword functions exactly the same as it does in C++. For example, we can give the name `point` to the type `vector<float, 3>` using the following syntax:

```
typedef vector<float, 3> point;
```

Then instead of writing:

```
vector<float, 3> myPoint;
```

...we can just write:

```
point myPoint;
```

Here are two more examples that show how to use the `typedef` keyword with a constant type and an array:

```
typedef const float CFLOAT;
typedef float point2[2];
```

16.3.7 Variable Prefixes

The following keywords can prefix a variable declaration:

- `static`—If a global variable is prefixed with the `static` keyword, it means that it is not to be exposed outside the shader. In other words, it is local to the shader. If a local variable is prefixed with the `static` keyword, it has the same behavior as a `static` local variable in C++. That is, it is initialized once when the function is first executed, and it maintains its value throughout all calls of the function. If the variable is not initialized, it is automatically initialized to 0.

```
static int x = 5;
```

- `uniform`—If a variable is prefixed with the `uniform` keyword, it means the variable is initialized outside the shader, by the C++ application for instance, and input into the shader.

- `extern`—If a variable is prefixed with the `extern` keyword it means the variable can be accessed outside the shader, by the C++ application for instance. Only global variables can be prefixed with the `extern` keyword. Non-static global variables are `extern` by default.

- `shared`—If a variable is prefixed with the `shared` keyword, it hints to the effects framework (see Chapter 19) that the variable will be shared across multiple effects. Only global variables can be prefixed with the `shared` keyword.

- `volatile`—If a variable is prefixed with the `volatile` keyword, it hints to the effects framework (see Chapter 19) that the variable will be modified often. Only global variables can be prefixed with the `volatile` keyword.

- `const`—The `const` keyword in HLSL has the same meaning it has in C++. That is, if a variable is prefixed with the `const` keyword, then that variable is constant and cannot be changed.

```
const float pi = 3.14f;
```

16.4 Keywords, Statements, and Casting

16.4.1 Keywords

For reference, here is a list of the keywords that HLSL defines:

asm	bool	compile	const	decl	do
double	else	extern	false	float	for
half	if	in	inline	inout	int
matrix	out	pass	pixelshader	return	sampler
shared	static	string	struct	technique	texture
true	typedef	uniform	vector	vertexshader	void
volatile	while				

This next set displays identifiers that are reserved and unused but may become keywords in the future:

auto	break	case	catch	char	class
const_cast	continue	default	delete	dynamic_cast	enum
explicit	friend	goto	long	mutable	namespace
new	operator	private	protected	public	register
reinterpret_cast	short	signed	sizeof	static_cast	switch
template	this	throw	try	typename	union
unsigned	using	virtual			

16.4.2 Basic Program Flow

HLSL supports many familiar C++ statements for selection, repetition, and general program flow. The syntax of these statements is exactly like C++.

The *return* statement:

```
return (expression);
```

The *if* and *if...else* statements:

```
if( condition )
{
    statement(s);
}

if( condition )
{
    statement(s);
}
else
{
    statement(s);
}
```

The *for* statement:

```
for(initial; condition; increment)
{
    statement(s);
}
```

The *while* statement:

```
while( condition )
{
    statement(s);
}
```

The *do...while* statement:

```
do
{
    statement(s);
}while( condition );
```

16.4.3 Casting

HLSL supports a very flexible casting scheme. The casting syntax in HLSL is the same as in the C programming language. For example, to cast a `float` to a `matrix`, we write:

```
float f = 5.0f;
matrix m = (matrix)f;
```

For the examples in this book, you will be able to deduce the meaning of the cast from the syntax. However, if you want more detailed information on the supported casts, in the DirectX SDK documentation, under the Contents tab, see DirectX Graphics\Reference\Shader Reference\High Level Shading Language\Type.

16.5 **Operators**

HLSL supports many familiar C++ operators. With a few exceptions noted below, they are used exactly the same way as they are in C++. These are the HLSL operators:

[]	.	>	<	<=	>=
!=	==	!	&&	||	?:
+	+=	–	–=	*	*=
/	/=	%	%=	++	––
=	()	,			

Although the operators' behavior is very similar to C++, there are some differences. First of all, the modulus % operator works on both integer and floating-point types. In order to use the modulus operator, both the left-side value and right-side value must have the same sign (e.g., both sides must be positive or negative).

Secondly, observe that many of the HLSL operations work on a per component basis. This is due to the fact that vectors and matrices are built into the language and these types consist of several components. By having the operations work on a component level, operations such as vector/matrix addition, vector/matrix subtraction, and vector/matrix equality tests can be done using the same operators that we use for scalar types. See the following examples.

Note: The operators behave as expected for scalars (that is, in the usual C++ way).

```
vector u = {1.0f, 0.0f, -3.0f, 1.0f};
vector v = {-4.0f, 2.0f, 1.0f, 0.0f};

// adds corresponding components
vector sum = u + v; // sum = (-3.0f, 2.0f, -2.0f, 1.0f)
```

Incrementing a vector increments each component:

```
// before increment: sum = (-3.0f, 2.0f, -2.0f, 1.0f)

sum++; // after increment: sum = (-2.0f, 3.0f, -1.0f, 2.0f)
```

Multiplying vectors component-wise:

```
vector u = {1.0f, 0.0f, -3.0f, 1.0f};
vector v = {-4.0f, 2.0f, 1.0f, 0.0f};

// multiply corresponding components
vector sum = u * v; // product = (-4.0f, 0.0f, -3.0f, 0.0f)
```

Comparison operators are also done per component and return a vector or matrix where each component is of type `bool`. The resulting

Part IV

"`bool`" vector contains the results of each compared component. For example:

```
vector u = { 1.0f, 0.0f, -3.0f, 1.0f};
vector v = {-4.0f, 0.0f,  1.0f, 1.0f};

vector b = (u == v); // b = (false, true, false, true)
```

Finally, we conclude by discussing variable promotions with binary operations:

- For binary operations, if the left side and right side differ in dimension, the side with the smaller dimension is promoted (cast) to have the same dimension as the side with the larger dimension. For example, if x is of type `float` and y is of type `float3`, in the expression (x + y) the variable x is promoted to `float3` and the expression evaluates to a value of type `float3`. The promotion is done using the defined cast. In this case we are casting scalar-to-vector; therefore, after x is promoted to `float3`, x = (x, x, x), as the scalar-to-vector cast defines. Note that the promotion is not defined if the cast is not defined. For example, we can't promote `float2` to `float3` because there exists no such defined cast.

- For binary operations, if the left side and right side differ in type, then the side with the lower type resolution is promoted (cast) to have the same type as the side with the higher type resolution. For example, if x is of type `int` and y is of type `half`, in the expression (x + y) the variable x is promoted to a `half` and the expression evaluates to a value of type `half`.

16.6 User-Defined Functions

Functions in HLSL have the following properties:

- Functions use a familiar C++ syntax.
- Parameters are always passed by value.
- Recursion is not supported.
- Functions are always inlined.

Furthermore, HLSL adds some extra keywords that can be used with functions. For example, consider the following function written in HLSL:

```
bool foo(in const bool b,    // input bool
         out int r1,         // output int
         inout float r2)     // input/output float
{
```

```
if( b )                   // test input value
{
    r1 = 5;               // output a value through r1
}
else
{
    r1 = 1;               // output a value through r1
}

// since r2 is inout we can use it as an input
// value and also output a value through it
r2 = r2 * r2 * r2;

return true;
}
```

The function is almost identical to a C++ function except for the in, out, and inout keywords.

- in—Specifies that the *argument* (particular variable that we pass into a parameter) should be copied to the parameter before the function begins. It is not necessary to explicitly specify a parameter as in because a parameter is in by default. For example, the following are equivalent:

```
float square(in float x)
{
    return x * x;
}
```

Without explicitly specifying in:

```
float square(float x)
{
    return x * x;
}
```

- out—Specifies that the parameter should be copied to the argument when the function returns. This is useful for returning values through parameters. The out keyword is necessary because HLSL doesn't allow us to pass by reference or pass a pointer. We note that if a parameter is marked as out, the argument is not copied to the parameter before the function begins. In other words, an out parameter can only be used to output data—it can't be used for input.

```
void square(in float x, out float y)
{
    y = x * x;
}
```

Here we input the number to be squared through x and return the square of x through the parameter y.

Part IV

- inout—Shortcut that denotes a parameter as both `in` and `out`. Specify `inout` if you wish to use a parameter for both input and output.

```
void square(inout float x)
{
    x = x * x;
}
```

Here we input the number to be squared through x and also return the square of x through x.

16.7 Built-in Functions

HLSL has a rich set of built-in functions that are useful for 3D graphics. The following table is an abridged list of them. In the next two chapters we will get practice using some of these functions. For now, just get familiar with them.

Note: For further reference, the complete list of the built-in HLSL functions can be found in the DirectX documentation, under the Contents tab, then DirectX Graphics\Reference\Shader Reference\High Level Shader Language\Intrinsic Functions.

Function	Description
abs(x)	Returns $|x|$
ceil(x)	Returns the smallest integer $\geq x$
clamp(x, a, b)	Clamps x to the range $[a, b]$ and returns the result
cos(x)	Returns the cosine of x, where x is in radians
cross(u, v)	Returns $\mathbf{u} \times \mathbf{v}$
degrees(x)	Converts x from radians to degrees
determinant(M)	Returns the determinant $\det(\mathbf{M})$
distance(u, v)	Returns the distance $\|\mathbf{v} - \mathbf{u}\|$ between the points $\mathbf{u}$ and $\mathbf{v}$
dot(u, v)	Returns $\mathbf{u} \cdot \mathbf{v}$
floor(x)	Returns the greatest integer $\leq x$
length(v)	Returns $\|\mathbf{v}\|$
lerp(u, v, t)	Linearly interpolates between u and v based on the parameter $t \in [0, 1]$
log(x)	Returns $\ln(x)$
log10(x)	Returns $\log_{10}(x)$
log2(x)	Returns $\log_{2}(x)$

Function	Description
max(x, y)	Returns x if $x \geq y$, else returns y
min(x, y)	Returns x if $x \leq y$, else returns y
mul(M, N)	Returns the matrix product **MN**. Note that the matrix product **MN** must be defined. If **M** is a vector, it is treated as a row vector so that the vector-matrix product is defined. Likewise, if **N** is a vector it is treated as a column vector so that the matrix-vector product is defined.
normalize(v)	Returns $\mathbf{v}/\|\mathbf{v}\|$
pow(b, n)	Returns b^n
radians(x)	Converts x from degrees to radians
reflect(v, n)	Computes the reflection vector given the incident vector **v** and the surface normal **n**
refract(v, n, eta)	Computes the refraction vector given the incident vector **v**, the surface normal **n**, and the ratio of the two indices of refraction of the two materials *eta*. Look up Snell's law in a physics book or on the Internet for information on refraction.
rsqrt(x)	Returns $1/\sqrt{x}$
saturate(x)	Returns clamp(x, 0.0, 1.0)
sin(x)	Returns the sine of x, where x is in radians
sincos(in x, out s, out c)	Returns the sine and cosine of x, where x is in radians
sqrt(x)	Returns $\sqrt{x}$
tan(x)	Returns the tangent of x, where x is in radians
transpose(M)	Returns the transpose $\mathbf{M}^T$

Most of the functions are overloaded to work with all the built-in types for which the function makes sense. For instance, `abs` makes sense for all scalar types and so is overloaded for all of them. As another example, the cross product `cross` only makes sense for 3D vectors, so it is only overloaded for 3D vectors of any type (e.g., 3D vectors of `int`s, `float`s, `double`s etc.). On the other hand, linear interpolation, `lerp`, makes sense for scalars and 2D, 3D, and 4D vectors and therefore is overloaded for all types.

Note: If you pass in a non-scalar type into a "scalar" function, that is, a function that traditionally operates on scalars (e.g., `cos(x)`), the function will act per component. For example, if you write:

```
float3 v = float3(0.0f, 0.0f, 0.0f);

v = cos(v);
```

Part IV

Then the function will act per component: $\mathbf{v} = (\cos(x), \;\; \cos(y), \;\; \cos(z))$.

The following examples show how some of these intrinsic functions might be called:

```
float x = sin(1.0f);        // sine of 1.0f radian.
float y = sqrt(4.0f);       // square root of 4.

vector u = {1.0f, 2.0f, -3.0f, 0.0f};
vector v = {3.0f, -1.0f, 0.0f, 2.0f};
float  s = dot(u, v);        // compute dot product of u and v.

float3 i = {1.0f, 0.0f, 0.0f};
float3 j = {0.0f, 1.0f, 0.0f};
float3 k = cross(i, j);      // compute cross product of i and j.

matrix<float, 2, 2> M = {1.0f, 2.0f, 3.0f, 4.0f};
matrix<float, 2, 2> T = transpose(M); // compute transpose
```

16.8 Summary

- We write HLSL programs in ASCII text files and compile them in our applications using the `D3DXCompileShaderFromFile` function.

- The `ID3DXConstantTable` interface allows us to set variables in the shader program from our application. This communication is necessary because variables used by the shader can change on a frame-to-frame basis. For example, if the view matrix changes in the application, we need to update the shader's view matrix variable with the new view matrix. We can do this update with the `ID3DXConstantTable`.

- For each shader, we must define an input and output structure that describes the format of the data that the shader inputs and outputs, respectively.

- Every shader has an entry point function that takes an input structure parameter that is used to pass input data into the shader. In addition, every shader returns an output structure instance that is used to output data from the shader.

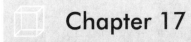

Chapter 17

Introduction to Vertex Shaders

A *vertex shader* is a program executed on the graphics card's GPU that replaces the transformation and lighting stage in the fixed function pipeline. (This is not 100 percent true, as vertex shaders can be emulated in software by the Direct3D runtime if the hardware does not support vertex shaders.) Figure 17.1 illustrates the section in the pipeline that the vertex shader replaces.

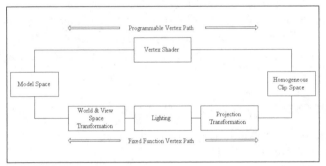

Figure 17.1: The vertex shader replaces the lighting and transformation stage of the fixed function pipeline.

From Figure 17.1 we see that vertices are input into the vertex shader in local coordinates and the vertex shader must output lit (colored) vertices in *homogeneous clip space*. (We didn't delve into the details of the projection transformation in this book for simplicity reasons. But the space to which the projection matrix transforms vertices is called homogeneous clip space. Therefore, to transform a vertex from local space to homogenous clip space, we must apply the following sequence of transformations: world transformation, view transformation, and projection transformation, which are done by the world matrix, view matrix, and projection matrix, respectively.) For point primitives, a vertex shader can also be used to manipulate the vertex size per vertex.

Because a vertex shader is a custom program that we write (in HLSL), we obtain a *huge* amount of flexibility in the graphical effects we can achieve. For example, with vertex shaders we can use any lighting algorithm that can be implemented in a vertex shader. We are no longer limited to Direct3D's fixed lighting algorithm. Furthermore, the ability to manipulate a vertex's position has a variety of applications as well, such as cloth simulation, point size manipulation for particle systems, and vertex blending/morphing. In addition, our vertex data structures are more flexible and can contain much more data in the programmable pipeline than they could in the fixed function pipeline.

Vertex shaders are still a relatively new feature, and many cards do not support them, especially the newer vertex shader versions that were released with DirectX 9. You can test the vertex shader version that your graphics card supports by checking the `VertexShader-Version` member of the `D3DCAPS9` structure and the macro `D3DVS_VERSION`. The following code snippet illustrates this:

```
// If the device's supported version is less than version 2.0
if( caps.VertexShaderVersion < D3DVS_VERSION(2, 0) )
    // Then vertex shader version 2.0 is not supported on this
    // device.
```

We see that the two parameters of `D3DVS_VERSION` take the major and minor version number, respectively. Currently, the `D3DXCompile-ShaderFromFile` function supports vertex shader versions 1.1 and 2.0.

Objectives

- To learn how we define the components of our vertex structure in the programmable pipeline
- To learn about the different usages for vertex components
- To learn how to create, set, and destroy a vertex shader
- To learn how to implement a cartoon rendering effect using a vertex shader

17.1 Vertex Declarations

Thus far, we have been using a flexible vertex format (FVF) to describe the components of our vertex structure. However, in the programmable pipe, our vertex data can contain much more data than can be expressed with an FVF. Therefore, we usually use the more descriptive and powerful *vertex declaration*.

Note: We can still use an FVF with the programmable pipeline if the format of our vertex can be described by it. However, this is for convenience only, as the FVF will be converted to a vertex declaration internally.

17.1.1 Describing a Vertex Declaration

We describe a vertex declaration as an array of D3DVERTEXELEMENT9 structures. Each element in the D3DVERTEXELEMENT9 array describes one component of the vertex. So if your vertex structure has three components (e.g., position, normal, color), then the corresponding vertex declaration will be described by an array of three D3DVERTEXELEMENT9 structures. The D3DVERTEXELEMENT9 structure is defined as:

```
typedef struct _D3DVERTEXELEMENT9 {
    BYTE Stream;
    BYTE Offset;
    BYTE Type;
    BYTE Method;
    BYTE Usage;
    BYTE UsageIndex;
} D3DVERTEXELEMENT9;
```

- Stream—Specifies the stream with which the vertex component is associated

- Offset—The offset, in bytes, to the start of the vertex component relative to the vertex structure of which it is a member. For example, if the vertex structure is:

```
struct Vertex
{
    D3DXVECTOR3 pos;
    D3DXVECTOR3 normal;
};
```

…the offset of the component pos is 0 since it's the first component. The offset of the component normal is 12 because sizeof(pos) == 12. In other words, the component normal starts at byte 12 relative to Vertex.

- Type—Specifies the data type. This can be any member of the D3DDECLTYPE enumerated type; see the documentation for a complete list. Some commonly used types are:

   ☐ D3DDECLTYPE_FLOAT1—A floating-point scalar

   ☐ D3DDECLTYPE_FLOAT2—A 2D floating-point vector

   ☐ D3DDECLTYPE_FLOAT3—A 3D floating-point vector

   ☐ D3DDECLTYPE_FLOAT4—A 4D floating-point vector

☐ D3DDECLTYPE_D3DCOLOR—A D3DCOLOR type that is expanded to the RGBA floating-point color vector (*r g b a*), with each component normalized to the interval [0, 1].

■ Method—Specifies the tessellation method. We consider this parameter advanced, and thus we use the default method, which is specified by the identifier D3DDECLMETHOD_DEFAULT.

■ Usage—Specifies the planned use for the vertex component. For example, is it going to be a position vector, normal vector, texture coordinate, etc.? Valid usage identifiers are of the D3DDECLUSAGE enumerated type:

```
typedef enum  D3DDECLUSAGE {
        D3DDECLUSAGE POSITION      = 0,  // Position.
        D3DDECLUSAGE BLENDWEIGHTS  = 1,  // Blending weights.
        D3DDECLUSAGE BLENDINDICES  = 2,  // Blending indices.
        D3DDECLUSAGE NORMAL        = 3,  // Normal vector.
        D3DDECLUSAGE PSIZE         = 4,  // Vertex point size.
        D3DDECLUSAGE TEXCOORD      = 5,  // Texture coordinates.
        D3DDECLUSAGE TANGENT       = 6,  // Tangent vector.
        D3DDECLUSAGE BINORMAL      = 7,  // Binormal vector.
        D3DDECLUSAGE TESSFACTOR    = 8,  // Tessellation factor.
        D3DDECLUSAGE POSITIONT     = 9,  // Transformed position.
        D3DDECLUSAGE COLOR         = 10, // Color.
        D3DDECLUSAGE FOG           = 11, // Fog blend value.
        D3DDECLUSAGE DEPTH         = 12, // Depth value.
        D3DDECLUSAGE SAMPLE        = 13  // Sampler data.
} D3DDECLUSAGE;
```

The D3DDECLUSAGE_PSIZE type is used to specify a vertex point size. This is used for point sprites so that we can control the size on a per vertex basis. A vertex declaration with a D3DDECLUSAGE_POSITIONT member implies that the vertex has already been transformed, which instructs the graphics card to not send this vertex through the vertex processing stages (transformation and lighting).

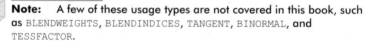

Note: A few of these usage types are not covered in this book, such as BLENDWEIGHTS, BLENDINDICES, TANGENT, BINORMAL, and TESSFACTOR.

■ UsageIndex—Used to identify multiple vertex components of the same usage. The usage index is an integer in the interval [0, 15]. For example, suppose that we have three vertex components of the usage D3DDECLUSAGE_NORMAL. We would specify a usage index of 0 for the first, a usage index of 1 for the second, and a usage index of 2 for the third. In this way we can identify each particular normal by its usage index.

Example vertex declaration description: Suppose the vertex format we want to describe consists of a position vector and three normal vectors. The vertex declaration would be specified as:

```
D3DVERTEXELEMENT9 decl[] =
{
{0,  0, D3DDECLTYPE_FLOAT3, D3DDECLMETHOD_DEFAULT, D3DDECLUSAGE_
  POSITION, 0},
{0, 12, D3DDECLTYPE_FLOAT3, D3DDECLMETHOD_DEFAULT, D3DDECLUSAGE_
  NORMAL,   0},
{0, 24, D3DDECLTYPE_FLOAT3, D3DDECLMETHOD_DEFAULT, D3DDECLUSAGE_
  NORMAL,   1},
{0, 36, D3DDECLTYPE_FLOAT3, D3DDECLMETHOD_DEFAULT, D3DDECLUSAGE_
  NORMAL,   2},
D3DDECL_END()
};
```

The `D3DDECL_END` macro is used to initialize the last vertex element in the `D3DVERTEXELEMENT9` array. Also, observe the usage index labels for the normal vectors.

17.1.2 Creating a Vertex Declaration

Once a vertex declaration has been described as a `D3DVERTEXELE-MENT9` array, we can obtain a pointer to an `IDirect3DVertex-Declaration9` interface using the method:

```
HRESULT IDirect3DDevice9::CreateVertexDeclaration(
    CONST D3DVERTEXELEMENT9* pVertexElements,
    IDirect3DVertexDeclaration9** ppDecl
);
```

- `pVertexElements`—Array of `D3DVERTEXELEMENT9` structures describing the vertex declaration we want created
- `ppDecl`—Used to return a pointer to the created `IDirect3D-VertexDeclaration9` interface

Example call, where `decl` is a `D3DVERTEXELEMENT9` array:

```
IDirect3DVertexDeclaration9* _decl = 0;
hr = _device->CreateVertexDeclaration(decl, &_decl);
```

17.1.3 Enabling a Vertex Declaration

Recall that flexible vertex formats are a convenience feature and internally get converted to vertex declarations. Thus, when using vertex declarations directly, we no longer call:

```
Device->SetFVF( fvf );
```

We instead call:

```
Device->SetVertexDeclaration( _decl );
```

Part IV

where `_decl` is a pointer to an `IDirect3DVertexDeclaration9` interface.

17.2 Vertex Data Usages

Consider the vertex declaration:

```
D3DVERTEXELEMENT9 decl[] =
{
{0,  0, D3DDECLTYPE_FLOAT3, D3DDECLMETHOD_DEFAULT, D3DDECLUSAGE_
   POSITION, 0},
{0, 12, D3DDECLTYPE_FLOAT3, D3DDECLMETHOD_DEFAULT, D3DDECLUSAGE_
   NORMAL,   0},
{0, 24, D3DDECLTYPE_FLOAT3, D3DDECLMETHOD_DEFAULT, D3DDECLUSAGE_
   NORMAL,   1},
{0, 36, D3DDECLTYPE_FLOAT3, D3DDECLMETHOD_DEFAULT, D3DDECLUSAGE_
   NORMAL,   2},
D3DDECL_END()
};
```

We need a way to define a map from the elements of the vertex declaration to the data members of the vertex shader's input structure. We define this map in the input structure by specifying a semantic (`: usage-type[usage-index]`) for each data member. The semantic identifies an element in the vertex declaration by its usage type and usage index. The vertex element identified by a data member's semantic is the element that gets mapped to that data member. For example, an input structure for the previous vertex declaration is:

```
struct VS_INPUT
{
    vector position   : POSITION;
    vector normal     : NORMAL0;
    vector faceNormal1 : NORMAL1;
    vector faceNormal2 : NORMAL2;
};
```

Note: If we leave off the usage index, it implies usage index zero. For example, POSITION is the same thing as POSITION0.

Here element 0 in `decl`, identified by usage POSITION and usage index 0, is mapped to `position`. Element 1 in `decl`, identified by usage NORMAL and usage index 0, is mapped to `normal`. Element 2 in `decl`, identified by usage NORMAL and usage index 1, is mapped to `faceNormal1`. Element 3 in `decl`, identified by usage NORMAL and usage index 2, is mapped to `faceNormal2`.

The supported vertex shader input usages are:

- `POSITION[n]`—Position
- `BLENDWEIGHTS[n]`—Blend weights
- `BLENDINDICES[n]`—Blend indices
- `NORMAL[n]`—Normal vector
- `PSIZE[n]`—Vertex point size
- `DIFFUSE[n]`—Diffuse color
- `SPECULAR[n]`—Specular color
- `TEXCOORD[n]`—Texture coordinates
- `TANGENT[n]`—Tangent vector
- `BINORMAL[n]`—Binormal vector
- `TESSFACTOR[n]`—Tessellation factor

Where n is an optional integer in the range [0, 15].

Note: Again, a few of these usage types are not covered in this book, such as `BLENDWEIGHTS`, `TANGENT`, `BINORMAL`, `BLENDINDICES`, and `TESSFACTOR`.

In addition, for the output structure, we must specify what each member is to be used for. For example, should the data member be treated as a position vector, color, texture coordinate, etc.? The graphics card has no idea, unless you explicitly tell it. This is also done with the semantic syntax:

```
struct VS_OUTPUT
{
    vector position : POSITION;
    vector diffuse  : COLOR0;
    vector specular : COLOR1;
};
```

The supported vertex shader output usages are:

- `POSITION`—Position
- `PSIZE`—Vertex point size
- `FOG`—Fog blend value
- `COLOR[n]`—Vertex color. Observe that multiple vertex colors can be output, and these colors are blended together to produce the final color.
- `TEXCOORD[n]`—Vertex texture coordinates. Observe that multiple texture coordinates can be output.

Where n is an optional integer in the interval [0, 15].

17.3 Steps to Using a Vertex Shader

The following list outlines the steps necessary to create and use a vertex shader.

1. Write and compile the vertex shader.
2. Create an `IDirect3DVertexShader9` interface to represent the vertex shader based on the compiled shader code.
3. Enable the vertex shader with the `IDirect3DDevice9::SetVertexShader` method.

Of course, we have to destroy the vertex shader when we are done with it. The next subsections go into these steps in more detail.

17.3.1 Writing and Compiling a Vertex Shader

First, we must write a vertex shader program. In this book we write our shaders in HLSL. Once the shader code is written, we compile the shader using the `D3DXCompileShaderFromFile` function, as described in section 16.2.2. Recall that this function returns a pointer to an `ID3DXBuffer` that contains the compiled shader code.

17.3.2 Creating a Vertex Shader

Once we have the compiled shader code, we can obtain a pointer to an `IDirect3DVertexShader9` interface, which represents a vertex shader, using the following method:

```
HRESULT IDirect3DDevice9::CreateVertexShader(
    const DWORD *pFunction,
    IDirect3DVertexShader9** ppShader
);
```

- `pFunction`—Pointer to compiled shader code
- `ppShader`—Returns a pointer to an `IDirect3DVertexShader9` interface

For example, suppose the variable `shader` is an `ID3DXBuffer` that contains the compiled shader code. Then to obtain an `IDirect3DVertexShader9` interface, we would write:

```
IDirect3DVertexShader9* ToonShader = 0;
hr = Device->CreateVertexShader(
        (DWORD*)shader->GetBufferPointer(),
        &ToonShader);
```

Note: To reiterate, the `D3DXCompileShaderFromFile` is the function that would return the compiled shader code (`shader`).

17.3.3 Setting a Vertex Shader

After we have obtained a pointer to an `IDirect3DVertexShader9` interface that represents our vertex shader, we can enable it using the following method:

```
HRESULT IDirect3DDevice9::SetVertexShader(
    IDirect3DVertexShader9* pShader
);
```

The method takes a single parameter where we pass a pointer to the vertex shader that we wish to enable. To enable the shader we created in section 17.3.2, we would write:

```
Device->SetVertexShader(ToonShader);
```

17.3.4 Destroying a Vertex Shader

As with all Direct3D interfaces, to clean them up we must call their `Release` method when we are finished with them. Continuing to use the vertex shader we created in section 17.3.2, we have:

```
d3d::Release<IDirect3DVertexShader9*>(ToonShader);
```

17.4 Sample Application: Diffuse Lighting

As a warm-up to creating and using vertex shaders, we write a vertex shader that does standard diffuse lighting per vertex with a directional (parallel) light source. As a recap, diffuse lighting calculates the amount of light that a vertex receives based on the angle between the vertex normal and the light vector (which points in the direction of the light source). The smaller the angle, the more light the vertex receives, and the larger the angle, the less light the vertex receives. If the angle is greater than or equal to 90 degrees, the vertex receives no light. Refer back to section 13.4.1 for a more complete description of the diffuse lighting algorithm.

We begin by examining the vertex shader code.

```
// File: diffuse.txt
// Desc: Vertex shader that does diffuse lighting.
//
//
// Global variables we use to hold the view matrix, projection matrix,
// ambient material, diffuse material, and the light vector that
// describes the direction to the light source. These variables are
// initialized from the application.
//
```

```
matrix ViewMatrix;
matrix ViewProjMatrix;

vector AmbientMtrl;
vector DiffuseMtrl;

vector LightDirection;

//
// Global variables used to hold the ambient light intensity (ambient
// light the light source emits) and the diffuse light
// intensity (diffuse light the light source emits). These
// variables are initialized here in the shader.
//

vector DiffuseLightIntensity = {0.0f, 0.0f, 1.0f, 1.0f};
vector AmbientLightIntensity = {0.0f, 0.0f, 0.2f, 1.0f};

//
// Input and Output structures.
//

struct VS_INPUT
{
    vector position : POSITION;
    vector normal   : NORMAL;
};

struct VS_OUTPUT
{
    vector position : POSITION;
    vector diffuse  : COLOR;
};

//
// Main
//

VS_OUTPUT Main(VS_INPUT input)
{
    // zero out all members of the output instance.
    VS_OUTPUT output = (VS_OUTPUT)0;

    //
    // Transform position to homogeneous clip space
    // and store in the output.position member.
    //
    output.position = mul(input.position, ViewProjMatrix);

    //
    // Transform lights and normals to view space.  Set w
    // components to zero since we're transforming vectors
    // here and not points.
    //
    LightDirection.w = 0.0f;
```

```
        input.normal.w   = 0.0f;
        LightDirection   = mul(LightDirection, ViewMatrix);
        input.normal     = mul(input.normal,   ViewMatrix);

        //
        // Compute cosine of the angle between light and normal.
        //
        float s = dot(LightDirection, input.normal);

        //
        // Recall that if the angle between the surface and light
        // is greater than 90 degrees the surface receives no light.
        // Thus, if the angle is greater than 90 degrees we set
        // s to zero so that the surface will not be lit.
        //
        if( s < 0.0f )
            s = 0.0f;

        //
        // Ambient light reflected is computed by performing a
        // component-wise multiplication with the ambient material
        // vector and the ambient light intensity vector.
        //
        // Diffuse light reflected is computed by performing a
        // component-wise multiplication with the diffuse material
        // vector and the diffuse light intensity vector.  Further,
        // we scale each component by the shading scalar s, which
        // shades the color based on how much light the vertex received
        // from the light source.
        //
        // The sum of both the ambient and diffuse components give
        // us our final vertex color.
        //

        output.diffuse = (AmbientMtrl * AmbientLightIntensity) +
                         (s * (DiffuseLightIntensity * DiffuseMtrl));

        return output;
}
```

Now that we have looked at the actual vertex shader code, let's shift gears and look at the application code. The application has the following relevant global variables:

```
IDirect3DVertexShader9* DiffuseShader = 0;
ID3DXConstantTable* DiffuseConstTable = 0;

ID3DXMesh* Teapot                      = 0;

D3DXHANDLE ViewMatrixHandle       = 0;
D3DXHANDLE ViewProjMatrixHandle = 0;
D3DXHANDLE AmbientMtrlHandle      = 0;
D3DXHANDLE DiffuseMtrlHandle      = 0;
D3DXHANDLE LightDirHandle         = 0;

D3DXMATRIX Proj;
```

We have variables to represent the vertex shader and its constant table. We have a teapot mesh variable, followed by a set of D3DXHANDLEs whose variable names describe the variable they refer to.

The Setup function performs the following tasks:

- Creates the teapot mesh
- Compiles the vertex shader
- Creates the vertex shader based on the compiled code
- Obtains handles to several variables in the shader program through the constant table
- Initializes several of the shader variables through the constant table

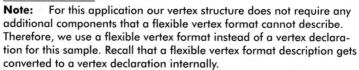

Note: For this application our vertex structure does not require any additional components that a flexible vertex format cannot describe. Therefore, we use a flexible vertex format instead of a vertex declaration for this sample. Recall that a flexible vertex format description gets converted to a vertex declaration internally.

```
bool Setup()
{
    HRESULT hr = 0;

    //
    // Create geometry:
    //

    D3DXCreateTeapot(Device, &Teapot, 0);

    //
    // Compile shader
    //

    ID3DXBuffer* shader      = 0;
    ID3DXBuffer* errorBuffer = 0;

    hr = D3DXCompileShaderFromFile(
        "diffuse.txt",
        0,
        0,
        "Main", // entry point function name
        "vs_1_1",
        D3DXSHADER_DEBUG,
        &shader,
        &errorBuffer,
        &DiffuseConstTable);

    // output any error messages
    if( errorBuffer )
    {
        ::MessageBox(0, (char*)errorBuffer->GetBufferPointer(), 0, 0);
        d3d::Release<ID3DXBuffer*>(errorBuffer);
```

```
    }

    if(FAILED(hr))
    {
        ::MessageBox(0, "D3DXCompileShaderFromFile() - FAILED", 0, 0);
        return false;
    }

    //
    // Create shader
    //

    hr = Device->CreateVertexShader(
        (DWORD*)shader->GetBufferPointer(),
        &DiffuseShader);

    if(FAILED(hr))
    {
        ::MessageBox(0, "CreateVertexShader - FAILED", 0, 0);
        return false;
    }

    d3d::Release<ID3DXBuffer*>(shader);


    //
    // Get Handles
    //

    ViewMatrixHandle = DiffuseConstTable->GetConstantByName(
                        0, "ViewMatrix");
    ViewProjMatrixHandle = DiffuseConstTable->GetConstantByName(
                            0, "ViewProjMatrix");
    AmbientMtrlHandle = DiffuseConstTable->GetConstantByName(
                        0, "AmbientMtrl");
    DiffuseMtrlHandle = DiffuseConstTable->GetConstantByName(
                        0, "DiffuseMtrl");
    LightDirHandle   = DiffuseConstTable->GetConstantByName(
                        0, "LightDirection");

//
// Set shader constants:
//

// Light direction:
D3DXVECTOR4 directionToLight(-0.57f, 0.57f, -0.57f, 0.0f);
DiffuseConstTable->SetVector(Device, LightDirHandle,
                            &directionToLight);

// Materials:
D3DXVECTOR4 ambientMtrl(0.0f, 0.0f, 1.0f, 1.0f);
D3DXVECTOR4 diffuseMtrl(0.0f, 0.0f, 1.0f, 1.0f);
DiffuseConstTable->SetVector(Device,AmbientMtrlHandle, &ambientMtrl);
DiffuseConstTable->SetVector(Device,DiffuseMtrlHandle, &diffuseMtrl);
DiffuseConstTable->SetDefaults(Device);
```

Part IV

```
// Compute projection matrix.
D3DXMatrixPerspectiveFovLH(
    &Proj, D3DX_PI * 0.25f,
    (float)Width / (float)Height, 1.0f, 1000.0f);

return true;
}
```

The `Display` function is quite simple. It tests for user input and updates the view matrix accordingly. However, because we perform the view matrix transformation in the shader, we must also update the view matrix variable within the shader. We do this using the constant table:

```
bool Display(float timeDelta)
{
    if( Device )
    {
        //
        // Update view matrix code snipped...
        //

        D3DXMATRIX V;
        D3DXMatrixLookAtLH(&V, &position, &target, &up);

        DiffuseConstTable->SetMatrix(Device, ViewMatrixHandle, &V);

        D3DXMATRIX ViewProj = V * Proj;
        DiffuseConstTable->SetMatrix(Device, ViewProjMatrixHandle,
                                     &ViewProj);

        //
        // Render
        //

        Device->Clear(0, 0, D3DCLEAR_TARGET | D3DCLEAR_ZBUFFER,
                      0xffffffff, 1.0f, 0);
        Device->BeginScene();

        Device->SetVertexShader(DiffuseShader);

        Teapot->DrawSubset(0);

        Device->EndScene();
        Device->Present(0, 0, 0, 0);
    }
    return true;
}
```

Also observe that we enable the vertex shader that we wish to use right before the `DrawSubset` call.

Cleaning up is done as expected; we simply release the allocated interfaces:

```
void Cleanup()
{
    d3d::Release<ID3DXMesh*>(Teapot);
```

```
d3d::Release<IDirect3DVertexShader9*>(DiffuseShader);
d3d::Release<ID3DXConstantTable*>(DiffuseConstTable);
}
```

17.5 Sample Application: Cartoon Rendering

As a second vertex shader sample, let's write two vertex shaders that
shade and outline a mesh in such a way that it appears as a cartoon-
style drawing. Figure 17.2 illustrates this:

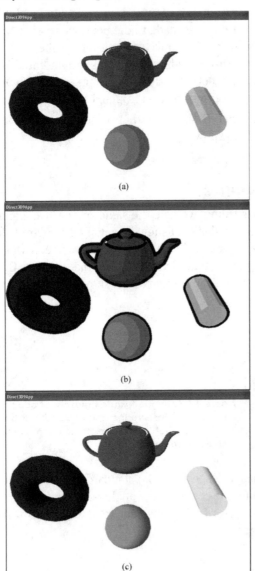

Figure 17.2: (a) Objects
shaded using cartoon shading (note the sharp transition
between shades). (b) To
enhance the cartoon effect,
the silhouette edges are outlined. (c) Objects shaded
using standard diffuse
lighting.

> **Note:** Cartoon rendering is a particular kind of *non-photorealistic rendering*, sometimes called *stylistic rendering*.

Although cartoon rendering isn't for all games, such as violent first-person shooters, it can enhance the atmosphere of some types of games when you want to impart a cartoonish feel. Furthermore, cartoon rendering is pretty easy to implement and allows us to demonstrate vertex shaders nicely.

We break cartoon rendering into two steps.

1. Cartoon drawings typically have few shading intensity levels with an abrupt transition from one shade to the next; we refer to this as *cartoon shading*. In Figure 17.2.a we see that the meshes are shaded using exactly three shading intensities (bright, medium, dark) and the transition between them is abrupt—unlike Figure 17.2.c, which has a smooth transition from light to dark.

2. Cartoon drawings also typically have their silhouette edges outlined, as Figure 17.2.b shows.

Each step requires its own vertex shader.

17.5.1 Cartoon Shading

To implement cartoon shading, we take the same approach as Lander describes in his article "Shades of Disney: Opaquing a 3D World" featured in the March 2000 issue of *Game Developer* magazine. It works like this: We create a grayscale luminance texture that contains the different shade intensities we desire. Figure 17.3 shows the texture that we use in the sample program.

Figure 17.3: Shade texture holds the shade intensities we use. Observe the abrupt transitions between shades and that the texture shade intensity must increase from left to right.

Then in the vertex shader we perform the standard diffuse calculation dot product to determine the cosine of the angle between the vertex normal $\hat{\mathbf{N}}$ and the light vector $\hat{\mathbf{L}}$, which is used to determine how much light the vertex receives:

$$s = \hat{\mathbf{L}} \cdot \hat{\mathbf{N}}$$

If $s < 0$, that implies the angle between the light vector and vertex normal is greater than 90 degrees, which implies that the surface receives no light. Therefore, if $s < 0$, we let $s = 0$. So $s \in [0, 1]$.

Now, in the usual diffuse lighting model, we use s to scale our color vector such that the vertex colors are darkened based on the amount of light that they receive:

diffuseColor $= s(r, \quad g, \quad b, \quad a)$

However, this will result in a smooth transition from light to dark shades. This is the opposite of what we desire for cartoon shading. We want an abrupt transition between a few different shades (around two to four shades works well for cartoon rendering).

Instead of using s to scale the color vector, we are going to use it as the u texture coordinate for the luminance texture that we spoke of earlier—the one depicted in Figure 17.3.

Note: The scalar s is of course a valid texture coordinate since $s \in [0, 1]$, which is the usual texture coordinate interval.

In this way the vertices won't be shaded smoothly but rather abruptly. For example, the luminance texture might be divided into three shades, as Figure 17.4 shows.

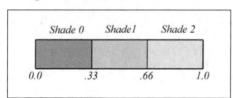

Figure 17.4: The shade used depends on the interval the texture coordinate falls in.

Then values of $s \in [0, 0.33]$ are shaded using *shade 0*, values of $s \in (0.33, 0.66]$ are shaded using *shade 1*, and values of $s \in (0.66, 1]$ are shaded using *shade 2*. Of course, the transition from one of these shades to the next is abrupt, giving us the desired effect.

Note: We turn off texture filtering for cartoon shading as well because the filtering attempts to smooth out the shade transitions. This is undesirable since we want abrupt transitions.

17.5.2 **The Cartoon Shading Vertex Shader Code**

We now present the vertex shader for cartoon shading. The primary task of the shader is merely to compute and set the texture coordinate based on $s = \hat{\mathbf{L}} \cdot \hat{\mathbf{N}}$. Observe that in the output structure, we have added a data member to store the computed texture coordinate. Also note that we still output the color of the vertex, though we don't modify it, and

Part IV

when the color is combined with the luminance texture, it appears
shaded.

```
// File: toon.txt
// Desc: Vertex shader that lights geometry so it appears to be
//       drawn in a cartoon style.

//
// Globals
//

extern matrix WorldViewMatrix;
extern matrix WorldViewProjMatrix;

extern vector Color;

extern vector LightDirection;

static vector Black = {0.0f, 0.0f, 0.0f, 0.0f};

//
// Structures
//

struct VS_INPUT
{
    vector position : POSITION;
    vector normal   : NORMAL;
};

struct VS_OUTPUT
{
    vector position : POSITION;
    float2 uvCoords : TEXCOORD;
    vector diffuse  : COLOR;
};


//
// Main
//

VS_OUTPUT Main(VS_INPUT input)
{
    // zero out each member in output
    VS_OUTPUT output = (VS_OUTPUT)0;

    // transform vertex position to homogenous clip space
    output.position = mul(input.position, WorldViewProjMatrix);

    //
    // Transform lights and normals to view space.  Set w
    // components to zero since we're transforming vectors.
    // Assume there are no scalings in the world
    // matrix as well.
    //
    LightDirection.w = 0.0f;
```

```
input.normal.w   = 0.0f;
LightDirection   = mul(LightDirection, WorldViewMatrix);
input.normal     = mul(input.normal, WorldViewMatrix);

//
// Compute the 1D texture coordinate for toon rendering.
//
float u = dot(LightDirection, input.normal);

//
// Clamp to zero if u is negative because u
// negative implies the angle between the light
// and normal is greater than 90 degrees.  And
// if that is true then the surface receives
// no light.
//
if(u < 0.0f)
    u = 0.0f;

//
// Set other tex coord to middle.
//
float v = 0.5f;


output.uvCoords.x = u;
output.uvCoords.y = v;

// save color
output.diffuse = Color;

return output;
}
```

A couple of remarks:

- We assume the world matrix doesn't do any scaling because if it does, it can mess up the length and direction of a vector that multiplies it.

- We always set the v texture coordinate to the middle of the texture. This implies that we are using only a single horizontal line in the texture, which implies we could use a 1D luminance texture instead of a 2D one. However, both 1D and 2D textures work. For the sample we have used a 2D texture rather than a 1D texture for no particular reason.

17.5.3 Silhouette Outlining

To complete the cartoon effect, we need to outline the silhouette edges. This is a bit more involved than cartoon shading.

Part IV

17.5.3.1 **Edge Representation**

We represent an edge of a mesh as a quad (built from two triangles)—see Figure 17.5.

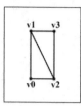

Figure 17.5: A quad to represent an edge

We choose quads for a couple of reasons: We can easily change the thickness of the edge by adjusting the dimensions of the quad, and we can render degenerate quads to hide certain edges, namely edges that are *not* silhouette edges. In Direct3D we build a quad out of two triangles. A *degenerate quad* is a quad built from two degenerate triangles. A *degenerate triangle* is a triangle with zero area or, in other words, a triangle defined by three vertices that lie on the same line (collinear). If we pass a degenerate triangle into the rendering pipeline, nothing is displayed for that triangle. This is useful because if we wish to hide a particular triangle we can simply degenerate it without actually removing it from our triangle list (vertex buffer). Recall that we only want to display the silhouette edges—not every edge of the mesh.

When we first create an edge, we specify its four vertices so that it is degenerate (Figure 17.6), which means the edge will be hidden (not displayed when rendered).

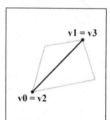

Figure 17.6: Degenerate quad describing the edge shared by the two triangles

Note that for the two vertices $\mathbf{v}_0$ and $\mathbf{v}_1$ in Figure 17.6, we set their vertex normal vector to the zero vector. Then when we feed the edge vertices into the vertex shader, the shader will test if a vertex is on a silhouette edge; if it is, then the vertex shader will offset the vertex position in the direction of the vertex normal by some scalar. Observe then that the vertices with a zero normal vector will not be offset.

Thus, we end up with a non-degenerate quad to represent the silhouette edge, as Figure 17.7 shows.

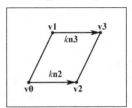

Figure 17.7: Vertices $\mathbf{v}_2$ and $\mathbf{v}_3$ on a silhouette edge being offset in the direction of their vertex normals $\mathbf{n}_2$ and $\mathbf{n}_3$, respectively. Observe that vertices $\mathbf{v}_0$ and $\mathbf{v}_1$ remain in their fixed position since their vertex normals equal the zero vector, thus no offset occurs for them. In this way the quad is successfully regenerated to represent the silhouette edge.

Remark: If we didn't set the vertex normals of vertices $\mathbf{v}_0$ and $\mathbf{v}_1$ to the zero vector, then those vertices would have been offset as well. But if we offset all four of the vertices describing a silhouette edge, then we have only translated the degenerate quad. By keeping vertices $\mathbf{v}_0$ and $\mathbf{v}_1$ fixed and only offsetting vertices $\mathbf{v}_2$ and $\mathbf{v}_3$ we regenerate the quad.

17.5.3.2 Testing for a Silhouette Edge

An edge is a silhouette edge if the two faces, $face_0$ and $face_1$, sharing that edge face in different directions relative to the viewing direction. That is, if one face is front facing and the other face is back facing, then the edge is a silhouette edge. Figure 17.8 gives an example of a silhouette edge and a non-silhouette edge.

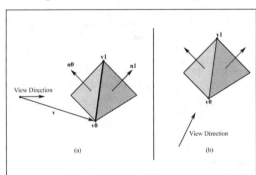

Figure 17.8: In (a), one face that shares the edge defined by the vertices $\mathbf{v}_0$ and $\mathbf{v}_1$ is front facing and the other face that shares the edge is back facing, thus the edge is a silhouette edge. In (b), the faces that share the edge defined by $\mathbf{v}_0$ and $\mathbf{v}_1$ are both front facing, and therefore the edge is *not* a silhouette edge.

It follows then that in order to test if a vertex is on a silhouette edge, we must know the normal vectors of $face_0$ and $face_1$ on a per vertex basis. Our edge vertex data structure reflects this:

```
struct VS_INPUT
{
    vector position    : POSITION;
    vector normal      : NORMAL0;
    vector faceNormal1 : NORMAL1;
    vector faceNormal2 : NORMAL2;
};
```

The first two components are straightforward, but we see two additional normal vectors, namely `faceNormal1` and `faceNormal2`. These vectors describe the two face normals of the faces that share the edge the vertex lies on, namely $face_0$ and $face_1$.

The actual mathematics of testing if a vertex is on a silhouette edge is as follows. Assume we are in view space. Let $\mathbf{v}$ be a vector from the origin to the vertex we are testing—Figure 17.8. Let $\mathbf{n}_0$ be the face normal for $face_0$ and let $\mathbf{n}_1$ be the face normal for $face_1$. Then the vertex is on a silhouette edge if the following inequality is true:

(1) $\quad (\mathbf{v} \cdot \mathbf{n}_0)(\mathbf{v} \cdot \mathbf{n}_1) < 0$

Inequality (1) is true if the signs of the two dot products differ, making the left-hand side negative. Recalling the properties of the dot product, the signs of the two dot products being different implies that one face is front facing and the other is back facing.

Now, consider the case where an edge only has one triangle sharing it, as in Figure 17.9, whose normal will be stored in `faceNormal1`.

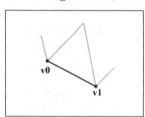

Figure 17.9: The edge defined by vertices $\mathbf{v}_0$ and $\mathbf{v}_1$ has only one face sharing it.

We define such an edge to *always* be a silhouette edge. To ensure that the vertex shader processes such edges as silhouette edges, we let `faceNormal2 = -faceNormal1`. Thus, the face normals face in opposite directions and inequality (1) will be true, indicating the edge is a silhouette edge.

17.5.3.3 Edge Generation

Generating the edges of a mesh is trivial; we simply iterate through each face in the mesh and compute a quad (degenerate, as in Figure 17.6) for each edge on the face.

Note: Each face has three edges since there are three edges to a triangle.

For the vertices of each edge, we also need to know the two faces that share the edge. One of the faces is the triangle the edge is on. For instance, if we're computing an edge of the ith face, then the ith face shares that edge. The other face that shares the edge can be found using the mesh's adjacency info.

17.5.4 The Silhouette Outlining Vertex Shader Code

We now present the vertex shader for rendering the silhouette edges. The primary task of the shader is to determine if the vertex passed in is on a silhouette edge. If it is, the vertex shader offsets the vertex by some defined scalar in the direction of the vertex normal.

```
// File: outline.txt
// Desc: Vertex shader renders silhouette edges.

//
// Globals
//

extern matrix WorldViewMatrix;
extern matrix ProjMatrix;

static vector Black = {0.0f, 0.0f, 0.0f, 0.0f};

//
// Structures
//

struct VS_INPUT
{
    vector position   : POSITION;
    vector normal     : NORMAL0;
    vector faceNormal1 : NORMAL1;
    vector faceNormal2 : NORMAL2;
};

struct VS_OUTPUT
{
    vector position : POSITION;
    vector diffuse  : COLOR;
};

//
// Main
//

VS_OUTPUT Main(VS_INPUT input)
{
    // zero out each member in output
    VS_OUTPUT output = (VS_OUTPUT)0;

    // transform position to view space
    input.position = mul(input.position, WorldViewMatrix);

    // Compute a vector in the direction of the vertex
    // from the eye.  Recall the eye is at the origin
    // in view space - eye is just camera position.
```

```
vector eyeToVertex = input.position;

// transform normals to view space.  Set w
// components to zero since we're transforming vectors.
// Assume there are no scalings in the world
// matrix as well.
input.normal.w      = 0.0f;
input.faceNormal1.w = 0.0f;
input.faceNormal2.w = 0.0f;

input.normal      = mul(input.normal,      WorldViewMatrix);
input.faceNormal1 = mul(input.faceNormal1, WorldViewMatrix);
input.faceNormal2 = mul(input.faceNormal2, WorldViewMatrix);

// compute the cosine of the angles between
// the eyeToVertex vector and the face normals.
float dot0 = dot(eyeToVertex, input.faceNormal1);
float dot1 = dot(eyeToVertex, input.faceNormal2);

// if cosines are different signs (positive/negative)
// then we are on a silhouette edge.  Do the signs
// differ?
if( (dot0 * dot1) < 0.0f )
{
    // yes, then this vertex is on a silhouette edge,
    // offset the vertex position by some scalar in the
    // direction of the vertex normal.
    input.position += 0.1f * input.normal;
}

// transform to homogeneous clip space
output.position = mul(input.position, ProjMatrix);


// set outline color
output.diffuse = Black;

return output;
}
```

17.6 Summary

- Using vertex shaders, we can replace the transformation and lighting stages of the fixed function pipeline. By replacing this fixed process with our own program (vertex shader), we can obtain a *huge* amount of flexibility in the graphical effects that we can achieve.
- Vertex declarations are used to describe the format of our vertices. They are similar to flexible vertex formats (FVF) but are more flexible and allow us to describe vertex formats that FVF cannot describe. Note that if our vertex can be described by an FVF, we can still use them; however, internally they are converted to vertex declarations.

■ For input, usage semantics specify how vertex components are mapped from the vertex declaration to variables in the HLSL program. For output, usage semantics specify what a vertex component is going to be used for (e.g., position, color, texture coordinate, etc.).

Chapter 18

Introduction to Pixel Shaders

A *pixel shader* is a program executed on the graphics card's GPU during the rasterization process for each pixel. (Unlike vertex shaders, Direct3D will not emulate pixel shader functionality in software.) It essentially replaces the multitexturing stage of the fixed function pipeline and gives us the ability to manipulate individual pixels directly and access the texture coordinate for each pixel. This direct access to pixels and texture coordinates allows us to achieve a variety of special effects, such as multitexturing, per pixel lighting, depth of field, cloud simulation, fire simulation, and sophisticated shadowing techniques.

You can test the pixel shader version that your graphics card supports by checking the `PixelShaderVersion` member of the `D3DCAPS9` structure and the macro `D3DPS_VERSION`. The following code snippet illustrates this:

```
// If the device's supported version is less than version 2.0
if( caps.PixelShaderVersion < D3DPS_VERSION(2, 0) )
    // Then pixel shader version 2.0 is not supported on this device.
```

Objectives

- To obtain a basic understanding of the concepts of multitexturing
- To learn how to write, create, and use pixel shaders
- To learn how to implement multitexturing using a pixel shader

18.1 Multitexturing Overview

Multitexturing is perhaps the simplest of the techniques that can be implemented using a pixel shader. Furthermore, since pixel shaders replace the multitexturing stage, it follows then that we should have a basic understanding of what the multitexturing stage is and does. This section presents a concise overview of multitexturing.

When we originally discussed texturing back in Chapter 6, we omitted a discussion on multitexturing in the fixed function pipeline for two reasons: First, multitexturing is a bit of an involved process, and we considered it an advanced topic at the time. Additionally, the fixed function multitexturing stage is replaced by the new and more powerful pixel shaders; therefore it made sense not to spend time on the outdated fixed function multitexturing stage.

The idea behind multitexturing is somewhat related to blending. In Chapter 7 we learned about blending the pixels being rasterized with the pixels that were previously written to the back buffer to achieve a specific effect. We extend this same idea to multiple textures. That is, we enable several textures at once and then define how these textures are to be blended together to achieve a specific effect. A common use for multitexturing is to do lighting. Instead of using Direct3D's lighting model in the vertex processing stage, we use special texture maps called *light maps*, which encode how a surface is lit. For example, suppose we wish to shine a spotlight on a large crate. We could define a spotlight as a `D3DLIGHT9` structure, or we could blend together a texture map representing a crate and a light map representing the spotlight as Figure 18.1 illustrates.

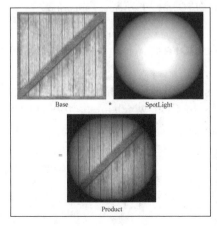

Figure 18.1: Rendering a crate lit by a spotlight using multitexturing. Here we combine the two textures by multiplying the corresponding texels together.

Part IV

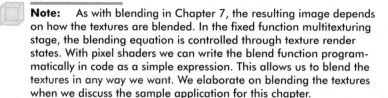

Note: As with blending in Chapter 7, the resulting image depends on how the textures are blended. In the fixed function multitexturing stage, the blending equation is controlled through texture render states. With pixel shaders we can write the blend function programmatically in code as a simple expression. This allows us to blend the textures in any way we want. We elaborate on blending the textures when we discuss the sample application for this chapter.

Blending the textures (two in this example) to light the crate has two advantages over Direct3D's lighting:

■ The lighting is precalculated into the spotlight light map. Therefore, the lighting does not need to be calculated at run time, which saves processing time. Of course, the lighting can only be precalculated for static objects and static lights.

■ Since the light maps are precalculated, we can use a much more accurate and sophisticated lighting model than Direct3D's model. (Better lighting results in a more realistic scene.)

Remark: The multitexturing stage is typically used to implement a full lighting engine for static objects. For example, we might have a texture map that holds the colors of the object, such as a crate texture map. Then we may have a diffuse light map to hold the diffuse surface shade, a separate specular light map to hold the specular surface shade, a fog map to hold the amount of fog that covers a surface, and a detail map to hold small, high frequency details of a surface. When all these textures are combined, it effectively lights, colors, and adds details to the scene using only lookups into precalculated textures.

Note: The spotlight light map is a trivial example of a very basic light map. Typically, special programs are used to generate light maps given a scene and light sources. Generating light maps goes beyond the scope of this book. For the interested reader, Alan Watt and Fabio Policarpo describe light mapping in *3D Games: Real-time Rendering and Software Technology*.

18.1.1 Enabling Multiple Textures

Recall that textures are set with the `IDirect3DDevice9::SetTexture` method and sampler states are set with the `IDirect3DDevice9::SetSamplerState` method, which are prototyped as:

```
HRESULT IDirect3DDevice9::SetTexture(
    DWORD Stage, // specifies the texture stage index
    IDirect3DBaseTexture9 *pTexture
);

HRESULT IDirect3DDevice9::SetSamplerState(
    DWORD Sampler, // specifies the sampler stage index
    D3DSAMPLERSTATETYPE Type,
```

```
     DWORD Value
);
```

Note: A particular sampler stage index *i* is associated with the *i*th texture stage. That is, the *i*th sampler stage specifies the sampler states for the *i*th set texture.

The texture/sampler stage index identifies the texture/sampler stage to which we wish to set the texture/sampler. Thus, we can enable multiple textures and set their corresponding sampler states by using different stage indices. Previously in this book, we always specified 0, denoting the first stage because we only used one texture at a time. So for example, if we need to enable three textures, we use stages 0, 1, and 2 like this:

```
// Set first texture and corresponding sampler states.
Device->SetTexture(    0, Tex1);
Device->SetSamplerState(0, D3DSAMP_MAGFILTER, D3DTEXF_LINEAR);
Device->SetSamplerState(0, D3DSAMP_MINFILTER, D3DTEXF_LINEAR);
Device->SetSamplerState(0, D3DSAMP_MIPFILTER, D3DTEXF_LINEAR);

// Set second texture and corresponding sampler states.
Device->SetTexture(    1, Tex2);
Device->SetSamplerState(1, D3DSAMP_MAGFILTER, D3DTEXF_LINEAR);
Device->SetSamplerState(1, D3DSAMP_MINFILTER, D3DTEXF_LINEAR);
Device->SetSamplerState(1, D3DSAMP_MIPFILTER, D3DTEXF_LINEAR);

// Set third texture and corresponding sampler states.
Device->SetTexture(    2, Tex3);
Device->SetSamplerState(2, D3DSAMP_MAGFILTER, D3DTEXF_LINEAR);
Device->SetSamplerState(2, D3DSAMP_MINFILTER, D3DTEXF_LINEAR);
Device->SetSamplerState(2, D3DSAMP_MIPFILTER, D3DTEXF_LINEAR);
```

This code enables `Tex1`, `Tex2`, and `Tex3` and sets the filtering modes for each texture.

18.1.2 Multiple Texture Coordinates

Recall from Chapter 6 that for each 3D triangle, we want to define a corresponding triangle on the texture that is to be mapped to the 3D triangle. We did this by adding texture coordinates to each vertex. Thus, every three vertices defining a triangle defined a corresponding triangle on the texture.

Since we are now using multiple textures, for every three vertices defining a triangle we need to define a corresponding triangle on each of the enabled textures. We do this by adding extra sets of texture coordinates to each vertex—one set for, and that corresponds with, each enabled texture. For instance, if we are blending three textures together, then each vertex must have three sets of texture coordinates

Part IV

that index into the three enabled textures. Thus, a vertex structure for multitexturing with three textures would look like this:

```
struct MultiTexVertex
{
    MultiTexVertex(float x, float y, float z,
                   float u0, float v0,
                   float u1, float v1,
                   float u2, float v2)
    {
        _x = x;    _y = y;   _z = z;
        _u0 = u0;  _v0 = v0;
        _u1 = u1;  _v1 = v1;
        _u2 = u2;  _v2 = v2;
    }

    float _x, _y, _z;
    float _u0, _v0; // Texture coordinates for texture at stage 0.
    float _u1, _v1; // Texture coordinates for texture at stage 1.
    float _u2, _v2; // Texture coordinates for texture at stage 2.

    static const DWORD FVF;
};
const DWORD MultiTexVertex::FVF = D3DFVF_XYZ | D3DFVF_TEX3;
```

Observe that the flexible vertex format flag D3DFVF_TEX3 is specified, denoting the vertex structure contains three sets of texture coordinates. The fixed function pipeline supports up to eight sets of texture coordinates. To use more than eight, you must use a vertex declaration and the programmable vertex pipeline.

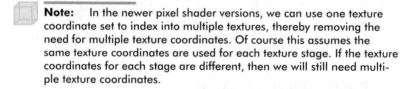

Note: In the newer pixel shader versions, we can use one texture coordinate set to index into multiple textures, thereby removing the need for multiple texture coordinates. Of course this assumes the same texture coordinates are used for each texture stage. If the texture coordinates for each stage are different, then we will still need multiple texture coordinates.

18.2 Pixel Shader Inputs and Outputs

Two things are input into a pixel shader: colors and texture coordinates. Both are per pixel.

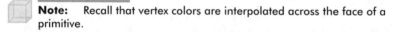

Note: Recall that vertex colors are interpolated across the face of a primitive.

A per pixel texture coordinate is simply the (u, v) coordinates that specify the texel in the texture that is to be mapped to the pixel in question. Direct3D computes both colors and texture coordinates per pixel, from vertex colors and vertex texture coordinates, before entering the pixel shader. The number of colors and texture coordinates input into the pixel shader depends on how many colors and texture coordinates were output by the vertex shader. For example, if a vertex shader outputs two colors and three texture coordinates, then Direct3D will calculate two colors and three texture coordinates per pixel and input them into the pixel shader. We map the input colors and texture coordinates to variables in our pixel shader program using the semantic syntax. Using the previous example, we would write:

```
struct PS_INPUT
{
    vector c0 : COLOR0;
    vector c1 : COLOR1;
    float2 t0 : TEXCOORD0;
    float2 t1 : TEXCOORD1;
    float2 t2 : TEXCOORD2;
};
```

For output, a pixel shader outputs a single computed color value for the pixel:

```
struct PS_OUTPUT
{
    vector finalPixelColor : COLOR0;
};
```

18.3 Steps to Using a Pixel Shader

The following list outlines the steps necessary to create and use a pixel shader.

1. Write and compile the pixel shader.
2. Create an `IDirect3DPixelShader9` interface to represent the pixel shader based on the compiled shader code.
3. Enable the pixel shader with the `IDirect3DDevice9::Set-PixelShader` method.

Of course, we have to destroy the pixel shader when we are done with it. The next few subsections go into these steps in more detail.

18.3.1 Writing and Compiling a Pixel Shader

We compile a pixel shader the same way that we compile a vertex shader. First, we must write a pixel shader program. In this book, we write our shaders in HLSL. Once the shader code is written we compile the shader using the `D3DXCompileShaderFromFile` function, as described in section 16.2.2. Recall that this function returns a pointer to an `ID3DXBuffer` that contains the compiled shader code.

Part IV

Note: Since we are using pixel shaders, we will need to remember to change the compile target to a pixel shader target (e.g., `ps_2_0`) instead of a vertex shader target (e.g., `vs_2_0`). The compile targets are specified through a parameter of the `D3DXCompileShader-FromFile` function. See section 16.2.2 for details.

18.3.2 Creating a Pixel Shader

Once we have the compiled shader code, we can obtain a pointer to an `IDirect3DPixelShader9` interface, which represents a pixel shader, using the following method:

```
HRESULT IDirect3DDevice9::CreatePixelShader(
    CONST DWORD *pFunction,
    IDirect3DPixelShader9** ppShader
);
```

- `pFunction`—Pointer to compiled shader code
- `ppShader`—Returns a pointer to an `IDirect3DPixelShader9` interface

For example, suppose the variable `shader` is an `ID3DXBuffer` that contains the compiled shader code. Then to obtain an `IDirect3D-PixelShader9` interface, we would write:

```
IDirect3DPixelShader9* MultiTexPS = 0;
hr = Device->CreatePixelShader(
        (DWORD*)shader->GetBufferPointer(),
        &MultiTexPS);
```

Note: To reiterate, the `D3DXCompileShaderFromFile` is the function that would return the compiled shader code (`shader`).

18.3.3 Setting a Pixel Shader

After we have obtained a pointer to an `IDirect3DPixelShader9` interface that represents our pixel shader, we can enable it using the following method:

```
HRESULT IDirect3DDevice9::SetPixelShader(
    IDirect3DPixelShader9* pShader
);
```

The method takes a single parameter where we pass a pointer to the pixel shader that we wish to enable. To enable the shader we created in section 18.3.2, we would write:

```
Device->SetPixelShader(MultiTexPS);
```

18.3.4 Destroying a Pixel Shader

As with all Direct3D interfaces, to clean them up we must call their `Release` method when we are finished with them. Continuing to use the pixel shader we created in section 18.3.2, we have:

```
d3d::Release<IDirect3DPixelShader9*>(MultiTexPS);
```

18.4 HLSL Sampler Objects

Textures are sampled in a pixel shader using the special `tex*`-related intrinsic functions of HLSL.

Note: Sampling refers to indexing a texel for a pixel based on texture coordinates for the pixel and the sampler states (texture filter states).

See section 16.7 for details on these functions. In general, these functions require us to specify two things:

- The (u, v) texture coordinates used to index into the texture
- The particular texture we want to index into

The (u, v) texture coordinates are, of course, given as input into the pixel shader. The particular texture that we want to index into is identified in the pixel shader by a special HLSL object called a sampler. We can think of a `sampler` object as an object that identifies a texture and sampler stage. For example, suppose that we were using three texture stages, which implies we need to be able to refer to each of these stages in the pixel shader. In the pixel shader, we would write:

```
sampler FirstTex;
sampler SecondTex;
sampler ThirdTex;
```

Direct3D will associate each of these `sampler` objects with a unique texture stage. Then in the application we find out the stage that a `sampler` object corresponds with and set the appropriate texture and sampler states for that stage. The following code illustrates how the application would set the texture and sampler states for `FirstTex`:

```
// Create texture:
IDirect3DTexture9* Tex;
D3DXCreateTextureFromFile(Device, "tex.bmp", &Tex);
.
.
.
// Get handle to constant:
FirstTexHandle = MultiTexCT->GetConstantByName(0, "FirstTex");
```

Part IV

```
// Get a description of the constant:
D3DXCONSTANT_DESC FirstTexDesc;
UINT count;
MultiTexCT->GetConstantDesc(FirstTexHandle, &FirstTexDesc, &count);
.
.
.
// Set texture/sampler states for the sampler FirstTex. We identify
// the stage FirstTex is associated with from the
// D3DXCONSTANT_DESC::RegisterIndex member:
Device->SetTexture(FirstTexDesc.RegisterIndex,
                   Tex);

Device->SetSamplerState(FirstTexDesc.RegisterIndex,
                        D3DSAMP_MAGFILTER, D3DTEXF_LINEAR);
Device->SetSamplerState(FirstTexDesc.RegisterIndex,
                        D3DSAMP_MINFILTER, D3DTEXF_LINEAR);
Device->SetSamplerState(FirstTexDesc.RegisterIndex,
                        D3DSAMP_MIPFILTER, D3DTEXF_LINEAR);
```

> **Note:** Alternatively, instead of using the sampler type, you can use the more specific and strongly typed `sampler1D`, `sampler2D`, `sampler3D`, and `samplerCube` types. These types are more type safe and ensure that they are only used with the appropriate `tex*` functions. For example, a `sampler2D` object can only be used with `tex2D*` functions. Similarly, a `sampler3D` object can only be used with `tex3D*` functions.

18.5 Sample Application: Multitexturing in a Pixel Shader

The sample application for this chapter demonstrates multitexturing using a pixel shader. The sample will texture a quad based on the "result" in Figure 18.2 by blending together a crate texture, a spotlight texture, and a texture that contains the string "Pixel Shader Sample."

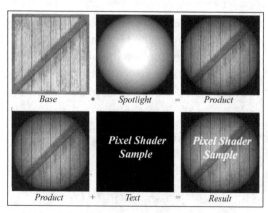

Figure 18.2: Combining the textures. Let **b**, **s**, and **t** be the colors of corresponding texels from the crate texture, spotlight texture, and text texture, respectively. We define how these colors are combined as $c = b \otimes s + t$, where $\otimes$ denotes component-wise multiplication.

This sample can be done without using pixel shaders. However, it is easy and straightforward to implement this application, and it allows us to demonstrate how to write, create, and use pixel shaders without getting distracted by the algorithm of some special effect.

Although we are only using three textures at once in this sample, it is worthwhile to go over the number of sampler objects that can be used with each pixel shader version. In other words, how many textures we can use at once depends on the pixel shader version that we use.

- Pixel shader versions ps_1_1 to ps_1_3 support up to four texture samples.
- Pixel shader version ps_1_4 supports up to six texture samples.
- Pixel shader versions ps_2_0 to ps_3_0 support up to 16 texture samples.

The pixel shader for multitexturing with three textures is implemented as follows:

```
//
// File: ps_multitex.txt
//
// Desc: Pixel shader that does multitexturing.
//

//
// Globals
//

sampler BaseTex;
sampler SpotLightTex;
sampler StringTex;

//
// Structures
//

struct PS_INPUT
{
    float2 base      : TEXCOORD0;
    float2 spotlight : TEXCOORD1;
    float2 text      : TEXCOORD2;
};

struct PS_OUTPUT
{
    vector diffuse : COLOR0;
};

//
// Main
//
```

Part IV

```
PS_OUTPUT Main(PS_INPUT input)
{
    // zero out members of output
    PS_OUTPUT output = (PS_OUTPUT)0;

    // sample appropriate textures
    vector b = tex2D(BaseTex,      input.base);
    vector s = tex2D(SpotLightTex, input.spotlight);
    vector t = tex2D(StringTex,    input.text);

    // combine texel colors
    vector c = b * s + t;

    // increase the intensity of the pixel slightly
    c += 0.1f;

    // save the resulting pixel color
    output.diffuse = c;

    return output;
}
```

First the pixel shader declares three `sampler` objects, one for each texture that we are blending. Next the input and output structures are defined. Notice that we don't have any color values input into the pixel shader; this is because we are using the textures exclusively for coloring and lighting; that is, `BaseTex` holds the color of our surface and `SpotLightTex` is our light map. The pixel shader outputs a single color value that specifies the color that we have computed for this particular pixel.

The `Main` function samples the three textures using the `tex2D` function. That is, it fetches the texel from each texture that is to be mapped to the pixel that we are currently computing based on the specified texture coordinates and `sampler` object. We then combine the texel colors with the statement `c = b * s + t`. Next we brighten the overall pixel color a bit by adding 0.1f to each component. Finally, we save the resulting pixel color and return it.

Now that we have looked at the actual pixel shader code, we shift gears and look at the application code. The application has the following relevant global variables:

```
IDirect3DPixelShader9* MultiTexPS = 0;
ID3DXConstantTable* MultiTexCT    = 0;

IDirect3DVertexBuffer9* QuadVB = 0;

IDirect3DTexture9* BaseTex      = 0;
IDirect3DTexture9* SpotLightTex = 0;
IDirect3DTexture9* StringTex    = 0;
```

```
D3DXHANDLE BaseTexHandle      = 0;
D3DXHANDLE SpotLightTexHandle = 0;
D3DXHANDLE StringTexHandle    = 0;

D3DXCONSTANT_DESC BaseTexDesc;
D3DXCONSTANT_DESC SpotLightTexDesc;
D3DXCONSTANT_DESC StringTexDesc;
```

The vertex structure for the multitexturing sample is defined as:

```
struct MultiTexVertex
{
    MultiTexVertex(float x, float y, float z,
                   float u0, float v0,
                   float u1, float v1,
                   float u2, float v2)
    {
        _x = x;   _y = y;   _z = z;
        _u0 = u0;  _v0 = v0;
        _u1 = u1;  _v1 = v1;
        _u2 = u2,  _v2 = v2;
    }

    float _x, _y, _z;
    float _u0, _v0;
    float _u1, _v1;
    float _u2, _v2;

    static const DWORD FVF;
};
const DWORD MultiTexVertex::FVF = D3DFVF_XYZ | D3DFVF_TEX3;
```

Observe that it contains three sets of texture coordinates.

The `Setup` function performs the following tasks:

- Fills the vertex buffer representing the quad
- Compiles the pixel shader
- Creates the pixel shader
- Loads the textures
- Sets the projection matrix and disables lighting
- Gets handles to the `sampler` objects
- Gets descriptions of the `sampler` objects

```
bool Setup()
{
HRESULT hr = 0;

//
// Create quad geometry.
//

Device->CreateVertexBuffer(
    6 * sizeof(MultiTexVertex),
    D3DUSAGE_WRITEONLY,
```

```
        MultiTexVertex::FVF,
        D3DPOOL_MANAGED,
        &QuadVB,
        0);

MultiTexVertex* v = 0;
QuadVB->Lock(0, 0, (void**)&v, 0);

v[0] = MultiTexVertex(-10.0f, -10.0f, 5.0f,
                       0.0f, 1.0f, 0.0f, 1.0f, 0.0f, 1.0f);
v[1] = MultiTexVertex(-10.0f,  10.0f, 5.0f,
                       0.0f, 0.0f, 0.0f, 0.0f, 0.0f, 0.0f);
v[2] = MultiTexVertex( 10.0f,  10.0f, 5.0f,
                       1.0f, 0.0f, 1.0f, 0.0f, 1.0f, 0.0f);

v[3] = MultiTexVertex(-10.0f, -10.0f, 5.0f,
                       0.0f, 1.0f, 0.0f, 1.0f, 0.0f, 1.0f);
v[4] = MultiTexVertex( 10.0f,  10.0f, 5.0f,
                       1.0f, 0.0f, 1.0f, 0.0f, 1.0f, 0.0f);
v[5] = MultiTexVertex( 10.0f, -10.0f, 5.0f,
                       1.0f, 1.0f, 1.0f, 1.0f, 1.0f, 1.0f);

QuadVB->Unlock();

//
// Compile shader
//

ID3DXBuffer* shader      = 0;
ID3DXBuffer* errorBuffer = 0;

hr = D3DXCompileShaderFromFile(
    "ps_multitex.txt",
    0,
    0,
    "Main", // entry point function name
    "ps_1_1",
    D3DXSHADER_DEBUG,
    &shader,
    &errorBuffer,
    &MultiTexCT);

// output any error messages
if( errorBuffer )
{
  ::MessageBox(0, (char*)errorBuffer->GetBufferPointer(), 0, 0);
  d3d::Release<ID3DXBuffer*>(errorBuffer);
}

if(FAILED(hr))
{
  ::MessageBox(0, "D3DXCompileShaderFromFile() - FAILED", 0, 0);
  return false;
}

//
// Create Pixel Shader
```

```
//
hr = Device->CreatePixelShader(
        (DWORD*)shader->GetBufferPointer(),
        &MultiTexPS);

if(FAILED(hr))
{
        ::MessageBox(0, "CreateVertexShader - FAILED", 0, 0);
        return false;
}

d3d::Release<ID3DXBuffer*>(shader);

//
// Load textures.
//

D3DXCreateTextureFromFile(Device, "crate.bmp", &BaseTex);
D3DXCreateTextureFromFile(Device, "spotlight.bmp", &SpotLightTex);
D3DXCreateTextureFromFile(Device, "text.bmp", &StringTex);

//
// Set projection matrix
//

D3DXMATRIX P;
D3DXMatrixPerspectiveFovLH(
            &P, D3DX_PI * 0.25f,
            (float)Width / (float)Height, 1.0f, 1000.0f);

Device->SetTransform(D3DTS_PROJECTION, &P);

//
// Disable lighting.
//

Device->SetRenderState(D3DRS_LIGHTING, false);

//
// Get handles
//

BaseTexHandle      = MultiTexCT->GetConstantByName(0, "BaseTex");
SpotLightTexHandle = MultiTexCT->GetConstantByName(0, "SpotLightTex");
StringTexHandle    = MultiTexCT->GetConstantByName(0, "StringTex");

//
// Set constant descriptions:
//

UINT count;

MultiTexCT->GetConstantDesc(
                BaseTexHandle,
                &BaseTexDesc,
                &count);
MultiTexCT->GetConstantDesc(
```

```
                    SpotLightTexHandle,
                    &SpotLightTexDesc,
                    &count);
MultiTexCT->GetConstantDesc(
                    StringTexHandle,
                    &StringTexDesc,
                    &count);

MultiTexCT->SetDefaults(Device);

return true;
}
```

The `Display` function sets the pixel shader, enables the two textures, and sets their corresponding sampler states before rendering the quad.

```
bool Display(float timeDelta)
{
if( Device )
{
    // ...camera update code snipped

    //
    // Render
    //

    Device->Clear(0, 0, D3DCLEAR_TARGET | D3DCLEAR_ZBUFFER,
                Oxffffffff, 1.0f, 0);
    Device->BeginScene();

    // set the pixel shader
    Device->SetPixelShader(MultiTexPS);
    Device->SetFVF(MultiTexVertex::FVF);
    Device->SetStreamSource(0, QuadVB, 0, sizeof(MultiTexVertex));

    // base tex
    Device->SetTexture(BaseTexDesc.RegisterIndex, BaseTex);
    Device->SetSamplerState(BaseTexDesc.RegisterIndex,
                            D3DSAMP_MAGFILTER, D3DTEXF_LINEAR);
    Device->SetSamplerState(BaseTexDesc.RegisterIndex,
                            D3DSAMP_MINFILTER, D3DTEXF_LINEAR);
    Device->SetSamplerState(BaseTexDesc.RegisterIndex,
                            D3DSAMP_MIPFILTER, D3DTEXF_LINEAR);

    // spotlight tex
    Device->SetTexture(SpotLightTexDesc.RegisterIndex, SpotLightTex);
    Device->SetSamplerState(SpotLightTexDesc.RegisterIndex,
                            D3DSAMP_MAGFILTER, D3DTEXF_LINEAR);
    Device->SetSamplerState(SpotLightTexDesc.RegisterIndex,
                            D3DSAMP_MINFILTER, D3DTEXF_LINEAR);
    Device->SetSamplerState(SpotLightTexDesc.RegisterIndex,
                            D3DSAMP_MIPFILTER, D3DTEXF_LINEAR);

    // string tex
    Device->SetTexture(    StringTexDesc.RegisterIndex, StringTex);
    Device->SetSamplerState(StringTexDesc.RegisterIndex,
                            D3DSAMP_MAGFILTER, D3DTEXF_LINEAR);
```

```
Device->SetSamplerState(StringTexDesc.RegisterIndex,
                        D3DSAMP_MINFILTER, D3DTEXF_LINEAR);
Device->SetSamplerState(StringTexDesc.RegisterIndex,
                        D3DSAMP_MIPFILTER, D3DTEXF_LINEAR);

    // draw the quad
    Device->DrawPrimitive(D3DPT_TRIANGLELIST, 0, 2);

    Device->EndScene();
    Device->Present(0, 0, 0, 0);
}
return true;
}
```

Of course we must remember to free our allocated interfaces in the `Cleanup` function:

```
void Cleanup()
{
    d3d::Release<IDirect3DVertexBuffer9*>(QuadVB);

    d3d::Release<IDirect3DTexture9*>(BaseTex);
    d3d::Release<IDirect3DTexture9*>(SpotLightTex);
    d3d::Release<IDirect3DTexture9*>(StringTex);

    d3d::Release<IDirect3DPixelShader9*>(MultiTexPS);
    d3d::Release<ID3DXConstantTable*>(MultiTexCT);
}
```

18.6 **Summary**

- Pixel shaders replace the multitexturing stage of the fixed function pipeline. Furthermore, pixel shaders give us the ability to modify pixels on an individual basis in any way that we choose and access texture data, thereby empowering us to implement many special effects that could not be achieved in the fixed function pipeline.

- Multitexturing is the process of enabling several textures at once and blending them together to produce a desired result. Multitexturing is typically used to implement a complete lighting engine for static geometry.

- The HLSL intrinsic `sampler` objects identify a particular texture/sampler stage. A `sampler` object is used to refer to a texture/sampler stage from the pixel shader.

Part IV

Note: Once you understand how to implement vertex and pixel shaders, you need some ideas of effects that can be implemented using them. The best way to get ideas of effects that can be achieved with vertex and pixel shaders is to study existing effects. The book *Direct3D ShaderX: Vertex and Pixel Shader Tips and Tricks* edited by Wolfgang Engel, also from Wordware Publishing, is a good start, as are NVIDIA's and ATI's developer sites, http://developer.nvidia.com/ and http://ati.com/developer/index.html, respectively. In addition, we recommend *CG: The Cg Tutorial* by Randima Fernando and Mark J. Kilgard. This book is an excellent tutorial to programmable 3D graphics using the high-level graphics language Cg, which is practically the same as Direct3D's HLSL.

Chapter 19

The Effects Framework

A rendering effect is typically composed of the following components: a vertex and/or pixel shader, a list of device states that need to be set, and one or more rendering passes. Furthermore, it is often desirable to have a fallback mechanism for rendering effects on different grades of graphics hardware (that is, to have several versions of an effect available that implements the same effect or attempts to implement the same effect as closely as possible, using the capabilities of different grades of hardware). It is clear that all these necessary tasks are associated with one effect. Therefore, it is a logical step to try to encapsulate these tasks into one unit.

The Direct3D effects framework provides such a mechanism for encapsulating tasks related to rendering effects in an *effect file*. Implementing effects in effect files has a couple of advantages. For one thing, it allows us to change the implementation of an effect without having to recompile the application source code. This makes the process of updating an effect easier, whether it is to fix a bug, make a simple enhancement, or take advantage of the latest 3D hardware feature. Secondly, it encapsulates all the components of an effect in one file.

This chapter guides you through the necessary information and steps to writing and creating an effect file. We note that effect files can be written in any ASCII file format just like our HLSL programs.

Objectives

- To gain an understanding of the structure and organization of an effect file
- To find out about some additional intrinsic objects in HLSL
- To learn how device states are specified in an effect file
- To learn how to create and use an effect
- To gain some experience working with the effects framework by studying some sample programs

19.1 Techniques and Passes

An effect file consists of one or more *techniques*. A technique is a particular way of rendering some special effect. So in other words, an effect file provides one or more different ways of rendering the same special effect. Why the need for several different implementations of the same effect? Well, some hardware might not support a particular implementation of an effect. Therefore, it is necessary to implement several versions of the same effect targeting different levels of hardware.

Note: For example, we might implement two versions of an effect, one implemented with shaders and one implemented with the fixed pipeline. In this way, users who have cards that support shaders can take advantage of the shader implementation, while those who do not can still use the fixed pipeline.

Being able to implement all versions of an effect in one effect file gives us more complete encapsulation of the overall effect, which is one of the goals of the effects framework—encapsulation.

Each technique contains one or more rendering passes. A *rendering pass* encapsulates the device states, samplers, and/or shaders used to render the geometry for that particular pass.

Note: Effects are not limited to use with the programmable pipeline only. For example, they can be used for the fixed function pipeline for controlling device states, such as lights, materials, and textures.

The reason for multiple passes is because some special effects are achieved by rendering the same geometry multiple times but with different device states, shaders, etc., for each particular pass. For example, recall that in Chapter 8 we had to render the same geometry multiple times per frame with different device states each time to achieve the reflection effect.

As an example, here is a skeleton of an effect file with two techniques, where the first technique consists of one pass and the second technique consists of two passes:

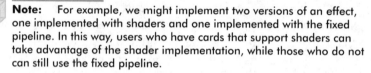

```
// effect.txt
...
technique T0
{
    // first and only pass for this technique
    pass P0
    {
        ...[specify pass device states, shaders, samplers, etc.]
    }
}
```

```
technique T1
{
    // first pass
    pass P0
    {
        ...[specify pass device states, shaders, samplers, etc.]
    }
    // second pass
    pass P1
    {
        ...[specify pass device states, shaders, samplers, etc.]
    }
}
```

19.2 More HLSL Intrinsic Objects

There are some additional built-in object types in HLSL. We didn't cover them earlier because they're used primarily in the effects framework.

19.2.1 Texture Objects

The HLSL intrinsic `texture` type represents an `IDirect3DTex-ture9` object. By using `texture` objects we can associate the texture for a particular sampler stage directly in the effect file. `Texture` objects have the following data members that can be accessed:

- `type`—The type of texture (e.g., 2D, 3D)
- `format`—The pixel format of the texture
- `width`—The width of the texture in pixels
- `height`—The height of the texture in pixels
- `depth`—The depth (if a 3D volume texture) of the texture in pixels

Aside: So far we have only used textures to store image data, but as you get into more advanced techniques, you will find that textures are used to hold arbitrary table info. In other words, textures are just tables of data; they don't have to contain image data necessarily. For example, in bump mapping we use what is called a *normal map*, which is a texture that contains normal vectors at each entry.

19.2.2 Sampler Objects and Sampler States

We discussed the `sampler` object in Chapter 18; however, the effects framework exposes the new `sampler_state` keyword. Using the `sampler_state` keyword, we can initialize a `sampler` object (that is, set the texture and sampler states for that sampler object directly within an effect file). The following example illustrates this:

```
Texture Tex;

sampler S0 = sampler_state
{
    Texture   = (Tex);
    MinFilter = LINEAR;
    MagFilter = LINEAR;
    MipFilter = LINEAR;
};
```

Here we have associated the texture `Tex` with the texture stage that `S0` corresponds with and also set the sampler states for the sampler stage that `S0` corresponds with. We have set all this directly and cleanly in the effect file!

19.2.3 Vertex and Pixel Shader Objects

The `vertexshader` and `pixelshader` HLSL intrinsic types represent vertex and pixel shaders, respectively. They are used in the effects framework to refer to the particular vertex and/or pixel shader that is to be used for a particular rendering pass. A `vertexshader` and/or `pixelshader` type can be set from the application through the `ID3DXEffect` interface with the `ID3DXEffect::SetVertex-Shader` and `ID3DXEffect::SetPixelShader` methods, respectively. For example, let `Effect` be a valid `ID3DXEffect` object, let `VS` be a valid `IDirect3DVertexShader9` object, and let `VSHandle` be a `D3DXHANDLE` that refers to a `vertexshader` object in the effect file; then we can initialize the vertex shader that `VSHandle` refers to by writing:

```
Effect->SetVertexShader(VSHandle, VS);
```

We look at `SetVertexShader` and `SetPixelShader` more when we examine how to set variables in the effect file from the application.

Alternatively, we can write the vertex and/or pixel shader directly into the effect file. Then using a special compiling syntax, we can set a shader variable. The following example illustrates how to initialize a `pixelshader` variable ps.

```
// Define Main:
OUTPUT Main(INPUT input){...}

// Compile Main:
pixelshader ps = compile ps_2_0 Main();
```

Observe that after the `compile` keyword we specify the version name, followed by the shader's entry point function. Note that when using this style to initialize a vertex/pixel shader object, the entry point function must be defined in the effect file.

Finally, we associate a shader with a particular pass, as follows:

```
// Define Main:
OUTPUT Main(INPUT input){...}

// Compile Main:
vertexshader vs = compile vs_2_0 Main();

pass P0
{
    // Set 'vs' as the vertex shader for this pass.
    vertexshader = (vs);

    ...

}
```

Or more compactly as:

```
pass P0
{
    // Set the vertex shader whose entry point is "Main()" as the
    // vertex shader for this pass.
    vertexShader = compile vs_2_0 Main();

    ...

}
```

> **Note:** It is worth mentioning, so that you are at least aware of it, that you can initialize a `vertexshader` and `pixelshader` type using this syntax:
>
> ```
> vertexshader vs = asm { /*assembly instructions go here */ };
> pixelshader ps = asm { /*assembly instructions go here */ };
> ```
>
> This syntax is used if you are writing your shaders in assembly language.

19.2.4 Strings

Finally, there is a string object that can be used as shown here:

```
string filename = "texName.bmp";
```

Although `string` types are not used by any functions in HLSL, they can be read by the application. This way, we can further encapsulate references to data files that an effect uses, such as texture filenames and XFile names.

19.2.5 Annotations

In addition to the semantic syntax we have already discussed, annotations may be attached to variables. Annotations are not used by HLSL, but they can be accessed by the application through the effects framework. They merely serve to attach a "note" to a variable that the application might want associated with that variable. Annotations are

Part IV

added with the `<annotation>` syntax. The following line illustrates this:

```
texture tex0 <string name = "tiger.bmp";>;
```

The annotation in this example is `<string name = "tiger.bmp";>`. This associates a string with the variable `tex0`, namely the filename that stores the texture data. Clearly, annotating a texture with its corresponding filename can be beneficial.

Annotations can be retrieved using the following method:

```
D3DXHANDLE ID3DXEffect::GetAnnotationByName(
    D3DXHANDLE hObject,
    LPCSTR pName
);
```

`pName` is the name of the annotation we want a handle to and `hObject` is the handle to the parent block the annotation is in, such as a technique, pass, or structure block. Once we have a handle to the annotation, we can get info about it by using `ID3DXEffect::GetParameterDesc` to fill out a `D3DXCONSTANT_DESC` structure. See the DirectX SDK documentation for details.

19.3 Device States in an Effect File

Usually, to execute an effect correctly, we must set device states, such as render states, texture states, materials, lights, and textures. To support the ability to encapsulate a complete effect in one file, the effects framework allows us to set device states in the effect file. Device states are set inside a rendering pass block, and the syntax looks like this:

```
State = Value;
```

For the complete list of states, search for "states" in the index of the DirectX SDK documentation, or from the Contents tab of the SDK, see DirectX Graphics\Reference\Effect Reference\Effect Format\States.

Consider the `FillMode` state. If you look it up as just mentioned in the SDK, it says the values are the same values as `D3DFILLMODE` without the `D3DFILL_` prefix. If we look up `D3DFILLMODE` in the SDK documentation we find the values `D3DFILL_POINT`, `D3DFILL_WIREFRAME`, and `D3DFILL_SOLID`. Thus, for the effect file we omit the prefix and obtain the following valid assignment values for the state `FillMode`: `POINT`, `WIREFRAME`, and `SOLID`. For example, we would write the following in the effect file:

```
FillMode = WIREFRAME;
FillMode = POINT;
FillMode = SOLID;
```

> **Note:** In the subsequent sections we will set several device states in the example programs. For the most part, the meaning of the state can be deduced from its name, but if you want more elaborate details, see the SDK documentation.

19.4 Creating an Effect

An effect is represented by the `ID3DXEffect` interface, which we create with the following D3DX function:

```
HRESULT D3DXCreateEffectFromFile(
    LPDIRECT3DDEVICE9 pDevice,
    LPCSTR pSrcFile,
    CONST D3DXMACRO* pDefines,
    LPD3DXINCLUDE pInclude,
    DWORD Flags,
    LPD3DXEFFECTPOOL pPool,
    LPD3DXEFFECT* ppEffect,
    LPD3DXBUFFER *ppCompilationErrors
);
```

- `pDevice`—The device to be associated with the created `ID3DXEffect` object

- `pSrcFile`—Name of the text file (the effect file) that contains the effect source code we want to compile

- `pDefines`—This parameter is optional, and we specify null for it in this book.

- `pInclude`—Pointer to an `ID3DXInclude` interface. This interface is designed to be implemented by the application so that we can override default include behavior. In general, the default behavior is fine, and we can ignore this parameter by specifying null.

- `Flags`—Optional flags for compiling the shaders in the effect file; specify 0 for no flags. Valid options are:

  - ☐ `D3DXSHADER_DEBUG`—Instructs the compiler to write debug information

  - ☐ `D3DXSHADER_SKIPVALIDATION`—Instructs the compiler not to do any code validation. This should only be used when you are using a shader that is known to work.

  - ☐ `D3DXSHADER_SKIPOPTIMIZATION`—Instructs the compiler not to perform any code optimization. In practice this would only be used in debugging, where you would not want the compiler to alter the code in any way.

- `pPool`—Optional pointer to an `ID3DXEffectPool` interface that is used to define how effect parameters are shared across other effect instances. In this book we specify null for this parameter, indicating that we do not share parameters between effect files.

■ ppEffect—Returns a pointer to an ID3DXEffect interface representing the created effect

■ ppCompilationErrors—Returns a pointer to an ID3DXBuffer that contains a string of error codes and messages

Here is an example call of D3DXCreateEffectFromFile:

```
//
// Create effect.
//

ID3DXEffect* Effect = 0;
ID3DXBuffer* errorBuffer = 0;
hr = D3DXCreateEffectFromFile(
    Device,             // associated device
    "effect.txt",       // source filename
    0,                  // no preprocessor definitions
    0,                  // no ID3DXInclude interface
    D3DXSHADER_DEBUG,   // compile flags
    0,                  // don't share parameters
    &Effect,            // return result
    &errorBuffer);      // return error strings

// output any error messages
if( errorBuffer )
{
    ::MessageBox(0, (char*)errorBuffer->GetBufferPointer(), 0, 0);
    d3d::Release<ID3DXBuffer*>(errorBuffer);
}

if(FAILED(hr))
{
    ::MessageBox(0, "D3DXCreateEffectFromFile() - FAILED", 0, 0);
    return false;
}
```

19.5 Setting Constants

As with vertex and pixel shaders, we need to initialize variables in the effect source code from the application source code. However, instead of using a constant table, as we did with vertex and pixel shaders, the ID3DXEffect interface has intrinsic methods for setting variables. We are not going to list all the methods for setting different types of variables here simply because there are too many of them. See the DirectX SDK documentation for the complete list. Here is an abridged listing:

``HRESULT ID3DXEffect::SetFloat(
D3DXHANDLE hParameter,
FLOAT f
);```	Sets a floating-point variable in the effect file identified by hParameter to the value f
``HRESULT ID3DXEffect::SetMatrix(
D3DXHANDLE hParameter,
CONST D3DXMATRIX* pMatrix
);```	Sets a matrix variable in the effect file identified by hParameter to the value pointed to by pMatrix
``HRESULT ID3DXEffect::SetString(
D3DXHANDLE hParameter,
CONST LPCSTR pString
);```	Sets a matrix variable in the effect file identified by hParameter to the value pointed to by pString
``HRESULT ID3DXEffect::SetTexture(
D3DXHANDLE hParameter,
LPDIRECT3DBASETEXTURE9 pTexture
);```	Sets a texture variable in the effect file identified by hParameter to the value pointed to by pTexture
``HRESULT ID3DXEffect::SetVector(
D3DXHANDLE hParameter,
CONST D3DXVECTOR4* pVector
);```	Sets a vector variable in the effect file identified by hParameter to the value pointed to by pVector
``HRESULT ID3DXEffect::SetVertexShader(
D3DXHANDLE hParameter,
LPDIRECT3DVERTEXSHADER9
pVertexShader
);```	Sets a vertex shader variable in the effect file identified by hParameter to the value pointed to by pVertexShader
``HRESULT ID3DXEffect::SetPixelShader(
D3DXHANDLE hParameter,
LPDIRECT3DPIXELSHADER9 pPShader
);```	Sets a pixel shader variable in the effect file identified by hParameter to the value pointed to by pPShader

We obtain handles to variables (also called effect parameters) using the following method:

```
D3DXHANDLE ID3DXEffect::GetParameterByName(
    D3DXHANDLE hParent, // scope of variable - parent structure
    LPCSTR pName         // name of variable
);
```

Its signature is the same as the ID3DXConstantTable::GetConstantByName method. Namely, the first parameter is a D3DXHANDLE that identifies the parent structure in which the variable we want a handle to lives. For global variables that have no parent structure, we specify null. The second parameter is the name of the variable as it appears in the effect file.

Part IV

As an example, let's show how to set some variables in the effect file:

```
// some data to set
D3DXMATRIX M;
D3DXMatrixIdentity(&M);

D3DXVECTOR4 color(1.0f, 0.0f, 1.0f, 1.0f);

IDirect3DTexture9* tex = 0;
D3DXCreateTextureFromFile(Device, "shade.bmp", &tex);

// get handles to parameters
D3DXHANDLE MatrixHandle = Effect->GetParameterByName(0, "Matrix");
D3DXHANDLE MtrlHandle   = Effect->GetParameterByName(0, "Mtrl");
D3DXHANDLE TexHandle    = Effect->GetParameterByName(0, "Tex");

// set parameters
Effect->SetMatrix(MatrixHandle, &M);
Effect->SetVector(MtrlHandle, &color);
Effect->SetTexture(TexHandle, tex);
```

Note: There are corresponding `ID3DXEffect::Get*` methods for each `ID3DXEffect::Set*` method that can be used to retrieve the value of a variable in the effect file. For example, to get a variable that is a matrix type, we would use this function:

```
HRESULT ID3DXEffect::GetMatrix(
    D3DXHANDLE hParameter,
    D3DXMATRIX* pMatrix
);
```

See the DirectX SDK documentation for a list of all methods.

19.6 Using an Effect

In this section and its subsections, we show how to use an effect once it has been created. The following steps summarize the overall process:

1. Obtain a handle to the technique in the effect file you wish to use.
2. Activate the desired technique.
3. Begin the currently active technique.
4. For each rendering pass in the active technique, render the desired geometry. Recall that techniques may consist of several rendering passes, and we must render the geometry once for each pass.
5. End the currently active technique.

19.6.1 **Obtaining a Handle to an Effect**

The first step to using a technique is to obtain a D3DXHANDLE to that technique. A handle to a technique can be obtained using this method:

```
D3DXHANDLE ID3DXEffect::GetTechniqueByName(
    LPCSTR pName // Name of the technique.
);
```

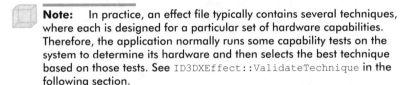

Note: In practice, an effect file typically contains several techniques, where each is designed for a particular set of hardware capabilities. Therefore, the application normally runs some capability tests on the system to determine its hardware and then selects the best technique based on those tests. See ID3DXEffect::ValidateTechnique in the following section.

19.6.2 **Activating an Effect**

Once the handle to the desired technique has been obtained, we must activate that technique. This is done with the following method:

```
HRESULT ID3DXEffect::SetTechnique(
    D3DXHANDLE hTechnique // Handle to the technique to set.
);
```

Note: Before activating a technique you will want to *validate* it with the current device. That is, you will want to ensure that the hardware supports the features the technique uses and the configuration of features the technique uses. You can use the following method to do so:

```
HRESULT ID3DXEffect::ValidateTechnique(
    D3DXHANDLE hTechnique // Handle to the technique to validate.
);
```

Recall that an effect file may have several techniques, each attempting to implement a particular effect using different hardware features, hoping that the implementation of at least one technique will work on the user's system. For an effect, you will want to iterate through each technique and run it through ID3DXEffect::ValidateTechnique so that you can verify which techniques are supported and which ones are not, and then act appropriately.

19.6.3 **Beginning an Effect**

To render geometry using an effect, we must place the drawing function calls between the ID3DXEffect::Begin and ID3DXEffect::End methods. These functions essentially enable and disable the effect, respectively.

```
HRESULT ID3DXEffect::Begin(
    UINT* pPasses,
    DWORD Flags
);
```

Part IV

- `pPasses`—Returns the number of passes in the currently active technique
- `Flags`—Any one of the following flags:
  - `Zero (0)`—Instructs the effect to save the current device states and shader states and then restore them after the effect is finished (when `ID3DXEffect::End` is called). This is useful because the effect file can change the states, and it may be desirable to restore the states prior to beginning the effect.
  - `D3DXFX_DONOTSAVESTATE`—Instructs the effect to *not* save and restore device states (excludes shader states)
  - `D3DXFX_DONOTSAVESHADERSTATE`—Instructs the effect to *not* save and restore shader states

19.6.4 Setting the Current Rendering Pass

Before we can render any geometry using an effect, we must specify the rendering pass to use. Recall that a technique consists of one or more rendering passes, where each pass encapsulates different device states, samplers, and/or shaders that are to be used for that pass. The rendering pass is specified with the following method:

```
HRESULT ID3DXEffect::Pass(
    UINT iPass // Index identifying the pass.
);
```

The rendering passes for a technique are labeled as $0\ldots n-1$ for n passes. Thus, we can iterate through each pass using a simple `for` loop and render the geometry for that pass. Section 19.6.6 shows an example.

19.6.5 Ending an Effect

Finally, after we have rendered the geometry for each pass, we disable or end the effect with `ID3DXEffect::End`:

```
HRESULT ID3DXEffect::End(VOID);
```

19.6.6 Example

The following code snippet illustrates the above five steps necessary to use an effect:

```
// In effect file:
technique T0
{
    pass P0
    {
        ...
```

```
        }
}
=====================================

// In application source code:

// Get technique handle.
D3DXHANDLE hTech = 0;
hTech = Effect->GetTechniqueByName("T0");

// Activate technique.
Effect->SetTechnique(hTech );

// Begin the active technique.
UINT numPasses = 0;
Effect->Begin(&numPasses, 0);

// For each rendering pass.
for(int i = 0; i < numPasses; i++)
{
    // Set the current pass.
    Effect->Pass(i);

    // Render the geometry for the ith pass.
    Sphere->Draw();
}
// End the effect.
Effect->End();
```

19.7 Sample Application: Lighting and Texturing in an Effect File

As a warm-up, let's create an effect file that handles lighting and texturing a 3D model. The sample runs entirely in the fixed function pipeline, implying that the effects framework is not limited to effects that use shaders. Figure 19.1 shows a screen shot of the Lighting and Texturing sample.

Figure 19.1: Screen shot from the Lighting and Texturing sample. The texture, material, and lighting states are specified inside the effect file.

Part IV

The effect file is implemented as follows:

```
//
// File: light_tex.txt
//
// Desc: Effect file that handles device states for lighting
//       and texturing a 3D model.
//


//
// Globals
//

matrix WorldMatrix;
matrix ViewMatrix;
matrix ProjMatrix;

texture Tex;

//
// Sampler
//

// Associated the texture 'Tex' with the texture stage 'S0'
// corresponds with and also set the sampler states for the sampler
// stage 'S0' corresponds with.
sampler S0 = sampler_state
{
    Texture   = (Tex);
    MinFilter = LINEAR;
    MagFilter = LINEAR;
    MipFilter = LINEAR;
};

//
// Effect
//

technique LightAndTexture
{
    pass P0
    {
        //
        // Set misc. render states.

        pixelshader    = null;  // No pixel shader.
        vertexshader   = null;  // No vertex shader.
        fvf = XYZ | Normal | Tex1; // Flexible vertex format
        Lighting       = true;  // Enable lighting.
        NormalizeNormals = true;  // Renormalize normals.
        SpecularEnable = false;  // Disable specular highlights.

        //
        // Set transformation states

        WorldTransform[0]  = (WorldMatrix);
        ViewTransform      = (ViewMatrix);
```

```
ProjectionTransform = (ProjMatrix);

//
// Set a light source at light index 0. We fill out all the
// components for light[0] because the Direct3D
// documentation recommends filling out all components
// for best performance.

LightType[0]          = Directional;
LightAmbient[0]       = {0.2f,  0.2f, 0.2f, 1.0f};
LightDiffuse[0]       = {1.0f,  1.0f, 1.0f, 1.0f};
LightSpecular[0]      = {0.0f,  0.0f, 0.0f, 1.0f};
LightDirection[0]     = {1.0f, -1.0f, 1.0f, 0.0f};
LightPosition[0]      = {0.0f,  0.0f, 0.0f, 0.0f};
LightFalloff[0]       = 0.0f;
LightRange[0]         = 0.0f;
LightTheta[0]         = 0.0f;
LightPhi[0]           = 0.0f;
LightAttenuation0[0] = 1.0f;
LightAttenuation1[0] = 0.0f;
LightAttenuation2[0] = 0.0f;

// Finally, enable the light:

LightEnable[0] = true;

//
// Set material components. This is like calling
// IDirect3DDevice9::SetMaterial.

MaterialAmbient  = {1.0f, 1.0f, 1.0f, 1.0f};
MaterialDiffuse  = {1.0f, 1.0f, 1.0f, 1.0f};
MaterialEmissive = {0.0f, 0.0f, 0.0f, 0.0f};
MaterialPower    = 1.0f;
MaterialSpecular = {1.0f, 1.0f, 1.0f, 1.0f};

//
// Hook up the sampler object 'S0' to sampler stage 0,
// which is given by Sampler[0].

Sampler[0] = (S0);
    }
}
```

In this effect file we are primarily setting device states, as covered in section 19.3. For instance, we set a light source and a material directly in the effect file. Furthermore, we specify transformation matrices and the texture and sampler states to apply. These specified states are then applied to any geometry that is rendered using technique `LightAnd-Texture` and rendering pass `P0`.

> **Note:** Observe that to refer to variables in an effect file, we must enclose them in parentheses. For example, to refer to matrix variables, we had to write `(WorldMatrix)`, `(ViewMatrix)`, **and** `(ProjMatrix)`. Leaving the parentheses off is illegal.

Since most of the necessary grunt work is done in the effect file, such as setting lights, materials, and textures, the application code is simply a matter of creating the effect and enabling it. The sample has the following relevant global variables:

```
ID3DXEffect* LightTexEffect = 0;

D3DXHANDLE WorldMatrixHandle   = 0;
D3DXHANDLE ViewMatrixHandle    = 0;
D3DXHANDLE ProjMatrixHandle    = 0;
D3DXHANDLE TexHandle           = 0;

D3DXHANDLE LightTexTechHandle = 0;
```

This is nothing interesting—just an `ID3DXEffect` pointer and some handles. The `LightTexTechHandle` is a handle to a technique, hence the substring "Tech" in its name.

The `Setup` function performs three primary steps: creates the effect, obtains handles to effect parameters and to the technique we are going to use, and initializes some of the effect parameters. Its abridged implementation is as follows:

```
bool Setup()
{
HRESULT hr = 0;

//
// ...[Load XFile Snipped]
//

//
// Create effect.
//

ID3DXBuffer* errorBuffer = 0;
hr = D3DXCreateEffectFromFile(
    Device,            // associated device
    "light_tex.txt",   // effect filename
    0,                 // no preprocessor definitions
    0,                 // no ID3DXInclude interface
    D3DXSHADER_DEBUG,  // compile flags
    0,                 // don't share parameters
    &LightTexEffect,   // return effect interface pointer
    &errorBuffer);     // return error messages

// output any error messages
if( errorBuffer )
{
    ::MessageBox(0, (char*)errorBuffer->GetBufferPointer(), 0, 0);
    d3d::Release<ID3DXBuffer*>(errorBuffer);
}

if(FAILED(hr))
{
```

```
        ::MessageBox(0, "D3DXCreateEffectFromFile() - FAILED", 0, 0);
        return false;
}

//
// Save Frequently Accessed Parameter Handles
//

WorldMatrixHandle=LightTexEffect->GetParameterByName(0,
                                              "WorldMatrix");
ViewMatrixHandle =LightTexEffect->GetParameterByName(0, "ViewMatrix");
ProjMatrixHandle =LightTexEffect->GetParameterByName(0, "ProjMatrix");
TexHandle        =LightTexEffect->GetParameterByName(0, "Tex");

LightTexTechHandle =
        LightTexEffect->GetTechniqueByName("LightAndTexture");

//
// Set effect parameters
//

// Matrices
D3DXMATRIX W, P;

D3DXMatrixIdentity(&W);
LightTexEffect->SetMatrix( WorldMatrixHandle, &W);

D3DXMatrixPerspectiveFovLH(
    &P, D3DX_PI * 0.25f, // 45 - degree
    (float)Width / (float)Height,
    1.0f, 1000.0f);

LightTexEffect->SetMatrix( ProjMatrixHandle, &P);

// Texture:
IDirect3DTexture9* tex = 0;
D3DXCreateTextureFromFile(Device, "Terrain_3x_diffcol.jpg", &tex);

LightTexEffect->SetTexture(TexHandle, tex);

d3d::Release<IDirect3DTexture9*>(tex);

return true;
}
```

The `Display` function is straightforward and performs the steps outlined in section 19.6:

```
bool Display(float timeDelta)
{
if( Device )
{
    //
    // ...[Camera update snipped]
    //

    // set the new updated view matrix
```

```
        LightTexEffect->SetMatrix(ViewMatrixHandle, &V);

        //
        // Activate the technique and render
        //

        Device->Clear(0, 0, D3DCLEAR_TARGET | D3DCLEAR_ZBUFFER,
                        0xffffffff, 1.0f, 0);
        Device->BeginScene();

        // set the technique to use
        LightTexEffect->SetTechnique( LightTexTechHandle );

        UINT numPasses = 0;
        LightTexEffect->Begin(&numPasses, 0);

        for(int i = 0; i < numPasses; i++)
        {
            LightTexEffect->Pass(i);

            for(int j = 0; j < Mtrls.size(); j++)
            {
                Mesh->DrawSubset(j);
            }
        }
        LightTexEffect->End();

        Device->EndScene();
        Device->Present(0, 0, 0, 0);
    }
    return true;
}
```

19.8 Sample Application: Fog Effect

One of the topics we regret not devoting a chapter to is Direct3D fog.
Fog effects add a new level of realism to the scene and can be used to
simulate certain types of weather conditions. Furthermore, fog can
greatly diminish far-clip plane visual artifacts.

Although we can't give it the attention it deserves, we do squeeze
in a brief fog sample here. Although we do not go into detail, we do
show and explain the Direct3D code, which is fairly intuitive.

Direct3D fog is part of the fixed function pipeline, and is controlled
through render states. The following effect file sets the necessary fog
states for vertex fog.

Note: Direct3D also supports pixel fog (also called table fog), which
is more accurate than vertex fog.

```
//
// File: fog.txt
//
```

```
// Desc: Effect file that handles device states for linear vertex fog.
//

technique Fog
{
    pass P0
    {
        //
        // Set misc render states.

        pixelshader      = null;
        vertexshader     = null;
        fvf              = XYZ | Normal;
        Lighting         = true;
        NormalizeNormals = true;
        SpecularEnable   = false;


        //
        // Fog states

        FogVertexMode = LINEAR;    // Linear fog function.
        FogStart      = 50.0f;     // Fog starts 50 units
                                   // away from viewpoint.
        FogEnd        = 300.0f;    // Fog ends 300 units
                                   // away from viewpoint.


        FogColor      = 0x00CCCCCC; // Gray colored fog.
        FogEnable     = true;       // Enable vertex fog.
    }
}
```

As you can see, linear vertex fog can be controlled through five simple render states:

■   FogVertexMode—Specifies the fog function to use for vertex fog. The fog function specifies how the fog increases with distance, as naturally fog is less thick near the viewpoint and becomes thicker as the distance increases. Valid assignment types are LINEAR, EXP, and EXP2. These functions are defined as:

LINEAR fog function: $f = \dfrac{end - d}{end - start}$

EXP fog function: $f = \dfrac{1}{e^{\,d\,(density)}}$

EXP2 fog function: $f = \dfrac{1}{e^{\,(d\,(density))^2}}$

(d is the distance from the viewpoint.)

Note: If you use the EXP or EXP2 fog functions, you do not need to set FogStart and FogEnd because they are not used in these types of fog functions; instead you must set the fog density render state (e.g., FogDensity = someFloatType;).

Part IV

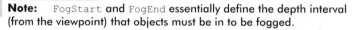

- `FogStart`—Marks the starting depth at which objects will begin to be fogged
- `FogEnd`—Marks the ending depth at which objects will stop being fogged

Note: `FogStart` and `FogEnd` essentially define the depth interval (from the viewpoint) that objects must be in to be fogged.

- `FogColor`—A `DWORD` or `D3DCOLOR` value type that describes the fog's color
- `FogEnable`—Specify `true` to enable vertex fog or `false` to disable vertex fog

Any geometry that we render using the fog.txt effect will have fog applied to it. In this way, we can control which objects get fogged and which ones don't. This is useful for only fogging certain areas. For example, generally if it is foggy outside, the insides of houses are not foggy. On the same note, certain parts of a geographic region may be foggy, but other parts may not be. Figure 19.2 shows screen shots taken from this section's sample program called Fog Effect.

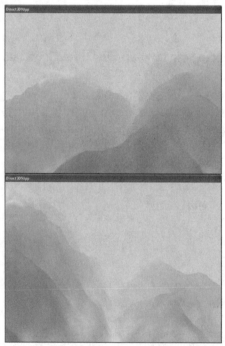

Figure 19.2: Screen shots from the Fog Effect sample. In this sample we use a linear fog function, and the fog render states are specified inside an effect file.

19.9 **Sample Application: Cartoon Effect**

The two effect file samples that we have shown so far did not use
shaders. Because shaders are typically an important part of special
effects, we want to show at least one example of them together. The
sample Cartoon Effect implements the cartoon shader as discussed in
Chapter 17, but this time using the effects framework. Following is an
abridged version of the effect file:

```
//
// File: tooneffect.txt
//
// Desc: Cartoon shader in an effect file.
//

extern matrix WorldMatrix;
extern matrix ViewMatrix;
extern matrix ProjMatrix;
extern vector Color;
extern vector LightDirection;
static vector Black = {0.0f, 0.0f, 0.0f, 0.0f};
extern texture ShadeTex;

struct VS_INPUT
{
    vector position : POSITION;
    vector normal   : NORMAL;
};
struct VS_OUTPUT
{
    vector position : POSITION;
    float2 uvCoords : TEXCOORD;
    vector diffuse  : COLOR;
};

// Cartoon Shader Function:
VS_OUTPUT Main(VS_INPUT input)
{
    ...[Implementation omitted for brevity.]
}

sampler ShadeSampler = sampler_state
{
    Texture   = (ShadeTex);
    MinFilter = POINT; // no filtering for cartoon shading
    MagFilter = POINT;
    MipFilter = NONE;
};

technique Toon
{
    pass P0
    {
        // Set P0's vertex shader.
        vertexShader = compile vs_1_1 Main();
```

```
            // Hook up the sampler object to sampler stage 0.
            Sampler[0] = (ShadeSampler);
    }
}
```

We note that the cartoon shader functions are defined inside the effect file, and we specify the shader to use for a particular pass using the syntax `vertexShader = compile vs_1_1 Main();` in the pass block. Device states are set as usual in the effect file.

19.10 EffectEdit

Before we conclude this chapter, we want to mention the EffectEdit program that ships with the DirectX SDK. It can be found in the \DXSDK\Samples\C++\Direct3D\Bin folder. Figure 19.3 shows a screen shot.

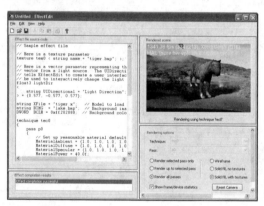

Figure 19.3: A screen shot of the EffectEdit program that ships with the DirectX SDK

The EffectEdit program is useful for testing and writing effect files. We recommend that you spend some time exploring this tool.

19.11 Summary

- Effect files encapsulate a complete effect, including possible hardware fallbacks for hardware with different capabilities and rendering passes. The effects framework is desirable because we can change effect files without recompiling source code and because it allows us to encapsulate an effect, making everything modular. Effect files can be used without shaders; that is, it is perfectly acceptable to make an effect file that uses the fixed function pipeline.

- A technique is a particular implementation of a special effect. Typically, an effect file will consist of several techniques that all implement the same effect but in different ways. Each implementation will utilize the capabilities of a specific generation of hardware. Thus, the application can choose the technique that is most fitting for the target hardware. For example, to implement multitexturing, we might define two techniques—one that uses pixel shaders and one that uses the fixed function pipeline. In this way, users with a pixel shader-capable 3D card can use the pixel shader technique, and users with a 3D card that does not support pixel shaders can still execute the effect in the fixed function version.

- A technique consists of one or more rendering passes. A rendering pass consists of the device states and shaders used to render the geometry for that particular pass. Multiple rendering passes are necessary because some special effects require the same geometry to be rendered several times, each time with different device states and/or shaders.

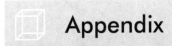
An Introduction to Windows Programming

To use the Direct3D API (application programming interface), it is necessary to create a Windows (Win32) application with a main window, upon which we render our 3D scenes. This appendix serves as an introduction to writing Windows applications using the native Win32 API. Loosely, the Win32 API is a set of low-level functions and structures exposed to us in the C programming language that enables our application and the Windows operating system (OS) to communicate with each other. For example, to notify Windows to show a particular window, we use the Win32 API function `ShowWindow`.

Windows programming is a huge subject, and this appendix introduces only what is necessary for us to use Direct3D. For readers interested in learning more about Windows programming with the Win32 API, the book *Programming Windows* (now in its fifth edition) by Charles Petzold is the standard text on the subject. Another invaluable resource when working with Microsoft technologies is the MSDN library, which is usually included with Microsoft's Visual Studio but can also be read online at www.msdn.microsoft.com. In general, if you come upon a Win32 function or structure that you would like to know more about, go to MSDN and search for that function or structure. Often in this appendix we direct you to look up a function or structure on MSDN for more elaborate details.

Objectives

- To learn and understand the event-driven programming model used in Windows programming
- To learn the minimal code necessary to create a Windows application that is necessary to use Direct3D

359

Note: We use a capital W to refer to Windows the OS, and a lower-case w to refer to a particular window running in Windows.

Overview

As the name suggests, one of the primary themes of Windows programming is programming windows. Many of the components of a Windows application are windows, such as the main application window, menus, toolbars, scroll bars, buttons, and other dialog controls. Therefore, a Windows application typically consists of several windows. These next few subsections provide a concise overview of Windows programming concepts that we should be familiar with before beginning a more complete discussion.

Resources

In Windows, several applications can run concurrently. Therefore, hardware resources such as CPU cycles, memory, and even the monitor screen must be shared among multiple applications. In order to prevent chaos from ensuing due to several applications accessing/modifying resources without any organization, Windows applications do not have direct access to hardware. One of the main jobs of Windows is to manage the presently instantiated applications and handle the distribution of resources among them. Thus, in order for our application to do something that might affect another running application, it must go through Windows. For example, to display a window, you must call `ShowWindow`; you cannot write to video memory directly.

Events, the Message Queue, Messages, and the Message Loop

A Windows application follows an *event-driven programming model*. Typically, a Windows application sits and waits (an application can perform idle processing—that is, perform a certain task when no events are occurring) for something to happen—an *event*. An event can be generated in a number of ways; some common examples are keypresses, mouse clicks, and when a window is created, resized, moved, closed, minimized, maximized, or becomes visible.

When an event occurs, Windows sends a *message* to the application for which the event occurred and adds the message to the application's *message queue*, which is simply a priority queue that stores messages for an application. The application constantly checks the message queue for messages in a *message loop*, and when it receives one it dispatches it to the *window procedure* of the particular window that the message is for. (Remember that an application can contain several windows within it.) The window procedure is a special function that is associated with each window of the application. (Every window has a window procedure, but several windows can share the same window procedure. Therefore, we don't necessarily have to write a window procedure for each window.) The window procedure is a function we implement that handles specific messages. For instance, we may want to destroy a window when the Escape key is pressed. In our window procedure we would write:

```
case WM_KEYDOWN:
    if( wParam == VK_ESCAPE )
        ::DestroyWindow(MainWindowHandle);
    return 0;
```

The messages that a window doesn't handle are usually forwarded to a default window procedure, which then handles the message.

To summarize, the user or an application does something to generate an event. The OS finds the application that the event was targeted toward, and it sends that application a message in response. The message is then added to the application's message queue. The application is constantly checking its message queue for messages. When it receives a message, the application dispatches it to the window procedure associated with the window for which the message is targeted. Finally, the window procedure executes instructions in response to the message.

Figure 1 summarizes the event-driven programming model.

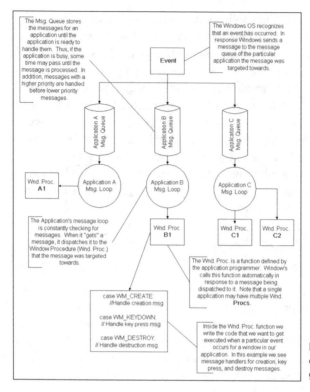

Figure 1: The event-driven programming model

GUI

Most Windows programs present a GUI (graphical user interface) that users can work from. A typical Windows application has one main window, a menu, a toolbar, and perhaps some other controls. Figure 2 shows and identifies some common GUI elements. For Direct3D game programming, we do not need a fancy GUI. In fact, all we need is a main window, where the client area is used to render our 3D worlds.

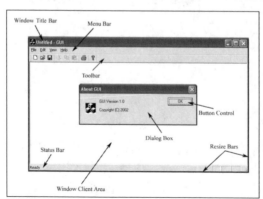

Figure 2: A typical Windows application GUI. The client area is the entire large white space of the application. Typically, this area is where the user views most of the program's output. When we program our Direct3D applications, we render our 3D scenes into the client area of a window.

Hello World Windows Application

Below is the code to a fully functional yet simple Windows program. Follow the code as best you can. The next section explains the code a bit at a time. It is recommended that you create a project with your development tool, type the code in by hand, compile it, and execute it as an exercise. Note that you must create a Win32 Application Project, *not* a Win32 Console Application Project.

```cpp
///////////////////////////////////////////////////////////////////////
//
// File: hello.cpp
//
// Author: Frank D. Luna (C) All Rights Reserved
//
// System: AMD Athlon 1800+ XP, 512 DDR, Geforce 3, Windows XP,
//         MSVC++ 7.0
//
// Desc: Demonstrates creating a Windows application.
//
///////////////////////////////////////////////////////////////////////

// Include the Windows header file, this has all the
// Win32 API structures, types, and function declarations
// we need to program Windows.
#include <windows.h>

// The main window handle. This is used to identify
// the main window we are going to create.
HWND MainWindowHandle = 0;

// Wraps the code necessary to initialize a Windows
// application. Function returns true if initialization
// was successful, else it returns false.
bool InitWindowsApp(HINSTANCE instanceHandle, int show);

// Wraps the message loop code.
int Run();

// The window procedure, handles events our window
// receives.
LRESULT CALLBACK WndProc(HWND hWnd,
                         UINT msg,
                         WPARAM wParam,
                         LPARAM lParam);

// Windows equivalant to main()
int WINAPI WinMain(HINSTANCE hInstance,
                   HINSTANCE hPrevInstance,
                   PSTR      pCmdLine,
                   int       nShowCmd)
{
    // First we create and initialize our Windows
    // application.  Notice we pass the application
    // hInstance and the nShowCmd from WinMain as
```

```
    // parameters.
    if(!InitWindowsApp(hInstance, nShowCmd))
    {
        ::MessageBox(0, "Init - Failed", "Error", MB_OK);
        return 0;
    }

    // Once our application has been created and
    // initialized we enter the message loop.  We
    // stay in the message loop until a WM_QUIT
    // message is received, indicating the application
    // should be terminated.
    return Run(); // enter message loop
}

bool InitWindowsApp(HINSTANCE instanceHandle, int show)
{
    // The first task to creating a window is to describe
    // its characteristics by filling out a WNDCLASS
    // structure.
    WNDCLASS wc;

    wc.style         = CS_HREDRAW | CS_VREDRAW;
    wc.lpfnWndProc   = WndProc;
    wc.cbClsExtra    = 0;
    wc.cbWndExtra    = 0;
    wc.hInstance     = instanceHandle;
    wc.hIcon         = ::LoadIcon(0, IDI_APPLICATION);
    wc.hCursor       = ::LoadCursor(0, IDC_ARROW);
    wc.hbrBackground =
        static_cast<HBRUSH>(::GetStockObject(WHITE_BRUSH));
    wc.lpszMenuName  = 0;
    wc.lpszClassName = "Hello";

    // Then we register this window class description
    // with Windows so that we can create a window based
    // on that description.
    if(!::RegisterClass(&wc))
    {
        ::MessageBox(0, "RegisterClass - Failed", 0, 0);
        return false;
    }

    // With our window class description registered, we
    // can create a window with the CreateWindow function.
    // Note, this function returns a HWND to the created
    // window, which we save in MainWindowHandle.  Through
    // MainWindowHandle we can reference this particular
    // window we are creating.
    MainWindowHandle = ::CreateWindow(
                        "Hello",
                        "Hello",
                        WS_OVERLAPPEDWINDOW,
                        CW_USEDEFAULT,
                        CW_USEDEFAULT,
                        CW_USEDEFAULT,
                        CW_USEDEFAULT,
```

```
                                   0,
                                   0,
                                   instanceHandle,
                                   0);

if(MainWindowHandle == 0)
    {
        ::MessageBox(0, "CreateWindow - Failed", 0, 0);
        return false;
    }

    // Finally we show and update the window we just created.
    // Observe we pass MainWindowHandle to these functions so
    // that these functions know what particular window to
    // show and update.
    ::ShowWindow(MainWindowHandle, show);
    ::UpdateWindow(MainWindowHandle);

    return true;
}

int Run()
{

    MSG msg;
    ::ZeroMemory(&msg, sizeof(MSG));

    // Loop until we get a WM_QUIT message.  The
    // function GetMessage will only return 0 (false)
    // when a WM_QUIT message is received, which
    // effectively exits the loop.
    while(::GetMessage(&msg, 0, 0, 0) )
    {
        // Translate the message, and then dispatch it
        // to the appropriate window procedure.
        ::TranslateMessage(&msg);
        ::DispatchMessage(&msg);
    }

    return msg.wParam;
}

LRESULT CALLBACK WndProc(HWND    windowHandle,
                         UINT    msg,
                         WPARAM  wParam,
                         LPARAM  lParam)
{
    // Handle some specific messages:
    switch( msg )
    {
        // In the case the left mouse button was pressed,
        // then display a message box.
    case WM_LBUTTONDOWN:
        ::MessageBox(0, "Hello, World", "Hello", MB_OK);
        return 0;

        // In the case the escape key was pressed, then
```

```
        // destroy the main application window, which is
        // identified by MainWindowHandle.
case WM_KEYDOWN:
        if( wParam == VK_ESCAPE )
            ::DestroyWindow(MainWindowHandle);
        return 0;

        // In the case of a destroy message, then
        // send a quit message, which will terminate
        // the message loop.
case WM_DESTROY:
        ::PostQuitMessage(0);
        return 0;
}

    // Forward any other messages we didn't handle
    // above to the default window procedure.
    return ::DefWindowProc(windowHandle,
                           msg,
                           wParam,
                           lParam);
}
```

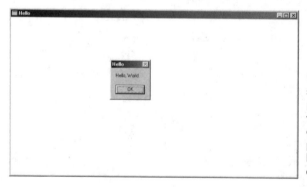

Figure 3: A screen shot of the above program. Note that the message box appears when you press the left mouse button in the window's client area.

Explaining Hello World

Let's examine the code from top to bottom, stepping into any function that gets called along the way. Refer back to the Hello World code listing throughout these subsections.

Includes, Global Variables, and Prototypes

The first thing we do is include the windows.h header file. By including the windows.h file, we obtain the structures, types, and function declarations needed for using the basic elements of the Win32 API.

```
#include <windows.h>
```

The second statement is an instantiation of a global variable of type HWND. This stands for "handle to a window." In Windows programming, we often use handles to refer to objects maintained internally by Windows. In this sample, we use an HWND to refer to our main application window maintained by Windows. We need to hold onto the handles of our windows because many calls to the API require that we pass in the handle of the window that we want the API call to act on. For example, the call UpdateWindow takes one argument that is of type HWND that is used to specify the window to update. If we didn't pass in a handle to it, the function wouldn't know what window to update.

```
HWND MainWindowHandle = 0;
```

The next three lines are function declarations. Briefly, InitWindows-App creates and initializes our main application window, Run encapsulates the message loop for our application, and WndProc is our main window's window procedure. We examine these functions in more detail when we come to the point where they are called.

```
bool InitWindowsApp(HINSTANCE instanceHandle, int show);
int  Run();
LRESULT CALLBACK WndProc(HWND, UINT, WPARAM, LPARAM);
```

WinMain

WinMain is the Windows equivalent to the main function in normal C++ programming. WinMain is prototyped as follows:

```
int WINAPI WinMain(
    HINSTANCE hInstance,
    HINSTANCE hPrevInstance,
    LPSTR     lpCmdLine,
    int       nCmdShow
);
```

- hInstance—Handle to the current application instance. It serves as a way of identifying and referring to this application. Remember that there may be several Windows applications running concurrently, so it is useful to be able to refer to each one.

- hPrevInstance—Not used in 32-bit Win32 programming and is 0

- lpCmdLine—The command line argument string used to run the program

- nCmdShow—Specifies how the application window should be displayed. Some common commands that show the window in its current size and position, maximized, and minimized, respectively, are SW_SHOW, SW_SHOWMAXIMIZED, and SW_SHOWMINIMIZED. See the MSDN library for a complete list of show commands.

If `WinMain` succeeds, it should return the `wParam` member of the `WM_QUIT` message. If the function exits without entering the message loop, it should return 0. The `WINAPI` identifier is defined as:

```
#define WINAPI __stdcall
```

This specifies the calling convention of the function, which means how the function arguments get placed on the stack.

Note: In the signature of `WinMain` in the Hello World sample, we use the type `PSTR` as the third argument instead of `LPSTR`. This is because with 32-bit Windows there are no longer "long pointers." `PSTR` is simply a `char` pointer (e.g., `char*`).

WNDCLASS and Registration

Inside `WinMain`, we call the function `InitWindowsApp`. As you can guess, this function does all the initialization of our program. Let's jump into this function and examine it. `InitWindowsApp` returns either true or false—true if the initialization was a success, false if something went wrong. In the `WinMain` definition, we pass a copy of our application instance to `InitWindowsApp` as well as the show command variable. Both are obtained from the `WinMain` parameter list.

```
if(!InitWindowsApp(hInstance, nShowCmd))
```

The first task at hand in the initialization of a window is to describe our window and register it with Windows. We describe our window with the `WNDCLASS` data structure. Its definition:

```
typedef struct _WNDCLASS {
    UINT     style;
    WNDPROC  lpfnWndProc;
    int      cbClsExtra;
    int      cbWndExtra;
    HANDLE   hInstance;
    HICON    hIcon;
    HCURSOR  hCursor;
    HBRUSH   hbrBackground;
    LPCTSTR  lpszMenuName;
    LPCTSTR  lpszClassName;
} WNDCLASS;
```

- `style`—Specifies the class style. In our example, we use `CS_HREDRAW` combined with `CS_VREDRAW`. These two bit flags indicate that the window is to be repainted when either the horizontal or vertical window size is changed. For the complete list of the various styles with descriptions, see the MSDN library.

```
wc.style = CS_HREDRAW | CS_VREDRAW;
```

- **lpfnWndProc**—Pointer to the window procedure function. This is how you associate your window procedure function with a window. Thus, the windows that are created based on the same WNDCLASS instance share the same window procedure. The window procedure function is explained in the section titled "The Window Procedure."

```
wc.lpfnWndProc = WndProc;
```

- **cbClsExtra** and **cbWndExtra**—These are extra memory slots that you can use for your own purpose. Our Hello World program does not require any extra space and therefore sets both of these to 0.

```
wc.cbClsExtra = 0;
wc.cbWndExtra = 0;
```

- **hInstance**—This field is a handle to our application instance. Recall that the application instance handle is originally passed in through WinMain.

```
wc.hInstance = instanceHandle;
```

- **hIcon**—Here you specify a handle to an icon to use for the windows created using this window class. There are several built-in icons to choose from. See the MSDN library for details.

```
wc.hIcon = ::LoadIcon(0, IDI_APPLICATION);
```

- **hCursor**—Similar to hIcon, here you specify a handle to a cursor to use when the cursor is over the window's client area. Again, there are several built-in cursors. See the MSDN library for details.

```
wc.hCursor = ::LoadCursor(0, IDC_ARROW);
```

- **hbrBackground**—This field is used to specify the background color of the client area of the window. In our sample code we call the function GetStockObject, which returns a handle to a brush of the color that we specified. See the MSDN library for other types of built-in brushes.

```
wc.hbrBackground =
    static_cast<HBRUSH>(::GetStockObject(WHITE_BRUSH));
```

- **lpszMenuName**—Specifies the window's menu. We have no menu in our application, so we set this to 0.

```
wc.lpszMenuName = 0;
```

- **lpszClassName**—Specifies the name of the window class structure that we are creating. This can be anything you want. In our application, we named it "Hello." The name is simply used to identify the class structure so that we can reference it later.

```
wc.lpszClassName = "Hello";
```

Once we have described our window, we need to register it with Windows. This is done with the `RegisterClass` function that takes a pointer to a `WNDCLASS` structure. This function returns 0 upon failure.

```
if(!::RegisterClass(&wc))
```

Creating and Displaying the Window

After we have registered a `WNDCLASS` variable with Windows, we can create a window based on that class description. We can refer to the `WNDCLASS` structure that describes the window that we want to create by the class name we gave it—`lpszClassName`. The function we use to create a window is the `CreateWindow` function, which is declared as follows:

```
HWND CreateWindow(
    LPCTSTR lpClassName,
    LPCTSTR lpWindowName,
    DWORD dwStyle,
    int x,
    int y,
    int nWidth,
    int nHeight,
    HWND hWndParent,
    HMENU hMenu,
    HANDLE hInstance,
    LPVOID lpParam
);
```

- `lpClassName`—The name (C string) of the registered `WNDCLASS` structure that describes the window that we want to create. Pass in the class name of the `WNDCLASS` we want to use for the creation of this window.

- `lpWindowName`—The name (C string) that we want to give our window; this is also the name that appears in the window's title bar.

- `dwStyle`—Defines the style of the window. `WS_OVERLAPPED-WINDOW`, which we use in the Hello World sample, is a combination of several flags: `WS_OVERLAPPED`, `WS_CAPTION`, `WS_SYSMENU`, `WS_THICKFRAME`, `WS_MINIMIZEBOX`, and `WS_MAXIMIZEBOX`. The names of these flags describe the characteristics of the window that they produce. See the MSDN library for the complete list of styles.

- `x`—The x position at the top-left corner of the window relative to the screen

- y—The y position at the top-left corner of the window relative to the screen
- nWidth—The width of the window in pixels
- nHeight—The height of the window in pixels
- hWndParent—Handle to a window that is to be the parent of this window. Our window has no relationship with any other windows; therefore we set this value to 0.
- hMenu—A handle to a menu. Hello World has no menu and specifies 0 for this argument.
- hInstance—Handle to the application with which the window will be associated.
- lpParam—A pointer to user-defined data

Note: When we specify the (x, y) coordinates of the window's position, they are relative to the upper-left corner of the screen. Also, the positive x-axis runs to the right as usual, but the positive y-axis runs downward. Figure 4 shows this coordinate system, which is called *screen coordinates* or *screen space*.

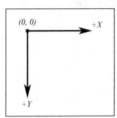

Figure 4: Screen space

CreateWindow returns a handle to the window that it creates (an HWND). If the creation failed, the handle will have the value of 0. Remember that the handle is a way to refer to the window, which is managed by Windows. Many of the API calls require an HWND so that they know what window to act on.

The last two function calls in the InitWindowsApp function have to do with displaying the window. First we call ShowWindow and pass in the handle of our newly created window so that Windows knows what window to show. We also pass in an integer value that defines how the window is to be initially shown (minimized, maximized, etc.). This value should be nShowCmd, which is an argument of WinMain. You can hardcode this value in, but it is not recommended. After showing the window, we should refresh it. UpdateWindow does this; it takes one argument that is a handle to the window we wish to update.

```
::ShowWindow(MainWindowHandle, show);
::UpdateWindow(MainWindowHandle);
```

If we made it this far in `InitWindowsApp`, then the initialization is complete; we return true to indicate everything went successfully.

The Message Loop

Having successfully completed initialization, we can begin the heart of the program, the message loop. In Hello World, we have wrapped the message loop in a function called `Run`.

```
int Run()
{
    MSG msg;
    ::ZeroMemory(&msg, sizeof(MSG));

    while(::GetMessage(&msg, 0, 0, 0) )
    {
        ::TranslateMessage(&msg);
        ::DispatchMessage(&msg);
    }
    return msg.wParam;
}
```

The first thing done in `Run` is an instantiation of a variable called `msg` of type `MSG`, which is the message structure that represents a Windows message. Its definition is as follows:

```
typedef struct tagMSG {
    HWND    hwnd;
    UINT    message;
    WPARAM  wParam;
    LPARAM  lParam;
    DWORD   time;
    POINT   pt;
} MSG;
```

■ `hwnd`—Identifies the window the message is for

■ `message`—A predefined constant value identifying the message (e.g., `WM_QUIT`)

■ `wParam`—Extra information about the message. This is dependent upon the specific message.

■ `lParam`—Extra information about the message. This is dependent upon the specific message.

■ `time`—The time the message was posted

■ `pt`—The (x, y) coordinates of the mouse cursor in screen coordinates when the message was posted

Next we enter the message loop. `GetMessage` will always return true unless a `WM_QUIT` message is posted; therefore, the loop continues until a `WM_QUIT` message is received. The `GetMessage` function retrieves a message from the message queue and fills in the members of our MSG structure. If GetMessage returns true, then two more functions get called: TranslateMessage and DispatchMessage. TranslateMessage has Windows perform some keyboard translations, specifically virtual key messages to character messages. DispatchMessage finally dispatches the message to the appropriate window procedure.

The Window Procedure

We mentioned previously that the window procedure is where we write the code we want to execute in response to a message that our window receives. In Hello World, we name the window procedure WndProc. It is prototyped as:

```
LRESULT CALLBACK WndProc(
    HWND hwnd,
    UINT uMsg,
    WPARAM wParam,
    LPARAM lParam
);
```

This function returns an integer of type LRESULT (which is a long) identifying the success or failure of the function. The CALLBACK identifier specifies that the function is a *callback* function, which means that Windows will be calling this function externally. As you can see from the Hello World source code, we never explicitly call the window procedure ourselves—Windows calls it for us when the window needs to process a message.

The window procedure has four parameters in its signature:

■ hwnd—Identifies the window the message is for

■ uMsg—A predefined value that identifies the particular message. For example, a quit message is defined as WM_QUIT. The prefix WM stands for "window message." There are over a hundred predefined window messages. See the MSDN library for details.

■ wParam—Extra information about the message, which is dependent upon the specific message

■ lParam—Extra information about the message, which is dependent upon the specific message

Our window procedure handles three messages: the WM_LBUTTON-DOWN, WM_KEYDOWN, and WM_DESTROY messages. A WM_LBUTTON-DOWN message is sent when the user clicks the left mouse button on the window's client area. A WM_KEYDOWN message is sent when a key is pressed. A WM_DESTROY message is sent when the window is being destroyed. Our code is quite simple; when we receive a `WM_LBUTTON-DOWN` message, we display a message box that prints out "Hello, World":

```
case WM_LBUTTONDOWN:
    ::MessageBox(0, "Hello, World", "Hello", MB_OK);
    return 0;
```

When our window gets a `WM_KEYDOWN` message, we test what key was pressed. The `wParam` passed into the window procedure specifies the *virtual key code* of the specific key that was pressed. Think of virtual key codes as an identifier for a particular key. The Windows header files have a list of virtual key code constants that we can use to then test for a particular key (for example, to test if the Escape key was pressed, we use the virtual key code constant `VK_ESCAPE`).

Note: Remember, the `wParam` and `lParam` parameters are used to specify extra information about a particular message. For the `WM_KEY-DOWN` message, the `wParam` specifies the *virtual key code* of the specific key that was pressed. The MSDN library will specify the information that the `wParam` and `lParam` parameters carry for each Windows message.

```
case WM_KEYDOWN:
    if( wParam == VK_ESCAPE )
        ::DestroyWindow(MainWindowHandle);
    return 0;
```

When our window gets destroyed, we post a quit message (which terminates the message loop).

```
case WM_DESTROY:
    ::PostQuitMessage(0);
    return 0;
```

At the end of our window procedure, we call the `DefWindowProc` function. This function is a default window procedure. In our Hello World application, we only handle three messages; we use the default behavior specified in `DefWindowProc` for all the other messages that we receive but don't necessarily need to handle ourselves. For example, Hello World can be minimized, maximized, resized, and closed. This functionality is provided to us through the default window procedure, as we do not handle the window messages to perform this functionality. Note that `DefWindowProc` is a Win32 API function.

The MessageBox Function

There is one last API function that we have not yet covered, and that is the `MessageBox` function. This function is a very handy way to provide the user with information and get some quick input. The declaration for the `MessageBox` function looks like this:

```
int MessageBox(
    HWND hWnd,          // Handle of owner window, may specify null.
    LPCTSTR lpText,     // Text to put in the message box.
    LPCTSTR lpCaption,  // Text to put for the title of the message
                        // box.
    UINT uType          // Style of the message box.
);
```

The return value for the `MessageBox` function depends on the type of message box. See the MSDN library for a list of possible return values and styles.

A Better Message Loop

Games are very different applications than traditional Windows applications, such as office type applications and web browsers. Games are not typically event driven in the usual sense, and they must be updated constantly. For this reason, when we actually start writing our 3D programs we will, for the most part, not deal with Windows messages. Therefore, we will want to modify the message loop so that if there is a message, we will process it. But if there is not a message, then we want to run our game code. Our new message loop is as follows:

```
int Run()
{
    MSG  msg;

    while(true)
    {
        if(::PeekMessage(&msg, 0, 0, 0, PM_REMOVE))
        {
            if(msg.message == WM_QUIT)
                break;

            ::TranslateMessage(&msg);
            ::DispatchMessage(&msg);
        }
        else
            // run game code
    }
    return msg.wParam;
}
```

After we instantiate `msg`, we enter into an endless loop. We first call the API function `PeekMessage`, which checks the message queue for a message. See MSDN for the argument descriptions. If there is a message, it returns true and we handle the message. If `PeekMessage` returns false, then we handle our own specific game code.

Summary

- To use Direct3D, we must create a Windows application that has a main window onto which we can render our 3D scenes. Furthermore, for games we create a special message loop that checks for messages, and if there are messages, it processes them; otherwise it executes our game logic.

- Several Windows applications can be running concurrently; therefore Windows must manage resources between them and direct messages to the applications that they were intended for. Messages are sent to an application's message queue when an event (keypress, mouse click, timer, etc.) has occurred for that application.

- Every Windows application has a message queue where the messages that an application receives are stored. The application's message loop constantly checks the queue for messages and dispatches them to their intended window procedure. Note that a single application can have several windows within it.

- The window procedure is a special callback function we implement that Windows calls when a window in our application receives a message. In the window procedure, we write the code that we want to be executed when a window in our application receives a particular message. Messages that we do not specifically handle are forwarded to a default window procedure for default handling.

Bibliography

Angel, Edward. *Interactive Computer Graphics: A Top-Down Approach with OpenGL*. 2nd ed. Addison-Wesley, 2000.

Blinn, Jim. *Jim Blinn's Corner: A Trip Down the Graphics Pipeline*, pp. 53-61. San Francisco: Morgan Kaufmann Publishers, Inc., 1996.

Eberly, David H. *3D Game Engine Design*. San Francisco: Morgan Kaufmann Publishers, Inc., 2001.

Engel, Wolfgang F., ed. *Direct3D ShaderX: Vertex and Pixel Shader Tips and Tricks*. Plano, Texas: Wordware Publishing, 2002.

Fraleigh and Beauregard. *Linear Algebra*. 3rd ed. Addison-Wesley, 1995.

Kilgard, Mark J. "Creating Reflections and Shadows Using Stencil Buffers," Game Developers Conference, NVIDIA slide presentation, 1999. (http://developer.nvidia.com/docs/IO/1407/ATT/stencil.ppt)

Lander, Jeff. "Shades of Disney: Opaquing a 3D World." *Game Developer* magazine, March 2000.

Lengyel, Eric. *Mathematics for 3D Game Programming & Computer Graphics*. Hingham, Mass.: Charles River Media, Inc., 2002.

Microsoft Corporation. Microsoft DirectX 9.0 SDK documentation. Microsoft Corporation, 2002.

Möller, Tomas, and Eric Haines. *Real-Time Rendering*. 2nd ed. Natick, Mass.: A K Peters, Ltd., 2002.

Mortenson, M.E. *Mathematics for Computer Graphics Applications*. 2nd ed. New York: Industrial Press, Inc., 1999.

Petzold, Charles. *Programming Windows*. 5th ed. Redmond, Wash.: Microsoft Press, 1999.

Prosise, Jeff. *Programming Windows with MFC*. 2nd ed. Redmond, Wash.: Microsoft Press, 1999.

Savchenko, Sergei. *3D Graphics Programming: Games and Beyond*, pp. 153-156, 253-294. Sams Publishing, 2000.

van der Burg, John. "Building an Advanced Particle System." *Gamasutra*, June 2000. (http://www.gamasutra.com/features/20000623/vanderburg_01.htm)

Watt, Alan, and Fabio Policarpo. *3D Games: Real-time Rendering and Software Technology*. Addison-Wesley, 2001.

Watt, Alan. *3D Computer Graphics*. 3rd ed. Addison-Wesley, 2000.

Weinreich, Gabriel. *Geometrical Vectors*, pp. 1-11. Chicago: The University of Chicago Press, 1998.

Wilt, Nicholas. *Object-Oriented Ray Tracing in C++*, pp. 56-58. New York: John Wiley & Sons, Inc., 1994.

Index

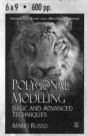

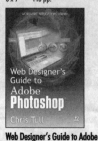
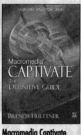
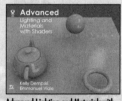

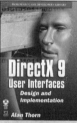